Forensic Psychology

FOR

DUMMIES®

Forensic Psychology FOR DUMMIES®

by Professor David Canter
Foreword by Ian Rankin

 **WILEY**

A John Wiley and Sons, Ltd, Publication

Forensic Psychology For Dummies®

Published by
John Wiley & Sons, Ltd
The Atrium
Southern Gate
Chichester
West Sussex
PO19 8SQ
England
www.wiley.com

For general information on our other products and services, please contact our Customer Care Department within the U.S. at 877-762-2974, outside the U.S. at 317-572-3993, or fax 317-572-4002.

For technical support, please visit www.wiley.com/techsupport.

Wiley publishes in a variety of print and electronic formats and by print-on-demand. Some material included with standard print versions of this book may not be included in e-books or in print-on-demand. If this book refers to media such as a CD or DVD that is not included in the version you purchased, you may download this material at http://booksupport.wiley.com. For more information about Wiley products, visit www.wiley.com.

British Library Cataloguing in Publication Data: A catalogue record for this book is available from the British Library

ISBN 978-1-119-97624-0 (pbk); ISBN 978-1-119-97736-0 (ebk); ISBN 978-1-119-97737-7 (ebk); ISBN 978-1-119-97738-4 (ebk)

Printed and bound in Great Britain by TJ International, Padstow, Cornwall

10 9 8 7 6 5 4 3 2 1

WILEY

About the Author

David Canter drifted into Forensic Psychology in 1986 when he was asked by Scotland Yard to give guidance to a major police investigation into a series of murders and rapes. The value of this guidance opened doors to many other police investigations and brought him into the work of psychologists in many other areas of legal activity. He became a Chartered Forensic Psychologist and developed postgraduate courses recognised by the British Psychological Society as a step towards chartered status. Hundreds of those who were his students now have senior jobs in universities, police forces and many other organisations around the world. He has been a Professor of Psychology at the University of Surrey in the South of England, where he was also Head of the Department, and at The University of Liverpool, where he now has Emeritus status. He is currently Professor of Psychology at the University of Huddersfield where he directs the International Research Centre for Investigative Psychology. He writes for major newspapers, notably *The Times*, and often contributes to radio and television news and documentary programmes in the UK and overseas. He wrote and presented a six part TV documentary series *Mapping Murder* that was broadcast around the world.

Dedication

For Rosie, Robin and Felix in the hope that what is dealt with in this book will always remain irrelevant to them.

Author's Acknowledgements

The work of many colleagues has been drawn on unashamedly in this book. It is not the *For Dummies* format to cite these directly. However, I would like to mention that I have found the work of my colleagues Kevin Browne and Donna Youngs, as well as more distant associates Curt and Anne Bartol to be of particular value. Graham Davies reviewed the draft thoroughly and I have incorporated his suggestions, although of course any errors are mine. The compendium put together by Jennifer Brown and the late Elizabeth Campbell, is also a masterwork that I found very useful. Lionel Haward, sadly missed, encouraged me in the early days of my involvement with the law, so his influence is never very far from this book. As ever, I am grateful to my agent, Doreen Montgomery, for her help. My obsession with getting this book written has been endured by Sandra Canter with her love, support and good humour that is taxed every time I take up one of my writing commitments.

Publisher's Acknowledgments

We're proud of this book; please send us your comments at http://dummies.custhelp.com. For other comments, please contact our Customer Care Department within the U.S. at 877-762-2974, outside the U.S. at 317-572-3993, or fax 317-572-4002.

Some of the people who helped bring this book to market include the following:

Acquisitions, Editorial, and Vertical Websites

Project Editor: Jo Jones

Commissioning Editor: Claire Ruston

Assistant Editor: Ben Kemble

Development Editor: Andy Finch

Copy Editor: Martin Key

Technical Editor: Graham Davies

Proofreader: Andi Sisodia

Production Manager: Daniel Mersey

Publisher: David Palmer

Cover Photos: © Kitch Bain / Alamy

Cartoons: Rich Tennant (www.the5thwave.com)

Composition Services

Project Coordinator: Kristie Rees

Layout and Graphics: Carl Byers

Proofreader: Lauren Mandelbaum

Indexer: Christine Karpeles

Special Help

Brand Reviewer: Jennifer Bingham

Publishing and Editorial for Consumer Dummies

    Kathleen Nebenhaus, Vice President and Executive Publisher

    Kristin Ferguson-Wagstaffe, Product Development Director

    Ensley Eikenburg, Associate Publisher, Travel

    Kelly Regan, Editorial Director, Travel

Publishing for Technology Dummies

    Andy Cummings, Vice President and Publisher

Composition Services

    Debbie Stailey, Director of Composition Services

Contents at a Glance

Table of Contents

Foreword

1 first encountered Professor David Canter's work and world in a book he published in 1994 called *Criminal Shadows*. Its subtitle was 'Inside the Mind of the Serial Killer', and it interested me because I felt it might help me get beneath the skin of the fictional criminals I was writing about in my 'Inspector Rebus' novels. That book was clear-sighted and level-headed. Hannah Arendt had already coined the term 'the banality of evil' to describe Nazism and the atrocities which took place in its name. Professor Canter explained that real-life serial killers are seldom like their rococo fictional equivalents. These killers tend towards the banal and colourless; they are lucky rather than preternaturally skilful – and they seldom play complicated mind games with their pursuers.

There is still a place for the likes of Hannibal Lecter in fiction, of course, but he and his ilk belong to the realm of legend and folk-tale. The book you are currently reading will explain why – but it will do a lot more. Professor Canter is an entertaining, comprehensive and comprehensible guide who pricks the myth (perpetuated in film, on TV, and in novels) of the forensic psychologist as a gifted but antisocial loner with drink and relationship problems. In real life, forensic psychologists look at why humans commit crimes and what types of crime they are likely to commit. They also ponder the nature of evil, and whether evil itself can ever be 'diagnosed'.

In this book you will find a clear explanation of terms such as psychosis, schizophrenia and sadism - terms bandied about in life as in fiction, but not always with any great degree of accuracy.

Professor Canter also looks at the ways in which we can tell if someone is lying, taking in everything from body language to brain-mapping. Forensic psychologists work with various law agencies and may be called upon to help with witness interviews. One of many fascinating cases discussed here concerns a kidnapped bus driver and the use of hypnosis to garner witness evidence.

As a criminal profiler, the author is well-equipped to debunk many of the common misconceptions around that specialism. Profiling can be helpful to the police, but it has to be used with care. Professor Canter cites the case of an attacker who had long fingernails on one of his hands. The investigating officers deduced that they were looking for a guitarist. Had this been a Sherlock Holmes story, they would undoubtedly have been correct, but there was actually another less obvious explanation.

Importantly, Professor David Canter also looks at how forensic psychology can aid victims of crime. Victims are often forgotten about, in life as in fiction. Here they are given due prominence.

Whether you are a serious student or have a casual interest, this book will deepen your knowledge of forensic psychology. I dare say crime writers will find it useful, too, even though we continue to portray our killers as exaggerated monsters with penchants for puzzles, fava beans and a nice chianti.

Ian Rankin

Introduction

. . . .

*I*n 1985, a senior police officer at Scotland Yard asked me to attend a meeting to plan an investigation into a series of rapes and murders committed around London. Up until that point during my work as a psychologist, I'd had very little contact with the police or criminals and was rather taken aback when asked whether I 'could help catch this man before he kills again'. I agreed to assist the investigation and its eventual success changed my life. As a result I was drawn ever more intensively into a wide range of police investigations, and then into commenting on psychological evidence presented in court. I began considering rehabilitation programmes for offenders and examining processes for assessing the possible risk they posed if they were released. I talked to killers and burglars and many other criminals and their victims.

I was now part of the burgeoning field of forensic psychology, reading its journals, giving keynote addresses at conferences, and debating with colleagues and students how many aspects of behavioural science (particularly psychology) were informed by, and carried consequences for, the full range of legal issues. I became increasingly enthusiastic about the evolving ways in which psychology is influencing all aspects of the legal process.

Since that fateful day, I discovered that many people, in all walks of life, have questions about what makes criminals tick, and how psychology can be used throughout the investigation, prosecution, treatment and rehabilitation of criminals and to help their victims. This book aims to answer those questions.

About This Book

In this book, I cover what happens from when a crime is first reported through to dealing with convicted offenders and, where possible, helping them to desist from future criminality. I include many examples of forensic psychology in action to bring the excitement of this professional activity to life.

Here are a few things, however, that you won't read about in this book: the motives that so delight crime fiction writers (greed, jealousy, revenge . . . in fact I avoid using the vague term 'motive' at all); whether criminals did (or didn't) get on with their mothers; or whether something is wrong with their biology. Instead, *Forensic Psychology For Dummies* gives you a much wider and more interesting landscape to explore. I go beyond the myths of such popular ideas as 'offender profiling' and deeper than whether criminals are born or made. In this book, I show you what forensic psychologists actually do, and why they do it in the ways that they do.

Although psychologists tend to drift into jargon, writing about most of what they do without technical terms is perfectly possible. On the few occasions when specialist words are needed, I make sure that their meaning is clear. So, if you know absolutely nothing of psychology, this book is for you. If you've read or studied any psychology before, many aspects are here presented in a new light. If you've already had some contact with forensic psychology or are considering it as a career path, the breadth of coverage provides a map to help you find your way.

Forensic psychology is a professional area of activity. So I do describe some of the requirements and challenges that professionalism creates. But even if you're only curious as to what all the fuss is about, knowing the underlying principles and processes may come in handy if ever you come into contact with a real-life forensic psychologist (they aren't usually scary, honest).

I think of books in a library as being in conversation with each other, drawing on what they're about and offering connections for others to pick up. *Forensic Psychology For Dummies* is part of a gaggle of books chatting to each other. Where you can get more detail elsewhere I make that clear, but bear in mind that I'm using my own point of view to cover what's written about in other books and, as in any conversation, not everyone agrees with each other. So if you want to check out what others have to say, by all means take a look at *Criminology For Dummies* by Stephen Briggs (Wiley) and *Forensics For Dummies* by Douglas P. Lyle (Wiley). Because forensic psychology has such close contacts with the law I mention the legal issues whenever I absolutely have to, but I'm a psychologist not a lawyer. So if you want to get to grips with all that stuff, do what I do and read *Law For Dummies* by John Ventura (Wiley), although be warned that it's about the law in the US and every country has its own way of doing legal things. Although the views of criminologists, political scientists, historians and anthropologists, to name just a few, are extremely valuable I don't engage with these disciplines. This book is about forensic psychology and psychologists focus on individuals and their relationships with others.

Conventions Used in This Book

I use a few conventions to help you find your way around this book easily:

- ✔ *Italic* highlights new, often specialist, terms that I always define nearby, and is also sometimes used for emphasis.
- ✔ **Boldfaced** text indicates the action part of numbered steps.

Although I keep the number of technical terms and jargon to an absolute minimum, all professional activities include words that have precise meanings for people within that profession. Mastery of these italicised terms enables you to bluff your way in any discussions of crime and criminals.

I try to avoid specific gender stereotyping, but the writing can get very lumpy if I do so all the time. Therefore, every now and then I refer to an individual offender as 'he'. The fact that the great majority of criminals, 80 per cent or more, are men means that referring to them as male is usually accurate. Of course, this assumption doesn't mean that women never commit crimes; it just keeps the writing simpler. If I need to refer to specifically female criminals, or make clear that a higher proportion of offenders than normal of a particular crime are female, I do so.

You should also note that a very high proportion of Forensic Psychologists are women, so sometimes it makes sense to refer to them as 'she' or 'her'.

I'd love this book to be a laugh-a-minute, but squeezing humour out of rape and murder, or even the more mundane crimes of burglary and robbery, is difficult if not inappropriate. Criminals themselves aren't comic (although some of them are clowns). As an expert in court I manage to get a smile out of the jury from time to time, and so whenever I can I do the same here. But please don't see these attempts to enliven the topic as implying that anything is other than serious.

What You're Not to Read

One of the problems with most books is that they start at page one and carry on in a straight line until they end on the last page. But ideas don't always sit along a line so neatly, and often you don't want to find out about things in the sequence that the writer wants to tell you.

This book is written to take account of such human foibles. In general, each chapter is self-contained and you can read the chapters in any order you like, although the book makes greater sense if you do read chapters in the numbered order. But to help out, I also make any information that you can safely skip easy to recognise. The grey boxes dotted throughout this book (known as *sidebars*) contain historical examples or more detailed theory that may otherwise break the flow of the text. You can skip them or just flick through to get the feel of what's going on.

Foolish Assumptions

I've lectured on psychology to many different audiences for nearly 50 years ('it don't seem a day too long, guv'), which helped me to keep a vision in my mind of you while writing this book. The word *Dummies* in the title means only that I assume you're not an expert in forensic psychology, but that you're intelligent enough to use this book in the way that works best for you. I assume that you have some combination of the following interests:

- ✔ You're fascinated by crime and criminals, but want to know more than you can get from fictional accounts or glib documentaries.

- ✔ You think that you may want to be a forensic psychologist, but are curious as to what it's all about.

- ✔ You know a little about the criminal justice system and wonder how the scientific study of people can contribute to it being more effective.

- ✔ You're studying psychology and are fed up with artificial laboratory experiments and details of which area of the brain lights up when people do odd things, and so you want to know what psychologists do in the real world.

- ✔ You're studying crime or the law, writing an article or book, or making a documentary, and you want to know more about psychology and how it connects with the law.

How This Book Is Organised

Except for the first and last parts, each part of this book deals with a different context in which forensic psychology happens. So you can choose the area that you're most curious about and start there.

Part 1: Nailing Forensic Psychology: A Moving Target

Forensic psychology is a rapidly expanding area and takes on different forms in different places. This part, therefore, gives you an 'efit' of forensic psychology to help you recognise it when you stumble across it. Chapter 1 examines what forensic psychologists do (and don't do) and who they deal with, Chapter 2 describes some of the aspects of what makes someone break the law and Chapter 3 shows how forensic psychology relates to the legal process.

Part II: Helping the Police Solve Crimes

Many fictional accounts of crime investigations use some sort of psychological intervention to help solve the case. In truth, this aspect is a minutely small part of what forensic psychologists do, but it does get the juices flowing and is a crucial point on your journey into the world of forensic psychology.

Getting good information from victims and witnesses during interviews (which I discuss in Chapter 4) isn't as easy as the movies may have you believe. Not everyone the police talk to tells the truth, and so detecting deception (or indeed bare-faced lying) is a challenging topic, to which I devote Chapter 5. Making use of the information the police do collect opens up the topic often referred to as 'offender profiling' (see Chapter 6). Chapter 7 covers the important but often neglected subject of helping the victims of crime and Chapter 8 discusses crime prevention and reduction.

Part III: Measuring the Criminal Mind

Like every science, forensic psychology relies on precise and reliable measurement. But people, especially criminals, aren't static lumps of material that can be plonked on a laboratory bench to have refined measuring tools applied to them. Therefore, various assessment procedures have been developed to weigh up important characteristics of offenders, such as determining their mental state and its relevance to the legal process, a subject I describe in Chapter 9. A small, but crucial, subset of criminals have no obvious mental problems and are often characterised by commentators as 'evil'. Chapter 10 looks directly at what this description can mean and offers a less sensational account.

Part IV: Viewing Psychology in Court

Forensic psychology started life as guidance to legal proceedings and is now a common feature of many court hearings. I describe how this process works in Chapter 11. The new developments, especially in the US, of guiding lawyers to be as effective and understandable as possible are covered in Chapter 12.

Part V: Helping and Treating Offenders

Many forensic psychologists end up in prison . . . to help prisoners, of course, and sometimes prison management. Chapter 13 looks at the different forms of psychological help and treatment that are now available for offenders. Two particularly important areas are violence and sex offending, and so they have their own chapters (14 and 15, respectively). Youngsters who become involved in crime pose a particular challenge and so I devote Chapter 16 to them.

Part VI: The Part of Tens

If you want to know more about the professional aspects of forensic psychology, I describe ten vital aspects in Chapter 17. Chapter 18 lists ten stages in the career of many people who become professionals in this area. But because forensic psychology is such a rapidly evolving profession, I also list ten areas that are emerging in Chapter 19. In Chapter 20, I describe ten great examples of cases in which forensic psychology successfully made a significant contribution.

Icons Used in This Book

This book uses different icons to highlight important information. Here's what they mean:

This icon indicates stuff that's really worth bearing in mind.

This icon indicates where I set the record straight on common misconceptions.

I use this icon to show you where I draw on my own experience to bring you real-life stories.

This icon tips you off to where I describe differences across the globe or where I focus on one country or jurisdiction.

This icon reveals unusual nuggets from the realms of criminal investigation and behaviour.

Where to Go from Here

You can read this book in any order you like, because I write it so that the text makes sense wherever you start. You can flick through and look at the cartoons (which to be honest is how I explore *For Dummies* books) or just go straight to the Part of Tens for some useful summaries. But if you're new to the subject, I think you'll get more out of it if you read Chapter 1 first. Most importantly, though, enjoy!

Part I
Nailing Forensic Psychology: A Moving Target

The 5th Wave   By Rich Tennant

"You're the one with the fancy forensic psychology degree; you tell me which one of them did it."

In this part . . .

The work done by forensic psychologists covers an increasingly wide range of topics; everything from exploring how to detect deception and malingering all the way through to helping families who have juvenile delinquents in their midst. Other examples are helping witnesses to remember and assessing how dangerous a person really is. These professional contributions occur in many different institutions: law courts, prisons, special secure hospitals for people sent there by the courts, in the community at large and on rare occasions even as part of police investigations. They concern themselves with all sorts of criminals from arsonists to terrorists and crimes starting with every letter of the alphabet in between.

At the heart of what forensic psychologists do is an understanding of criminals, their actions and the causes of their behaviour. This links to many other people who are interested in criminals such as criminologists, lawyers and even doctors and geographers. The difference is that psychologists focus on the person rather than patterns of crime, with that person's thoughts and emotions rather than physical or sociological processes. To get started, there is a lot of ground to clear about what forensic psychology is and the basis of what forensic psychologists do. In this part, I map out the fundamentals to get you ready for the more detailed stuff later.

Chapter 1

Discovering the Truth about Forensic Psychology

. . . .

In This Chapter

▶ Figuring out what forensic psychology is and isn't

▶ Seeing where forensic psychology happens

▶ Understanding how forensic psychologists know what they know

▶ Finding out who forensic psychologists work with

. . . .

If you think that you know what forensic psychology is, this chapter may well have a few surprises in store. The abundance of police movies, TV series and crime novels give you a great picture of what forensic psychologists do – sometimes wrongly. Yes, police movies and TV series are truly criminal in content, but often only in terms of their inaccuracies and simplifications! Forensic psychology is an ambitious and diverse discipline and in this chapter I take a look at some specifics of the profession to sort out the reality from the fiction.

Whatever activity a forensic psychologist is involved in, he's arriving at logical conclusions using systematic, scientific procedures. The forensic psychologist's work is founded as much as possible on objective research, which isn't always easy to do for reasons I discuss in this chapter.

Grasping What Forensic Psychology Is Not

You know the typical crime movie plot, which goes something along the following lines: the detectives in the film are stumped (you'd have no plot if they found the criminal sitting crying at the crime scene). The serial killer has killed again (why are most killers in films serial killers?) and the pressure is on to find him (or more rarely, her). Enter the forensic psychologist, usually grudgingly, just when he's having enough problems, with drink, his girlfriend, or both. He visits the crime scene and magically knows what the murderer was thinking, why he killed, and how the police can catch him. But the killer refuses to talk, and so the heroic forensic psychologist settles down for an intellectual battle of wits leading to the criminal revealing all. (Along the way of course the forensic psychologist loses custody of his darling daughter, his girlfriend walks out on him again, and he returns to the bottle.)

I'm no scriptwriter, but I'm sure the scene is familiar to you. Well, as this book and this chapter shows, the typical crime storyline has more to do with Conan Doyle's fictional detective Sherlock Holmes, and all the well-known fictional sleuths following in his footsteps, than with the work of the present-day forensic psychologist.

Often, the best way of understanding the details of a professional activity is to clear the area around the profession and so establish what it's not. This approach is particularly important for forensic psychology, which shares friendly, neighbourly relationships with many other areas and professions. You'd certainly be forgiven for thinking, for example, that forensic psychology is the same as criminology.

Journalists mistakenly often refer to me as a criminologist, even though I'm no expert on changes in the pattern of crime over the centuries or between different countries, and I know little about the effects of different forms of punishment on the prevalence of crimes or the effectiveness of different crime prevention strategies.

I know only a little about crime as a general area, but have spent my entire career as a forensic psychologist taking a lot of interest in criminals. And yet, as a forensic psychologist, I may criticise general considerations of how to cut crime or treat offenders, but journalists generally have little understanding about what I know about how criminals act and think.

Forensic psychologists don't:

- ✔ Study broad trends in criminality.
- ✔ Examine how the legal system works.
- ✔ Solve crimes.

Finding out that forensic psychology isn't forensics

Forensic psychology isn't *forensics*, which is the application of science in legal investigations, such as the chemistry of poisons, the physics of bullets, determining the time of death or how a person was killed. In other words, all the aspects of the Crime Scene Investigation featuring in so many TV crime series.

The examination of the scene of a crime and the exploration of the forensic evidence that can be drawn from the crime is sometimes useful to a forensic psychologist, for example in challenging an offender's claim in therapy.

Although in some crime fiction the forensic scientist may offer up opinions about the mental state of the offender or similar speculations to keep the storyline moving, this activity is quite different to forensic psychology.

Distinguishing forensic psychology from psychiatry

Psychologists aren't *psychiatrists* – doctors treating mental illness and related matters, which some legal systems call 'diseases of the mind'. Psychiatrists are allowed to prescribe drugs and other forms of medical treatment and specialise in working with people who have problems in relating or their ability to deal effectively with others and the world around them.

To help their patients, psychiatrists may use talking therapies as well as medical interventions. Treatment can include the type of intensive psychotherapy initiated by Sigmund Freud, called *psychoanalysis*. When they're not prescribing pills, electric shock therapy, or brain surgery and are treating their mentally ill patients by non-invasive means, psychiatrists are drawing on psychological research.

Although some overlap exists between forensic psychology and forensic psychiatry, most of the topics in this book – such as testimony, measuring aspects of personality and mental state, giving guidance on court procedures, and many aspects of the psychological treatment of offenders – are carried out by forensic psychologists. When psychiatrists are involved in assessment and treatment, I believe that they're practising forensic psychology. They may not agree, however.

Recognising What Forensic Psychology Is

Psychologists start out studying general psychology, focusing on such things as memory, learning, personality, and social interaction. Psychology students examine which bits of the brain light up when different activities are engaged in and the biological and genetic basis of human experience. Therefore they do study some of the areas that medical students explore, but in far less detail.

After finishing general undergraduate training, psychologists can specialise in a number of different areas of psychology, including occupational, educational, health, or even environmental psychology. Psychologists do further training, if they want to get a professional post in one of these areas. (In Chapter 18, I list the stages in becoming a professional forensic psychologist.)

Psychologists working at providing assessment and therapy with mentally ill people are called *clinical psychologists,* and their activities overlap with those of psychiatrists. In times past there was quite a turf war going on between clinical psychologists and psychiatrists, but in recent years both professions have come to respect each other and recognise the value of working together.

Some psychiatrists specialise even further and work mainly with patients brought to them through the legal system. They're known as *forensic psychiatrists*. The medical profession is held in such high regard by the courts that at one time only psychiatrists were allowed to give evidence on the mental state of defendants. That has changed over the last decade or two and now psychologists often provide expert evidence in court.

The term *forensic* originally meant 'of service to the court' but its meaning has broadened out to cover anything connected to crime, criminals and the court of law. *Psychologists* focus on how people think, feel and act. However, a forensic psychologist may explore many different aspects of a crime, and the easiest way to approach his role is by thinking of crime as a process. This process is described in this section.

Step 1: Crime starts with a criminal

A crime occurs or is created by the criminal. The crime may involve the victim suffering direct personal violence or indirectly, as in a burglary of their home when they aren't present (the experience isn't indirect, I just mean that no direct personal confrontation is involved). A number of psychological issues are relevant at this stage, notably the characteristics of the criminal and how they see or create the opportunities for crime. The consequences for victims of crime (an increasingly important area of forensic psychology) are important too, although often forgotten about in crime fiction and sometimes in real life. (Flip to Chapter 7 for more about helping victims.)

As a forensic psychologist, I'm interested in the implications of different kinds and styles of crime. Do some crimes require more intelligence or are some likely to be a product of anger or lack of self-control? The recurring debate about whether criminals are born or made (often called the 'nature versus nurture' controversy) is central to these considerations. You can find out more about 'nature or nurture' in Chapter 2.

Where the term forensic psychology comes from

A little Latin is a useful thing. The word *forensic* comes from the Latin *forens*, meaning the Forum, which was the meeting place for sorting out your differences in ancient Rome. The Forum is the origin of the modern court. Now anything that provides help or a service to a court of law is known as *forensic*. That's why you have forensic scientists, forensic pathologists, and even forensic archaeologists. They draw on their own experience and knowledge to give evidence in court that helps the judge and jury make decisions. Originally, only psychologists who gave expert evidence in court were called forensic psychologists, but nowadays any psychologist who helps with anything to do with legal procedures, policing or offenders may be called a forensic psychologist, even if they never set foot in a court of law.

The term *forensic* has become so widespread that it's now attached to any psychologist who has anything to do with crime, criminals or their victims in a way that's relevant to detection, trials, treatment or imprisonment, or the impact of crime. Now the term *forensic* has gone as far as including those psychologists who help in selecting people to become police officers although their work doesn't involve anything at all to do with legal proceedings. *Forensic* now includes the crime psychologist (I prefer that to 'criminal psychologist' because that sounds as if a dodgy psychologist is being mentioned!), police psychologist, investigative psychologist, and prison psychologist – all terms that overlap with forensic psychologist. To add to this confusion the label takes on different meanings in different countries because different legal systems allow different sorts of expert intervention. I explain some of these differences where they're especially relevant in the book.

So forensic psychology is like many terms in common use – difficult to define precisely but you recognise it when you see it.

Don't get too het up about defining the term forensic psychology and instead look at what forensic psychologists do and where they do it. Some experts may think that I cast the net too wide in this book and others may think that I leave out important areas. But I'm sure they all agree that forensic psychology is a fascinating and vibrant part of modern psychology.

Step 2: Reporting of the crime

Most reports consist of a person giving a verbal account of the crime and, if an investigation follows, the crime scene is examined (the job of trained crime scene investigators). A victim or witness in a police interview gives an account of the crime with the interviewer attempting to get the interviewee to remember as clearly as possible what happened. (I discuss witnesses and interviews in more detail in Chapter 4.) Psychologists have been studying memory for well over 150 years and nowadays a lot is known about how the memory works, which is relevant to improving police interviews.

When a suspect is interviewed (and some witnesses), issues of lying and other forms of deception may come into play. (I describe these issues in further detail in Chapter 6.) The possibility of detecting lying and deception is likely to be a great help, and plenty of psychologists have had a go at this tricky problem. Establishing if you're being told the truth is especially important where a person may be making a false allegation that a crime occurred, or in the unexpected, but not uncommon, false admission to a crime.

Step 3: Investigation gets underway

A few forensic psychologists may help with many aspects of police procedures, most famously by 'offender profiling'. I put this term in inverted commas because, as I discuss in Chapter 5, the technique isn't what sensational fiction suggests. Sure, from time to time a person crops up on TV or in the newspapers putting himself forward as a profiler, suggesting he's a modern Sherlock Holmes. But if profilers are doing the job properly, they aren't basing their proposals on instinct and intuition, or even the brilliant insights that made Holmes so admired, but using established scientific procedures.

Profiling procedures are still in their infancy and their predictions only weakly successful. Profiling is best understood as a small part of the much broader growth in the psychological study of criminals, their victims and various aspects of the legal process. These studies are trying to find out what it's about an individual that leads him to offend (or at least to offend more seriously than the average citizen). Forensic psychologists look at what goes on in interviews during investigations in order to improve the information the investigators have to work with.

A lot of forensic psychology is concerned with helping people who've become criminals to find a way out of their life of crime or at least to cope with their imprisonment in a way that's less personally destructive.

Some developments over the last decade that draw on geographical analysis as well as behavioural analysis show the huge gap between the brilliant but flawed profiler and the neutral scientific process. The question of how investigators make decisions is also a fascinating psychological one, but still rarely studied.

Step 4: An offender is apprehended

The forensic psychologist gets down to work at this stage. He or she assesses the individual's ability to understand the legal process, or whether any aspects of his (see this book's Introduction for why I use the male pronoun throughout) mental state mean that he was unable to be aware of the nature or consequence of his actions. Assessments help the court to decide if the person is fit to stand trial and whether aspects of his mental capacity need to be taken into account during the trial. An assessment can also influence what the court decides is to happen to the defendant if he's convicted.

Step 5: Conviction for a crime

If a person is convicted, he may undergo a variety of punishments or indeed 'treatments'. Psychologists may be active in helping him through those punishments and in providing various forms of assistance. Most commonly, help is given if the person has some obvious psychological problems. Alcoholism is a typical example of the problem a person may be struggling with that leads him into crime. Violence between people who are intimates, often called 'domestic violence', is another area where an offender can be helped to deal with his personality and interpersonal issues. Sexual offending (which I discuss in Chapter 15) is a further activity that may grow out of the offender misunderstanding the impact or significance of his actions, and which psychotherapeutic interventions can help.

Treatment and other interventions with offenders is one of the fastest growing areas of forensic psychology. I talk about treatment and interventions for offenders in Part V.

Step 6: After the trial

Psychological assessments of criminals go on long after the trial is over, in prisons and in other places dealing with offenders. These assessments are the bread and butter of the day-to-day work of the majority of forensic psychologists. Assessments are made up of a variety of different, standard procedures that have been developed over the years to measure aspects of an offender's personality, intellect, experience, attitudes and actions. Go to Chapter 9 to find out how these measuring procedures are developed.

A particularly interesting aspect of assessment is the consideration of individuals who have no obvious mental illness or other intellectual problems, but who clearly have difficulty in relating effectively to others. At the extreme such people may be called 'evil' and they pose a challenge to psychological assessment. Various approaches to this issue have been explored but the dominant one is to think of the person as having a *personality disorder,* the main example being *psychopathy.* I cover these issues a little more in Chapter 2 and give over the whole of Chapter 10 to personality disorders.

Considering the court process raises many intriguing psychological and social psychological questions, but answering them is difficult and greatly influenced by the differences between different legal systems. For example, many courts throughout the world don't have juries: legally trained professionals, magistrates or judges make all the decisions. Where juries do exist, important differences arise in how psychological issues are dealt with and, crucially from the point of doing research, how possible it is or isn't to examine how the court operates.

Not all legal activity concerns criminal acts

In my overview of the areas of activity of forensic psychology, I talk about 'crime' and 'offending'. But that isn't the only legal process in which psychology is relevant.

Courts consider a host of other events, usually referred to as *civil proceedings* and in which no-one is charged with a crime but there's a disagreement that requires a court of some sort to decide upon. One example is a coroner's court in which the cause of death is to be determined. Family courts in which custody of children may be the central issue are places where you often find psychologists assessing the parents or the children, their relationships or other related matters.

I think of some proceedings as *quasi-legal.* They're rather like courts of law but don't carry the same weight or formality. Examples include employment tribunals, where a person is perhaps claiming wrongful dismissal, reviews of a person's disability in relation to an accident claim, or a claim for disability benefits from the state. As well as possible medical aspects, these examples may also feature significant psychological issues.

I also use the terms 'police' or 'investigation' in a rather loose way. Many of the people carrying out investigations aren't police officers, but may be insurance or arson investigators, customs and excise, tax collectors or other government agencies involved in aspects of law enforcement. All these areas are increasingly drawing on forensic psychology.

In the US, issues around proceedings are more open. The delightful film, based on the John Grisham novel *The Runaway Jury* pushes to the extreme the ways in which some knowledge of individual personality processes and social dynamics can influence juries. The attorney used this advice in the film to try and choose a jury that would give him the verdict he wanted and then to manipulate the way he presented arguments to them so they would take his side. I won't tell you how it all pans out in case you want to watch the film or read the book, but you can be sure it was not as you might expect.

Plenty of professional psychologists in the US, while not going as far as the characters in the film, do endeavour to help attorneys in selecting who should be eliminated from a jury and how to present the case to take account of how and what a jury understands of a case.

Reviewing the origins of forensic psychology

Although professional forensic psychologists have only been operating in any numbers over the past 25 years, activity that can be recognised as forensic psychology is as old as modern psychology, going back to the latter half of the nineteenth century. Indeed, just about any development in scientific psychology quickly finds an application in some aspect of the legal process. Many well-known psychological studies started in the university and found their way into court as evidence. (I describe some of these landmark cases in Chapter 20.) Also, clinical practitioners working directly with patients have also contributed to developments in forensic psychology. In this section, I review these two parallel disciplines of psychology.

The academic strand

All the applications of psychology to crime and law that I discuss in this section have their origins in the research laboratories of universities. New procedures have come from the products of careful study independently of the cut and thrust of legal debate or the challenges of a particular case. Later on, these procedures were applied directly to actual cases as illustrated in the nearby sidebar 'Defending a mayor from a charge of obscene behaviour'.

The law deals with all aspects of people in all the situations they find themselves. No surprise, therefore, that every major area of psychology and every significant psychologist has found relevance in some consideration of crime, criminality, investigation and prosecution. As a result, the links of psychology to the law are most notable in those countries where psychologists have been most numerous and active. Sigmund Freud, for example, told judges in Vienna in1906 that they needed to be aware of how witnesses can inadvertently distort information because of unconscious processes.

ANECDOTE

Defending a mayor from a charge of obscene behaviour

Professor Lionel Haward (1920–98) is the father of forensic psychology in the UK and gave evidence in many cases, often using procedures derived from experimental psychology as the basis for his evidence.

One particularly interesting (not to say amusing) case was when Haward acted for the defence of a local mayor who was accused of indecent exposure in a public toilet. This charge resulted from two police officers following up complaints of indecent activities by hiding themselves in a cubicle in the public conveniences, peering through a grill in the door.

The defendant claimed that he'd been wearing a pink scarf at the time and that the enthusiastic police officers, keen to make an arrest, were so primed to expect indecency that they misinterpreted this innocent apparel for a part of his anatomy!

Haward set up an experiment in which naïve subjects were shown photographs under limited lighting conditions of the mayor wearing his scarf. The subjects were given the expectation that something untoward was illustrated in the pictures and asked to indicate when they saw it and what it was.

Haward found that one picture in every eight was believed to represent an indecent act. Haward offered these results together with an explanation of the psychological processes involved and citation of other studies illustrating the power of expectancies on the interpretation of ambiguous images. The attorney used this report as the basis for invalidating the police evidence. The mayor was acquitted.

As early as 1908, Harvard Professor of Psychology Hugo Münsterberg published a book with the modern sounding title *On the Witness Stand*, in which he described the various ways in which the discoveries of the newly emerging discipline of psychology were of relevance to expert evidence in court. Many of the topics discussed are still relevant today, such as the fallibility of witnesses' memories, false confessions and how the court process itself can influence what people admit to. (Check out Chapter 4 for much more on memory and witnesses.) In Germany in 1909, where psychological research was also very active, Clara and William Stern published a book that considered children's ability to remember and give effective testimony as well as examination of the various psychological processes that may give rise to false testimonies.

A recurring interest in the psychology of lying and deception and the possibility that physiological changes in the person can reveal such deception was an early application of laboratory-derived ideas to forensic considerations. In 1915, William Marston, a student of Münsterberg, introduced the first 'lie detector' that measured a person's blood pressure when answering questions about a past event. Within a few years similar procedures were being used successfully in criminal investigations. This laid the groundwork for many procedures that are in use today. I talk much more about deception in Chapter 6.

Following on from the work of the early pioneers in psychological research, an increasing number of psychological studies of relevance to the law were carried out. Examining psychological issues relating to testimony and deception have become the cornerstone of this work. But broader issues such as beliefs about rape, or social psychological aspects of jury decision-making, have now taken this far beyond those explorations a century ago.

The clinical strand

Alongside the academic explorations of human behaviour and experience that I describe in the preceding section, people working directly with patients in a clinical context have, from early in the 20th century, contributed to various aspects of legal proceedings.

Lionel Haward was a clinical psychologist carrying out therapy with patients. Some of his patients came to him through the courts, for assessment or treatment, and out of that contact he was called on to give expert evidence. He drew on psychological procedures as illustrated in the sidebar 'Defending a mayor from a charge of obscene behaviour', but as with most clinical psychologists his main contribution to court procedure was from the point of view of a clinician offering an informed, objective opinion about a patient.

Giving testimony

One of the founders of modern, scientific psychology was J. McKeen Cattell, working at Columbia University in the 1890s. He was very interested in how people remember and how accurately they could recall what had happened. He thus set in motion the study of the psychology of testimony that has grown ever since and thrives today.

The assessment of an individual for the courts is usually traced back to a famous case in 1843 when Daniel McNaughton shot Edward Drummond. Apparently McNaughton thought he was shooting Sir Robert Peel, who was the leader of the Tory party at the time. McNaughton said that the reason for the shooting was that:

> *The Tories in my native city have compelled me to do this. They follow and persecute me wherever I go, and have entirely destroyed my peace of mind.*

This claim was taken to mean that McNaughton was mentally disturbed, causing a furore in the British legal system at the time.

To understand this case, I need to introduce a couple of legal Latin terms.

For a person to be convicted in most places in the world, certain conditions need to be satisfied:

- **Actus reus** – meaning that the act did actually occur (or some crime was committed because an action did not occur).

- **Mens rea** – meaning that the individual knew what he was doing, knew that it was wrong and did it intentionally.

In their wisdom, lawyers think of mental disturbances as (simplistically) implying that the person isn't guilty if his mind isn't guilty. (They have a neat Latin phrase for this, but I think you've had enough Latin for now!) When lawyers start talking about the mind, though, they open the door to psychologists and psychiatrists, who are more than ready to comment on other people's minds and how in contact with reality they are.

Now, back to the McNaughton case. At the time, convicting someone who didn't appreciate the significance of his own actions, or whose actions weren't under his rational voluntary control, was considered uncivilised. The confusion in the existing law that required only the second condition of *mens rea* to be met, but didn't detail how that can relate to mental disturbance, led to a clarification of the law in what became called the McNaughton Rules. The rules recognised that a 'disease of the mind' can exist in which the person couldn't have voluntary and conscious control over his actions or be really aware of their significance. Therefore, on the basis of *mens rea*, McNaughton was found not guilty of murder.

The idea that the mind (rather than the brain) is an organ that can be diseased, like the liver or heart, shows how subtle (or possibly ignorant!) lawyers can be. Plenty of illnesses of the brain don't affect a person's ability to voluntarily and consciously commit a crime. Similarly, many disturbed mental states can't be linked directly to brain disease. So a seemingly straightforward legal requirement opened the doors to professionals who worked with mentally ill patients to give guidance to the court on whether the defendant was in a psychologically sound state at the time of the crime to be legally responsible for his actions. This situation is still a central issue on which psychologists and psychiatrists give guidance to the court.

Another case, this time from the US, helps to illustrate this situation of clinical psychology helping the legal system. When Christopher Simmons was a few months shy of his 18th birthday, he carefully planned and carried out the murder of Shirley Crook. Simmons was given a death sentence when convicted. However, the American Psychological Association supported his appeal against the death sentence by reviewing studies of teenagers. They stated that juveniles under the age of 18 didn't have the mental ability to take full moral responsibility for their actions, and therefore couldn't be regarded as having *mens rea*. The US Supreme Court accepted this advice and overturned the death penalty. (Turn to Chapter 16 for more on crime and juveniles.)

The consideration of the mental state of the defendant has produced many other issues on which the court welcomes guidance, including:

✔ Deciding whether, due to intellectual ability or mental state, the defendant can understand the court procedures well enough to be fit to plead.

✔ Determining the ability of children to be witnesses and the most effective procedures for involving them in court cases (see Chapter 4).

✔ Predicting the likely risk that an offender may pose in the future and hence implications for his sentencing.

✔ Deciding whether an offender's mental condition is likely to be responsive to treatment.

✔ Helping with the support and assistance to victims (I look at this in Chapter 7).

Examining the Building Blocks of Forensic Psychology

Academic and clinical approaches to psychology may differ. For example, academics research more general aspects of human psychology, such as perception, personality or memory while clinicians are concerned with examining the thoughts, feelings and actions of their patient in the clinic. However, for the forensic psychologist, the academic and clinical strands have never been totally distinct. Nowadays the two strands overlap in many different ways. This raises the interesting question of how forensic psychologists know what they know.

The chief difference between the layman and the professional is that the professional can draw on the body of objective knowledge and findings that come from established scientific procedures. Therefore in this section, I look at the basis on which forensic psychologists form an opinion. Having some knowledge of how this process works, helps to give you a clearer picture of the nature of forensic psychology.

Experimenting

Imagine that you want to show that a particular procedure such as detecting lying really works. The most reliable way of doing this is by using the long-established scientific procedure of the carefully controlled experiment. This experiment needs to demonstrate that the procedure detects when people are lying better than the chance probability of, say, throwing a dice, and also that the scientific procedure can detect the truth better than chance.

The challenge in setting up these types of experiments is that ethical limits often exist on what the subjects in an experiment can be asked to do. For example, you can't ask people to commit a real crime, mix them in with others who didn't and then see if you can spot the liars. You have to set up some sort of artificial situation, which means that, no matter how realistic you make it, the same emotional pressures don't exist as, for example, in a real murder case where the murderer is desperately trying to avoid being found out.

Other difficulties come from getting a reliable comparison between the conditions that are of interest and some neutral comparable circumstances. An important example is in experiments that are trying to improve interview procedures. What do you compare any new interview procedure with? How do you measure the differences between new and comparison procedures? As in the example of lying, interviewing people about a serious event you know is fictitious can be fruitless, but if you interview people about actual events there may be something special about those events and how they're remembered that means they aren't typical of other situations. Does it make any difference whether you're interviewing people who have experienced a burglary in contrast to a violent assault?

These questions show how complicated setting up carefully controlled experiments in the area of forensic psychology can be.

Overall, many experiments are rather artificial. They use students pretending in various ways, or people are shown videos rather than experiencing actual events directly. Attempts to repeat the results in real situations aren't always successful.

Nonetheless, some of the basic issues, especially in the area of testimony have been opened up by using carefully controlled academic experiments.

Studying in the field

Studies carried out in real life situations are generally regarded as producing results that can be applied more readily to other real circumstances. The most common form of study is in evaluating the impact of a particular intervention, such as a treatment programme for alcoholics or a screening procedure for selecting prison staff. Ideally such studies also require careful comparisons, at least with what happened before the intervention, but preferably with other established procedures.

These studies can explore many related processes in large scale analyses such as, for example, when considering the impact on future criminality of different ways of dealing with criminals. The results from this specific research merge with more general areas of criminality. Psychologists expect to pay particular attention to making sure that like is compared with like and carrying out detailed analysis of who was being dealt with in each of the forms of treatment or punishment. Often the impact of any intervention with an offender depends more on the nature of the offender – his age or how deep he's in a criminal culture – rather than exactly what punishment or treatment he gets.

Assessing and measuring

The focus on individuals and understanding their particular psychology is such a central aspect of forensic psychology that a great deal of research and practice revolves around assessing the characteristics of individuals. In Part III I go through some of the processes that are used to develop assessment instruments. For now, you just need to know that this measuring is far from a casual activity.

When forensic psychologists decide that measuring an aspect of a person is useful, they take care to define the aspect precisely. It may be sexual fantasies, psychopathy, malingering, suggestibility, general levels of deviance or a whole host of other crucial aspects that may be relevant to some area of how the judicial system deals with such people.

Having decided on what to examine, the psychologist then forms and tries out careful statements, possibly in a questionnaire to be answered, or guidance of what's to be observed in an interview or information gathered from records about the person. In some cases, the respondent may be asked to perform tests, or physiological measurements may be made of the person under certain conditions. An example is measuring if a man gets an erection when viewing different forms of sexually explicit pictures as a way of finding out his sexual preferences.

After the procedure is developed, it's tested in several ways with different samples of people so that the procedure can be effectively calibrated. Eventually, after a number of studies of the procedure in actual use, a court of law may accept it as providing a measure that can guide the court's deliberations or as the basis for determining treatment regimes or parole.

The two key aspects of reliability and validity are required before the measurement instrument can be trusted. Psychological assessment measurements can't be taken at face value and have to be demonstrated through research:

- ✔ **Reliability:** How consistently the procedure measures what it measures. For example, a measuring tape made out of elastic isn't reliable because it gives a different length for the same object every time it's used.

- ✔ **Validity:** How well the procedure measures what it claims to measure. A measure of sexual fantasies that was in fact assessing how much pornography a person watched can be misleading, although asking the person about what he liked watching may indicate sexual preferences.

Validity is more difficult to establish than reliability because validity requires a careful definition of what the measurement is supposed to be measuring.

There are lots of other aspects of psychological measurements that are important before they can be used with confidence, but two are enough for now. You can find out about other psychological measurements in Part III.

Studying individual cases

Many breakthroughs in medicine come from the study of an individual person. Working from a single case is much easier for doctors, because usually the majority of human bodies are more or less physically the same: two arms, two eyes, the same sort of kidneys and liver (give or take a few beers!).

In contrast, an individual's psychological make-up is distinctly different from the next person's, and even if many similarities exist, everybody *thinks* that they're unique. For this reason, psychologists frown on a single study as a way of making discoveries and then applying the discovery to numberless people. However, single cases are very useful in illustrating results drawn from other scientific procedures, which is how I use case-studies throughout this book.

Getting theoretical

I don't want you to think that forensic psychology is all numbers and observation and prisoners filling in questionnaires. None of these ways of collecting information about people makes much sense unless accompanied by explanation and understanding of what the forensic psychologist is doing. In science such insights come from what is broadly known as 'theory'.

Psychological theories aren't idle speculations or impossible suggestions in the way that the word theory is often used in daily life. In the study of psychology, *theories* consist of carefully defined ideas that are related to each other in an argument, which is then tested by obtaining some information (usually called data) from actual situations.

So, when you ask whether criminals are born or created by their experiences, called the 'nature or nurture' question, you're really asking which of the two broad theories about the origins of crime is most plausible.

As I show throughout this book, when you start to define more clearly what key concepts mean and you look for the evidence, the theories usually become more subtle and more complicated. But that's what makes forensic psychology so fascinating.

Professional ethics

All of the activities that forensic psychologists are engaged in carry serious consequences, both legally and professionally. A person's life or freedom can hang on what the psychologist says. There are therefore many constraints and guidelines for what forensic psychologists do. I explore ten of these in Chapter 17.

Working with Others: People and Places That Forensic Psychologists Encounter

Forensic psychologists don't spend their time locked in prison cells chatting to serial killers. They find themselves interacting with a great range of people in various ways:

✔ **Patients:** Some people are assigned to forensic psychologists through the legal process and offered therapy or given help in other ways to cope with any psychological problems.

✔ **Clients:** People, without personal problems, buying into assistance from forensic psychologists on matters such as getting help with setting up selection procedures, say for prison officers or policemen who work on sexual assault cases, or giving advice on interviewing procedures that may be used in many different sorts of investigations.

✔ **Witnesses:** In some cases witnesses may need special help to cope with the legal process or even to remember more clearly what happened. Young children can pose special problems to the courts. Forensic psychologists may be brought in to help with these matters.

✔ **Other professionals:** Fellow professionals can turn to the forensic psychologist to assist in throwing light on the circumstances of a case or for help in understanding the actions of an individual. Assessing future risk is a particularly important service in this regard, as I describe in Chapter 10.

The following sections list some of the settings and groups of people where the forensic psychology makes an important contribution.

In the courts

Forensic psychologists carry out the following tasks, for example, in relation to criminal cases:

✔ Giving help in selecting jury members or giving lawyers guidance on how to present a case, especially in the US.

✔ Evaluating the competence of a defendant to stand trial.

✔ Providing risk and other assessments that can influence the sentencing of a convicted person.

- Assessing whether a convicted person is mentally sound enough to face the death penalty (in the US).

- They can act for the prosecution or the defence. I've done both, although not in the same trial of course.

In civil cases and in quasi-legal settings, including industrial and employment tribunals or internal reviews of employees, forensic psychologists carry out the following tasks, for instance:

- Evaluating child custody cases.

- Assessing whether child abuse occurred.

- Appraising competency of key individuals.

- Gauging psychological effects of trauma, personal injury, product liability, harassment and professional negligence.

- Reviewing judgements made about behavioural material, such as offensive communications.

Depending on the jurisdiction, forensic psychologists can also offer the same sort of help and expertise in criminal cases.

With victims

Forensic psychologists provide help to victims by:

- Educating and assisting those who are responsible for notifying relatives of a victim's death.

- Treating victims or witnesses of crime.

- Training people who supply services to victims.

In prisons, 'special hospitals' and correctional institutions

The sorts of tasks that forensic psychologists carry out in institutions include:

- Helping to select personnel for employment in the prisons.

- Providing support, especially in stress management, for those working in institutions.

✔ Evaluating programmes in use or proposed programmes for helping offenders from re-offending, such as the anger management and sexual awareness programmes I describe in Part V.

✔ Contributing to decisions about how prisoners are classified and suitable placements in appropriate institutions or on the different sorts of programmes I discuss in Chapters 13 to 16.

With the police

Forensic psychologists sometimes do the following in criminal investigations:

✔ Give guidance on the search for an unknown offender.

✔ Train and assist in interviews of victims, witnesses and suspects.

✔ Advise on dealing with mentally ill people.

✔ Offer guidance on handling domestic violence.

Forensic psychologists may also:

✔ Supply counselling services for police officers involved in shooting or other traumatic incidents.

✔ Give support in hostage negotiations.

Chapter 2

Exploring the World of the Criminal

In This Chapter

▶ Understanding who criminals are

▶ Knowing the explanations for what makes a criminal

▶ Examining the relationship between mental illness and crime

▶ Considering what prevents people committing crimes

*W*hen I first went into a prison – with a colleague to interview some inmates, I hasten to add – I was struck by the fact that she kept all her keys for unlocking the various doors in a special leather pouch. The idea was to foil some clever prisoner noting a key dangling on a belt, memorising it and secretly setting about making a copy to aid his escape. A highly unlikely scenario, but even so a picture flashed through my mind of the dangling key and a brilliantly demonic criminal who needed to be second-guessed at every turn.

Forensic psychology doesn't focus on this sort of offender for the simple reason that you so rarely meet them in real life. In this chapter, I look at the different sorts of *real* people who become criminals and offer you reasons as to how offenders get that way. I show the limitations of the over-simplistic 'nature or nurture' debate and suggest that much more is involved in a person becoming an offender than how his genes fit or whether he loves his mother. A particularly important aspect of someone becoming an offender is the difference between personality disorders and mental illness and how both relate, or don't. Of course, not everyone turns to a life of crime and so I also talk about what stops the majority of people from breaking the law.

Defining Criminals and Crimes

If I ask you, 'How does a person become a criminal?', you may well answer 'He commits a crime.' Correct, but that begs the question of what's illegal.

For example, in some countries, as in many countries in the past, consentual homosexual activity is against the law, inviting imprisonment or even execution. Another example is the world of financial management, where business practice can vary significantly from one country to another, so that what's acceptable in one country is considered fraud in another.

People are labelled as *criminals* because they break the law and not because of some inherent characteristic of the person.

This section takes a look at some basic terms and aspects of crimes and criminals (which turn out to be more complicated than you may think), and I hope explains and corrects a few myths and misconceptions.

Getting caught (or not)

Being labelled a criminal means getting caught and convicted of a crime. I'm always amused by the TV police drama where the story ends with the roll of dramatic music as the culprit gives himself away quite unintentionally during the police interview or in the way he tied the victim's shoelaces. Rarely does the storyline take into account whether the evidence is going to stand up in a court of law, or if a good defence attorney can show that the evidence means something quite different to what the detective claims.

Early ideas about identifying criminals

Cesare Lombroso (1835–1909) was one of the first people in modern times to study criminals and criminality, and although many of his ideas are now discredited, he left a mark on how people think of criminals even today. Lombroso tried to identify what's distinct about criminals, and his efforts contributed to the (of course, wrong) idea that criminals are some sort of subspecies of society. He also claimed that criminals had distinct bodily features, being above or below average height with 'projecting ears, thick hair, a thin beard, enormous jaws, a square and projecting chin and large cheekbones'. He suggested that criminals were heavier than non-criminals or markedly lighter, pigeon-breasted, with an imperfectly developed chest and stooping shoulders. Criminals were also flat-footed! He even produced an *Atlas of Criminal Types* showing you what a poisoner, for example, or an assassin looked like.

Lombroso's idea was that criminals are less evolved than the rest of society, and closer to being animals. A few careful studies comparing non-criminals (university students actually) with criminals soon showed how mistaken Lombroso was. But the idea that criminals are of a certain type and can be characterised in obvious ways still hangs on, as I know every time a journalist asks the silly question: 'Can you just tell me the typical profile of a serial killer/robber/rapist/fraudster.'

In real life things are somewhat different. In most countries statistics show that, of burglaries reported to the police, only one in every ten burglars is caught; and possibly as many as six out of every ten burglaries aren't even reported. An even smaller proportion of rape allegations lead to a rapist being convicted. The figures for murder are more encouraging in that only a handful out of every hundred murders remain unsolved, at least in Western countries. This success is often because the murderer is known to the victim and so can be readily tracked down, and he may even give himself up (it's not unusual that it's the killer who calls the police and admits the crime).

Experts call unreported and unsolved crimes the *dark figure* of crime – a bit like dark matter in the universe that astrophysicists know exists but they can't see. These hidden crimes may be similar to solved crimes or they can be very different. However, many explanations of crime that are based on studies of convicted criminals can be distorted by the characteristics of the offenders whose crimes are reported. The fact is that not all criminals share these characteristics. No doubt some very astute, capable people do turn to crime – like the Tom Ripley character in Patricia Highsmith's novels – and constantly get away with it so that they don't regularly feature in criminal psychology research.

When studying the personality of criminals, experts are usually dealing with people who are convicted. The offenders have been caught and (typically) are in prison, because that's where researchers can find them and ask them to fill in questionnaires or do psychological tests. Psychologists can't always tell you therefore what the characteristics are of every person committing a crime, only about those they have access to.

What's deemed to be a crime, the sheer diversity of crimes, and who gets caught and convicted, have significant implications for the forensic psychologist. Under the right circumstances, just about anyone can be labelled a criminal (in certain cultures, even committing adultery can result in someone being treated as a serious criminal). Therefore, great care is needed when discussing the causes of criminality (as I'm doing in this chapter) because there are so many ways and reasons for a person to become designated as a criminal.

Careering towards criminality

Sometimes people refer to persistent offenders as 'career criminals' and as having 'criminal careers'. These terms are misleading, because they imply that a life of crime is similar say to working your way up in a legal organisation. Films about the Mafia give you the idea that members climb a ladder of criminality, like starting as an office boy running errands for the boss and ending up in charge of the whole mob. Although some highly organised criminal groups do exist (such as the Chinese Triads), the vast majority of criminals don't experience anything like a career.

A more useful way to think of 'career criminals' is as persons living on ill-gotten gains. The criminal has no legitimate way of earning a living and devotes himself to crime in the same way as most people have conventional jobs. The term 'criminal career' refers to the range of crimes a person commits over an extended period of time.

You won't find a criminal starting off on a training course, although some people think that prison can provide training in how to commit crime as younsgters mix with more experienced offenders. Fortunately, there's no such thing as becoming junior management of a criminal gang, and then getting promoted to sales manager, and eventually joining the board.

Identifying different forms of similar crimes

In general, there's a difference between crimes involving the taking of property (*property crimes*) and those involving direct interaction with other people (*crimes against the person*). Although this separation is a helpful summary, try asking your friends whether arson is a property crime or a crime against the person and the answers you get are likely to show the limitations of the separation. You need to know a lot more about some crimes before you can accurately place the crime into a category.

Are criminals specialists or versatile?

Criminals aren't usually specialist offenders, choosing to concentrate on being a devious fraudster, an axe-wielding maniac, a cat-burglar who climbs up drainpipes to enter a house, a bank robber, and so on. Studies show that the great majority of people (particularly youngsters) who commit enough crimes to end up in prison are pretty versatile. When I looked into the criminal backgrounds of convicted rapists, for example, I found that eight out of every ten had previously been convicted for some non-violent crime, notably burglary. (Although the vast majority of burglars don't commit sexual assaults.) Older criminals can be a bit more

specialist, but even an experienced cat-burglar doesn't shin up a drainpipe if the front door is left open.

Studies of criminals show that those willing to get involved in violent crime form a distinct subset of the general mass of offenders. Some criminals have more aggressive and confrontational personalities. The majority of offenders, especially burglars, prefer not to take on the occupants of a house.

The other subgroup that tends to be distinct are those who carry out sexual crimes, such as rape or indecent exposure.

I think of all crime as doing violence to a person, whether overtly as in assault, rape or murder, or implicitly as in burglary or many types of fraud. I refer to burglary and robbery a lot in this book because they're such common crimes, and I want to help you to avoid making the mistake I made when I first started out, in thinking that the two crimes are the same thing.

Most legal systems make an important distinction between entering a building and stealing without contact with the occupier (*burglary*) and coming into contact with someone and stealing using the threat of or actual violence (*robbery*).

To complicate matters, some forms of burglary do involve contact with the owner of the stolen goods but not in a threatening or violent manner, as when a person knocks on the door and asks for assistance but then steals something when the occupant isn't looking. Other forms of theft also exist, including various types of fraud and not returning lost property.

These subtle distinctions give you some idea of the many diverse legal definitions there are for the hundreds of things that the law deems to be illegal. This creates a problem for the psychological study of crime because legal refinements, and the distinctions that keep lawyers in business, are often not the distinctions that are relevant or useful to understanding what a person has done or why.

Lawyers and forensic psychologists are interested in different aspects of crime and criminals. They use different terms, or may give different meanings to the same term, such as insanity, which I discuss in Chapter 1.

Important behavioural variations exist within any legally defined crime. Take the following two examples. First, a bank can be robbed in a haphazard, risky way or the offence can be very carefully planned to avoid violent confrontation. The same law is broken in both cases, but the psychology involved is very different. Second, think about the even more contentious example of child sexual abuse. Abuse can occur over time in an unthreatening way, by leading the child to believe that the deed is acceptable, or the assault on the child can be violent. The consequences and implications of these acts may be different for understanding (but, of course, not condoning) the offender and possibly even for the nature of the traumatic effects on the victim.

Throughout this book I use the legal term to describe the criminal act being discussed, but every now and then I try to get to grips with the important behavioural details. Therefore, a person with a number of crimes on his record is called a *serial* criminal and his crimes as a *series*. The term *series* applies to all series of crimes, such as burglary or robbery, not just the favourite of crime fiction, the serial killer. For the forensic psychologist the serial offender is often the most interesting criminal to study. A serial offender may have drifted into crime, or been involved in illegal activity, for a long time, but although he may not think of himself as a criminal, you and I probably recognise him as such.

Criminal characteristics

Criminals are a varied bunch of people, but research shows that there are some general characteristics typical of the average criminal, no matter what the crime:

- They're most often men (about 80 per cent for most crime types).

- They're usually in their mid- to late teens.

- They come from dysfunctional family backgrounds.

- They have family or friends who've been convicted of crimes.

- They probably didn't do well at school.

Of course, plenty of convicted criminals don't have these characteristics (and they sometimes write their autobiographies just to show how capable and misunderstood they are). People from good family backgrounds can end up as murderers or major fraudsters, but they're the exception rather than the rule.

Without doubt, social, economic, political and cultural influences affect the prevalence of crime, but, hey, I'm a forensic psychologist and want you to get to know about the factors relating to characteristics of individuals. To find out more about criminals and crimes check out *Criminology For Dummies* by Stephen Briggs (Wiley).

Committing a Crime: What Leads Someone to Break the Law

Stephen Sondheim's tongue-in-cheek lyric from that great musical *West Side Story* and used to such brilliant effect, seeks to boldly shift any blame for the seriously bad behaviour of the youthful hooligans and delinquents squarely onto society (the full lyrics are available at www.westsidestory.com/lyrics_krupke.php).

Sondheim enjoys sending up the argument so often put forward for excusing criminal behaviour. But as with all explanations for crime, the fact that plenty of people from similar circumstances never become criminals exposes its flaws. In this section, I take a look at several of the suggested causes for crime and try to find out what gives rise to a person becoming a habitual criminal, committing one sort of crime after another, over a few hours, days or a number of years.

You may notice in the section 'Defining Criminals and Crimes', that I didn't get round to discussing what causes a person to become a criminal (or not). In fact, almost anyone is capable of committing a crime in a given situation – and probably everyone does from time to time, like filching the coloured paper from the office stationery cupboard to make party hats, or driving over the speed limit.

Most people, most of the time, avoid doing anything seriously criminal. Even in very difficult circumstances, when survival may depend on breaking the law, many people resist.

It's suprising how people act in an emergency, such as being caught in a building on fire. I've seen people put their lives in danger so as not to break the law. For example, when a fire alarm sounds in shops or a restaurant, and even with smoke visible, many people queue up or wait to pay their bill rather than just running for the exit.

Giving birth to criminals?

Under the heading 'Defining Criminals and Crimes', I talk about how different legal systems define crime differently and the many different sorts of crimes that exist, from impulsive and violent crimes to crimes requiring intelligent planning so as to avoid violence. Some criminals may work alone and some criminals operate in a group. Therefore, stating a general cause for criminality that holds true around the world and that gives rise to the many different types of crime is impossible.

Perhaps you're thinking, 'that's all very well, but what causes a person to commit a crime . . . is it nature or nurture . . . is somebody born a criminal or does he become that way through having the skills, experience and opportunity?'

The causes of crime lie partly in inherited characteristics and partly in upbringing and circumstances. Both aspects of a person can combine together to produce an offender. For example, consider someone with little intellectual ability, for whom school is one big turn-off, who finds more interest and excitement in mixing with his older brothers who're already committing crimes. Is it nature or nurture that makes him a criminal?

More likely, some general personality characteristics – such as the desire for excitement, impulsivity and low intelligence – open up the social pathways that can lead to becoming a criminal. But of course tendencies such as seeking excitement can also be channelled into more productive activities such as sports (although sporting activities also need self-discipline, hard work and so on). Similarly, plenty of capable, resourceful people grow up in a criminal culture and become gang bosses, when in a different situation and having alternatives they may well have become politicians (assuming you accept the wide difference between the two occupations!).Wanting money can play a part in someone being drawn into criminal activities. Crimes involving financial gain, especially theft, can be caused by a real financial need. However, the average burglar generally makes little money from a burglary (what he makes from selling stolen goods is invariably only a fraction of the real value of the items). Many thieves see burglary as an exciting opportunity and not a carefully considered way of making money.

Calculating the actual financial rewards of burglary is difficult. The opportunity exists for insurance claims being distorted by the victim of a burglary exaggerating their claim (crime feeding on crime).

In contrast to burglary, a carefully planned identity theft is more likely to attract a criminal looking to acquire a steady income. The criminal need have no direct contact with the victim, who's more than likely in a different country. He may tell himself that everything's covered by insurance and so cares nothing about the victim's feelings.

Keeping bad company

Mixing with bad company can so easily lead a person off the straight and narrow. The interesting question, though, is what leads some people into bad company in the first place.

Of course, some people are 'born' into a life of crime. Family and close friends are criminals and so a person discovers how to be a criminal as he grows up, whatever his own psychological make-up.

Crime movies are fond of depicting the dark underworld of the criminal community and the difficulty of quitting and becoming a law-abiding citizen. A type of moral code exists within the criminal community, but the code is a distortion of what's legally acceptable. The many countries in which corruption is endemic show clearly that what a community accepts can be at variance with what the law requires.

In some cases, certain aspects of personality may make a person more prone to accept the opportunities provided by criminal contacts. The person joins in because of the excitement or status a life of crime provides, when a more cautious person likely turns away. This is particularly true of young offenders as I show in Chapter 16.

Abusing substances

Alcoholism and drug abuse are problems closely associated with criminals and crime, although neither conditions are usually regarded as being a form of mental illness and are certainly not a defence in law. However, alcoholism and drug abuse can rapidly lead to crime through:

- Needing a lot of money to feed the habit.
- Making the addict more impulsive, violent or disinhibited.
- Bringing addicts into contact with criminals for the supply of the substances.

How female offenders differ from males

Statistics record that men commit eight out of every ten crimes. The crimes that women commit are generally different from those of men. Women commit far fewer violent crimes and are less likely to be involved in gang crimes or have long careers as criminals. If a woman commits a crime, it's more likely to be fraud of one sort or another, except of course for the illegal activity dominated by women – prostitution (although here, again, who ends up convicted of prostitution varies enormously depending on the local laws).

The criminal justice system tends to deal with convicted women differently from convicted men, with court decisions often being more lenient for women. This leniency is sometimes because of the effect on children of being separated from their mother while she's in prison, or even the assumption that women aren't inherently wicked and that there are some exonerating circumstances which can lower the severity of a woman's sentence. Not uncommonly, people assume that for a woman to commit a crime she must be mentally disturbed, and so she may get a sentence that's regarded as a form of treatment. Courts accept a whole host of psychological conditions as explanations for a woman's illegal actions, which I talk about in Chapter 11.

Sometimes the leniency of the courts can only be put down to a form of 'chivalry', with the judge taking pity on an apparently defenceless, seemingly harmless woman as against the glowering, burly, tattooed man!

Not all alcohol and drug addicts become criminals. If the person who's addicted can afford to pay for his addiction through legitimate means and manages his intake so that it doesn't interfere with his work, he may never become a criminal other than in the act of purchasing illegal drugs. These addicts are more likely to destroy their relationships and health, becoming a social burden rather than a criminal.

As well as alcoholism or drug addiction causing crime, the opposite may also be true: criminals becoming addicts. From the proceeds of crime a criminal can afford to get hold of substances previously out of reach and by mixing with addicted criminals he gets drawn into addiction himself. Drugs may well be easier to obtain in prison than outside, and so a term inside can open the way to addiction.

Passing it on in the blood

Every now and then a pundit comes up with yet another attempt to explain the causes of crime by citing some aspect of the criminals' biological or physiological make-up. These include:

- Brain damage or dysfunction
- Genetic inheritance
- Hormones, especially testosterone and low serotonin levels
- Physical stature

One bizarre suggestion is that the cause of crime is in the water! Apparently, some indicators suggest that increased levels of the chemical silicon fluoride in drinking water are related to higher rates of violent crime.

The problem with accepting any of these reasons as a primary cause of criminality is that plenty of other people sharing the same aspects never commit crimes. So although physiological characteristics may sometimes contribute indirectly, they're unlikely to be the direct cause of crime.

Blaming Darwin

A curious idea that's sometimes aired is that an evolutionary advantage exists to many forms of crime, especially crimes against the person: violent humans are more likely to survive and pass on their genes.

The claim is that if men in prehistory raped then that behaviour increased the likelihood of offspring being conceived and born and thus increasing the genetic availability of whatever genes made rape more likely in the first case. Some criminologists even claim that murder is part of the human evolutionary make-up, because when limited food is around for hunter-gatherers or fertile women are scarce, killing off competitive males increases the chances of survival.

Fascinating though these evolutionary theories may be, they still don't explain away the most prevalent types of crime, burglary and other forms of theft. I believe the evolutionary arguments to be amoral: pseudoscience dressed up in Darwinian clothes. Although evolution may have some general validity in terms of the prevalence of violence throughout human history, the theories never tell you why one brother can be a murderer and another an upright citizen.

Investigating the case of the extra chromosome

Other biological influences that are argued to be the cause of criminality are the basic components of inheritance: chromosomes.

As you probably know, women have two X chromosomes (they're called that because they're X-shaped when viewed under a microscope) but men are different (glad you noticed); they're missing one of the X chromosomes and have a Y chromosome instead. Therefore, what makes men by nature aggressive is often assumed to be down to the Y chromosome.

It wasn't the syndrome that did it

Some men have an added X chromosome; being XXY, which is called the Klinefelter's syndrome. Although some males with this syndrome may appear slightly more effeminate and sadly may suffer from illnesses rare in men, no evidence exists that a person with Klinefelter's syndrome is more docile or less criminal than other men. Indeed, in one tragic case a man with Klinefelter's killed two children. The children had been teasing him mercilessly because of his appearance, and he hit out at them more violently than intended with disastrous consequences.

This idea of the Y chromosome causing aggressive behaviour seems oversimplistic, but this didn't stop some experts of a biological turn of mind getting very excited when they discovered that some offenders were endowed with an additional Y chromosome, being XYY. 'Aha!' they shouted 'That explains why they're criminal . . . they're wearing unusual genes.' When the excitement died down and serious research was carried out, researchers found that plenty of violent criminals had perfectly normal chromosomes and that most people with the XYY anomaly never hurt a fly.

Thinking about crime

Psychologists are fond of the term *cognition,* which refers to a person's thought processes and includes how he or she thinks about themselves, others and the world around them. The particular way a person or group thinks is sometimes called a *cognitive style,* and some experts say what gives rise to becoming a criminal is a person's cognitive style. Talking about the criminal mind as if it's an especially effective organ is misleading. The fictional James Bond villain who's brilliantly masterminding the destruction of the world, having an evil desire for power, is the stuff of the blockbuster crime novel and movie and in no way the sort of criminal you find discussing his attitude to violence in a prison group programme.

Studies of persistent criminals show that they often have a particular way of thinking about themselves and their crimes:

- **Denial of criminality:** This is the direct statement that it didn't happen or not as the victim claimed. 'She wanted sex. It was consensual' would be one example of this. Or in many cases simply 'it was not me who killed her'.

- **Justification:** 'It was them or me.' This thinking is that the criminal owes it to his associates to show who's in charge. Or even the view that he's entitled to take what he believes society owes him. An example is the excessive insurance claim such as in: 'The insurance companies are all rogues and I've been paying my premiums for years without making any claims, so I have a right to get some money back from them.'

The technical term *hostile attribution bias* is useful here as in: 'Who are you looking at!' Many criminals seem highly sensitive to ambiguous comments or gestures that assume they're aggressive, when no accusation of aggression is intended.

✔ **Minimisation:** 'I didn't really hurt her.' This thinking is seeking to minimise the impact or severity of the crime.

A rape victim was telling me that before the rapist climbed back out of the window of her apartment, he said to her: 'You shouldn't have left your window open. Someone could've come in and attacked you,' thus denying to himself that he'd done anything wrong or in anyway injured the traumatised survivor of his assault.

✔ **Rationalisation:** 'Never give a sucker an even break.' Rationalising in this way shifts the blame onto the victim because she was asking for the crime to happen to her, for example, by leaving her purse where anyone can take it.

Another intriguing suggestion that's gaining in popularity is that criminals develop a personal narrative in which they see themselves as heroes or victims, professionals or adventurers. This way of thinking – which seems to mix aspects of self-denial and justification – allows them to maintain their criminal lifestyle.

The thought processes of people who commit crimes are revealed by what they say about their crimes and how they think about their actions, and those things tend to be along the lines of what people often say to themselves in lesser situations. For example, have you ever thought to yourself that your employer isn't going to miss a couple of paper clips and anyway the company made a huge profit this year?

What makes these thought processes part of the cognitive style of criminals is the *application* of them to more extreme situations in which the various denials can never be defended.

Getting personal with the personality of many criminals

Many criminals show a number of common personality traits as well as having shared thought processes (which I list in the section 'Thinking about crime').

Psychologists use the term personality specifically to describe the innate characteristics of a person (do not confuse with a TV personality or celebrity!). In psychology, everyone has a personality that can be studied and measured, like other characteristics that I describe in Part III.

When talking about the personality traits of criminals, I'm referring to aspects of personality that everyone shares to some degree, but which in criminals are, on average, more exaggerated. For example, research shows that many criminals are more extrovert and neurotic than the law-abiding general population.

Here are some shared aspects of the personality of many criminals:

- **External locus of control:** People differ in their thinking on whether fate rules their lives or whether they have control over what happens to them. Psychologists call the dominant influence on a person's life the *locus of control*. Research has identified criminals not taking responsibility for their actions as having an *external locus of control*, the criminal claiming that his actions are someone else's fault (as in the Officer Kruptke song I quoted earlier). The research results aren't clear-cut, however, because some criminals are the opposite and believe that they have a right to take what they want (that is creating your own destiny). This belief is particularly true of another Hollywood favourite, the bank robber.

- **Lack of empathy:** Some criminals don't have the ability to feel what others are feeling. The consequences can be that the criminal doesn't realise the effects of his actions; for example, a burglar or rapist not realising the trauma he's causing the victims. This is similar to *denial of criminality* that I mention in the section 'Thinking about crime', except that lack of empathy is an aspect of personality rather than a thought process. The person is genuinely unable to appreciate what others are going through.

- **Lack of self-control:** Impulsivity or the reluctance to delay gratification have often been associated with criminality, especially among younger offenders and drug users. But then again, lack of self-control doesn't apply to someone who spends months planning a bank robbery.

- **Search for excitement:** Do you thirst to go bungee jumping or racing fast cars? Do you prefer wild parties instead of staying at home reading a book? Do you get bored seeing the same old faces and never dream of going to the same film twice? If you answer yes to all these questions, you're a *sensation seeker* and possibly a risk taker too. Many criminals are sensation seekers, especially the younger ones. They enjoy the excitement of committing the crime and getting away with it. So, when you think about it, the boredom of prison must be particularly punishing for the sensation seeker.

Such personality characteristics are present in people in all walks of life, but do seem to be more common in criminals than non-criminals.

Investigating Mental Disorder and Crime

Having a *mental disorder* is about how a person feels, thinks or acts that reflects some abnormal distress or disability that's not part of normal development or usual within any given culture. (*Personality* describes a normal range of ways of dealing with the world. I talk about personality characteristics typical of many criminals in the section 'Getting personal with the personality of many criminals'.)

There are two main forms of mental disorder. The first is a mental illness in which the person's thoughts and feelings are deeply disturbed and the person may be out of contact with reality. The second form of mental disorder is subtler, and known as *personality disorder.* Having a personality disorder means having an extreme type of personality that marks out a person as not dealing with others in the way most people think of as normal or acceptable.

Here are a few examples to highlight the differences between the two forms of mental disorders:

- ✔ A person who thinks that external issues, such as upbringing, have shaped his life isn't in any way 'disordered'; he's just exhibiting an aspect of his *personality*, like being an extrovert or a neurotic (see the section 'Getting personal with the personality of many criminals').

- ✔ A person (like Daniel McNaughton who I mention in Chapter 1) who thinks that the Tories want to destroy him and so tries to kill a leading member of the Tory party is suffering a *mental illness,* and is likely to be regarded by the courts as insane and therefore 'Not Guilty by Reason of Insanity'.

- ✔ Possibly the first person to be found 'Not Guilty by Reason of Insanity' was James Hadfield who tried to assassinate King George III at the Drury Lane Theatre in London in 1800. The claim made was that Hadfield was suffering from the delusional belief that he, Hadfield, had to die at the hands of others. Trying to kill the king, he thought, was a sure way of getting himself killed.

- ✔ A person who's totally unable to empathise or relate to other people in an acceptable way is described as having a *personality disorder*. One widely discussed personality disorder is *psychopathy*, which I describe briefly in the next paragraph. But there are also other personality disorders listed in Chapter 10.

Note that *psychopathy* is a term applied to people who are impulsive and lack empathy or self-control; some may jump quickly to violence or be superficially charming and ready to take advantage of another's weaknesses. I discuss the term in more detail in Chapter 10 when I look at how psychopathy can be measured.

I have a problem with the idea that someone's personality can be 'disordered'. I find it difficult to understand how what a person is can be broken in some way, because being disordered suggests seeking some ideal, probably God-given, personality that people simply don't match up to. But that's you, me and everyone, isn't it?

However, labels such as 'sadism', 'narcissism' and 'borderline personality disorder' are used in court to explain why a person was unable to help doing what he did, as if he has a disease or a psychosis.

Having a personality disorder doesn't label someone as a potential criminal, but a higher proportion of people with a personality disorder are likely to get into trouble than people whose personalities aren't thought to be 'disordered'.

In Chapter 10 I discuss how experts measure psychopathy and its implications for understanding criminality and also the different types of personality disorders. For now, my aim is to help you get your head around some of the major terms that come into play in this area. Also, try to clear your mind of the single-minded killer of the movies, who's completely devoid of any emotions and just wants to wander around killing people, more or less for the sake of it.

Enjoying the urge to hurt: Sadism

Sadism is a sexual preference in which consenting adults enjoy inflicting pain on one another. One party, a *masochist,* enjoys being hurt, and the other, a *sadist,* enjoys doing the hurting, hence the activity of sado-masochism. Although not my idea of fun, the activity is legal and practised with the opportunity for the masochist to say 'enough is enough' and the other party, the sadist, to stop.

You have to be careful using the term *sadism* in a criminal sense. Consensual sado-masochism is rather different from the personality disorder clinically described as *sadism,* in which being cruel and demeaning to another person, humiliating them and causing them suffering gives pleasure to the sadist. A person with sadistic personality disorder is likely to be fascinated by weapons and violence and find aggression to others amusing. Although the term comes from the writings of the Marquis de Sade (who put forward the abuse of others as a philosophical argument, for which he was appropriately imprisoned), people with sadistic personality disorder don't dress their liking in such abstract clothing.

Sadism arises when investigating the causes of serial killing. A serial killing often involves sexual attacks as well as killing, and the victim is killed so that she can't be a witness. These are different serial killers from those who are sadists in the true sense and enjoy hurting others.

Loving yourself: Narcissism

You may remember the Greek myth in which the beautiful youth Narcissus falls deeply in love with his own reflection in a pool and after hopelessly trying time and again to get hold of his image, eventually pines away. The idea that someone so in love with his own image that he shuns all other relationships became known as narcissism, and such a person *narcissistic*.

Experts have taken this useful, mildly disparaging word, and turned it into a nasty clinical condition. *Narcissism* is now a recognised personality disorder that describes someone wholly preoccupied with success, hypersensitive to criticism, self-important and who feels entitled to admiration. At the extreme, a person who's narcissistic can be so furious with being ignored or his desires not being satisfied that he attacks or rapes to get what he thinks is his due.

If you know someone like that and want a peaceful life, best not tell him he has a personality disorder called 'narcissism'!

Sitting on the fence: Borderline personality disorder

A *borderline personality disorder* is the label given to someone who has unstable moods, difficulty forming relationships, gets intensely angry without any obvious reason and fears abandonment. A person with borderline personality disorder isn't obviously mentally ill. He often can cope reasonably well on a day-to-day basis, but is likely to be often unhappy because those around him aren't relating to him as he wants. Because of this he may drift in and out of various criminal activities, violent and non-violent, as a way of trying to cope with his emotional confusions.

Suffering psychosis

People who know that they're doing something wrong and are clearly in touch with reality, are described in law as being *mens rea* (you can find more on *'mens rea'* in Chapter 1). When committing a crime, the criminal is fully aware that his action is wrong. (Some professionals are unsure whether a person with a personality disorder does have *mens rea*, but that's something to be sorted out in court.)

The general public sometimes assumes that a person who commits a horrific crime for no obvious reason, and which is therefore 'mindless' or 'pointless', must be out of touch with reality, insane, mad or suffering from a mental illness.

Yet, the most inexplicable of criminals – such as 'serial killers' who appear to wander around killing people more or less at random for no obvious reason – are rarely regarded in court as mentally ill and therefore unfit to face a trial. This situation is difficult to understand until you realise that the courts' definition of mental illness is rather different and more specific than what the term means in everyday life. For most courts (as with the anecdote about Daniel McNaughton in Chapter 1), the 150-year-old idea that the person has to exhibit a 'disease of the mind' to be declared criminally insane still exists. This section discusses what does count as 'insane' in court.

Psychosis is the legally accepted mental illness that goes beyond the person feeling anxious and sad and beyond what is called functioning psychopaths. Broadly, the psychotic person must have at least one of the following symptoms:

- ✔ **Intense paranoia:** Believing that others, sometimes unknown and invisible, are seeking to hurt him and disturb him, possibly even controlling his mind.

- ✔ **Hallucinations:** Seeing or hearing things that don't exist and believing that they're present.

- ✔ **Delusions:** A belief in some unlikely set of circumstances, most notably that he's the Prime Minister or Napoleon (although the latter is unlikely as he's been dead a long time).

Although a person may experience some of the symptoms of psychosis some of the time, the symptoms are only considered significant and part of an underlying illness when they become extreme and/or deeply disturbing, such as having schizophrenia. (Check out the sidebar 'Sorting out Jekyll from Hyde').

Sorting out Jekyll from Hyde

The term schizophrenia is widely misused in day-to-day conversation to suggest a 'split personality'; the pleasant civilised Dr Jekyll by day and dangerous, destructive Mr Hyde at night. *Schizophrenia* is a psychosis, which can be paranoid, hallucinatory, delusional, or any combination. Neither is schizophrenia *bi-polar disorder*, in which the person has extreme mood swings, which used to be called *manic-depressive psychosis*. The mood can swing from deep depression to hyperactive, irrationally optimistic behaviour.

Multiple personality – in which a person behaves as a completely different person from one occasion to the next, each character apparently being unaware of the other – is extremely rare. Its exotic and potentially dramatic nature, however, caused the few recorded occurrences to take on mythical properties, giving rise to books and films. Many experts are deeply suspicious of the phenomenon of multiple personality as a mental illness, especially when used as a defence in court.

Extreme depression can also be a psychotic state, and is far more than just feeling very sad. Severe depression can be associated with intense feelings of despair and lack of self-worth, and even lead to being suicidal.

A form of mental illness that courts sometimes do accept is called *automatism*. Here the person acts automatically without being aware of what he's doing, such as what's commonly called 'sleep walking'. Automatism has been allowed as a defence in some challenging cases.

An ex-soldier claimed that he saw a man hurting a child and that caused him to relive an experience in battle, so that he moved into involuntary automatic mode and killed the man.

A person who commits a crime and the courts deem the person to be psychotic and not responsible for his actions may send the person to a special institution that can manage, and possibly treat the condition, rather than sending the person to prison. In general, psychoses such as schizophrenia aren't a major cause of crime. The mass media are ready to point out that a killer is schizophrenic, implying that's why he acted violently, but the media ignore the fact that the vast majority of people with a psychosis are much more a danger to themselves than anyone else. So although many people in prison have some form of mental illness, only a small percentage are suffering from a psychosis. That number may be higher than in the population at large, but who's to say that this isn't because of how people with psychosis are treated by the rest of society instead of psychosis being a direct cause of crime.

Understanding Why Not Everyone Is a Criminal

Although *Forensic Psychology For Dummies* talks mainly about criminals, most of the population shuns a life of crime. Even in some social subgroups where criminals are widespread – and accepting that social and psychological factors may increase the risk of criminality – the great majority of people (including those from the most underprivileged communities), don't commit serious crimes. In this section, I take a look at why there aren't more criminals in society.

Perhaps you argue that most people don't commit crimes because they're afraid of being caught. Evidence exists that property crimes can be cut by making burglary and robbery more difficult to carry out and easier to detect, something I talk about in Chapter 8. Violent crime is more likely to be a product of the personality of the offender and the culture he's part of, including having some of the personality disorders I discuss in the section 'Investigating Mental Disorder and Crime' earlier in this chapter. A person who relates well to others and can control his temper, in a society where violence isn't tolerated, isn't likely to commit violent crimes.

Of course, most people are good citizens because they've been brought up to observe the law and so avoid committing crimes. However, there are people out there committing crimes who are never caught and charged. So, exactly what proportion of the community is likely to commit a crime in the knowledge that they can get away with it, despite knowing right from wrong, is an open question.

Just about every psychological aspect of criminality I talk about in this chapter is present to some degree in most of the population – and with most people having been convicted of nothing more than a traffic offence.

Factoring in protective factors

So many things can cause a person to become a criminal; the list is long. But if you'd like a broader sociological perspective get hold of *Criminology For Dummies* by Stephen Briggs (Wiley) where you can find out a lot more about the causes of crime, such as deprivation and class conflicts. Yet people earmarked as potential criminals don't all turn out bad. There are certain aspects of daily life – known as *protective factors* – that help to cut the pernicious influences that can give rise to a person becoming a criminal:

✔ **Close relationship with a family member:** Feeling alone in the world is an ingredient for believing that you don't need to accept society's restraints. A close relationship with a family member or a teacher you admire gives you roots in the community and the feeling of self-respect that can prevent you from drifting into crime.

✔ **Good educational environment:** Education is the key to so much in a person's development even if you're not brilliantly clever. Enjoying a level of educational attainment gives you self-respect; the ability to express your own capabilities protects you from a life of crime.

✔ **Job satisfaction:** If you like your job, you're more likely to experience self-worth and also you're less likely to want to risk losing your job by committing a crime.

✔ **Positive relationships with non-criminals:** Beyond the satisfaction that comes from having good relationships with individual family members and teachers, being part of an overall group of law-abiding individuals is as much a barrier to criminality as being part of a criminal gang is a pathway into the underworld of crime (see the earlier section 'Keeping bad company').

✔ **Sociability:** If you get on with other people and relate to them well, you feel confident in yourself and are more able to resist the temptations of undesirables and bad company. Crime becomes less attractive as an option.

Of course, knowing right from wrong does help to keep people on the straight and narrow. But that knowledge comes from the people you mix with.

Lacking the opportunity

Absence of opportunity is a good way of preventing a crime being committed. One school of thought argues that society can tackle crime by using *target hardening*: that is, reducing the opportunities and possibilities for crime to a minimum. Target hardening is about making a crime more difficult to carry out, such as having measures in place to make it harder to steal and defraud and the perpetrator believing he can get away with it. I explore target hardening in more detail in Chapter 8.

Fearing being caught

Punishments for crime exist to deter people from committing the crime. But the punishment only has any power if people think that they're going to get caught. Therefore, the effectiveness of law enforcement is important in stopping people becoming criminals.

When a person commits a crime and gets away with it, he's developing criminal skills and is more likely to be on the path to a criminal career. Some people have similar characteristics to a criminal but direct these personal traits into something more socially acceptable; for example, the hard-headed businessman who takes advantage of others without having any feelings of guilt for the consequences. The suggestion has been widely canvassed that some people who are successful in the cut-throat world of big business are best thought of as *psychopaths* – people lacking in empathy who callously and without remorse insist on getting their own way.

Aging: 'I'm too old for all this!'

The good news is that aging can act as a deterrent to crime. There comes a stage in life when you feel committing a crime simply isn't worth the effort. Crime is a young person's activity (see Figure 2-1). Physical prowess, risk-taking and believing you can get away with it and not end up in prison is typical of young men, a way of thinking not nearly so common in older people.

If a person commits a crime early in life, he's likely to suffer the consequences and wants to put that experience behind him. A settled lifestyle with a spouse and children is a good enough reason to avoid taking risks and any possibility of doing time in prison.

Figure 2-1: An example of age distribution of offenders cautioned in English courts in 2002

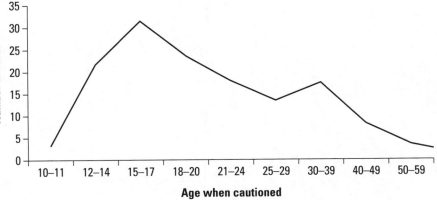

Chapter 3

Providing Expert Evidence: Forensic Psychology and the Law

*F*orensic psychology hooks inevitably into the legal process, not least when practitioners are called to give expert testimony in court cases. Therefore, to understand how the discipline works you have to understand the legal process and how expert evidence fits into it. In this chapter, I provide a basic summary of how the law works and some general differences in how it operates in various countries, which in turn affect how forensic psychology expert witnesses fulfil different roles in different courts. I also demonstrate what being an expert witness entails and the ways in which the forensic psychologist can contribute in and around the courts.

In some countries, especially in Eastern Europe and non-English speaking places, people with a medical training still dominate the process of giving psychological evidence. They may be psychiatrists or even general medical practitioners. The preference for people with medical training as experts on psychological matters, such as fitness to plead, rather than psychologists used to be true in the UK and US, but forensic psychologists have certainly found their way into the legal limelight in the US ever since the early 1960s and are ever more present these days in the UK, Australia and Canada.

Understanding That Legal Systems Vary Worldwide

The central message of this section is that each country (or sometimes part of a country) has a different way of doing the law. Well, you wouldn't expect things to be otherwise, would you! After all, human beings invented legal systems and because their histories and cultures vary, inevitably their institutions vary too. These variations make different assumptions about human beings and incorporate different sorts of protections to make sure that justice is done.

Throughout this chapter (and book) I refer to *jurisdiction.* By this term, I mean an area in which a particular set of laws hold sway. The word can also mean the sorts of laws that an authority has the power to enforce.

To illustrate, the Federal Bureau of Investigation (FBI) in the US has jurisdiction only over crimes that occur on government property or across state lines, or nationwide crimes such as serial killing, unless other state or city jurisdictions call them in for advice. In the UK, the Scottish legal system is quite distinct from that in the rest of the UK. Scotland is a different jurisdiction.

Facing up to an opponent: The adversarial system

If you love Hollywood and TV court-case movies, you're familiar with the idea of a courtroom. A judge sits up on a high chair, much like a throne, in the middle of the court. The accused stands on a boxed-in platform nearby, lower than the judge, witnesses stand or sit on the other side of the judge. Across the room are two rows of people, the *jury*, who listen to the trial as it progresses and eventually present their verdict.

This is typical of what are known as Crown Courts in England and Wales and Federal and State courts in the US. In fact the great majority of court cases in many countries take place without a jury in front of what are called Magistrates. Typically these are three people who act as judges but aren't trained lawyers, assisted by a legal advisor. There are a number of other types of courts that occur in different places but this is not a book on the law, so I'll stay with what happens in the Crown Courts with a jury because that is where the role of the psychological expert is clearest.

The legal process used in most courts in the UK, the US and most Anglo-Saxon countries is known as the *adversarial system,* because at its heart is the adversarial nature of the defence and prosecution sides, played out before a judge or magistrates, and sometimes a jury that watches as a series of witnesses are questioned.

Initially the *prosecution* brings forward its witnesses. The prosecution officially represents the state or country; in the UK this is the queen. So much so that the most experienced and senior prosecutors are known as Queen's Counsel. This prosecuting barrister (known as the prosecution attorney in the US) first questions the witnesses called by the prosecution, during a process known in the UK and Australia as providing *evidence in chief.* The US tends to use more informal terminology. This questioning is to reveal the facts of the case as the prosecution would wish the court to see them.

Next, in the *cross-examination,* the defence barrister (defence attorney in the US) challenges the prosecution witnesses' accounts. They may try to challenge the reliability of the witness or the clarity of what they have said as you'll see in Chapter 11. Sometimes, subsequently, a barrister asks one of 'his or her' witnesses a few more questions for clarification in the light of what the person said during cross-examination. Then the defence witnesses are brought in, with the defence first questioning the witnesses to provide the facts as the defence would like to court to see the. The prosecution barrister follows with a cross-examination that again has the objective of undermining the defence witnesses' account of the facts. After all the witnesses have been dealt with, the prosecution and defence summarise the evidence as they see it. Then the judge does an overall summing up emphasising the legal issues the jury needs to take into account. The jury is then hidden away to make a decision about innocence or guilt, and in some jurisdictions also to determine the sentence a person gets when convicted.

Don't assume that the cut and thrust in the courtroom, so beloved of film-makers, is typical of most court cases. In my experience they're remarkably tedious, conducted in an extremely polite manner, going over minute detail interminably. Also, a lot happens outside the courtroom, or out of hearing of the jury.

Considerable debate takes place about what evidence can be presented, with the defence and prosecution bargaining over which witnesses can be called and what aspects of their evidence can be put before the jury.

In addition, reports are prepared for both the prosecution and the defence that provide background information. Many aspects of these reports may not find their way into court but barristers can draw on them to influence the case they make and how they make it.

In the adversarial system the only thing that counts as evidence is what's revealed in court. Mounds of documents and reports may have been prepared in support of the case, but only what's said in court in front of the jury can be taken into account.

Many times I've written lengthy reports for court cases, but have not been allowed to present the information to the court as, for example, I would when lecturing to students. Instead I can only answer the questions the barristers ask. Sure, these questions are based on my report, but if the barrister doesn't ask about aspects that I regard as crucial, the court may never hear that information in order to take it into account.

In the adversarial system, when the case is presented in front of a jury, it's the jury that makes the final decision guided on the principles of law by the judge. Generally speaking, the judge determines the sentence when a person is found guilty, but various expert reports may guide the judge on what sentence to give.

In the UK, the police carry out the investigation into a crime and the initial preparation of the evidence. The Crown Prosecution Service (CPS) then brings (or decides not to bring) prosecutions in criminal cases.

The CPS has some similarities to the District Attorney's office in the US, but the complications of the US legal system are so great I don't try to summarise them here.

The main point is that under most adversarial systems, the police carry out the investigations and then pass the evidence over to lawyers to conduct the prosecution. The police are in contact with the lawyers as the investigation proceeds, but in the vast majority of cases people with formal legal qualifications don't have an active role in the initial investigation. This system is very different to most inquisitorial systems, as I describe in the next section.

Keeping things brief in court: The inquisitorial system

When I mentioned to some Dutch colleagues how long I've had to sit around UK courts waiting to hear whether a judge would allow my evidence to be presented before the jury – the days and weeks that even the simplest court case can take – they laughed and said they knew from watching the televised O.J. Simpson murder trial.

They assured me that nothing like that could happen in courts in The Netherlands. Under their *inquisitorial system,* the whole process is conducted in front of one or more judges – generally known as *magistrates* – without any jury. The great majority of the legal process is carried out through written documents with the court case usually being a relatively brief discussion of what the documents contain. The prosecution leads the case with some representation from defence lawyers, but the to-ing and fro-ing battle that's central to the UK and US adversarial legal process (as I describe in the preceding section) isn't common under their system.

Furthermore, an attorney officially leads criminal investigations, and the police are answerable to this person in providing evidence for a prosecution. This attorney often acts as the prosecutor in any following court case, which means that a much closer link exists between the prosecution and the investigators than in the adversarial system.

The distinction between the adversarial and inquisitorial systems that I sketch in this and the preceding sections is hugely simplified. For example, some UK and US courts have no juries, such as appeal courts where cases are brought to challenge an earlier conviction or most coroners' courts that consider the cause of death. Also, in many inquisitorial jurisdictions, versions of the jury system operate. In the French system, for instance, the judge can sit in the jury room with the jurors while they're making their decisions, to ensure that they do so legally and sensibly.

Examining the US system: Constitution, federal and state laws

The US has a greatly elaborated legal system, with some laws that apply across all states (*federal laws*) and other laws that are state-specific, although they may be modelled on some general framework on which all states draw. In fact, some parallels exist in the UK, where Scotland has its own distinct legal system and some aspects of the legal process have been modified from time to time in Northern Ireland.

Unlike the UK, where the law is embedded in many centuries of case examples that have shaped what's acceptable, the US has the formidable Constitution and Bill of Rights that specifies in admirable detail the basic principles on which the legal system is founded (although the legal precedents of cases are certainly still relevant). The Constitution provides a framework of 7 articles and 27 amendments that lay out how the country is to be run and provide benchmarks against which any laws can be measured.

With the variety of jurisdictions comes some important flexibility in the US legal system. For example, certain states have courts specifically set up to deal with offenders with mental illnesses. Variations in sentencing and what may be allowed as evidence, as well as issues relating to jury selection and other aspects of the legal process, can all have a significant impact on the roles that experts, especially forensic psychologists, can play. For example, virtually all the advice on jury selection that I describe in Chapter 12 is offered by psychologists in the US because much more room exists for choosing a jury than in the UK and other countries with a jury system. Although some of the issues discussed in Chapter 12 are relevant outside of the US, the legal system there does mean that they can usually only be applied in the US.

To take another example that I consider in more detail in Chapter 11, evaluation of whether a person understands the legal proceedings enough to be given the death penalty can be a challenge for forensic psychologists in countries where the death penalty still exists. This difficulty does not occur in the UK which no longer has the death penalty.

Against this background of variation, the detailed US Constitution provides a firm reference point that allows many challenges to legal outcomes, which can have implications for how forensic psychologists contribute.

Considering the implications for forensic expertise

The very brief outline of variations in legal systems in this section make clear that what forensic psychology expert witnesses can do in court is shaped by the nature of the particular legal system to which they're contributing. Of particular importance is whether the evidence is presented in front of a jury, people who are assumed to be non-expert with no particular understanding of the issues at hand (as is usual under the adversarial system), or is presented to one or more magistrates (often the case in the inquisitorial system).

Judges and magistrates are assumed to be professionals who can make up their own mind and can accept or dismiss evidence in an objective way. (Whether they really can or not is, of course, a fascinating topic that some researchers have studied with rather less rosy results than the judiciary may like to hear, as I consider in Chapter 12.) This means that expert evidence that may be allowed when no jury is present may not be allowed if a case is being held in front of a jury. This precaution is to ensure that the jury makes the decision rather than the expert, an issue I discuss in more detail in the later section 'Detailing the Dangers: Ensuring Trial by Jury and not Trial by Expert'.

ANECDOTE

Courts differ on what expert evidence they accept

In one case in England, a man was charged with the murder of his wife, even though a suicide note was found. The court didn't allow any psychological evidence to be presented about the mental state of the deceased wife. As a result, no discussion was allowed in court about whether she may have been depressed and likely to take her own life, which weakened the case of the accused considerably. In a case in Northern Ireland, a man charged with the murder of his son, wife and daughter claimed that his son had gone berserk and killed his mother and sister (the defendant's wife and daughter) before killing himself. In this case, psychological evidence was allowed that suggested the deaths were the result of a carefully planned execution by the father. In both cases, the men were convicted of the murders.

In inquisitorial systems, therefore, experts are often given more free rein than in the adversarial system in front of a jury, including civil and quasi-legal processes where judgements aren't so much about guilt and sentencing but more aimed towards determining solutions in disputes. These variations between courts and legal systems also help to explain why expert forensic psychology evidence can play a significant role in one place but never get a look-in somewhere else, say in a different state or a different country. The matter is complicated further (as it so often seems to be with legal matters) by what any particular court regards as expertise, something I explore in the next section.

Using Your Experience and Knowledge: What Is an Expert Witness?

When experts (such as forensic psychologists) appear in court proceedings, in essence they're witnesses like any others. They take an oath to tell the truth and are bound to honour the court and its procedures. One crucial exception, however, distinguishes experts from other witnesses. Experts are allowed to give opinions whereas other witnesses can only provide an account of the facts as they know them. Experts have to defend their opinions and explain the basis on which they reach them. They're closely examined on whether they really do have the expertise to offer the opinions they present in court.

Experts, however, can't offer an opinion on just anything they happen to know about. What they comment on has to be something that the judge or jury can't know themselves.

This reality was brought home to me in a case concerning the likelihood that a victim committed suicide, the implication being, of course, that if she didn't, she was murdered. The victim hadn't given any overt indication that she intended to kill herself, but I knew of a number of cases of irrefutable suicide in which the person gave no prior hints of wanting to end their life. I thought that this knowledge was relevant to the court, but the judge ruled that a jury of ordinary people would have enough experience in their daily lives to make their own mind up from witnesses about the character of the deceased as to whether she'd intended to kill herself or not. So I wasn't allowed to provide evidence on this aspect.

Being called as an expert in criminal proceedings

Here's a summary of some criteria to be met for expert testimony to be admissible in court:

- ✔ The subject matter must be something a typical juror (or judge) would not usually know about or understand.

- ✔ The expert must have the qualifications and experience to be able to give the court assistance.

- ✔ The expertise must be objectively established and generally accepted by other experts within that area of knowledge.

- ✔ The value in helping to form an opinion about the evidence must be greater than the likely negative influence on the decision about the defendant.

Although the defence and prosecution lawyers argue about the expert evidence when presented, the judge decides whether the court accepts the expert opinion at all. He decides whether it provides information distinct from what the jury already knows and is of sufficient reliability and relevance to the case.

A particularly tricky decision for the judge is to weigh up the value of the offered expert evidence (known as its *probative values*) against how damaging it may be to the defendant (known as its *prejudicial value*). For example, if the evidence is of only marginal probative value but may be very detrimental, a judge won't allow it. How valuable expert testimony is also depends on how well-founded it is.

As a consequence, a key pointer in determining the acceptability of expert evidence is the notion of *reliability*. In other words, is what the expert offers expertise or just opinion? Various legal guidelines on this aspect have emerged over the years, as I discuss in the following sections.

US rulings

The US legal profession features rather more formal guidelines than other countries, which emerge from previous court decisions. Very significant as regards expert witnesses is a 1923 case (*Frye versus United States*) in which a man accused of murder wanted to bring evidence from a polygraph (lie detector) test (which I discuss in Chapter 5) to show he was telling the truth. But the court didn't allow that evidence to be presented. The ruling in that case on the inadmissibility of the polygraph evidence became the formal statement of what constitutes expert evidence:

> *The rule is that the opinions of experts or skilled witnesses are admissible in evidence in those cases in which the matter of inquiry is such that inexperienced persons are unlikely to prove capable of forming a correct judgment upon it, for the reason that the subject matter so far partakes of a science, art, or trade as to require a previous habit or experience or study in it, in order to acquire a knowledge of it. When the question involved does not lie within the range of common experience or common knowledge, but requires special experience or special knowledge, then the opinions of witnesses skilled in that particular science, art, or trade to which the question relates are admissible in evidence.*

One curious aspect of this clarification is that the 'expert' under this ruling doesn't need to have any special qualifications to offer an opinion, just experience or knowledge not normally available to other people. This means, for example, that a police officer who has arrested many people for the possession of drugs can offer an opinion on whether the quantity of drugs found on a particular person is likely to be for personal use only or is so much that they're for sale, making the person likely to be a supplier rather than just a user.

In some countries the requirement for being an expert for the court is much stricter. In France, for instance, experts are usually on a registered list.

But how is new expertise that comes along to be evaluated, such as the 'lie detector polygraph' in the Frye case in 1923? Well, the judge in that case was clear about the need to determine the soundness of the expertise. He said:

> *Just when a scientific principle or discovery crosses the line between the experimental and demonstrable stages is difficult to define. Somewhere in this twilight zone the evidential force of the principle must be recognized, and while courts will go a long way in admitting expert testimony deduced from a well-recognized scientific principle or discovery, the thing from which the deduction is made must be sufficiently established to have gained general acceptance in the particular field in which it belongs.*

In other words, no new-fangled idea is to be allowed as evidence just because someone claims it works. Only when the scientific community, from which that sort of evidence comes, generally accepts what's being claimed does the court allow it. The polygraph has never reached that acceptable standard and so has never been allowed in court.

This 'Frye Standard' still holds in some US states, but overall it was regarded as too restrictive, and so a different standard for judging whether expert evidence was acceptable was introduced following the case of *Daubert versus Merrill Dow Pharmaceuticals Inc.*

In 1993, Jason Daubert claimed that the birth defects he was born with had been caused by the chemical Bendictin sold by Merell Dow. He brought evidence from laboratory and animal studies to support his claim. His evidence was challenged as not being generally accepted by the relevant scientific community, but in the course of a complicated legal process the US Supreme Court determined that the original Frye Standard was no longer the law and that the crucial issue was:

> *If scientific, technical, or other specialized knowledge will assist the trier of fact to understand the evidence or to determine a fact in issue, a witness qualified as an expert by knowledge, skill, experience, training, or education, may testify thereto in the form of an opinion or otherwise.*

This statement changed the rules and led to Daubert's evidence being admissible. Now what mattered was whether the person giving evidence was expert enough, not the general acceptance in the scientific community of the procedure being drawn on. In the curious way of the law, the effect was to make the judge the person who decides on whether evidence is sound enough to be acceptable instead of the scientific community from which the expert comes.

The Daubert ruling seems less stringent than the Frye Standard, and you'd expect courts to be more open to developments in science that aren't yet established enough to gain general acceptance by the scientific community. In many court cases, the judge reviews the proposed expert evidence and decides whether or not to admit it. Instead of opening the floodgates to all sorts of novel scientific discoveries, however, the indications are that judges have become more conservative since Daubert. Few judges want to be the first to allow a new form of evidence that may later be shown to be rubbish! But some do, which is why expertise may be accepted in some courts but not in others.

UK approaches

In contrast to the US system of an overarching set of guidelines, the UK courts rely much more on what happened in previous cases, often known as *precedent* (although of course 'rules of evidence' and other frameworks can be drawn on). In general, UK courts are much more cautious about what's allowed as expert evidence than in the US, which is why many forms of evidence (notably the syndrome evidence I discuss in Chapter 11) is much more likely to emerge in a US court first, long before it sees the light of day in the UK.

In Britain, a judge determines whether any expert is allowed to give evidence, and draws on his own understanding of the expertise involved. As far as psychology is concerned, this tends towards acceptance of views that appear to have strong medical roots. So a psychiatrist claiming that psychopathy (which I examine in Chapter 10) is a medical condition over which the defendant has no control, and therefore the person needs to be regarded as a patient rather than a criminal, probably gets a hearing from the judge. A psychologist proposing that a person can plan suicide without indicating this intention to anyone is far less likely to be listened to as there is no medical basis to the opinion.

Appearing as an expert in civil proceedings

Many courts don't operate in as formal a way as criminal courts and other legal settings that deal with crimes from burglary to murder. Civil courts often operate as if they're informal courts, and they're not bound by the same legal constraints. They can deal with a great mix of matters, including the following cases:

- ✔ Child custody
- ✔ Contract challenges
- ✔ Divorce
- ✔ Personal injury compensation
- ✔ Professional negligence
- ✔ Sexual harassment
- ✔ Unfair dismissal

In some US states, notably Oregon, a need exists to determine whether a person has the mental competence to request assistance in hastening their own death. Increasingly, psychologists are active in providing guidance to such proceedings and so in this section I mention some of the issues that distinguish this sort of expert evidence.

One crucial point is that, whereas in most criminal cases the defendant has to be found guilty *beyond all reasonable doubt*, in civil proceedings the burden of proof is much weaker, often phrased as *on the balance of probabilities*. Therefore, a much wider range of expertise is allowed into these legal deliberations.

Another important aspect of non-criminal proceedings is that the people to whom the psychologist's evidence relates are likely to be rather different from the run-of the-mill criminals seen in most criminal courts. Youngsters, or *juveniles* as they're known in legal parlance, are often dealt with in a much more informal context, as are children who are at the heart of child-custody hearings. The psychologist therefore has to guide the court on such sensitive and complex matters as relationships between parents and children, or how amenable a youngster is to rehabilitation.

These varied forms of consultation to civil courts make special demands on forensic psychologists that aren't nearly so apparent in criminal proceedings:

✔ Care must be taken in how an individual is labelled, because this can become part of their file and can shape their life as well as how the justice system deals with them. Labelling someone with conditions such as autism and Asperger's syndrome (I consider the assessment of young offenders in Chapter 9), for instance, can give all the wrong signals and blight what a person can do for many years to come.

✔ The expert has to be willing and knowledgeable not only about the problem a person has that led them to the court, but also what can be done about it. Informing those present of the approaches and 'treatments' available can be more important than assigning any diagnostic label.

✔ Relationships between people, such as children and their parents or youngsters and their lawyers, are often an important part of the psychologist's assessment. This is much more difficult to evaluate than the mental state of an individual. It requires skills in relating to people and enabling them to be honest with you that aren't so crucial in many criminal cases.

✔ Often much more heated emotion is associated with the proceedings, especially in child-custody litigation. The psychologist may be very vulnerable to challenges about his ethics or expertise arising from the intense passions involved.

Keeping Your Lips Sealed: What an Expert Can't Comment On

As I explain in the preceding sections (possibly at more length than you expect!), much legal debate exists about who's an expert and what can be allowed as expert evidence. Of course, the expertise must be relevant to the case in question, but additional constraints surround this issue that you need to understand if you're to appreciate how some psychological expertise gets into court and some doesn't.

Staying within your competence

Although some people may like to present themselves as all-knowing authorities on many things (you see them on TV often enough!), professional humility is crucial for a forensic psychology expert witness to be effective in court and avoid committing perjury or even contempt of court. Experts have to stay within their area of expertise.

This fact may seem obvious, but remember that the person deciding who a court accepts as an expert (and what that expertise is to cover) isn't a professional in the area in question but in the law, that is, a judge or magistrate. The court therefore often relies on experts themselves to indicate when they're being asked to comment on something outside their competence.

For example, an expert on the use of language (who I mention in Chapter 5) was asked to offer an opinion on the probability of a particular form of words being used. But although the expert knew about language, he didn't know much about statistics and how to calculate probabilities.

ANECDOTE

A case of getting his numbers wrong

When standing in the witness box, experts can be tempted to offer an opinion on something outside their area of expertise, such as providing a statistical calculation.

In 1999 Sally Clark was convicted of the murder of her two children. The expert testimony from Sir Roy Meadows was crucial in her conviction. Sir Roy was a highly respected British paediatrician who had testified in more than 300 cases relating to children's illness and death. The defence claimed that the children died from 'cot death' or *sudden infant death syndrome* (SIDS). But Sir Roy gave evidence that the chances of two children dying from SIDS in one family were 75 million to 1.

To come to this figure, he'd multiplied the probability of one child dying from SIDS by the chances of another child dying. This calculation, however, contained a basic error of which the court was unaware, but which the Royal Statistical Society demonstrated for Sally Clark's later appeal. The statistical experts looked at a variety of cases in which more than one cot death had been experienced by a family and showed that, sadly, Sir Roy's assumption that the two cases were totally unrelated wasn't valid.

You can't just multiply the probabilities of the combination of two events occurring when some potential link exists between them. For example, you may see a bald man in a red sports car and from knowing the probability of bald men and the probability of red sports cars simply multiply these probabilities to find out how rare the combination is. But if bald men like to buy red sports cars, the combination's going to be far more frequent.

The statisticians calculated that the chances of two such terrible deaths happening in one family were closer to 100 to 1, probably because of some genetic aspect to the deaths. The appeal court concluded that if the jury had had that information they may not have found Sally guilty so she won her appeal.

Avoiding the ultimate question

Psychology experts in court must avoid answering what lawyers call 'the ultimate question' – whether the defendant is innocent or guilty. The expert is very likely to have formed an opinion on this point, but get their knuckles wrapped by the judge if they drift into offering such an opinion. In some cases, expert testimony may not be allowed into the court simply because it's seen as getting too close to offering a decision that's the court's prerogative.

Sometimes the expert opinion may not seem to do the court's work for it, but actually it does. The most obvious example is when the psychology expert's opinion comments on whether a key witness may be lying, or may not have the memories claimed. For although the opinion isn't directly commenting on guilt or innocence, the implication of the opinion is so clear that it would sway the court too much.

In general, judges prefer to form their own opinion about whether a person is telling the truth or not, and encourage the jury to do the same, instead of relying on an expert opinion.

Remaining unprejudiced

As I mention in the earlier section 'Being called as an expert in criminal proceedings', judges are always concerned that expert evidence may prejudice the jury to assume the defendant is guilty even though that evidence doesn't deal directly with the facts of the case. This is particularly problematic for many aspects of psychological evidence.

I once gave evidence for a defendant who was accused of rape and murder. He made clear to me that he was 'a stud'. He claimed he picked up women from a local nightclub on a regular basis and had consenting sex with them, and so he had no reason to rape anyone. This admission seemed important evidence to present to a jury, but his lawyers believed (I'm sure correctly) that the account of such a promiscuous existence would lead the jury to see the defendant as an unsavoury character and assume that if he could behave like that he was capable of rape as well. As it happens, the jury would've been right. He eventually confessed to the rape.

Detailing the Dangers: Ensuring Trial by Jury and not Trial by Expert

When considering the legal context of giving expert evidence, forensic psychologist witnesses need to remember that they're advisers to the court and not the judge or the jury! This situation can often be a challenging requirement.

An experienced forensic psychologist once told me about a case in which, although he wasn't sure whether the person he'd examined was guilty or not, he was certain that the individual was a very dangerous man and should be locked up for a long time! Fortunately, he didn't say this in court because he'd have got into serious trouble!

Most legal systems are very aware of the overly influential nature that an expert's testimony can bring to the court's decisions and, as I explain in the earlier section 'Being called as an expert in criminal proceedings', go to some trouble to try and neutralise it. Often this requires disallowing evidence that the expert (and perhaps many observers) think is exactly what the jury needs to know. This problem is particularly significant in much forensic psychology evidence.

Unlike the evaluation of physical evidence, such as a blood sample or a fingerprint, psychologists are never dealing with some distinctly separate aspect of an individual. No matter how hard you try to divide a person up and only deal with a particular aspect of his mental state, you're always commenting in a way that's relevant to the person as a whole.

Therefore, a jury can take even the most limited comment on the characteristics of an individual as indicating something very important that spills over into other deliberations. A defendant, for example, may be a good worker and highly intelligent, but if the forensic psychologist lets slip that the person has 'psychopathic tendencies', the court would re-interpret many aspects of his activities in that light and in a negative way.

A major reason for the caution is the undue influence expert testimony may have over the jury. Many jurors may be in a daunting courtroom for the first time, and reaching a decision about guilt or innocence can make people anxious. If an assured, articulate, authoritative person confidently presents information to the court that implies guilt on the basis of their expertise, especially if that expertise is rather difficult to fathom and seems to come from the particular genius of that expert, many jurors may accept that expert's opinion rather than worrying about working out their own. At least, courts believe this can happen, hence their caution.

Accepting the restrictions of being an expert in court

The potential significance of a forensic psychologist's expert testimony was brought home to me by a prisoner I spoke to who told me that he avoided psychologists like the plague. His reason was understandable. From his point of view, a psychologist could form an opinion about him and his actions but he would have no possibility of influencing that opinion. He may have determined to give up any future criminal activity and lead a totally honest life, but if the psychologist formed a view that this stated intention was all window-dressing and that the man was inherently criminal, he'd have extreme difficulty challenging that opinion.

The problem for the psychologist is compounded by the fact that they're not investigators and so may have great difficulty getting all the details of a case. If called in by the defence, for example, information that doesn't support the defence case may not be given to the psychologist.

Experienced forensic psychology experts learn to discover what may be hidden from them and seek ways of obtaining all the crucial information.

In my early days providing expert testimony, I naïvely assumed that everything would be laid out before me and that I'd be able to offer the court an opinion on anything I thought I was competent to say. I soon realised after just a few cases that the rules of legal proceedings are somewhat different. The expert in court isn't playing by the same rules she or he would in other areas of professional life. Experienced experts find ways of using the court process to get their message across, as I eventually did, but less experienced ones may be bamboozled by the legal process. Not all experts are the same. If you're seeking an expert to provide evidence on your behalf, the expert you end up with can be crucial. You don't always get the expert you deserve.

The frustrations of a need-to-know basis

In one case I was asked to assess the written material of a man who was accused of killing his wife. I wanted to talk to him in person to get to understand more of his way of thinking about things, but because the prosecution had called me in, the defence wouldn't allow me to talk to him.

From the other side, when called in by the defence in a suspicious suicide, I wasn't allowed to interview prosecution witnesses who knew the deceased, and who may have helped me understand the victim's mental state. By denying me that access, the prosecution made sure that my opinion wouldn't be put before the jury.

Criticising the role of forensic psychology experts in court

Some people have raised the following criticisms about the use of forensic psychologists as experts in court:

- ✔ Their opinions are so powerful that they inappropriately dominate the legal proceedings.

- ✔ They can offer opinions on the 'ultimate issue', something that the court should determine.

- ✔ They're biased by the financial incentives of giving evidence (experts are paid for their time, often quite handsomely).

- ✔ They may have professional relationships with defendants or witnesses that are external to the court process, for example, through therapy or consultancy.

- ✔ They're under pressure from the lawyers to offer evidence that suits their side of the case.

- ✔ They can fall into the trap of competing with an opposing expert and so overstate their case.

- ✔ They may display a lack of awareness of sources of bias in the evidence.

Part II
Helping the Police Solve Crimes

The 5th Wave   By Rich Tennant

"We're thinking of pleading 'Not Guilty By Reason of Naivety.'"

Part II

Helping the Police Solve Crimes

In this part . . .

Sometimes psychologists move into areas that most people think are really the provenance of the police; interviewing witnesses, deciding if a suspect is lying, helping victims or even considering how to prevent crime. The role in this area that has caught the public imagination is 'offender profiling', which is usually presented as some almost magical skill of a gifted individual. In all of these areas psychological processes can help the police to be more effective. In this part the psychological theories and methods that underpin these contributions are described and I blow away some of the myths that fiction writers live by.

Chapter 4

Interviewing Witnesses and Victims

Committing a crime and not being detected is thought of as the perfect crime (well, at least in crime fiction). Until someone reports a crime it doesn't appear on the radar. Seeing the report of a crime on TV you're always given what appears to be a clear picture of what's happened and when. Yet even a video recording of a crime is open to interpretation. For example, in the UK people have been shot because a police sharpshooter claims to have seen a gun, but none is later found. Or, you come home to find that your home has been burgled and everything is upside down but the nature of the crime is open to question until you can give an accurate description of what's been taken. At every stage of the legal process a description of what's actually happened is required, usually, by a witness or witnesses making a statement to the police or lawyers. But it can also be a suspect being interviewed and being asked where he was and what he was doing at the time of the crime.

In this chapter, I walk you through the psychology of interviewing people as part of an investigation (talking to a patient in therapy, for example, is something quite different). When a witness has seen something or someone they may be asked to identify the object or person. I also consider this eyewitness testimony. I don't worry in this chapter about the complicating factor of deliberate lying and deception (something I cover in Chapter 5). I discuss the process and experience of interviewing witnesses, suspects and victims by investigators. Interviews are accounts of what people remember. So I also examine how human memory works, including the ways in which memory can be unreliable, and I describe the issues of helping people remember what may be traumatic incidents, particularly when the person is very distressed.

Understanding the Nature of Interviews: Why Are You Asking Me That?

Interviewing is all about getting an accurate account of an event. But when the police interview someone, they want to do more than just find out what's actually happened. They also need to find answers to the questions:

- Is the incident a criminal offence?
- Where can I find further evidence?
- Are there any other witnesses or victims?
- How does this witness's account coincide with any other witnesses?
- Did the victim contribute to the crime in any way?
- Are the victims or witnesses telling the truth?

Clearly, the interview is much more than a chat between friends. The recording of the interview – whether a written account or an audio or video recording – is a legal document that many people draw on. Forensic scientists will use it to see if it points to where there may be evidence. If a victim says 'he grabbed my sleeve' then the scientists know to look closely there for DNA. The defence and the prosecution draw on the interview to prepare their cases for court.

The necessity of having a complete and accurate account of an interview was brought home to me once after interviewing a man charged with a serious crime. My object had been to get to know the suspect and find out as much as I could about his background to draw on for his defence. I had to provide the court with a full audio recording of the interview, but I turned the recording off immediately when the interview was over. This made the recording seem to stop suddenly. I therefore had to make clear that I had not deliberately cut out something that was relevant to the case.

Interviewing and its connection to other sources of information

Interviews with victims, witnesses and suspects aren't the only sources of information available to an investigation and to the courts. All of the sorts of forensic science information that TV shows like *CSI* and *Silent Witness* draw on are used in real cases too. I don't discuss those here because you can glean a lot about forensic science from those shows as well as many other books.

When it's available you can also use:

- **Biological evidence:** Blood stains, semen, excreta and so on.
- **Crime scene records:** Especially photos or videos.
- **Geographical information:** Plus related location information.
- **Impressions:** Fingerprints, tyre tracks or 'ear prints'.
- **Personal records:** Diaries, suicide notes and computer information like e-mails or Facebook pages.
- **Records:** From hospitals, births, deaths and medical treatments.
- **Traces:** Fibres, soil particles, gunshot residue and so on.

Any or all these pieces of evidence can be used to get a fuller picture of the crime and those involved, and together with the interview, for example, can test the claims made by victims, witnesses or suspects.

Managing the process: Interviews as conversations

When you're carrying out an interview you're making use of the witness's memory. The purpose of an interview is to draw out facts about a crime from a person who has some special connection with it; the interview is a live event and not just a theoretical exercise as in a laboratory experiment.

An interview consists of two or more people involved in a dialogue, and so one way of thinking about the process is as *conversation management.* By forming a friendly, but professional, working relationship with the person being interviewed, the interviewer can encourage confidence and honesty.

Establishing rapport is important, but you also need to have the flexibility to move the questions carefully in relation to the answers being given, rather than bulldozing through the questions you think you ought to be asking. Doing so can be difficult with a reluctant witness, or one who's anxious about what's going on. A traumatised victim may be in an emotional state that makes answering questions clearly very difficult. They may need careful encouragement and to be given time to respond.

As an interviewer, you can develop rapport by:

- Explaining clearly what the interview is for and how you're carrying out the interview.
- Listening carefully.

 ✔ Showing respect.

 ✔ Being non-confrontational.

 ✔ Understanding the respondent's anxieties.

Responses to questions can also be influenced by social pressures, such as the desire by people being interviewed to please the interviewer, wanting to help because of the seriousness of a situation even though they may not have much to offer, or when rapport or a relationship develops with police officers involved in the case, so they go out of their way to imply their memory is clear when it's really very vague.

Pressure on a witness to remember the details of an event can cause mistaken recollections because of the witness desiring to appear correct, observant, helpful and not foolish. For example, a witness who's keen to help may be trying hard to guess what the police want to hear and so they persuade themselves that what they're remembering corresponds with what's required.

Combating the possibility of witnesses saying what they think the interviewer wants to hear rather than what they really remember is a subtle business. Letting them give an account of what they remember without too much direct prompting, saying things like 'tell me what happened' rather than 'did you see him punch her?' is part of good interview technique. But there is a lot more to it than that, which is why all sorts of interview frameworks have been developed that I discuss later in this chapter and in the next.

Remembering That Memory Can Mislead

Researching how the memory works is a hot topic in psychology and has been for over 150 years. No surprise, therefore, that forensic psychologists have been exploring witness and victim memories since the earliest days. (In Chapter 20 I give you an example of the role and significance of memory in an internationally famous trial.)

Try this little test. Can you remember what you had for breakfast three days ago? If I ask you to describe what the table looked like (assuming you weren't eating on the run and indeed you had breakfast), are you likely to give me a different answer if I provide a list of possible settings and ask you to tick a box? Or, how do you go about explaining to someone who always has breakfast in bed, what breakfast looks like sitting at a table?

What I'm getting at is that your account takes on two crucial aspects:

✔ **The act of remembering:** You have to remember what happened, which isn't simply a matter of taking out some sort of 'mind movie' and playing it to the person who's asking the questions. Then you need to put together a description, drawing on your verbal skills and what you can dig out of your memory.

✔ **The situation:** What you say depends on who's asking the questions. You may give a different account to a close friend to the one you would give to a police officer. How questions are asked will also influence how you answer. If you are given a list of possible answers to choose from you may choose one even though none of them really fits the situation you remember, but if you are asked to describe what you remember in your own words you may struggle to find the exact words.

You may think that a question is a question is a question, but not so. How you phrase a question can unwittingly direct the answer. An *open question* is one that doesn't give any hint of supplying an answer: for example, 'What did you have for breakfast?'. In contrast, a *closed question* gives the respondent possible answers, such as the yes/no kind ('Did you have breakfast today?'), or more detailed such as 'Which of the following did you have for breakfast: cereal, eggs, coffee, juice?'. The problem with the closed question is that the questioner is assuming what the possible answers can be. If you had chapatti and banana for breakfast, a closed question isn't going to reveal that fact.

Asking open-ended questions is the art of good investigative questioning.

Going back over a crime with a witness and getting them to remember the details relies heavily on their working memory, which is often less than perfectly reliable. Psychological studies of witness memories show that things can go wrong in many different ways, not least because of a witness lying (turn to Chapter 5 for more on lying and detecting deception). 'Interrogation' (meaning asking a question) is a word you often hear when referring to police interviews, implying a challenging confrontation with a suspect. But, the main purpose of an interview with a witness, victim or suspect is to get a description of who did what, where and when. The event you're asking about is in the past and it's rare to have an on-the-spot record of what happened. An *explanation* of what happened may also be needed, to determine whether a crime's been committed and if the suspect being interviewed knew what he was doing: remembering why he did what he did. This explanation may be arrived at after the event, opening the way for the witness's statement to be legally challenged.

ANECDOTE

Requiring a photographic memory!

Courts of law are good at assuming that all witnesses and defendants have a good memory of what happened. Here's one example. I was giving evidence in a trial in which a report I'd written 20 years earlier was drawn on, but I hadn't been given advance notice of this fact. I was expected to remember the details of the report without being allowed to look over the document itself. Also, in the same trial, something I said in the morning was raised with me in the afternoon, as if I had total recall of everything I was saying and the exact words I was using.

The earliest studies of memory show how quickly ordinary memories decay and fade away, but the attorneys questioning me were keen to act as if no such memory decay exists. As a witness I was expected to remember everything without having any prompting. Of course not all courts work exactly like this, but any admission of a lack of clarity of memory can be used to challenge the veracity of what the witness is saying. (Skip to Chapter 12 if you want to see how this works in court proceedings.)

Recalling past events

Research shows that memory isn't like taking an old photograph out of a box, which may have just faded a bit with age.

You have two types of memory working very differently from each other:

- **Long-term memory:** You're drawing on your long-term memory when remembering a past event such as a crime.
- **Short-term memory:** Your short-term memory is your immediate memory – your working memory – like a scratch pad where you make a note or jot down a phone number before throwing it away.

The effectiveness of your long-term memory for an event or experience depends on:

- How long ago the event was.
- How much attention you were paying to the event at the time.
- How memorable the event was.
- Whether there are any cues to help you in remembering.

You can help a witness or victim remember the event by offering useful cues such as taking them back to the context of the event (called *context re-instatement*). For example, if you're being asked to recall what you ate in a particular restaurant, it's much easier to remember if you go back to the restaurant, rather than trying to remember from a distance. Going back to where you were at the time of the crime is useful for jogging your memory of the event. The process can add detail and clarity rather than changing the fundamental aspects of the memory itself.

Sometimes a significant event has an overwhelming and emotional impact on you, called a *flashbulb memory*. Like, where you were and how you heard about the 9/11 Twin Towers attacks or, if you're my age, where you were and how you heard of the death of John F. Kennedy or John Lennon.

A difference exists between identification testimony and other forms of testimony. When you're asked to select (say, from a police line-up or a set of photographs) a person who you saw and who's associated with a crime, it's usually referred to as *eyewitness testimony* (see the later section 'Looking into Eyewitness Testimony'). Choosing from a presented selection in this way is very different from generating your own account of what happened in a police interview.

Forgetting: Why do people fail to remember?

Forgetting the details of an event involves two processes:

- ✔ **'Recording' the memory:** If you didn't notice or pay much attention to the initial information, you tend not to 'store' the information effectively. The more unusual, memorable or emotionally significant the event, the more it attracts your attention, and so you're more likely to remember the details.

- ✔ **'Retrieving' the memory:** After committing the information to memory, you then need to 'retrieve' that information. The process of retrieval is vulnerable because your memories can be distorted, as delving into your memory isn't simply like playing a record. Remembering is an active process of generating a report of the bits of information that are stored. There may even be some assistance from general experience and logic of what is possible. 'I usually have eggs for breakfast so I suppose I did three days ago. There are no eggs left so I guess I ate them all then.'

Remembering anything that you experienced more than a few moments ago means *reconstructing* past events (something I talk about more fully in the later section 'Filling in the gaps: Errors in memory'). Reconstructing draws upon various strategies based on your knowledge and assumptions of what happens where and when (your preconceptions, in other words). The more the event follows your day-to-day expectations, the more you're reconstructing what you *think* happened rather than any direct memory of what really *did* happen. The result is that you may inadvertently alter the facts and leave some out (forget them).

Unwittingly altering facts

Cognitive dissonance is the process of a person wanting to make actions agree with their attitudes and beliefs, or indeed just needing to resolve conflicting thoughts. For example, if you're thinking of yourself as a good witness, you're intent on giving a clear account of what happened even if your memory isn't so clear – such as remembering being very frightened by an attacker and so assuming that he was very large.

Decaying over time

Psychologists studying memory found that memories of a past event become rapidly worse and less detailed over time. This *decay over time* starts soon after the event and then the loss of memory levels off. In general the longer the delay between an event and your attempt to remember it, the less complete and accurate your account is going to be. For example, this decay can easily apply to a witness taking part in a police line-up or viewing a set of identification photographs.

The decay isn't the same for everything though. I can still remember I was doing the washing up listening to the radio when I heard of John Lennon's death. (It wasn't the unusualness of my doing the washing up, but being at Liverpool University when The Beatles were in their prime meant they were part of my formative years.) However, I can't remember if it was my turn to do the washing up last Wednesday or not. Regular actions and events don't stick out in the same way as special or unusual ones.

Your memory doesn't normally improve over time and most of your forgetting takes place close in time to the event. Within a few days most of the forgetting that's going to take place has already happened. This forgetting occurs even when you're at some pains to 'store' the memory by rehearsing it. Also, as you get older, retrieving information from memory becomes slower, without doubt. However, what you forget, and what you have difficulty remembering does depend on the many aspects I mention throughout this chapter.

Filling in the gaps: Errors in memory

You deal with the incremental loss of memory for events over time by *reconstructing* what happened. The processes of reconstructing those memories that do not stand out for the sorts of special emotional or distinct qualities I mention earlier can include:

✔ Connections you're holding between places and events.

✔ Your experiences of patterns typical of various sorts of activities.

✔ What you know about people and activities.

Memories are open to distortion from existing preconceptions, and from information discovered and events occurring after the experiences being remembered. Typically, these distortions aren't deliberate or conscious: you genuinely believe that what you're remembering is what occurred.

Post-event information can affect a witness's memory and even cause the person to include non-existent details into a previously acquired memory.

One unexpected consequence of these distortions is that a witness's report in a criminal case can get more complete and less ambiguous each time the witness repeats what happens. So the account being heard in court appears to be more accurate, perhaps many months after the initial somewhat confused report given to the police. This process of *filling in* can be an efficient way of remembering, but can also be unreliable. The witness may be distorting or reconstructing the memory to fit information that becomes available after the event, such as who's suspected of the crime. The witness may be doing so for the best of intentions, conscientiously constructing parts of an unclear memory to make it seem more plausible.

Attempts to 'remember better' (such as using context re-instatement, which I describe in the earlier section 'Recalling past events') don't necessarily lead to an increase in accuracy. The person is likely to remember far more, but there can still be plenty of errors in what is remembered. The witness may still be drawing unconsciously on assumptions of what's likely to have happened and filling in with spurious details.

The need for a witness to make their recollection consistent, probable and harmonious can cause them to fill in the gaps (incorrectly) and repress information that blurs the issue or creates conflicts.

Example of a Loftus experiment

Witnesses were shown a video of a car accident in which a car drives through a stop sign. Half of the witnesses were asked 'How fast was the car going when it ran the stop sign?' Fifty-three per cent recalled seeing a stop sign. The other half of the witnesses were asked 'How fast was car A going when it turned right?': only 35 per cent of these witnesses remembered seeing a stop sign. Simply mentioning the stop sign greatly increased the likelihood that a witness remembered it.

Facing up to false memories

False memories occur when you remember something that didn't in fact happen. In a crime investigation, one of the most direct ways in which false memories occur is when a witness is offered an answer, which is implied by the phrasing of the question.

Elizabeth Loftus, a leading psychologist, carried out experiments showing that people can come to believe that they remember something by being led to believe it happened (see the nearby sidebar 'Example of a Loftus experiment').

The law recognises false memory by limiting the use of 'leading' questions that imply what answer the witness is expected to give. The most extreme leading questions are those implying guilt, such as the famous example: 'When did you stop beating your wife?' But a subtler leading question that implies an answer 'What did you see the defendant carrying from the shop?' is likely to be challenged by any good defence lawyer. The question implies the defendant was indeed carrying something, possibly leading the witness in trying to think of something he *may* have seen. A better question is 'Did you see the defendant leaving the shop?' or 'What did you see?'

An experiment in encouraging false memories

Spend 30 seconds memorising the 14 words below. After 30 seconds, cover the list and then write down as many of the words as you can remember.

Wheel	Road
Driving	Traffic
Travel	Passenger
Engine	Fuel
Highway	Tyre
Steering	Journey
Van	Train

Check the words you've written down against the list of words. Are there any words on your list that aren't on my list? Did you add extra words such as, auto, car or anything else to do with travel? If so, they're false memories. This exercise shows that your added words tend to be connected with vehicles or travel, because each of the listed words is associated with travelling. When recalling the words from the list, you draw on the commonly associated meanings of these words to help you in remembering. But by using that as a cue you actually add words that aren't on the list but you possibly thought ought to have been.

ANECDOTE

Extreme example of false memories

In the US, the daughters of Paul Ingram 'recovered' memories of their father abusing them. Ingram was a Christian fundamentalist and Chief Civil Deputy in a Sheriff's department and he agreed to be intensively interrogated, using techniques similar to those used in hypnosis (which I describe in the later section 'Using investigative hypnosis'). During investigative hypnosis Ingram 'recovered' memories of having brutally raped his daughters over a long time and of having led a satanic cult that sacrificially murdered hundreds of babies. He was sentenced to 20 years in prison although there was no evidence that he'd done any of the crimes. No babies were missing and no bodies found. Ingram later denied his confession but was only released after serving his sentence.

Recovered memories are another aspect of false memories that are contentious. These particular forms of false memory came to the fore with a number of well-publicised accounts of people supposedly 'remembering' that they'd been abused as children many years earlier, although they'd apparently long forgotten that abuse. Such 'memories' usually emerge during the course of psychotherapy. Of course, as I mention earlier there are processes that can improve the details of what is remembered. That is different from what I am calling 'recovered memories' here.

Assisting Witnesses and Victims to Remember

Getting as much relevant information as you can from an interview in a criminal investigation is vitally important. Psychologists have developed ways of maximising the information you get during an interview. In this section, I describe two such approaches (cognitive interviews and hypnosis) and give you guidelines on how children are best interviewed.

Letting someone speak: The cognitive interview

You can carry out a successful and effective interview by:

✔ Helping the interviewee in trying to remember what happened. Anything that can help the memory process is of value.

✔ Establishing a good relationship between the interviewer and the interviewee (the 'conversation management' that I talk about in the earlier section 'Managing the process: Interviews as conversations'). You need to be as supportive and helpful as possible so that more effective information is likely to be obtained.

The *cognitive interview* has been developed to enhance both of these aspects of interviewing by suggesting that you try:

✔ Establishing rapport.

✔ Listening actively.

✔ Encouraging spontaneous recall.

✔ Asking open-ended questions.

✔ Pausing after responses.

✔ Avoiding interrupting.

✔ Asking for detailed descriptions.

✔ Encouraging the person to concentrate on the question.

✔ Encouraging the use of imagery.

✔ Recreating the original context of the event.

✔ Adopting the witness's perspective.

✔ Asking relevant questions.

✔ Encouraging multiple retrieval attempts.

Cognitive interviewing stresses the importance of making full use of different mental processes. Therefore you need training and preparation before carrying out a cognitive interview. This type of interview is also time-consuming and sometimes difficult to put into practice. For these reasons, cognitive interviewing is being used more in research studies than in real-life police investigations.

Interviewing suspects

Questioning someone who's suspected of a crime is rather different from interviewing a victim or witness. What they say may be used in evidence against them. (The more challenging matter of whether they may not be telling the truth is dealt with in the next chapter.) So the law in most countries tries to control how those interviews take place. One problem though is that police interrogators may have the belief that the purpose of their questioning is to gain a confession. This can lead to people admitting to crimes they have not committed.

Dealing with false confessions

Sometimes a person is guilty of confessing to committing a crime when he's innocent. This strange situation can come about in a number of ways:

- Through being drunk or on drugs at the time of the crime and so having no actual memory of what happened, and therefore being susceptible to suggestions.

- Having a mental illness, such as schizophrenia, making it difficult for the person to distinguish fantasy from reality.

- Someone with a learning disability not understanding enough of what's happening.

- Cultural differences in which what an authority figure says is accepted without question, causing a person from this culture to accept they have done what they've been told they've done.

- A person who may be being threatened or coerced into making a confession.

- Someone with a personality that's susceptible to the influence of others, which is shown by recognised personality tests.

In the UK, police officers are trained in an interview procedure that emphasises that the point of questioning a suspect is to find the truth, not necessarily to get a confession.

Recognising the importance of improving police interview procedures, authorities in England and Wales have introduced the PEACE system, which draws on ideas from the cognitive interview. PEACE gives weight to what the police do before and after the interview as well as highlighting the importance of engaging with the respondent: building rapport and listening carefully. The aim is to encourage the interviewee to give an uninterrupted account in response to open questions of the kind, 'Tell me what you remember'. PEACE is a mnemonic for:

- **Preparation and Planning**

- **Engage and explain purpose of interview and process**

- **Account – free recall**

> ✔ Clarify, challenge and conclude
>
> ✔ Evaluate – new lines of inquiry?

Although the use of PEACE has had beneficial effects on police interviewing, there are still police officers interrupting and asking focused, closed questions. In part, this seems to be because the PEACE framework goes against the grain of police culture, which is to make forceful assumptions about an event and then use the interview to get confirmation of that assumption.

Using investigative hypnosis

What is hypnosis? Now, that's a big question! You may believe that it's a special trance-like state that reaches aspects of consciousness that aren't reached any other way. Or, you may think it's just a form of relaxed concentration that allows people to focus on certain things more clearly.

Experts frown on the stage hypnotist who's apparently making people do silly things against their will. Research studies show that it's difficult to get someone to do things against their will while under hypnosis, but you can certainly confuse the person. Also, not everyone can be readily hypnotised. As part of my forensic psychology training, I attended hypnosis sessions, but I never got into anything other than a slightly edgy, quiet state; and yet I can fall asleep during a classical music concert without any difficulty!

But whatever hypnosis really is, there is no doubt that in special circumstances it can help witnesses or victims to remember more clearly what they saw. It's only used very rarely when it's thought that a person may be able to remember some crucial detail if carefully helped. It has the risk like any intensive interview process of distorting what is remembered, therefore many safeguards are recommended if hypnosis is being used in a criminal investigation. For example, the hypnotist has to be fully trained and must have no other involvement in the investigation, and the hypnosis session must be always fully recorded by audio or preferably video.

There are a number of stages to follow in investigative hypnosis:

1. **Preparation:** Reviewing what's already known about the crime and the witness or victim and finding out what needs to be known.

2. **Introduction:** Telling the person being hypnotised what is going to happen and why.

3. **Induction of the hypnotic state:** Can include eye fixation, looking upwards while closing the eyes, deep breathing, muscle relaxation and repeated instructions to relax.

4. **Deepening the state:** Increasing the comfort of the person being hypnotised, using images of being on a sunny beach or other relaxing location.

5. **Drawing out information:** Reminding the witness of the crime scene and then getting the person to give a further account of what happened. A witness can be prompted at this stage to go into yet more detail. A post-hypnotic suggestion can also be used to help the witness remember other material, to help a further interview.

6. **Bringing the person out of the hypnotic state:** Using instructions to make the person feel calm, relaxed, normal in every way and fully awake.

Investigative hypnosis is a powerful procedure, but is open to all the problems, confusion and influences that I discuss in the earlier section 'Facing up to false memories' and related matters. Because of this, many courts don't allow information obtained under hypnosis to be used as evidence.

Helping children tell what happened

Children become involved in criminal proceedings for many reasons: as victims, witnesses, and as defendants. There have been swings of opinion on whether children should be allowed to give evidence at all and much debate about how to involve them in court. These days young children (often what is 'young' will depend on the maturity of the child and the views of the judge) rarely appear in the actual courtroom and in the UK they are generally interviewed in a separate room, with the interview being video-recorded. This arrangement makes for less intimidating surroundings and the interview is more likely to be successful.

An interview supporter, interpreter or intermediary may be used in an interview to make sure that the child understands what's being asked of them. Such a person is referred to as an *appropriate adult*. Props, such as dolls, may also be employed during the interview.

When interviewing children, you need to follow four main stages:

1. **Establishing rapport with the child.**

2. **Getting the child to provide a free flowing, uninterrupted narrative of what happens in their own words.**

3. **Asking specific questions based on that free narrative.**

4. **Obtaining closure (for example, post-interview counselling).**

There's a lot of debate about whether children can be regarded as reliable witnesses and, if so, at what age a child is able give a clear and reliable account. In Chapter 5, I look at how experts examine children's statements for validity. This is an important issue because in certain cases children are the only witnesses.

ANECDOTE

Forensic hypnosis in use

Twenty-six children on board a school bus were kidnapped at gunpoint with their driver in California in 1976. The children were held captive underground, but managed to dig themselves out. However, none of the victims was able to give any useful details to the investigating FBI.

The bus driver, Ed Ray, agreed to be hypnotised and under hypnosis remembered all but one of the digits of the number plate of the kidnappers' white van, leading to the conviction of the three men.

Looking Into Eyewitness Testimony

Witnesses are essential in a criminal investigation, providing on-the-spot and relevant evidence in court proceedings. An *eyewitness's testimony* is often vitally important in catching a criminal, and yet problems can arise about the accuracy of eyewitness evidence.

The reasons for errors in identifications are complex and not fully understood, but many academic studies point to relevant factors such as the length of time between the alleged event and the identification.

A witness can feel the pressure to perform. When a witness is brought in by the police to an identification parade the witness is likely to assume that the police have a suspect in mind or even in custody. He therefore feels he has to pick someone, even if the officer showing the photographs or running the line-up is careful not to force the issue.

Also, line-up administrators can sometimes unintentionally communicate their knowledge about which line-up member is the suspect and which members are fillers, through giving verbal and non-verbal cues. This tendency has been confirmed by a study in which some line-up administrators were given assumptions that one person was the culprit, but other administrators were given the assumption it was a different person. The person identified in the line-up varied depending on the assumption the administrator had been given!

REMEMBER

There are important differences between *recalling* an event, which draws heavily on the need to reconstruct what happened (as I discuss in the earlier section 'Remembering That Memory Can Mislead'), and *recognition* when you're faced with choosing an option. For example, you may not be able to recall a name but can readily choose the correct name from those on offer.

Although recognition is generally more accurate than recall, recognition is still open to distortions, for example:

- ✔ **Age:** Witnesses are most accurate when calculating the age of someone of a similar age, being familiar with that age group. And, the greater the difference between the age of the witness and the age of the offender, the less accurate a witness's estimate of the offender's age is likely to be.

- ✔ **Height:** Witnesses are often poor at judging heights, and as with age, the greater the difference in height between the offender and the eyewitness, the less accurate the estimate.

- ✔ **Build:** Witnesses have difficulty at judging the build of a person, with judgements being heavily influenced by clothing.

- ✔ **Clothing:** Witnesses' descriptions of the style of clothing are usually reasonably accurate, but a description of the colour of the clothing is often less accurate.

Eyewitness identifications aren't nearly as accurate and reliable as the public and the courts believe. As an example, an experiment was undertaken in which a person goes into a convenience store drawing attention to themselves by paying for their purchases all in pennies. Soon afterwards the salesperson views a photo spread and identifies the 'customer'. The percentage of correct identifications in such exercises ranges from 34 to 48 per cent and the percentage of false identifications from 34 to 38 per cent. Even after quite a short interval, an eyewitness is as likely to be as incorrect as correct when attempting to identify strangers.

Eyewitnesses are most accurate when identifying someone from a familiar and similar situation to themselves.

The innocence project

Scary but horribly true! In 1999, in the US, eyewitness identifications led to 75,000 prosecutions. DNA is now offering a much more reliable way of identifying a suspect and shows just how dodgy many legal eyewitness identifications are. One study shows that of the 62 persons acquitted by DNA evidence, 52 had been imprisoned on the basis of faulty eyewitness identification. Researchers hold a growing belief that the majority of false convictions are due to mistaken eyewitness testimony.

Lack of relationship between confidence and accuracy

A witness talking with great confidence about what they can remember doesn't mean that they're being any more accurate in what they're saying than someone who seems much less confident. There's no evidence of a simple link between confidence and accuracy. Furthermore, confidence increases over time, especially if the witness is giving the same account to different people, and so any relationship between confidence and accuracy grows less and less.

Also, if a police officer confirms to a witness that what the witness says agrees with other facts known to the police, the witness's confidence increases further, although the accuracy of what's being said doesn't.

A witness is more likely to recognise a person or event accurately if the happening was particularly memorable or striking. For example, you're more likely to remember a person's clothing, race or age if it stands out in contrast to that of other bystanders. Novel events, such as a ballerina tripping during a performance, or even more memorable, a politician admitting he's made a mistake, are more readily noted and remembered because the event is so rare and unusual.

Assessing eyewitness accuracy

Mnemonics, in which a memorable word is used to summarise a set of other facts, is a powerful aid to memory. Two colleagues of mine, Graham Wagstaff and Mark Kebbell, have created the mnemonic ADVOKATE to summarise the key factors influencing a witness's ability to remember the details of an event:

- **A**mount of time under observation – the longer a witness observes an event, the better the event is remembered.

- **D**istance of the witness from the person or event – being closer to the person or the event means that a witness is likely to be better at storing and remembering details.

- **V**isibility – the more visible the event, the better the witness is likely to recall it.

- **O**bstruction – the fewer obstructions to a witness's view, the better the event is remembered.

- **K**nown or seen before – if a witness has seen the offender before, they're more likely to remember that person when they see that person again in a different situation.

- ✔ **Any reason to remember** – if something is striking or novel, it's more likely to make a strong impression on the witness.

- ✔ **Time lapse** – the greater the length of time between an event and the witness's attempts to recall it, the worse their memory for that event is likely to be.

- ✔ **Errors or discrepancies** – if parts of a witness's testimony are inaccurate, other aspects of the testimony are also likely to be inaccurate.

If someone's pointing a knife or gun at you, the chances are that you're looking at the weapon rather than at the face of the attacker. Stress, fear, violence or the presence of a weapon will help you remember more clearly what is happening, but some of the details may be left out because you're noticing what's important to your survival and not the information that can help to identify your attacker.

Understanding unconscious transference

Human memory is much more readily influenced than you, may realise and constantly striving to make things fit together and make sense. Memory can be distorted by exposure to similar situations or people between the present event and its recall. Also, because recognition is helped by being in the situation where the things being recalled happened, an out of context witness can be aware that a person seems familiar but be confused about where he knows that person from. This process is called *unconscious transference*, where the witness remembers seeing a person but wrongly assigns that person to the criminal context.

Difficulties of cross-racial identification

Witnesses are usually good at saying whether they have been attacked by someone from their own ethnic group or a different one. However, they're less accurate in describing the specific racial group to which an individual belongs.

Cross-racial identification seems to be more difficult for a witness than same-race identification. Studies show that people from one racial background have more difficulty in identifying individual members of another race than they do members of their own race. In one experiment, researchers put together 72 photographs of black and white males and females. Each subject viewed 24 of the slides, chosen at random. After a five-minute break, the participants viewed all 72 photographs in random order, and were asked to identify the faces that they'd seen before. Both blacks and whites were significantly better at recalling faces of their own race. Many studies confirm this fact, now called an ORB – 'Own Race Bias'.

Even after having only a short exposure to someone, that person can be fixed in your unconscious, and then seem familiar to you in an entirely different situation. A witness, having come upon a random character, may well store that image in their mind and later reproduce the image in a different setting. For instance, if the witness to a crime is shown photographs of suspects, and the random character looks familiar, the familiarity may get interpreted by the witness as being the person they saw at the time of the crime. However, in fact, the familiarity is because they happened to have observed a random character just before the crime took place. The image of the random character has become tied up with what the witness remembers of the crime. Unconscious transference can also take place when a witness identifies a suspect from a line-up just after seeing a similar-looking person (for example, in a set of photos). The apparent familiarity may be mistakenly related back to the crime or incident rather than back to the photographs. The chances of a mistaken identification increase dramatically in these situations.

How widely unconscious transference occurs is unclear, as is what degree of familiarity with the other person is necessary – and under what circumstances – for it to surface. Psychologists all agree that unconscious transference needs to be watched out for when considering witness testimony.

In an experiment to demonstrate unconscious transference, 50 students were told a story with six characters, one of whom was a criminal. The students were shown pictures of each character, who were all generally similar in appearance. Three days later, the students were asked to choose the criminal at the centre of the story from a set of photos. In the sets of photos that didn't include the criminal's picture, 60 per cent of the students chose a photo of a character who's face seemed familiar but wasn't the criminal of the story.

Here's an example of unconscious transference in an actual case.

At the railway station the ticket clerk was robbed at gunpoint. He later identified a sailor as his assailant. On the day of the robbery, however, the sailor was away at sea. The forensic psychologist reviewing the case realised that the sailor had been an obvious victim of unconscious transference. The ticket clerk picked him out from the police line-up because his face was familiar. As it turned out, the sailor was based near the railway station and had bought train tickets from the same clerk on three different occasions before the robbery took place.

Minimising bias: Good practice recommendations

To cut the risk of bias in police line-up identifications, the American Psychological Association recommends the following:

- ✔ **Double-blind testing:** The person managing the line-up should have no knowledge of the identities of the persons in the line-up or of the culprit.

- ✔ **Keeping eyewitnesses informed:** The eyewitnesses should be told whether the culprit is going to be present in the line-up.

- ✔ **Lookalikes:** Make sure that the persons selected in the line-up resemble the description of the suspect given by the eyewitness.

- ✔ **Confidence of the eyewitness:** To be assessed and recorded at the time of identification.

- ✔ **Impartiality:** Make no comment about the person the eyewitness chooses.

Sometimes the recommendations of the American Psychological Association on bias are completely disregarded by the court. For example, a judge or attorney may ask the witness 'Is the person who you saw leaving the premises with the stolen goods here in court?' And the witness is face-to-face with the accused standing in the dock. This is a situation in which:

- ✔ The suspect is put at a disadvantage.

- ✔ The court assumes that the suspect appeared in the police identification process.

- ✔ Only the one suspect is presented to the witness in the court proceedings.

- ✔ A witness who's feeling insecure or unsure about his testimony can hide behind the legal formalities.

Asking a witness to identify the person standing in the dock as the person he saw at the time of the crime is an unsafe and unsound means of seeking witness corroboration, and yet many jurisdictions around the world use this procedure with great confidence.

Earwitness testimony

Earwitness? Yes, you're reading that correctly! A neglected but developing area of research into witness testimony is how a person remembers and reproduces what he hears as well as what he sees at the time of the crime. Your memory for both what you see and hear can decay rapidly, and so weaken the reliability of the accuracy of a witness's testimony. This can be a crucial aspect, say, of recognising a voice that made offensive or threatening phone calls. How well can you identify another person's voice? When I answer the phone I can sound very much like my son, much to the consternation of his girlfriends.

I've not come across any studies of witness testimony for smells yet although an awareness of smells can be important in what a victim remembers. In one rape case I was involved in, the victim said that her assailant smelled very clean. It later turned out that the assailant had just played in a football match and had probably showered shortly before attacking his victim.

Chapter 5

Exposing Liars and Detecting Deception

. . . .

In This Chapter

▶ Revealing the essentials of lying and deception

▶ Getting to know about detecting lies

▶ Hearing about criminal deception

▶ Finding out about interviewing suspects

▶ Studying documents for ciminal evidence

. . . .

Although most people tell the truth a lot of the time, deceptions do occur every now and then, such as telling that little white lie, from the highest of motives, because you want to avoid hurting your best friend's feelings. Or you may even hide the truth because life would get just too complicated if you had to explain all the details. But dishonesty isn't the default characteristic of the majority of people in most situations.

Things are a bit different though in the world of crime and criminal investigations. You can't assume that everyone is trying their best to tell the truth and nothing but the truth. Police investigators have to assume that suspects may try to weave a web of lies. They may deny guilt or, even more problematically for detectives and prosecutors, confess a guilt that's false.

Filtering out the truth and detecting deception is a major challenge for any investigation. In this chapter I take a look at the nature of lying and the ways that people set out to deceive, and the tools available to help to disentangle truth from lies. I also delve into the business of interviewing criminals, and the difficulties faced when trying to get at the truth when examining documents.

Understanding the Nature of Lying

It's not that easy to lie. (Skip to the next section to discover the difficulties.) So people lie in many different ways:

- ✔ The most obvious is saying something false as if it were true.
- ✔ Leaving out key facts in an account when those facts are likely to reveal the truth.
- ✔ Hiding the truth by giving misleading information.
- ✔ Providing a partial account by omitting certain facts.
- ✔ Telling the truth in an exaggerated way making it sound unbelievable.

Surprisingly, many suspects will admit to their crimes. The majority of convictions come because the culprit confesses. But you also need to understand that some suspects are *more likely* to tell lies than tell you the truth, simply because of the type of person that they are, such as:

- ✔ A psychopath telling you lies even when telling the truth isn't going to harm him or cause him any problems. Telling lies can be just a habit that he has without thinking about it.

- ✔ In extreme forms of psychosis, the person has difficulty in distinguishing between what's real and what's imaginary. This situation raises an interesting philosophical question. Can a person who believes his neighbours are reading his thoughts and poisoning his cat and complains about this to the police be regarded as a liar? This poses a challenge for investigators if they have no understanding of psychosis. It can also make legal proceedings fraught, because the defence could challenge anything the person claims even though some of it may be genuine.

- ✔ An adult with a learning or mental disability, or a young child, may not be able to tell the difference between the actual facts and what they want the facts to be. Also, as any parent can tell you, a child from a remarkably young age is quite clever at deceiving you if it serves their purpose or they thinks it's fun. Because of this problem, it's possible that such individuals may not be allowed to give evidence in court.

- ✔ Before my grandson was even a year old, he liked to play a game of putting out his hand to me and pretending he was giving me a present, and then pulling his hand away, giggling furiously as I tried to get hold of it. An example of deception being practised from a very early age?

- ✔ In certain social groups, there's a deep-seated fear of figures of authority. Therefore, a suspect may agree to having been in a particular place simply because a police officer is telling him that's the case. This tendency raises issues about more forceful techniques of discovering lying and deceit that I discuss later in this chapter in 'Interrogating suspects'.

Discovering the difficulties of successful deception

You may be surprised to find that being a successful liar isn't all that easy. This fact becomes clear when you think about the emotional and intellectual demands that people who are lying place upon themselves:

- ✔ A liar has to create a lie, requiring imagination.
- ✔ A liar has to hold the untruth together with the known facts.
- ✔ A liar has to develop the untruth around plausible possibilities.
- ✔ A liar has to think through how to make the deception plausible, which can be intellectually challenging.
- ✔ A liar has to be careful not to give himself away when he's believed, by some response, such as smirking, that may seem inappropriate to the interviewer.

Sticking fast to the lie is the most difficult aspect of lying. For example, if someone offers you a vast sum of money in exchange for doing nothing, you don't need any sophisticated lie-detecting equipment to know there's a catch. You simply know that the world doesn't work like that, providing free lunches willy-nilly!

Experienced fraudsters know that people may be suspicious of what they're offering, which is why the fraudster couches his claims in plausible scenarios (such as, 'Your address came up in a lottery that you didn't know about'). In the later section 'Plausibility' I describe the procedures you can follow for testing the truth and reliability of a statement being given in court.

Summarising why detecting deception is so difficult

Any lie-detection procedure takes into account the intellectual and emotional demands that lying requires (as I describe in the preceding section 'Discovering the difficulties of successful deception'). The nitty-gritty of detecting a lie is in testing the plausibility of the claims the suspect is making. But if a liar truly believes he's telling you the truth none of the intellectual or emotional aspects of lying exist and the usual procedures for detecting deception are unlikely to work.

Hardened liars are experts in using strategies to reduce the likelihood of being detected:

✔ The lie is rehearsed so that there's no need to invent a lie on the spot with all the associated risks of getting details wrong or saying something implausible.

✔ The lie is built upon something that actually happened, so that most of the details are true and don't need to be invented and are plausible. Only some crucial aspects of the lie are untruthful.

✔ The liar avoids giving any details to cut out the risk of tripping himself up.

You can make things much harder for a suspect you think is lying by asking for as much detail as possible. The more the liar has to invent, the more chance he's going to reveal inconsistencies in his story.

Detecting Lies: Some Attempted Procedures

Lie-detection procedures have been developed for interviewing suspects in a criminal investigation, helping to weed out the lies, and leave the truth exposed.

You have to bear in mind that none of the lie-detection procedures that I describe in this section are completely accurate or foolproof. Indeed, some procedures can mislead you into thinking that you've detected lying when the opposite is the case.

There are four general approaches you can take in detecting lying or deceit:

✔ **Physiological approach,** which records the physiological changes in a person's body when answering specific questions.

✔ **Behavioural approach,** looks at the way a person is behaving to see whether the person is showing any of the emotional or stressful aspects of lying (see the earlier section 'Discovering the difficulties of successful deception').

✔ **Semantic assessment,** which carefully examines the words the person is using and the possible meanings in the answers the person is giving under questioning.

✔ **Legal approach,** where a person is being questioned in a court of law and being put through a detailed examination of the plausibility of his statement.

Lie-detector procedures like the physiological, behavioural, semantic and legal approaches are concerned with testing the truthfulness of what the person is saying while he's giving his account of the event. These procedures don't include a careful investigation that can show that a person's *alibi* – the claim not to have been at the crime scene – is false. Nor do these procedures have the means of examining the impossibility of the person doing what he claims to have done or not done – for example, because that person has a physical disability, or the journey he claims to have taken could not have been completed in the time available. You need to test the credibility of what the person is claiming independently to find out if the person's story is true.

Testing the validity of a lie-detector procedure can be problematical. For example, you set up an experiment in which you get a person to simulate committing a crime. Then the person is questioned using a lie-detection procedure. But in an artificial situation, the reactions of the suspect and the truthfulness or otherwise of the suspect's statement doesn't carry the same high stakes as in real life where not being believed could mean a long prison sentence.

Getting true-life examples of the validity of lie-detector procedures can throw up many ethical and legal problems. In the real world, getting adequate comparisons with what is likely to have happened in a criminal investigation if the lie-detector procedure hadn't been used is often impossible. Companies selling lie-detection equipment or software typically avoid providing important comparison data. So although the company claims their product can show that a lot of deceptions were uncovered using their (often expensive) system, no-one can tell you if the lie-detector system really did add value. I discuss this anomaly in more detail, later in this chapter, in the section 'Combating insurance fraud'.

Using physiological approaches

Monitoring the physiological reactions of a suspect to detect whether he's telling the truth or lying has been in use for some years (something I talk about in Chapter 1). The aim of the physiological approach is to pick up on what's technically known as *arousal*: a heightened energising of the nervous system and muscles. Arousal is shown by an increase in heart rate and the rate of breathing, as well as by a change in the skin's ability to conduct electricity because of an increase in sweating. The person's voice can also become higher pitched and more erratic.

The problem for the forensic psychologist is that the heightened responses can also be a sign of a general emotional reactions produced by the anxiety of being questioned, especially if the person fears he's wrongly being thought of as a liar.

Recently, a TV show demonstrated the unreliability of the physiological approach for testing lying. Celebrities were asked tricky questions to find out if the answers they were giving were true or false. The interrogator maintained that his lie-detection system showed that some of the celebrities were lying – but the celebrities hotly denied the accusation.

Likely the celebrities were reacting emotionally to the crassness of the questions being asked – in front of millions on live TV. The experiment was dropped from further shows.

Companies selling physiological lie-detector tests often claim that the lie-detector can tell the difference between testing normal anxiety and the anxiety associated with lying. For example, the claim is that as the test continues normal anxiety disappears and the emotions associated with lying show at particular points when lies are being told. But variations between individuals in their response to the questioning can mask such subtleties.

Displaying heightened emotional responses isn't the same as lying. All physiological lie-detection procedures are in fact detecting only emotional responses, such as the anxiety of the person being interviewed thinking that he isn't going to be believed. Because a physiological lie-detector can be unreliable in detecting whether a person is lying, few courts allow their findings as evidence. (For more on the physiological approach see the section 'The polygraph'.)

The polygraph

The polygraph is a machine used for measuring small physiological changes in the body at one and the same time: heart rate, breathing, sweating and so on. It's the best known procedure for detecting lying (and is usually just called a *lie-detector*). Originally, the polygraph recorded these physiological changes using pens running across a moving sheet of paper, which is where the name *polygraph* comes from, meaning many lines. Polygraph machines have since been computerised: so the magic of pens bouncing across paper with a dramatic, crunchy upsurge when a 'lie' was being told is no more.

In an attempt to separate normal heightened emotional responses from the responses associated with lying, the polygraph is used alongside the *guilty knowledge procedure*. Under the guilty knowledge procedure the suspect is asked simple 'yes' or 'no' questions that contain a mixture of information that only the suspect can possibly know, together with unbiased questions that act as a sort of basis for a truthful answer. The comparison between the physiological responses to the questions containing the guilty knowledge and the unbiased questions is used to detect if the person is lying.

Scientific studies show that the guilty knowledge procedure is the most reliable procedure on the market for detecting lying, although not always giving valid results. Importantly, the guilty knowledge procedure is much better at showing when a person *isn't* lying than showing when he is.

Primitive lie-detectors

In early societies, some curious practices were followed in order to test if a person was being false. For example, it was the custom to use 'magic rice' to find out if a person was lying. The suspected person was deemed a liar if he wasn't able to swallow the magic rice, but if he did he was pronounced innocent. Anyone in a highly emotional state was almost bound to have a dry mouth and be unable to swallow, spelling doom for the suspect. Then there was the bizarre ritual of the witch-finder – a woman suspected of being a witch was dunked in the pond – with the idea that if she was innocent she drowned and if she survived it proved without doubt she was a witch. Doing little for the cause of justice!

As long as the guilty knowledge procedure spots no suspicious reactions, that person is likely to be telling the truth. So, although most courts don't allow a polygraph test to be presented as evidence of guilt, it can sometimes be a useful way of eliminating a suspect from the investigation because of the person being shown to be telling the truth.

When setting up a polygraph test using the guilty knowledge procedure you need to know a lot about the circumstances of the crime as well as understanding how much only the suspect can possibly know (difficult if a lot of information about the crime has become public knowledge). Also, the suspect has to be carefully briefed about what happens during a polygraph test and how the procedure works.

There may not be much that only the suspect would know so other types of polygraph tests are sometimes used. For example, a suspect's physiological reactions when presented with incriminating information may be compared with his reactions when asked innocent questions about things that many people do wrong. This is far less reliable than the guilty knowledge test. What is your likely reaction to being wired up to a polygraph and being asked bluntly 'Have you ever lied to avoid being found out about something you did wrong?' Like me, I think your heart is likely to start thumping and you're gasping for breath, even though most people would be expected to say 'yes' to this question. And yet, a hardened criminal is quite capable of responding in a relaxed manner: 'Yeah. Sure. Haven't you?'

There are many ways of cheating on the polygraph test (websites are devoted to telling you how to do so). In general, if a person's emotional responses are haphazard, or they set up some distraction such as having a stone in their shoe that's hurting them, or because they're having difficulty in focusing on the question, the polygraph machine is unable to detect the difference in responses to crucial questions.

Anyone making a living out of polygraph testing tells you that the key to a valid test is in establishing a working relationship with the person being tested. Having rapport with your subject determines how much he believes in the result of the procedure, sometimes to the point of admitting to his guilt without even needing to read the output.

Voice stress analysis

Voice stress analysis is a recent computer product on the market for detecting if a person is telling you the truth while speaking on the phone. The product is controversial and mostly used by companies dealing with insurance claims for detecting if the customer is making a false claim. The idea behind voice stress analysis is that any sound has measurable *frequency*. A sound with a high pitch has a rapid frequency; a low pitch a much slower frequency. So, an analysis of the frequency picks up any heightened emotional responses in the caller's voice.

Voice stress analysis faces lots of problems (hence the controversy). You know yourself that the pitch of your voice changes if you have a cold, or at different times of day. And, women generally have higher pitched voices than men, as well as pitch changing with age. As yet, I haven't been able to get any answers to how voice stress analysis deals with these matters.

I once asked a voice stress analysis salesman for the research results of the product and in return received a load of abuse down the phone. I didn't need his voice stress analysis equipment to tell me how angry he was with me for thinking that his product was less effective than he was claiming!

My concern is that voice stress analysis can be used by inexperienced and untrained call handlers, who simply watch the indicator on their screen (that's supposedly indicating whether a person is telling the truth or not) instead of the call handler listening carefully to what the customer's saying and how plausible they sound. In other words, does the use of voice stress analysis distract from the less hi-tech approach of carefully challenging what the person is claiming?

Truth drugs

Administering *truth drugs* (making the subject under questioning less wary in his replies because he's in a highly relaxed state, induced by special drugs) to detect lying and deceit was popular for a short while in the second-half of the 20th century. The favoured drugs were sodium amytal or sodium pentothal, which are essentially sedatives. However, the reliability of truth drugs is questionable as a person in a dreamlike state is just as likely to be fantasising as telling the truth.

Under international law, using truth drugs to detect lying is regarded as a form of torture. Judges forbid evidence gained from using truth drugs.

Brain 'fingerprinting'

Scientists are now able to produce a map of the electrical and related activity in the different parts of the brain, which commercial companies call *brain fingerprinting*. Mapping electrical activity in the brain is a more sophisticated lie-detection procedure than those I've already talked about (see the earlier sections 'The polygraph' and 'Voice stress analysis'). Brain fingerprinting consists of putting a number of electrical detectors on a suspect's head and mapping the pattern of electrical activity across the brain while the person is answering questions during a crime investigation.

The technique of brain fingerprinting is similar to the guilty knowledge procedure used with polygraph testing, except that this time the person being interviewed is shown pictures relevant to the crime mixed up with unrelated images, with the technique picking up on the images the suspect is particularly sensitive to.

Brain fingerprinting doesn't require the suspect to speak. The procedure is claimed to work without the person needing to make a verbal statement, in which he may be lying or telling the truth.

There's a lot of scepticism about using brain fingerprinting as a way of determining guilt or innocence. Some experts believe that commercial organisations are being misleading by naming it 'fingerprinting', using the term as a way of claiming similarities to the different and accurate fingerprinting procedure used in criminal investigations.

Yet, growing evidence suggests that, under carefully controlled conditions, brain-mapping has a part to play in determining a suspect's innocence or guilt because of the suspect's trust or faith in the procedure which as a result can produce a confession. Brain-mapping is an advanced version of physiological testing and is likely to be used more and more as the equipment becomes cheaper and less cumbersome.

Brain-mapping research

Early research studies show that some parts of the brain are particularly active during lying – for example, when a group of people were told they could keep £20 if they were successful in lying about the cards they were holding in their hands. The results of these studies allowed the researchers to decide with a high degree of accuracy whether a person was lying. Studies since then claim 100 per cent accuracy in detecting lying. Brain-mapping evidence has been used to support the guilt of a person accused of murder, as well as the innocence of others.

Observing carefully: Behavioural approaches

You can find out a lot about what a person's thinking and saying from the way they're behaving. In the game of poker, where you have to decide whether another player is bluffing or has a great hand, such non-verbal clues are called a 'tell' (such as, a person shuffling their legs or scratching their ear showing that they're lying). Using these clues to detect deception is fraught with difficulties. Studies show that looking at the way a person is behaving, and what he's saying, as a means of determining whether he's lying is more complicated than it first appears.

Non-verbal leakage (body language)

You can't help thinking the term *non-verbal leakage* sounds a bit rude (conjuring up the image of a young child squirming because of needing the toilet but denying it furiously – although come to think of it the squirming *is* a form of non-verbal leakage and if correctly understood can indeed stop other forms of leakage!). The idea is that people show you what they're feeling from the way that they behave, but they are not doing this consciously – as when a person threatens you by waving his fist in your face – they are doing it inadvertently. It's unconsciously 'leaking' from them.

This non-verbal leakage is an aspect of *body language*. You express many things without the use of words, sometimes deliberately: a shrug of the shoulders, looking away, glaring into someone's eyes. There are claims that some aspects of this non-verbal communication can be used to indicate lying.

Using body language to determine lying is unreliable in that everyone has their own way of behaving when telling a lie and that behaviour can change from situation to situation. Even poker players are aware that not every player has the same 'tell'; you have to watch a person playing over time to spot if the 'tell' is special to that individual.

STRANGE BUT TRUE

How do the experts do?

Studies show that professionals, such as police officers, are no better at detecting deception than the man in the street. Typically both groups have success in detecting truth or lying accurately in just over half the cases studied (only marginally better than guessing by tossing a coin). The only professional groups that do significantly better at detecting lying are members of the Secret Services. Spies seem to get it right in nearly three out of every four cases.

Some people assume that a guilty person is likely to be more nervous when lying and shows his stress through displaying more hand movements, slower speech and general fidgeting. But studies show that the opposite is the case. A person under pressure of maintaining the lie is concentrating harder on the lie, with the result that he displays *less* non-verbal leakage than you may expect. On the other hand, a person who's telling the truth is so often concerned to show that he's telling the truth that his body language may become more animated and exaggerated.

Body language is a gripping metaphor for communicating through gestures, facial expressions and other bodily movements. But these movements are not a **language** in the same way the written and spoken word is. They can add emphasis, as when people thump the table, but these movements and gestures do not provide an account of what is claimed that can be open to logical scrutiny of how plausible it is.

Micro-twitches

Paul Ekman, has spent over 40 years studying how people express emotions, focusing on the small changes in facial muscles that go with what a person's feeling. These *micro-twitches* often last only a fraction of a second and you can see them best from watching a slow-downed video recording. Ekman claims that micro-twitches show what a person is feeling even when trying to hide their emotions. They are not really part of body language because they are only visible under very special scrutiny.

Giving a false smile to hide what you're really feeling is the most obvious micro-twitch. Ekman's theory claims that although the muscles round the mouth are indicating pleasure the facial muscles around your eyes are showing the opposite.

As a result of Ekman's research micro-twitches are now being used for detecting lying and deceit. The problem is that these tiny facial muscles can only show strong emotions, such as anger, fear or surprise. If strong emotions can be proved to link directly to truthfulness or lying, micro-twitches can be valuable in detecting deception. For example, the suspect may be asked how he feels about his victim, and says that he liked her, while his wrinkling nose is indicating disgust. Or, when the suspect is asked directly if he's lying and he denies it, but the micro-twitches around his mouth are showing that he himself doesn't believe in what he's saying.

Paul Ekman warns against the danger of ignoring the value of micro-twitches as a way of detecting lying, calling it the 'Othello Error'. Remembering how Othello in Shakespeare's play refuses to believe Desdemona's protestations of innocence, totally ignoring her anguished face, and then killing her out of jealousy – so the investigator needs to bear in mind that the workings of the facial muscles have a part to play in helping get at the truth when you're interviewing a suspect in a crime investigation. The practice of observing micro-twitches as a way of detecting malicious intent is now being used in public places such as airports. However, this practice is being questioned on the grounds that a particular facial expression can be because of a person's culture in which such expressions are normal, as much as being a sign of what the person's thinking and feeling. There are also people who have a general dislike of authority and show this dislike in their facial expressions despite being innocent of any crime.

Aldert Vrij and his colleagues carried out an experiment for observing the rate of blinks before and after a person was telling a lie. Vrij found that the relative differences in the rates were much larger for liars than truth-tellers. As the experiment was small, having only 13 people in each group, the results are open to question.

Paralinguistic cues

What a person's telling you, and the actual meaning of what they're saying, is often less to do with *what's* being said than *how* it's being said. Because these aspects of speech run parallel to one another, they're called *paralinguistic cues*, such as:

- Indulging in pauses, of varying length and frequency.
- The number of mispronunciations or inappropriate words.
- Speed of delivery, either very fast or very slow.
- Inappropriate non-verbal utterances, such as laughter.
- Filled pauses, for example, 'eh', 'erm' and so on.

Computer programs have been set up to measure the frequency of paralinguistic cues and the relationship to a person's emotional state. Researchers have found that big differences exist between people in their paralinguistic characteristics. If these variations are allowed for, paralinguistic cues can produce results that give a reasonably accurate indication of a person's emotional response, most notably fear. But whether or not this relates to lying, depends on the individual and whether or not the circumstances of their utterances are so demanding that these cues will be revealing.

Studying semantic assessment

When you're looking closely at a suspect's statement and you believe that he's deliberately setting out to deceive, you're dealing with what I call the *semantic assessment* of deception. Semantic assessment involves examining each significant word in the statement for meaning and how that word is being expressed. In this section, I look at what you need to do when you're carrying out a semantic assessment, the difficulties you can come up against when trying to get to grips with what's being said, and the plausibility of the statement.

Experts have drawn up useful checklists setting out the valid points you need to keep in mind when carrying out a semantic assessment of a suspect's statement. Some countries, notably Germany, use these checklists for examining children's accounts of sexual abuse. The idea behind these checklists is that what you describe from actual experience will contain information that is usually not present when you invent a description.

Here are the sorts of things that you should look for to determine if a statement is an imaginative creation or the truth:

- ✔ Is there an overall logic to the account in which each aspects makes sense with every other aspect?
- ✔ Is the way the statement is given disorganised or does it have a clear unfolding structure to it?
- ✔ Does it have enough convincing detail?
- ✔ Is the context in which the event occurred clear?
- ✔ Where other people are present, how well are the interactions with them described?
- ✔ Is any conversation reproduced in a plausible way?
- ✔ Are unexpected complications described?
- ✔ Are there any unusual details?
- ✔ Are some of the details given superfluous to the main account?
- ✔ Does the person giving the statement describe aspects of what they were thinking or feeling at the time?
- ✔ Are there spontaneous corrections?
- ✔ Is there an admission of lack of memory?
- ✔ Does the person making the statement raise doubts about what happened?

This list of questions isn't without its critics and certainly isn't foolproof. It doesn't, for example, show the difference between a partially truthful account from an untruthful one, especially if the untruthful version is built upon something that actually happened, but not to the suspect or witness or not at the time claimed. As I discuss in Chapter 4, memory fades quickly over time and so the lack of clarity in what a liar says can be mistaken for a sign that he's telling the truth. Plus, memories of a traumatic event can leave an indelible mark and can be much sharper than the answers to these questions may lead you to expect.

Don't do that, do this!

Aldert Vrij and his colleagues have been looking into ways of exploiting the intellectual demands made on a person when inventing and maintaining a lie. Vrij claims that if you ask a suspect to carry out two separate tasks at the same time, putting pressure on his thought processes, more signs of lying become apparent – for example, asking the suspect to play a computer game while making his statement, or giving an account of what happened in reverse chronological order. By putting on this additional pressure many of the weaknesses in the plausibility of what is being said can come to the surface.

Looking at legal approaches

For the forensic psychologist the most common way of finding out the truth of a suspect's statement and detecting deception is during the court proceedings. Courts rely heavily on their own tried and tested approaches to getting at the truth, despite research showing the many difficulties associated with detecting lying and deceit.

Power of court proceedings

Lawyers have great confidence in the ritual of the court as the best way of extracting the truth from the person standing in the witness box. The witness or defendant has to swear an oath and is then examined closely in front of the judge, jury (if one is present), members of the public and sometimes even victims. This confidence comes partly from the belief that if a ritual is powerful enough, a person feels compelled to tell the truth. Indeed, the swearing of an oath comes from times in which a belief in God's wrath was so strong that a person feared divine punishment if he lied under that oath.

Getting to the truth in a court of law relies on the effectiveness of the questioning of witnesses and the defendant. In many jurisdictions, the defendant may not be open to questioning, which was the case in British courts until quite recently, because of the belief that a defendant can't be expected to be telling the truth.

In the US the view that a person is never put in a position where he can incriminate himself is enshrined in the Fifth Amendment to the US Constitution: 'nor shall be compelled in any criminal case to be a witness against himself'.

Plausibility

The court proceeding puts a great deal of emphasis on the plausibility of a person's statement. To establish the truth of a statement the court has to refer to what's generally expected to be possible or typical for a person's lifestyle or set of circumstances. Forensic psychologists therefore look at statements in terms of what the person may be expected to know and how ready the person is in giving that information, including:

- Assessing the clarity or vagueness of the evidence.
- Working out if the evidence is being presented in a logical sequence.
- Deciding whether the witness or defendant is willing to answer questions directly.
- Considering how the evidence relates to the general pattern of similar events.
- Assessing whether irrelevant information is likely to distract from the central issue.
- Looking at whether the evidence contains too many references to people in general rather than specific persons.
- Checking if the witness or defendant's evidence contains a lot of modifiers, such as 'sometimes', 'probably' and so on.

Ways in Which Lying Is Used to Commit Crime

Some crimes depend a lot on lying and deceit. In this section I take a look at three criminal activities that make full use of misrepresenting the truth – insurance fraud, false allegations and extortion – and how forensic psychology can help to get at the truth.

Corroborative evidence

A lawyer often looks for additional evidence that supports, or *corroborates,* the claims of those persons involved in the court case. If this additional evidence is only indirect, such as finding a weapon that can be related to a crime rather than having evidence that the defendant used the weapon, it's known as *circumstantial* evidence. However, such evidence can be strong enough to gain a conviction, even in very serious cases.

Combating insurance fraud

Have you ever been in a position of making an insurance claim that wasn't strictly accurate? For instance, claiming items on your insurance after being burgled, and then to your horror finding the items later on, and leaving it at that. Of course, you're more likely to be one of the majority of citizens who'd never do anything so underhand, but sadly, otherwise totally law-abiding people do sometimes break the law by defrauding on insurance claims.

Many reasons exist why generally honest people lie in this way. A person may, wrongly, justify an insurance claim by saying he's been paying insurance premiums for years and now it's time for payback. Or he may argue that it doesn't hurt anyone (untrue because everyone suffers by paying higher premiums as a consequence) and the insurance company makes lots of profits. A dishonest claim can even be a sort of revenge for another claim that was turned down in the past.

Many of the excuses you find yourself giving for having committed insurance fraud – denial, justification, minimisation and rationalisation – are similar to those that the hardened criminal gives for his actions (as I discuss in Chapter 2).

Committing insurance fraud is often seen as easy pickings: too many people think that they can get away with it. Over recent years insurance companies have tried to improve their ability to detect fraudulent claims (such as the method I describe in the earlier section 'Voice stress analysis'). Companies also use more direct approaches, like asking for original copies of documents and sending inspectors round to check out claims. But an insurer's business is dependent partly on how willing and ready the company is in dealing with a claim, so many would rather not check the claim too thoroughly and just bump up the premiums instead.

Those insurance companies that are aware of the importance of detecting lying immediately a claim is made have started using procedures like the one I've developed: the *Fraud Indicating Behaviours System* (FIBS). (Yes, you're likely thinking the acronym's the best part.) The following FIBS list gives you a framework for detecting deception. You can see from the list how I've turned my ideas about lying (including those I discuss in the earlier sections 'Understanding the Nature of Lying' and 'Detecting Lies: Some Attempted Procedures') into a simple system that you can use with only a little training. Insurance companies using FIBS are reporting a dramatic reduction in fraudulent insurance claims.

FIBS asks the following questions (I don't tell you how the responses are used to determine fraud, so as not to give the game away):

✔ **Reaction: What is the claimant's reaction to the event?**

- How emotional was his reaction?

- Does his reaction seem unusual?

- Did he carry out his own investigation?

✔ **Detail: What sort of detail does the claimant give about the event?**

- Are there gaps in the time of his account?

- Does he put the event in context?

- Is irrelevant information offered?

- Does his account have an obvious chronological sequence?

- Were there unexpected complications?

- Is there possible corroboration, say from other people?

✔ **Style: How does the claimant communicate the information?**

- Does he avoid answering?

- Are his answers consistent?

- Are his answers hesitant?

- How co-operative is he?

- How inquisitive is he about what he's being asked?

- Does he spontaneously correct what he's saying?

Discovering false allegations

Bringing a false allegation against a person is a particularly pernicious form of deception, especially when someone is accusing another person of a heinous crime such as sexual abuse or rape. Some evidence shows that false accusations of rape may occur in at least one out of every ten allegations.

In the case of rape, making a false allegation is quite a separate problem from determining whether consent to sexual activity took place. A false allegation is the dishonest claim that unwanted sexual activity occurred when there's clear evidence that both parties consented to the activity or that the activity never took place at all.

Reasons for making false allegations of rape can be because the person is:

✔ Looking for financial gain: for example, compensation.

✔ Seeking to gain support from other people by being seen as a 'victim' who needs help.

✔ Needing to excuse inappropriate behaviour, such as getting drunk and having a fling that's later regretted.

✔ Hoping the authorities can change the person's circumstances (one example may be when wanting to get different welfare housing).

✔ Wanting to hurt or discredit a person or institution.

✔ Creating difficulties in a relationship or as part of a job (as a form of blackmail).

✔ Claiming false (as in recovered) memory (a topic I discuss in Chapter 4).

The major problem with rape investigations is that victims are often reluctant to come forward. A high proportion of rape victims never report that they have been sexually assaulted. They may fear that they will not be believed. Being aware that only a small minority of rape allegations are false helps the police to take all allegations seriously. In fact, in many jurisdictions, the police assume the allegation is true unless there is overwhelming evidence that it isn't.

Tackling extortion

Extortion is illegally getting hold of money by compulsion. For example, a well-known company receives an anonymous letter threatening to poison the company's products, unless money is paid or some other action taken. The threat can have a major impact on the company if any hint that the company is being threatened reaches the public. This situation falls under the category of *extortion*. Therefore, careful examination of the threatening communication is crucial in deciding what steps to take.

Fortunately, the majority of people writing threatening letters never follow through on their threats. Often the act of writing is just an expression of anger or frustration, malice or spite. Against that backdrop, the task is to detect the minority of letters indicating a real determination to put the threat into action.

I've been involved in several cases of threatening letters and now know the signs to look for in establishing whether the threat is genuine or false. Clearly, making these signs available to the general public is inappropriate, but I can say that the signs draw upon a careful analysis of the credibility of the threat and the benefits and costs to the writer of carrying out the threat. Meticulous study of the form of words in which a threat is expressed can be of great value in understanding the sort of person the writer is, his background and knowledge. For instance, consider what the writer's really trying to achieve. Is it really money he's after or to cause havoc? What sort of person the writer's likely to be can also be gleaned from the way he writes. The crucial question, though, is the probability of the person actually carrying out the threat (check out the later section 'Examining Documents to Help Solve Crimes' for more information).

Interviewing Suspects to Sort Truth from Lies

Witnesses are generally in the habit of trying to tell the truth as they understand it when being interviewed. However, you can't make that assumption when interviewing suspects. Interviewing procedures are established in some places that make it easier to find out if the suspect is telling the truth. However, you need to keep in mind that such interviewing procedures can be fraught with problems.

Dealing with false confessions

A suspect confessing to a crime he didn't commit is a serious problem for police investigators. You have to get at the truth to avoid the person being wrongly imprisoned (often the person is vulnerable and needing help such as psychiatric treatment rather than custody) and, of course, wrongful imprisonment means letting the guilty person go free.

In 1980, when Sean Hodgson was 30 years old he told a prison chaplain that he'd murdered a barmaid. He withdrew the confession at his trial a year later, saying he was a 'pathological liar' who'd falsely confessed to countless crimes. But Hodgson spent nearly 30 years in prison until DNA evidence cleared him.

You may think that a person who's being tortured or coerced is more than likely to confess to a crime of which he's innocent. But many examples exist of people confessing without any such pressures. Police investigators have to be on the alert all the time for such possibilities in even fairly common crimes such as burglary. False confessions can happen because the person is:

✔ **Craving attention,** believing that he can gain notoriety or glory from admitting to a crime.

✔ **Feeling confused about what he did** and/or where he was at the time of the crime, especially if he's a habitual criminal and was under the influence of alcohol or drugs.

✔ **Suffering from a serious mental condition** and may not be aware of the real situation as against something he imagined or interpreted wrongly.

✔ **Accepting what he's being told.** Ghisli Gudjonsson, a forensic psychologist who has made a special study of how some people will accept what they've been told, calls this tendency *suggestibility*. He has developed a special way of measuring how prone someone is to suggestibility. It consists of asking people questions, then giving them suggestions in relation to their answers and seeing if they accept them. This procedure has been used in court cases to support the innocence of people who initially confess.

> ✔ **Wanting to get out of an awkward situation,** like having been put in a cell and just wanting to get home, possibly not realising the serious consequences of confessing.

In many parts of the world today, and in the past in most places, the main cause of false confessions was physical or mental intimidation or torture. The whole basis of the Inquisition in the Middle Ages was to torture people until they confessed their sins. This is less so now in the UK since the introduction of the PEACE interview process (described in Chaper 4) and the tape-recording of interviews of suspects.

Curiously, in high-profile murder cases or other crimes hitting the headlines, you find people confessing to the crime who couldn't possibly have done it. For example, in 1932 when the son of the famous aviator Charles Lindbergh was kidnapped, nearly 200 people confessed to the crime. More recently in 1986 more than 100 people confessed to the murder of the Swedish Prime Minister Olaf Palme.

Police investigators are aware of this phenomena, which is why crucial facts about a case are kept secret so that anyone confessing to the crime is required to show his knowledge of these decisive facts.

Encountering the IEE approach in the US

Paul Ekman and his colleagues in the US have drawn up a set of pointers called 'Improving Interpersonal Evaluations for Law Enforcement and Evaluations' – better known as the IEE approach – for helping the police interviewer decide the truthfulness of what's being said. A simple ABC list summarises what's involved in IEE:

- ✔ **A**wareness: Knowledge of ways in which information can be inaccurate.

- ✔ **B**aselines: Study of the normal mode of behaviour of the respondent.

- ✔ **C**hanges: Note reactions of the respondent that are different from the baseline.

- ✔ **D**iscrepancies: Observe variations in reactions in different channels of communication.

- ✔ **E**ngagement: Create a comfortable context for continuing rapport.

- ✔ **F**ollow-up: Explore corroborating evidence from other sources.

The IEE is a set of guidelines for establishing the truth in a police interview and draws on Ekman's work of how people reveal their emotions while under stress, which I describe in more detail in the earlier section 'Micro-twitches'.

Confessions around the world

People being presented with (false) evidence are sometimes willing to confess; teenagers are particularly vulnerable to this pressure. Although not exactly coercion, such subterfuge isn't allowed under UK law but is acceptable in the US.

In many countries, corroborative evidence is required before a confession is acceptable in the court. One notable exception is China where a large number of convictions are based on confessions.

In India, for many years, it was common practice by the police to beat or threaten a confession out of a suspect. But now a law has been passed whereby no confession obtained in the presence of a police officer is allowed as evidence in court.

The nearest equivalent UK police interview guidelines to the IEE is the English and Welsh PEACE, created with the help of forensic psychologists to improve the quality of interviews and combat false confessions.

Interrogating suspects

In the US, there are fewer constraints on police practice when obtaining a confession or getting vital information out of a suspect than in the UK. Certain US police procedures would raise eyebrows if they were tried out in a British court. For example, in the US you have *interrogations* as well as the more benign sounding *interviews,* the difference being:

- ✔ An interrogation aims at obtaining a confession or evidence leading to a conviction.

- ✔ A police interview aims at revealing the truth in as much detail as possible.

Before the introduction of the PEACE procedure that I describe in Chapter 4 the UK police also had a 'confession culture' in which the purpose of interviewing a suspect was to gain a confession.

During an interrogation the interviewer works at persuading the suspect that it's in his best interests to confess, by direct challenges or using spurious techniques (like trying to uncover lies by using lies) which can include:

- ✔ Using undercover police officers for obtaining a confession. In Britain, it's illegal for undercover police officers to entrap people or force a confession, but in Canada such undercover operations are often used to force a confession from a suspect.

✔ Underplaying or even lying on the part of the police about the seriousness of the offence. For example, saying the murder victim survived, or offering the possibility that the killing was an accident.

✔ Telling downright lies, such as saying that uncontroversial evidence of guilt exists or that a co-defendant has already confessed.

The Reid interrogation technique

Fred Inbau and John Reid, two experienced US law enforcement officers, have developed a procedure now widely used in North America, laying out nine steps for carrying out a persuasive interrogation:

1. **Being confrontational:** The suspect is told positively that he committed the alleged crime. The idea is that an innocent person immediately and without hesitation denies the offence, whereas a guilty person is evasive.

2. **Developing a theme:** The suspect is given reasons for thinking that the crime is less serious than he believes. This is an attempt to let the suspect 'off the hook' psychologically, making him feel more secure and less intimidated.

3. **Handling denials:** Denials are stopped short in their tracks and the suspect is told to listen to what the interrogator has got to say. This is a way of preventing the suspect thinking his denials carry any weight or of getting into his stride in advancing those denials.

4. **Overcoming objections:** The interrogator overcomes the objections the suspect is giving as an explanation or reason for his innocence and so undermines the suspect's confidence in his own innocence, making him more vulnerable to the assertions of the interrogator.

5. **Getting hold of and keeping the suspect's attention:** When the suspect shows signs of fatigue, the interrogator reduces the psychological (and if necessary physical) distance between himself and the suspect to regain the suspect's full attention.

6. **Handling suspect's passive mode:** When a suspect's resistance looks about to break down, the interrogator focuses on the suspect's main reasons for committing the crime, in order to show signs of understanding and sympathy. The interrogator appeals to the suspect's sense of decency and honour and possibly religious convictions, using the well-established psychological principle of rewarding behaviour that you want to encourage.

7. **Presenting an alternative question:** The suspect is presented with two possible alternatives for committing the crime, one face-saving and the other a repulsive or callous motivation.

8. **Having the suspect tell in his own words various details of the offence:** When the suspect accepts one of the alternatives he's asked to go into the story in further detail.

9. Converting an oral confession into a written confession:

This gives a further opportunity for ensuring the confession is clear and legally watertight.

There's a lot of controversy surrounding the use of the Inbau and Reid technique. Some challenges relate to the legality of the whole process of misleading a suspect. Others relate to its likelihood of inducing false confessions. But perhaps the greatest challenge to its usefulness is the claim by some who have studied the technique closely that it just doesn't work.

Extreme procedures

Sometimes you hear an interrogation being described as 'extreme'. In reality this is another way of saying that torture is being used: someone is being beaten as a way of getting them to give up information. The moral dilemma put forward is whether torture is acceptable if the information obtained can save one or many lives. However, this argument assumes that torture is a productive way of actually obtaining the truth.

Most experts agree that using torture as a means of getting at the truth is counterproductive. Inflicting extreme physical or mental pain can result in obtaining misleading information or nothing of use at all. Everyone involved is alienated, making it extremely difficult to build any future rapport that may lead to opening up to the truth.

Examining Documents to Help Solve Crimes

Forensic psychology is helpful when examining documents (handwritten, typed or even made from letters stuck together that have been cut out of newspapers) that can be used as valuable evidence in a criminal investigation. Such documents include threatening letters, suicide notes, confessions, declarations in wills and a range of other written material that can play an important part in helping to solve a crime.

The job of examining a document closely is often to find out if it shows criminal intent or is setting out to deceive, such as:

- ✔ Making a misleading claim: for example, snake oil curing warts.
- ✔ Describing an event that can lead to extortion or blackmail.
- ✔ Having dubious authorship: the writer of the text isn't who he claims to be, as in a forged confession or suicide note.

Sometimes the text offers particular potential as evidence. The following examples are all cases where the written record is the most important part of the crime. In some cases it's the crime itself. Unlike a crime scene, such as a murder scene, where the detailed actions of the offender have to be worked out from what can be observed, there are some crimes where a document is the actual crime. So the document can be regarded as a 'crime scene' and studied as closely as a room with a body in it. Here are some crimes where the document is the crime:

- ✔ A threatening letter written by the offender giving details of the crime he's planning to commit. Threatening someone is against the law, so the letter is the crime. As mentioned earlier, when considering 'extortion' the examination of this type of letter does also include an assessment of whether the threat is likely to be carried out, but even if it isn't, it's still a criminal act.

- ✔ A suicide note declaring the reasons for the person taking their own life counts as valuable evidence if found with a dead body. It can help to show what the person was thinking and feeling and possibly indicating that no other accomplices were involved in the crime. A suicide note is an invaluable record of the state of mind of the person immediately before they took their life, or even a record of what other people were thinking or saying. The genuineness of the note needs to be considered, not just whether the victim wrote it but whether the note does indicate they intended to take their own life. There are cases in which a suicide note was found but the Coroner (who deals with the cause of death) decided the person did not commit suicide.

- ✔ A written confession is taken seriously and treated as important evidence by the courts and public alike. The fact that the person has described in his own words his actions that lead to incriminating himself is significant. What he's written is seen as providing evidence of his guilt. But as I mention earlier there is still the need to consider carefully the conditions under which the confession was written. Was it beaten out of him or was he cheated into writing it?

Many other types of crime can involve the offender leaving a written record of his actions and intentions. Stalking is one, in which offensive letters can play an important part in documenting the crime. Another is business fraud where correspondence shows who the persons involved were or how the offender was distorting crucial documents.

In all these cases the authorship and genuiness of the document has to be established. It's not unknown for people to write offence letters to themselves or to invent a correspondence to imply they're being stalked.

Give-away words

In one criminal case, an anonymous incriminating diary was compared to the known writing of a suspect. The prosecution claim was that the diary was written by the suspect and therefore the incriminating evidence in it showed he was guilty of the crime. This claim was supported by a linguist who drew attention to a number of misspellings that were found in both documents (for example, 'breath' instead of 'breathe', and 'its' instead of 'it's'). These misspellings were consistent with how the words are pronounced. A number of profanities were common to both sets of text, such as 'ass', 'butthole' and 'screwed', as well as further similarities in the way time was recorded and how the writer expressed his emotions. The linguist used these comparisons to propose that the two sets of writing came from the same author.

But even with such glaring examples, the forensic psychologist challenged the possibility that the misspellings and other features were definitive signs of the documents being written by the same author. For example, most people in the suspect's circle often misspelled 'breathe' and 'it's' and the profanities were common words in their vocabulary. Without knowing how widespread the suspect's way of expressing himself was and if it was common to the community in which he lived and worked, the forensic psychologist argued that such matches can be taken only as a useful indicator and not as hard proof that the documents were by the same person.

Entering the world of document experts

The psychological examination of a document by a forensic psychologist is rather different from many other ways in which documents can be examined. The forensic psychologist focuses on the meanings of the document and what is known about lying and the indicators of truthfulness. But there are other ways of determining if a document is genuine that use very different sorts of knowledge and skills. Police investigators draw on these to help them in their task.

Linguists

Linguists are experts in how language is shaped and being used. They can comment on the usual or particular meaning and usage of the words. For example, they can advise whether the person who received the document could reasonably be expected to regard it as a genuine threat. That is important because the law requires the victim to experience the threat if it's to be considered a crime. Or, in the case of a trademark dispute, whether the text in the branding is making claims that people will assume to be indicating something, but that what it indicates can be shown to be false or dishonest. The dispute here is over what the words mean in common use.

Psycholinguists overlap with (and sometimes challenge the conclusions of) linguists. This is a distinct branch of psychology that is only rarely to do with anything criminal or illegal. A psycholinguist is concerned with the relation of the words to what's going on in a person's mind. In some cases the psycholinguist explores the idiosyncrasies of the way a person is expressing what he's saying. Forensic psychologists can draw on psycholinguistics to challenge the linguist, who looks at language in general. I give an example in the nearby sidebar 'Give-away words'.

If the way a person writes is influenced by his education and upbringing and the community in which he lives, the way he expresses himself in writing will not be entirely distinct for any individual. For writing to make sense it must draw on what people in that culture understand. So there will always be aspects of writing that are common to people in the same sub-group and possibly some aspects that are distinct for that person.

People use quite different grammar and vocabulary when speaking than when they're writing. No one speaks in the tidy sentences you use when writing. The way you communicate also varies from one situation to another: you find yourself speaking differently in the pub to the way you speak when giving evidence in court. Or, your academic essay is written in a completely different style from when you're texting friends. Some aspects of the way a person writes may cross over into different situations, but generally your style of communicating is surprisingly dependent on what you're actually communicating about and to whom. This means that any general techniques for characterising the way a person communicates in all situations – talking to friends, sending e-mails to the boss, writing an essay for an exam – are doomed to failure.

Can people hide how they write?

Criminals sometimes try to hide or distort how they express themselves when writing to avoid detection or a document being used in evidence against them. But trying to hide your style of writing can end up with you revealing more than you want to hide. For example, less skilled writers have difficulty imitating more sophisticated writers and the competent writer often has difficulty in hiding his own particular skill.

Once, in a murder case, I advised the prosecution that a suspect kept a detailed diary in which her visit to the victim was recorded in a very casual manner. Nearly all the other entries in the diary were recorded in careful and precise language that was very different from this particular entry, showing that she wouldn't normally have expressed visiting the victim in the way she did. A careful analysis of the entries in the diary showed that this key entry was strikingly different, mainly because the style of the entry was so laid-back and unremarkable. What I did was a psycholinguistic analysis, informed by my broader experience as a forensic psychologist who knows something of how criminals may try to hide their activities.

The prosecution counsel drew on this evidence to shape his cross-examination but the diary was never presented directly as evidence. The suspect was convicted of the murder.

Careful reading

The forensic psychologist always has to consider carefully the *content* of a document: *what* a person's writing about as much as the style of writing. By careful reading of a document you can explore what's going on in the writer's mind as well as how they're expressing it.

For example, a genuine suicide note often has a distinctly different psychological tone to a faked suicide note. A genuine suicide note is usually longer and more explanatory, showing clearly that the writer has internalised the decision to take their own life. The note's purpose is to make it clear that this decision is entirely their own and that no one else is to blame.

I've sometimes had the job of reviewing anonymous letters, mostly ones threatening or insulting an organisation. From studying the letters I've even been able to tell the company the name of the person who wrote it. No, I don't use magic, just careful reading of the document to identify its purpose, that is after ignoring all the profanities and highly-charged language. When you read of a person having been unfairly treated by the organisation, you don't need to be blessed with second sight to work out that the person referred to in the anonymous letter is the writer himself. And you know you've got your man when the author gives away his identity by offering you so much personal detail that you're left in little doubt. (Flip to Chapter 6 to see the parallels with the letters sent by the 'Mad Bomber of New York'.)

Always bear in mind when examining a threatening letter the possibility that the person receiving the letter *is* the anonymous author, especially when details of a very personal nature are revealed.

Chapter 6

Profiling Offenders and Distinguishing the Types of Crimes They Commit

In Thomas Harris's bestselling thriller, *The Silence of the Lambs*, which became a 1991 blockbuster film, Clarice Starling is a novice FBI agent trying to catch a serial killer. To help her she visits the brilliant, but disturbingly violent, Dr Hannibal Lecter in prison, in order to discover from him the likely characteristics of the serial killer. For many people, this film was their introduction to the notion of 'offender profiling'. Dr Lecter was portrayed as having brilliant insights into the killer's mind because, well, he was a killer himself and, umm, he was brilliant. The fun bit though is that, if you read the book carefully or look beyond the fabulous acting in the film, very cleverly Harris doesn't have Dr Lecter give any clear indications about the serial killer that are much help to Clarice. Hannibal just gives hints and does more to psych out Clarice than ever help her catch the killer. Although it's clear Lecter could have helped Clarice he chooses not to!

Despite Clarice's lack of real help, the idea of FBI agents using convicted killers as sources to help them solve crimes gained a hold in the popular imagination. Along with this interest came the idea that 'offender profilers' were some sort of geniuses able to see into the very souls of criminals and so solve crimes where the police failed.

I like to keep the terms 'profile' and 'profiling' in quotation marks because there has been a lot of misunderstanding, drawn from fictional accounts of how psychologists could help the police. The term 'profiling' implies a very special process carried out by unusually clever people, 'profilers', but as I make clear in this chapter a lot of their contributions are much more mundane – and what's of value to the police is the key guidance offered to an investigation instead of the number of details in a 'profile' or pen-picture. As I say at the start of Chapter 1, the notion of 'profiling' owes much more to the great granddaddy of fictional detectives, Sherlock Holmes, than to any real-life sleuths.

In this chapter, you will discover the facts of 'offender profiling'; the fascinating questions that are at the heart of what psychologists offer to criminal investigations, and how the struggle to answer these questions opens up the new field of investigative psychology. Part of understanding criminals involves understanding the crimes that they commit (and how they do so), therefore investigative psychology is very much part of forensic psychology, drawing from the broader topics that I cover in the rest of this book. However, to contribute to investigations you need to be aware of how crimes and criminals differ, so in this chapter I also guide you through the different categories of crimes.

Investigating 'Offender Profiling'

An experienced homicide detective used to say to people who asked him for a 'profile' of the killer, 'Do ya want a profile or do ya want me to help you catch the bad guy?' This statement neatly demonstrates the confusion over what a 'profile' is.

The popular notion is that an 'offender profile' gives police investigators some pointers as to where to target their investigations, describing the likely personality, lifestyle, motivations and other characteristics of an offender: in other words a sort of speculative pen-picture of the perpetrator. But although that may be fun in fiction it is not a lot of use in an investigation. What detectives need are specific directions to channel their search, or guide how they interview a suspect, not general chat about the unknown criminal's personality or family relationships. In this section, I provide the facts on 'offender profiling', using a number of real-life, often famous, cases as illustration, including the one that dragged me into this whole murky area.

I suppose, if the detectives have no idea at all about where to look or who the criminal is likely to be, a pen-picture may get them started. But look at the issue this way: surely a much more useful approach is to ask, 'Have you asked around at any local hostels where offenders recently let out of prison are staying?' Though hardly a detailed 'profile' of the possible offender, this suggestion may be the only pointer the police need. Giving such advice on where to find the criminal, rather than describing the individual's characteristics, has always been a large part of the contributions of experts in helping the police.

Because the useful guidance given to detectives by people who draw on psychological ideas is often much more direct than pen-pictures and personality profiles, many who help the police these days don't call themselves 'profilers', but instead like to be called something like 'behavioural investigative advisors', or just 'crime consultants'. In this guise they can advise on investigative procedures, such as checking carefully through potential suspects, or giving priority to house-to-house inquiries in particular areas (this is particularly assisted by 'geographical offender profiling' which I discuss in the later section 'Locating offenders geographically').

These advisors may have a background in forensic psychology, but will often not be the sort of qualified forensic psychologists that I describe in Chapter 18. They may even avoid the term 'psychologist' altogether and just call themselves 'behavioural scientists'. Yes I know it's getting a bit complicated, but the problem is that the term 'offender profiler' isn't a legal or professional label. It has more currency in the mass media and fiction than in any professional gathering. People who want to claim they have some special powers may call themselves 'profilers', but that doesn't mean they're forensic psychologists or know much about the sorts of things I describe in all the other chapters in this book.

A very brief history of 'offender profiling'

People have always been ready to draw on their own particular expertise to tell detectives about the criminal they're looking for, particularly crime writers.

An early instance of someone 'profiling' a case was Edgar Allan Poe, famous for his dark stories of murder and mayhem. In 1850, he wrote the *Mystery of Marie Roget*, which, although presented as a fiction set in Paris, was intended to be a contribution to the investigation of the murder of Mary Rogers in New York in 1842. From the crime scene details, Poe concluded that a gang of villains killed the hapless Mary, which contrasted with the police view that it was suicide. They didn't take kindly to his suggestions, but as the case was never conclusively solved, it's still anyone's guess as to who was correct.

Conan Doyle also offered 'profiles' on various real-life crimes troubling the police, although no indication exists that they took any notice of his advice or that it was ever much use. Yet this shows, as with Poe, that helping the police was regarded as an act of imagination rather than some scientific endeavour. This belief lingers on, adding to the general mythology that 'profiling' is a dark art, which owes more to the brilliance of the person producing the 'profile' rather than any systematic procedure.

Jack the Ripper

Perhaps the first true professional 'offender profile' in modern times was a report from a medical officer, Dr Thomas Bond, who carried out autopsies and advised the police on the murders that became known as the work of Jack the Ripper (killer of at least five women working as street sex workers in the Whitechapel area of London in 1888). Dr Bond offered the following opinion:

> *The murderer must have been a man of physical strength and great coolness and daring. There is no evidence he had an accomplice. He must in my opinion be a man subject to periodic attacks of homicidal and erotic mania. The character of the mutilations indicates that the man may be in a condition sexually that may be called Satyriasis. It is of course possible that the homicidal impulse may have developed from a revengeful or brooding condition of mind, or that religious mania may have been the original disease but I do not think either hypothesis is likely. The murderer in external appearance is quite likely to be a quiet inoffensive looking man probably middle-aged and neatly and respectably dressed. I think he might be in the habit of wearing a cloak or overcoat or he could hardly have escaped notice in the streets if the blood on his hands or clothes were visible.*
>
> *Assuming the murderer be such a person as I have just described, he would be solitary and eccentric in his habits, also he is likely to be a man without regular occupation, but with some small income or pension. He is possibly living among respectable persons who have some knowledge of his character and habits and who may have grounds for suspicion that he is not quite right in his mind at times. Such persons would probably be unwilling to communicate suspicions to the police for fear of trouble or notoriety, whereas if there were prospect of reward it might overcome their scruples.*
>
> Notes of examination of body of woman found
> murdered and mutilated in Dorset Street,
> date stamped 16 November 1888, MEPO 3/3153.

By modern standards this description is perfectly sensible, except for the allusion to Satyriasis and erotic mania, which aren't common medical terms these days (although 'heightened sex drive' may be an acceptable substitute term). Today's experts may also debate whether the violent mutilations that gave the killer the nickname 'ripper' are more likely to relate to sadism or indeed psychosis (which I discuss in Chapter 2) rather than sexual desires.

For comparison, here's Conan Doyle's 'profile' for Jack the Ripper and his advice to the police:

- He's been in America.
- He's educated, not a toiler.
- He's accustomed to the use of a pen.

✔ He likely has a rough knowledge of surgery.

✔ He probably clothes himself as a woman to approach victims without arousing suspicion and to escape the crime without detection.

✔ He'll have written letters over his own name (meaning, with his real name on them) or other documents that could be traced to him.

✔ Facsimiles of his handwriting from letters sent to the police should be published in the newspapers because someone may recognise the handwriting.

The Jack the Ripper murders have never been solved to everyone's satisfaction, although theories abound. Until they're solved, no one can tell how valid the 'profiles' were. One thing's certain though: they weren't much use in getting the villain caught!

The mad bomber of New York

The most famous modern 'offender profile' was of 'The mad bomber of New York'. This instance stimulated the myths of the power of 'profiles' because it was claimed to have solved a serious crime series.

Over a 16-year period in the 1940s and 1950s, homemade bombs were left in public places around New York. Letters claiming to come from the bomber were sent to the *New York Herald Tribune* saying that the bombs would continue until the Consolidated Edison Company 'brought justice for the bomber'. They didn't say exactly what sort of justice but it was clear the writer of the letters felt he'd been badly treated by Consolidated Edison. The police kept information about these bombings relatively quiet, but when they called in the psychiatrist James Brussel he recommended that they use the news media to see whether anyone was able to identify the bomber. You didn't need to be a genius (or even a psychiatrist) to realise that the perpetrator was somewhat peeved with Consolidated Edison, but Brussel gave this simple idea some impetus. From an examination of the letters the bomber had sent, and other information about his actions, Brussel proposed that the person possessed the following characteristics:

✔ Male (because most bombers are male).

✔ Has knowledge of metalworking, pipefitting and electricity.

✔ Suffered an injustice by Consolidated Edison, which had rendered him chronically ill.

✔ Suffers from an insidious disorder, paranoia, and has a persistent and chronic disorder.

✔ Is pathologically self-centred.

✔ Has no friends, male or female; is a loner.

✔ Symmetric athletic body type, neither fat nor skinny.

✔ Is middle-aged (due to onset of illness and duration of bombings).

✔ Good education, likely high-school educated but not college.

✔ Unmarried, possibly a virgin.

✔ Distrusts and despises male authority; hates father.

✔ Never progressed past the Oedipal stage of love for his mother due to her early death or separation from him.

✔ Lives alone or with female mother-like relative.

✔ Lives in Connecticut, is of Slavic descent, Roman Catholic and attends church.

✔ Neat, tidy and clean-shaven.

✔ Quiet, polite, methodical and prompt.

✔ Has chronic illness, heart disease, cancer or tuberculosis; most probably heart disease.

✔ Would be wearing a buttoned double-breasted suit when caught.

Despite Brussel's rich description, it was an assiduous clerk at Consolidated Edison, Alice Kelly, who led to the bomber's capture. She read the newspaper reports and decided to look through the company's special files on those employees who had earlier made threats as part of their requests for compensation. This search drew attention to George Metesky who'd been injured at the factory in 1931. The correspondence in these files showed similarities of wording to the anonymous letters the bomber had been sending to the police, leading the police to him and his eventual conviction.

So, although much of what Brussel proposed about the bomber turned out to be quite accurate, it didn't really assist the investigation. The crucial point was that the bomber was an angry ex-employee, which investigators had assumed from the beginning (derived from what the bomber had written in his letters and where he had put bombs). Brussel's claim that Metesky had sexual desires for his mother was far less useful in finding the bomber than Alice Kelly's diligent search through the records that contained details of employees who had openly threatened the company. In addition, most men in those days wore double-breasted suits, generally worn buttoned!

The railway murderer

This case is the one that set me on the path to writing this book, when I produced an 'offender profile' for a major investigation into many rapes, and three murders, that took place near railway stations, and were committed across London between 1982 and 1985.

The police claimed that they had a number of possible suspects but only one, John Frances Duffy, fitted my 'profile'. They therefore put him under surveillance and obtained enough evidence for a conviction. The success of the 'profile' that helped to identify John Duffy as the offender thus opened the way to the new science of investigative psychology, which I describe in the later section 'Delving into Investigative Psychology'.

Here's the 'profile' I produced to assist the police investigation:

- Lived in the area of early offences in 1983.
- Arrested after October 1983 for violence, not necessarily sexual.
- Lives with wife/girlfriend – childless.
- Aged mid- to late 20s.
- Light hair.
- 5 foot 9 inches tall.
- Right handed.
- He has an 'A' secretor blood type (this was in the days before DNA).
- Semi-skilled.
- No public contact.
- Keeps to himself, with one or two close friends.

The ideas that I used to produce the 'profile' of John Duffy are all derived from my *consistency principle,* which is that what an offender does in a crime is an expression of how he behaves in other non-criminal situations. Of course, his actions during a crime are more extreme than in other situations, but they're still consistent with them. Therefore, what he does in a crime can be taken as a direct indication of the sort of person he is.

Various, more detailed, aspects follow from this conclusion:

- The *familiarity* that a person exhibits in the crime reveals what he's normally familiar with. So, in this case, the area of his criminal activity would relate to places he knew from his usual activity (this relates to the routine activity theory that I describe in the later sidebar 'Staying close to home'). Duffy's crimes spread out across London, however, and so I hypothesised that initially he'd attacked near to areas he was familiar with, and then begin to look for opportunities farther afield, where he wouldn't be recognised. His behaviour, as described by his victims, had become more planned and determined, which also fitted this idea. This insight led to the conclusion that his earliest attacks would be the best indicators of where he was based. This process is an early development of 'geographical offender profiling', which I discuss in the later section 'Locating offenders geographically'.

✔ His *emotional responses* in the crime would be an indicator of his emotions in other situations. This offender was a man violently attacking young women, and so it was reasonable to assume that he would be known as a violent person. The point here was to draw attention to his violence rather than the sexual nature of the crimes. Such violence was likely to have previously brought him to police attention.

✔ His *social interaction* in the crime revealed that he was able to initially relate to his victims before he attacked them. This suggested that he was able to have a relationship with a woman that wasn't entirely vicious. Perhaps naïvely on my part, I assumed they wouldn't have had any children otherwise he wouldn't have attacked young women as he did. Since that time (a quarter of a century ago) I've realised that married men with children can be much nastier than I ever thought possible.

✔ His *intellectual ability* as revealed in his planning of the crimes indicated that he would have a job that wasn't a low-level manual one but had some skill associated with it, like being a carpenter (which he was).

✔ His *skills* may also have been relevant, for example in understanding the details of how he bound and controlled his victims, but were less obvious in this case than in many others.

✔ His *criminal habits,* that were the crimes themselves, suggested that the suspect didn't normally relate well to other people, and like many violent sex offenders had very few friends and little contact with other people.

I drew the other information in the 'profile' from witness descriptions and the forensic results of the police. They were carefully studied to provide a coherent set of the most probable information that the police could work with.

As I hope the case illustrates, the number of pointers in a 'profile' aren't necessarily of direct help to the investigation, but they do provide the key guiding points. You may get dozens of irrelevant details right (such as the car he drives, his background in burglary and his knowledge of firearms) and yet get one crucial fact wrong (such as the fact that a woman rather than a man committed the crimes). Clearly, in this case the 'profile' would be useless, which is why the current preference is a move away from providing a 'pen-picture' to giving guidance on all aspects of an investigation.

Demythologising 'profiling'

The notion of 'offender profiling' is so prevalent in popular culture that a number of myths about it have been absorbed into the public consciousness. For the record, none of the following claims are true:

✔ 'Offender profiling' is an invention of the late 20th century.

✔ 'Offender profiling' was initiated by the FBI.

✔ The Americans are current world leaders in 'profiling'. I guess people assume this because so much publicity is given to what goes on in the US. If any country has the most highly trained and focused behavioural investigative advisors it's probably the UK.

✔ The emergence of 'offender profiling' was isolated from any other scientific developments.

✔ Only odd crimes with curious psychological aspects are open to 'profiling'.

✔ 'Offender profiling' can only be applied to serious serial crimes, notably serial murder and serial rape.

✔ 'Offender profiling' is essentially an art dependent on the intellectual gifts of the person producing the 'profile'.

✔ The FBI did serious scientific studies on which they base their 'profiles'.

✔ Serial killers are always educated white men.

✔ Serial killers can be categorised as organised or disorganised.

✔ 'Offender profilers' solve crimes.

Staying close to home

Routine activity theory is a common idea in criminology, and means that criminals often choose their crime locations from places in which they're routinely located: on the way to work, near the pubs they use and so on. They're thought to see the opportunities for crime when going about their non-criminal activities. Although this idea has a lot to recommend it, from a psychologist's point of view it's the familiarity they have with an area that's crucial. This familiarity can even come from other sources such as maps or even criminal colleagues.

In addition, of course, habitual criminals may seek out areas beyond where they're based in order to find opportunities for crime. One burglar interviewed had been stealing golfing equipment from golf clubs around the UK. When asked how he knew where to go, he said that he simply used maps for golf enthusiasts (that show where all the golfing establishments are) to find opportunities for thieving.

Delving Into Investigative Psychology

As I describe in the earlier section 'Investigating "Offender Profiling', giving a detailed account of an offender's inner psychology isn't a lot of help to investigators (although it can be useful in guiding how to approach interviewing a suspect and sometimes helps detectives to get a feel for the sort of person they are looking for). However, some knowledge of the offender's psychology can be useful to prosecuting lawyers in court, because they can use this insight to help the jury understand how and why a crime was committed. (Of course, similarly, the defence can use the same information to argue that the defendant couldn't have committed the crime.)

The myths surrounding the whole idea of 'profiling' and its weaknesses led me to identify a branch of psychology that contributed to police investigations on a much broader front than just producing pen-pictures of unknown villains. I call this practice *investigative psychology,* which is the subject of this section.

Think of it this way. Creating a 'profile' of an offender requires getting details of the crime and then making some 'if...then' assumptions. For example, as I did in the Railway Murderer case, you may say 'if a man has been violent to women in these crimes then the police may know someone who has been violent to women on other occasions'. This 'if...then' conjecture is an *inference.* You are *inferring* features of the culprit from aspects of the crime. Such inferences require an understanding of criminals and how they act, which makes it part of forensic psychology. Developing these inferences requires much more than some clever insights into the criminal mind. It draws on the many different aspects of scientific psychology that I describe in the rest of this chapter as well as other chapters in this book.

When you are making inferences about an offender you are using what is known about his actions. But as a scientist you cannot just accept the information you are given. You want it to be as reliable and valid as possible. So an important part of *investigative psychology* is developing and improving ways of getting information in investigations. (Yes, the things discussed in chapters 4 and 5 on interviewing and detecting deception are an aspect of investigative psychology).

Investigative psychology isn't just an interesting academic pursuit (although it's very interesting and it's taught in many universities). It's aimed at being useful. It therefore also explores how to help investigations, which means understanding something of how detectives think. The information from psychology that can be given is therefore more than just basic 'offender profiling'. It covers all the ways in which psychology can contribute to investigations. The following sections give some more details of how this all works.

Following the investigative cycle

To see how psychology can contribute to all aspects of police investigations, understanding how police investigations unfold is useful. They usually follow a cycle of activity (see Figure 6-1):

1. *Information* **comes to the notice of the police that a crime has been committed.** How the police get the best information through interviewing and dealing with deceit are matters that investigative psychologists can help with (as I describe in Chapters 4 and 5).

2. *Inferences* **are made on the basis of that information.** This is the development by psychologists of the 'if...then' propositions that I discuss in the paragraph earlier in this chapter.

3. *Actions* **result from these inferences that may generate more information.** Investigative psychologists can guide these actions and produce techniques the police can use like the geographical profiling systems I describe in the section 'Locating offenders geographically'.

The cycle continues until enough information is obtained to take a culprit to court.

Figure 6-1:
A simplified illustration of the stages an investigation goes through.

Despite what you see in crime fiction, psychologists very rarely get actively involved in investigations. They may pop in and give a few hints, but they contribute far less than the Crime Scene Investigation (CSI) experts who deal with fibres and fingerprints, blood splatters and all those forensic science matters.

At every stage of this cycle, psychologists can contribute:

✔ Most information is collected through interviews with victims, witnesses or suspects. Chapters 4 and 5 show how psychologists can improve those processes.

✔ The inference process is best thought of as an 'if . . . then . . . so' activity. For example, '*if* the criminal is moving around a particular area picking opportunities for crime *then* he's likely to be familiar with this area when not committing crimes and *so* house-to-house inquiries in the area may be useful'. The production of 'profiles' are all derived from inferences.

✔ The inferences that psychologists make about criminals are informed assumptions, not definite conclusions. They may be supported by previous research that shows, for example, the probability that a person will commit a burglary within a mile of his home. Or they may be derived from some general principles, such as that offenders who use guns have some background and experience in using guns. But these are always just possibilities, never hard and fast facts. Many circumstances can modify the reliability of these proposals (as I discuss in the later section 'Facing the challenge of contingencies').

✔ The actions that the police carry out can be assisted by decision-support systems such as the process of geographical 'profiling' (check out the later 'Locating offenders geographically' section).

By *actions* I mean the pattern of activities and salient characteristics of a crime. This usage isn't to be confused with the popular term 'M.O.' (that stands for *modus operandi* and literally means 'way of doing things'). M.O. is intended to refer to the habitual way in which an offender operates. But this assumes that offenders have fixed styles of carrying out a crime and that these are different from the styles of offenders carrying out similar crimes, which is rarely the case. For example, certain aspects of all burglaries may well be similar but some rare events (like using the toilet in the burgled house) can be very unusual.

So, although certain unusual behaviours of an offender can sometimes be used to help characterise his actions (and may then be called his M.O.), he may not always do them. Hence I leave the term 'M.O.' to the amateur sleuths and I stick with exploring a criminal's actions.

In order to help in the criminal investigative cycle, psychologists need to have a full understanding of the sorts of things that detectives need to know that various psychological sources can answer (see Table 6-1).

Table 6-1 The Questions That Detectives Need Answering

Aspect	Question
Salience	Of all the things that happen in any crime, what are those aspects that are most important in understanding the nature of the crime and on which any inferences can be made?
Differentiating cases	What aspects of a crime are distinct about it and help to separate it from other similar crimes?

Aspect	Question
Linking cases	What cases can be linked together as likely to be the work of the same individual(s)? This may be achieved by forensic evidence, witness descriptions or similarities in the criminal's actions.
Eliciting suspects	Where can possible suspects be found? This may imply targeted searches of police records, or hunting on the ground through house-to-house inquiries (see 'Locating offenders geographically' later in this chapter) or from police informants.
Prioritising suspects	Which of the suspects should be closely examined first? Limited police resources mean that suspects have to be put in some sort of order.

Profiling equations

The inferences that make up 'offender profiles' can be thought of as rather like mathematical equations that link the 'Actions' in a crime to 'Characteristics' of the offenders. So I call them A → C equations. The → here implies that there may be any of a number of relationships between actions and characteristics. The mythbuster gives more detail. One important aspect of investigative psychology is trying to unravel these equations to come up with useful inferences.

It's rare for one simple aspect of a crime to imply one simple characteristic of the offender. The 'clue' so favoured by fiction writers that opens the way to the offender (such as a suspect using the word 'cell' for his 'mobile phone' showing he lived in the US where that term is the usual one) may come from forensic evidence such as fibres and body fluids, but when dealing with criminal actions it's usually the pattern of actions that points the way, not one specific action.

- ✔ **Actions** in the profiling equations mean all the information about the crime that the police have before they know who did it: for example, the place and time of the offence, as well as the details of the victim and what actually happened.

- ✔ **Characteristics** in the profiling equations mean all the information that's of use to the police in solving the crime, such as where the offender may be living or what other crimes he has been convicted of that'll be recorded in police databases.

Inferring isn't an exact science

In one rape case I worked on, the victim reported that the offender had long fingernails on his right hand but short ones on his left hand. Detectives became excited when they remembered that some guitar players keep their nails like this. So were we looking for a sexually violent guitarist? No. When he was caught, police found that he had no musical talents at all, but in fact worked replacing tyres on cars, which seemed to result in him wearing down the nails on one hand more than on the other.

Unfortunately, no necessary simple equation exists in which one Action can always be used reliably to infer one Characteristic. The anecdote in the nearby sidebar 'Inferring isn't an exact science' illustrates this point. Sometimes combinations of Actions offer the possibility of the various likely Characteristics. So possessing a firearm and using it with accuracy and confidence, for example, may imply that a person's a firearm enthusiast or that he's had military training.

Facing the challenge of contingencies

Contingencies are those aspects of the circumstances in which a crime occurs that can influence what inferences can be made about that crime. So any investigative psychologist trying to derive inferences needs to take account of these. The following aspects challenge the possibility of developing a simple 'profiling' equation (see the preceding section):

✏ One feature of a crime can change the implications of many others. For example, the actions during a burglary committed at night, when the occupant is likely to be in the house, have rather different implications from a daytime burglary.

✏ Combinations of features can change each other's implications. For example, setting fire to a building after it has been burgled suggests a different inference (such as the fire being set to destroy evidence) from setting fire to a building that has symbolic significance, such as a school.

✏ Events outside the control of the offender may distort what inferences can be made. This would be the case where a victim unexpectedly fights back and so the offender's actions are in part a reaction to the victim. Or if the offender is disturbed during the crime, his actions may not indicate fully what he intended to do.

✏ Opportunities may occur for the crime that the offender may not have anticipated. He may have intended to climb a drainpipe to get into the building, thus allowing inference of his particular skills, age and so on, but found the door open and so didn't need to.

Hearing the stories people tell themselves: Criminal narratives

One interesting way of understanding what criminals are doing that investigative psychologists have been developing is to think of the personal stories criminals tell themselves about their lives. These narratives can be used as a basis for inferences as well as assisting in guiding interview strategies.

The following four criminal narratives have been suggested as being prevalent in the minds of different criminals:

- **Being on an Adventure:** Offender sees crime as an exciting escapade in which he overcomes adversity to win the rewards that are due to the victor.

- **Being on a Heroic Mission:** The mission may be avenging insult to his honour or even fighting for the honour of his family or others. Whatever the precise nature, he casts himself in the role of justified hero.

- **Being a Tragic Victim:** This offender feels that he's always the fall guy and that his crime was just him trying to cope, but it all went wrong. He doesn't see himself as a criminal at all, but as misunderstood and picked-on.

- **Doing a Professional Job:** Some criminals that I talk to, usually older ones, say that crime is just what they do: it may even have lost some of its excitement for them. But they're proud of committing their crimes effectively, for instance, doing a bank robbery without anyone getting hurt.

Narrative not motive

Criminal narratives are rather different from the idea of 'motive', which is so enjoyed by fiction writers. In fact, courts don't need to know the motive for a crime. The judge and jury just need to know that the crime was committed by the defendant and he knew what he was doing and its implications. The term 'motive' is such a slippery one that I avoid using it throughout this book. It can mean an explanation, a purpose, a reason, an unconscious urge, the set of actions it was part of (such as 'we were all drunk and having a laugh') and some form of narrative (as in 'I don't let people push me around'). The term's ambiguity also makes it very difficult to determine.

The classic motives in thrillers such as revenge, jealousy or greed, never go the whole way in explaining why the particular crime was the way of achieving that motive. Furthermore, in real life often more than one such explanation exists and the criminal himself may not be fully aware of why he committed the crime.

Locating offenders geographically

One of the most useful pieces of information that detectives can get is the geographical location where the culprit may be found. This information allows the prioritisation of suspects by putting them in order of how near they are to that location. It allows the linking of crimes to a common offender and also enables the police to put up surveillance in designated locations or to carry out careful house-to-house inquiries in a targeted area. When they need to do a trawl of possible suspects by using DNA matches, an indication of the area in which the offender may have lived at the time of the offence can help to limit the number of people whose DNA needs to be matched. For all these reasons investigative psychologists consider *where* a crime occurs as well as what happens in the crime. They can use this to make inferences about the criminal and where he may be based.

I did an elementary form of geographical 'offender profiling' when I proposed that John Duffy had lived in the area circumscribed by the first three crimes of the series (see the earlier section 'The railway murderer'). However, since that time computer programmes have been developed to indicate the likelihood of an offender living in any particular location.

As an example, take a look at Figure 6-2, which shows the locations of bombs left in an extortion campaign across London. The points are the locations on a map of where the bombs were left. By looking at the distances criminals typically travel to commit their crimes, a computer programme calculates the likelihood of where on the map the bomber's home could be, and then joins up the areas that have the same probability. This is like height contours on an ordinary map, but instead of height this map shows how probable it is that the offender is living in any location. The figure shows two areas that have high probabilities, one to the East and one to the West. The police put surveillance on ATM points in the West and caught the culprit, Edgar Pearce, who lived near to where he was caught. The high probability area to the East surrounds where his ex-wife lived, who he still visited.

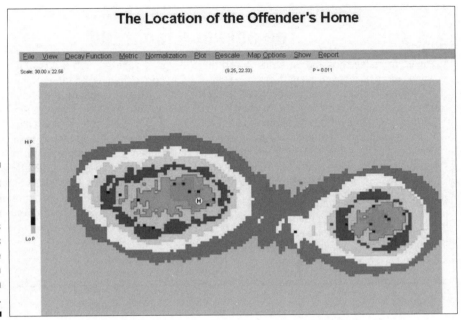

Figure 6-2:
A map
showing the
locations
of bombs
left in the
London
extortion
campaign.

Distinguishing between Crimes

Crucial to 'profiling' an offender is gaining an understanding of the type of criminal acts that the person carries out. Therefore, as part of 'profiling' offenders directly (a subject I cover in the earlier sections of this chapter), forensic psychologists have to examine and understand the different sorts of crimes that people commit, identifying the distinguishing characteristics of a crime: for example, the willingness (or not) of a person to use violence is central to making an investigative inference. Doing so requires an understanding of how crimes that notionally appear similar (and may even have the same legal label) differ from each other in important behavioural ways.

Of course, certain basic aspects remain common across most crimes of a certain type (a burglary involves stealing from a property, a rape involves a sexual assault). But the forensic psychologist needs to be able to distinguish more subtly between crimes, identifying the *less* common indicative actions of different styles of behaviour.

The advance fee fraud

You've probably received an e-mail (or in the olden days a fax or even a letter), or know someone who has, that says millions of dollars exist in some account and you can have a goodly proportion of it if you co-operate with the sender. It may be explained that the money is in a bank account because the original account holder has died and there are no relatives, or any of a number of other marginally plausible reasons.

If you respond to this offer of these windfall millions, you're asked for a relatively small sum of money to set up an account, to bribe someone, or for some other reason. This is the 'advance fee' that gives the fraud its name.

If you're rash enough to provide some initial fee, you're then asked for more money and yet more. Experts estimate that people who get sucked into this trap can lose on average as much as $30,000 before they realise that they'll never see any of their money or anyone else's ever again. Some people try to follow this up by direct contact with the fraudsters, who then become threatening and violent. Some authorities claim that a number of otherwise unexplained murders occur each year of victims trying to get their money back.

Dealing with property crimes

Experts often use the technical term *acquisitive crime* to describe all those crimes in which something of value is taken without permission of the owner. In such cases the owner is always directly or indirectly caught up in the crime. So the most crucial difference between crimes is whether only property is taken or a victim is confronted by the criminal. This distinction between property crimes and person crimes is central to understanding criminal actions.

The consistency principle that I describe earlier in this chapter (in 'The railway murderer' section) draws attention, for instance, to familiarity and the typical way of dealing with other people that you'd expect to be common in criminal and non-criminal situations. Consequently, whether the offender engages directly with the victim or avoids such contact has key psychological implications.

Within the category of acquisitive crime, a wide range of variations exists. For example, a span of scenarios can be identified, from having contact with the victim (as is characteristic of robbery), through burglary (in which the victim may or may not be present), through to the modification of documents in which no direct contact is ever made (as may be the case in many frauds). This set of stages implies a reduction in the willingness to use physical threats to obtain the property and an increase in the skills of manipulation of opportunities.

Forensic psychologists need to proceed with caution, though, because many combinations are possible. For example, some fraudsters start off very distant from their victims, but having made contact can start using threats of violence as in the nearby sidebar 'The advance fee fraud'.

Fraud

Broadly speaking, people become major fraudsters through one of two dominant routes: they spot loopholes in systems and then gain access to them in order to obtain vast sums of money; or they're in a position of trust and find that they need some money, which isn't readily available from personal funds. You may be surprised to discover that the first group is in the minority. Notorious examples such as Frank Abagnale do exist (see the nearby sidebar 'Catch me if you can . . . oh, you did!'), but they're extremely unusual.

The more usual way in which serious fraud happens is that a person abuses a position of trust and, say, steals from a company or organisation. Sometimes the person has gambling debts or just a desire for the good life, but very often the theft is to save face in unexpected financial circumstances.

One fraudster said that his business collapsed when apartheid suddenly came to an end in South Africa. He employed many people and didn't want them to lose their jobs. He therefore took a little money from a source he shouldn't have, hoping that the business would get better and he could pay it back. But things got worse and he took more money. Eventually he'd acquired £50,000 fraudulently before he was caught.

Forensic psychologists know that this sequence of small betrayals of trust leading to bigger and bigger fraud until it gets out of control is a common pattern.

Catch me if you can . . . oh, you did!

The most successful US fraudster ever was Frank Abagnale, who cashed $2.5 million in bad cheques across 26 countries over five years. Before he was 20 years old, he managed to impersonate an airline pilot well enough to be allowed to travel on over 250 flights for free and pass himself off as a sociology professor, doctor and attorney. He was eventually caught but allowed out of prison on condition that he help the FBI catch other fraudsters. Eventually he became a millionaire legitimately through advising companies on how to detect and avoid fraud. His story was made into the movie *Catch Me If You Can* in which Leonardo di Caprio played Abagnale brilliantly.

Tying weapons to offenders

One of my students did a remarkable study of criminal weapon use in her native Brazil, where criminals use a wide variety of weapons. She went into prisons and asked 120 offenders what weapons they used and why. She found that the weapons were chosen for their symbolic significance for the offenders and related to their personality and consequently the types of crimes they committed.

The very aggressive offenders whose crimes were an expression of emotional feelings, such as those with the tragic or heroic personal narratives (that I describe in the earlier section 'Hearing the stories people tell themselves: Criminal narratives'), and who had dominating and extrovert personalities, were more likely to use knives and weapons that involved direct contact with the victims. They used these weapons to commit rape and murder. Those who used firearms, which kept them at a distance from their victims, were more likely to be involved in acquisitive crimes for which their weapons were just to control their victims rather than hurt them.

Burglary

A huge psychological difference exists between a burglar who takes precautions to avoid contact with the occupant of a building and one who doesn't mind or even relishes such confrontation. In general, the former is most common. The majority of burglars go to a lot of trouble: they watch a house to make sure that everyone has left and knock on the door first to make sure no one answers. If someone does, they just ask for a fictitious person and apologise and leave, saying they have the wrong address.

Some burglars who avoid confrontation are nonetheless interested in the occupants of the building. They rummage through drawers without taking anything and may even destroy property unnecessarily just to insult the occupants. The courts take account of this, treating it as a more serious form of burglary than just stealing a handbag left by an open window.

The professional burglar may avoid domestic buildings entirely and focus on the opportunities provided by commercial premises. One young offender that I spoke to made clear that although his aim was to obtain goods of value to sell on, he really saw the crime as an adventure in which he was challenging the police. The owners of the warehouses he burgled were of no significance to him. What mattered to him was whether he could get away before the police caught him (he didn't and they did!).

Arson

The key to understanding arson is the nature of the target that's set on fire. Broadly, four sorts of targets exist and each carries different implications for the inferences that a forensic psychologist makes:

- ✔ **Domestic buildings in which people may be present.** The people are likely to be the target and the arsonist is acting out a narrative of a heroic mission to wrong some hurt he suffered.

- ✔ **Institutions such as schools or hospitals.** These places have symbolic significance for the arsonist and may often be related to some mental disturbance he experienced.

   The term *pyromania* is sometimes used to describe someone who gets pleasure from watching buildings on fire and so carries out a series of arson attacks. He may get excitement from the arrival of the fire-fighters and the whole dramatic event. Some experts even think that sexual arousal may be involved in this excitement.

- ✔ **Vehicles and other locations related to crimes that he has committed.** Here, arson is a strategy of the criminal who sees himself as a professional getting rid of the forensic evidence.

- ✔ **The arsonist himself.** A fire in which the arsonist gets hurt or even killed may well be a painful form of (attempted) suicide, most likely carried out by someone known to be mentally ill.

- ✔ **Arson for profit** is the term given to setting fire to buildings in order to claim the insurance, especially for failing businesses, or unwanted buildings that nobody wants to buy.

Working on violent crimes

Experts make a general distinction between different kinds of violence that's crucial to the forensic psychologist's work:

- ✔ **Expressive violence:** The act is an outburst of some emotional feelings.

- ✔ **Instrumental violence:** Violence is being used as means to an end.

People's relationship to violence can be heavily connected to the culture in which they're raised. Without doubt, certain subcultures exist in which violence is seen as a dominant means of communication and an expected form of interaction. It may surprise you to know that even in modern developed countries like the UK and US there are subcultures for which violence is a normal aspect of daily life. This is grippingly illustrated in Mikey Walsh's bestselling autobiography *Gypsy Boy*, but this is just one of many books that lift the lid on the violent worlds into which some people are born.

I was talking to one young man, as part of preparing his defence for a violent attack and rape that left his victim dead. He grew up in a poor part of Nigeria. He told me that when he was naughty his mother called local soldiers in to beat him up. With such an upbringing, it can't be a surprise that he exploded into violence when denied what he wanted, although that's in no way an excuse.

Whether a person grows up surrounded by violence like Walsh, some individuals have especially aggressive personalities, or short fuses. This may be one of the ways of expressing themselves they learned from their family and associates, but it can also be part of their personal narrative in which they feel that they have to defend themselves against any hint of insult by an act of violence. These aggressive people may offer many forms of justification for their violent behaviour (as I explain in Chapter 2).

Helping people to develop other ways of dealing with frustration and anger is challenging, but plenty of ways to try and do so are available (as I describe in Chapter 14).

Rape

The significance of the victim to the offender takes on a different perspective when considering sexual assaults than it does in burglary or arson (crimes I discuss in the earlier section 'Dealing with property crimes'). As in other types of crime there are many different aspects to rape. Although rapists use their victims to achieve sexual gratification, this isn't the only or even necessarily the psychologically most significant aspect of rape. Sexual assaults are often coloured with anger and frustration and the desire to control the victim. They may even be mainly an attempt to show where the power lies in a relationship.

Although some individuals get sexually aroused by the control they exert over their victims, and the pain they produce (as I mention in Chapter 2 in my discussion on sadism), that isn't what usually drives a rapist to be violent to his victim. Some rapists mistakenly believe that the victim will enjoy the violent encounter. They think they're involved in an acceptable relationship with a woman. In fact, it's not unknown for potential rapists to run away from a victim who fights and screams, but many victims are so traumatised by the attack that they're unable to do that.

Many rapists have regular sexual partners and aren't obviously sexually frustrated, although they're likely to have been violent to that partner even if the victim doesn't report it. A few rapists do have a very high sex drive that they have difficulty controlling, but that's not an explanation for why they rape women.

Forensic psychologists consider three ways in which rapists make use of their victims:

- **Victim as Object:** When the attacker treats the victim as just an opportunity for his sexual gratification, it matters little to the offender who the victim is or what her reactions are. All he wants to do is to control her enough to be able to carry out the sexual act. This rapist may well have a broad-ranging criminal background, as a thief or involved in other forms of criminality.

- **Victim as Vehicle:** Here the victim represents some aspect of 'womenhood' that the offender wants to control or have power over. Victims may represent women that he feels slighted him in the past or women that he believes are unavailable to him in any other way. Typically, these attackers have little ability to relate to women and may not have a regular sexual partner.

- **Victim as Person:** These are rapists for whom the victim is a significant person, perhaps their regular sexual partner or someone they've been stalking. The rapist may totally misunderstand the nature of his actions, believing the victim wants the sexual act.

Men can be victims of rape too, by other men or even by women. Such victims may be very reluctant to report the crime because of public attitudes. Such men and their male attackers aren't necessarily homosexual.

I explore attempts to treat sexual offenders in Chapter 15.

Murder

Murder is, of course, a catch-all term, and it's more useful in forensic psychologist work to understand and use more precise terms:

- **Homicide** is the killing of one person by another. This act may not be murder if the killing is lawful, such as in self-defence.

    Apparently, ten or more legal ways exist of killing someone in the state of Texas.

- **Contract killing** is when a third party is hired or urged to kill a person on behalf of another person. Films make much of the professional contract killer who's anonymous to the person who hires them and who moves around the world killing to order. Although such people undoubtedly exist in organised crime syndicates, more usually the contract killer is someone known to the person hiring him or at least known to someone they know. Quite often, though, unwittingly the 'friend of a friend' is actually an undercover police officer who has insinuated himself into a criminal network in order to find out who's trying to supply contract killers. He then has the evidence to convict the person who asked him to kill.

- ✔ **Serial killers** kill a number of people (most experts require three murders before they place a criminal into this unattractive league) over a period of time, with so-called cooling-off periods in between. These cooling-off periods can be as short as a day or so, or as long as a number of years.

- ✔ **Spree killers** kill a number of people in one intense activity. They walk into a store and shoot everyone they can before being stopped. School shootings, like the one at Columbine, Colorado in 1999, are typical of the activities of spree killers.

- ✔ **Mass murder** is the sort of thing that violent dictators perpetrate, killing hundreds, thousands or even millions of people. They can't do this slaughter on their own of course, and so it tends to be part of an organised process in which many killers participate. Sometimes it's a cult that kills all its followers, as happened at Jonestown, Guyana in 1978, or the cult may set out to kill members of the public, like the sarin gas attack on the Tokyo subway transport system in 1995.

Murder can occur in a number of different situations, and understanding these helps to clarify the nature of the particular killing:

- ✔ **Domestic violence:** Although this usually involves the man killing the woman, vice versa also happens. This violence can arise out of an enduring violent relationship in which both people involved attack each other from time to time, or circumstances in which one partner is habitually violent. The violent person's behaviour may be aggravated by the use of alcohol or other drugs that reduce normal inhibitions.

- ✔ **Juvenile homicide:** This typically emerges out of a group event in which the victim and the killer could just as readily be the other way round, if one had been quicker or slower to react. Of course, this can happen with adults too, but usually it happens with gangs of youths. These homicides often emerge out of masculine competitiveness, perceived defence of reputation and the quest for respect.

- ✔ **Confrontational homicide:** This can result from criminal challenges and is often embedded in violent subcultures in which honour and machismo are at a premium. The offenders can be directly instrumental in the desire to remove a competitor or to demonstrate power over others.

- ✔ **Crime-related homicide:** This is when a significant witness, as to a rape or bank robbery, is killed in the belief that this act reduces the likelihood of being caught and convicted. Sometimes, this category of murder involves a threat that gets out of control.

Terrorism

Many crimes are committed by people who claim they're fighting for a cause, which makes it very difficult to define acts of terrorism except in relation to what the perpetrators claim as the purpose of those actions. This is rather different from all other considerations of crime in which the actions themselves define the crime rather than the proposed reasons for those actions.

The aim of terrorism

The central idea of terrorism was articulated clearly in the 19th century by anarchists as 'Propaganda of the Deed'. In other words, what's crucial is the way in which their actions are interpreted (their symbolic meaning) instead of any direct impact on the functioning of society. The intention is to generate a violent reaction from the state so that mayhem ensues.

Most governments these days are aware of this intention and deal with terrorist atrocities cautiously, so as not to provoke further reactions from people who may get caught in a vicious governmental response to terrorism, and so support the terrorists' cause.

When considering terrorists as criminals who claim to be using robbery, murder or fraud to further political or ideological objectives, forensic psychologists can reflect on the same differences in styles that I describe earlier in this section for other crimes. For example, some terrorist groups are extremely confrontational, while others try only to attack targets that they regard as legitimate and some even try to avoid loss of life.

From a forensic psychology point of view, the important matters to establish are the details of what individual terrorists are doing and to understand their personal narratives (something I describe in the earlier section 'Hearing the stories people tell themselves: Criminal narratives'), instead of being seduced by the rhetorical propaganda of their leaders.

Organised crime

Terrorist groups are the most obvious examples of organised criminals. They have a network of contacts that work together in a co-ordinated way to carry out crimes. But don't fall into the trap of thinking that all criminal networks have similar strict hierarchies and structures; in fact, growing evidence suggests that not even terrorist groups are as tidily organised as is often assumed.

Maintaining an illegal organisation is rather difficult. Everything has to be secret and no one can be trusted unless they're close family members or part of a powerfully coercive subculture, such as the Chinese Triads. As a consequence, the notorious criminal organisations such as the Mafia are a rarity among criminal networks, and even they're not as tightly structured as the movies would have you believe.

The idea that illegal organisations have the same sort of structure as a legal one, with a chief executive, a board of directors, managers or departments, and clear lines of command is very misleading. They tend to be very volatile groupings drawing on different mixes of individuals for different crimes. The individuals involved have all the variations in their personality and styles that I discuss throughout this chapter. Consequently, the actions that occur in a crime known to be part of a particular criminal network, tell you something about the individuals carrying out that crime.

One interesting way of studying criminal networks is to look at who's in contact with whom and to represent the result as a network chart (as shown in Figure 6-3). This approach allows investigators to identify the key individuals and cliques as well as determining who's on the periphery of the network and so may be most open to informing to the police. Investigative psychologists can also establish the coherence of the network and how tight and interconnected it is to help determine its vulnerability to police interference.

For the example in Figure 6-3, the three target individuals provide the basis for a loosely knit gang that incorporates 19 people in total. Putting these three people out of action, say by imprisonment, would drastically reduce the network's ability to function.

Investigative psychologists can also provide inferences about the characteristics of those involved in terrorist attacks in much the same way they can for any other crime. This can be particularly helpful in indentifying who in a terrorist group may be least committed to the terrorist cause and so may be willing to withdraw from the group and help the police.

Figure 6-3:
Illustration of a network of associates in a criminal gang. The light grey circles named Targets 1, 2 and 3 are well known prolific offenders. The lines join them to other individuals with whom they have been arrested.

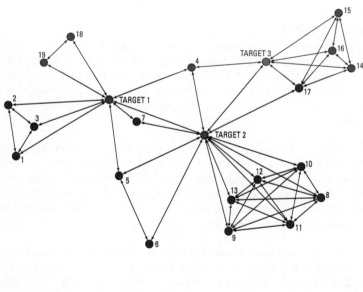

Questioning Whether This Chapter Should be Published

One question I'm often asked is whether I'm giving too much of the game away by publishing accounts of how investigative psychology works. I still remember the row I had with a government official who said that publishing would just make criminals more savvy and difficult to catch. In reply, I asked her whether she'd have kept the potential use of fingerprints to solve crimes a secret if she could. Without hesitation, she said 'yes!'.

I disagree with her for many reasons, but a main one is that in a democratic society it's essential that no group has secret control of information that can be used to entrap others. Another reason is that secret science is inevitably bad science: if people disagree with what I write in this book, they can test their ideas and mine, show which are correct and allow everyone to benefit from the published results.

Perhaps the most important reason, though, is that crime grows out of criminals' lack of awareness and insight into the implications and consequences of what they're doing. When informed, criminals can change their activities. For example, out of the blue I got a letter from a prisoner in a South African prison who'd read my book *Criminal Shadows* (on which I draw throughout this book). This man had a long history of violence in and out of prison. He wrote that when he read my book he realised that he'd always thought of himself as a tragic victim and that that was inappropriate. Having gained that insight, he was now on the road to a productive, violence-free life.

Chapter 7

Understanding Victims of Crime and Their Experiences

*A*ll too often in writing about crime – in fact and in fiction – the focus is on the criminal. Open any of the thousands of academic books about crime and you very rarely find a section on the victims and how to help them. Similarly, crime fiction nearly always focuses on the villain and catching him: the consequences of his actions for the victims and their families are rarely mentioned (unless the plot has a vengeful hero seeking retribution).

Over the last few years some experts have started to redress this imbalance by considering the consequences of being a victim and how to help those who experience crimes. Although forensic psychologists are often part of these considerations there are many other professional groups they may work with. These include criminologists, psychotherapists, psychiatrists, police officers and social workers, all of whom bring their own particular perspectives to bear on helping victims. These groups draw on the insights from forensic psychology, that I describe in this chapter, whether they have a professional forensic psychologist who's part of their team and who has qualified as I describe in chapter 18, or not. This study of victims is known as *victimology,* and covers issues such as who becomes a victim and the resulting social and political implications, while also examining the legal processes that are in place to assist victims.

In general in this chapter I write about victims of crimes. But the experiences of victims of accidents overlap with these. If you have the great misfortune to be knocked down by a car the police will probably assume that it was a crime and the driver will be charged with dangerous driving or something similar.

You will be appropriately angry at what you have suffered and if you are very unlucky you may experience some trauma similar to that experienced by people who are knocked down by a robber who steals their belongings. So there is no simple distinction between victims of crimes and victims of accidents. Therefore in some parts of this chapter I comment on the forensic psychology of accident victims as well as focussing mainly on crime victims.

In my opinion, however, too few of these studies deal directly with the experiences of victims and the psychological assistance they may need. In this chapter, I focus on the typical victims of crime and the impact on them of suffering from the acts of criminals. This aids understanding of what victims suffer, which is crucial for all the professional groups who seek to help them.

When I identify what typifies people who are victims of crime, of course I'm in no way blaming them for what they suffer. My hope is that by understanding their vulnerabilities the many different professions who help victims (as well as society in general) can do more to assist them and reduce crime.

Suffering at the Hands of Criminals: Who Become Victims of Crime?

Determining with accuracy how many crimes take place or who's most likely to be a victim isn't easy, mainly because not all crimes are reported to the police and the way in which reported crimes are recorded varies considerably from one law enforcement area to another. For example, the police may record some criminal acts that the public would see as serious, in such a way that they go into a category of minor offences.

Experts believe that only two sorts of crime are always reported to the police and so reasonably accurate figures are available only for the following:

- **Murder:** because that's a crime hard to avoid if a body is found.
- **Car theft:** because the owner wants the insurance money and usually does have insurance because of legal requirements.

To get more accurate figures, therefore, many countries carry out crime surveys in which a carefully selected sample of the population is asked to indicate in confidence whether they've experienced any crimes in the previous year. These surveys invariably show a much larger number of crimes than are officially recorded, and researchers estimate that on average only about half of all crimes find their way into official records. Crime surveys pick up on otherwise unreported crimes, such as less serious crimes and criminal acts in areas where people don't see any point in reporting them because they believe that nothing is going to be done about it. These surveys therefore help forensic psychologists to get a better picture of what crimes actually occur and the sorts of people who are victims but may not be recorded in official statistics drawn from crimes reported to the police.

In order to identify victims of crimes – which is the aim of this section – crime surveys, and not official police reports, provide the most accurate information.

Identifying the victims

Crime surveys show that not everyone is equally likely to be on the receiving end of a crime. In general, two contributory factors influence how likely people are to become victims:

- ✔ **Personal characteristics and vulnerabilities:** If you have a disorganised lifestyle, don't look after your property or are less able to look after yourself, criminals may take advantage of that situation.

- ✔ **Location:** Inevitably, if you live in or often visit a high-crime area, you're more likely to get caught up in a crime.

More specifically, here's a list of attributes, locations and circumstances that increase the likelihood of becoming a victim of crime:

- ✔ **Attractiveness:** Where the target object is so valued that the offender can sell it on to others, for example, an expensive car or the latest mobile phone. Clearly, the items under this category are ever-changing as new desirable objects come onto the market.

  You may think that attractiveness can also apply to victims of sexual assaults, but no clear evidence suggests that women who are generally regarded as attractive have a higher probability of being victims of such crimes. Although younger women are more likely to suffer rape than older women, this is just as likely to be a consequence of lifestyle – that is, being out and about, mixing with a variety of people – than any special attractiveness to rapists.

- ✔ **'Deviant' place:** Locations where crime can flourish, such as where high numbers of people meet at the same time and place: for example, a lot of crime is committed around football matches.

  If the police don't patrol such places, they can become known as *crime hot spots,* where people are at a higher risk of victimisation.

- ✔ **Proximity:** Where the offender can access the target geographically or by person-to-person interaction.

> Criminals select some victims simply because they're near to where the offender operates. (This fact is the other side of the coin to locating offenders from knowing where the crimes are, something I discuss in Chapter 6.)
>
> ✓ **Vulnerability:** Where a lack of protection of property, or the reduced ability of a person to resist an attack, increases the risk of being a victim. The elderly, very young or infirm, or those with learning disabilities, may all be more at risk if they're in the wrong place at the wrong time.

In the UK, the following groups are more than twice as likely to be burgled than the average household:

> ✓ Young households
>
> ✓ Lone parents
>
> ✓ The unemployed

In the UK and US, teenagers and young adults are twice as likely to experience violent crime compared with the rest of the population. In general, as people get older they're less likely to experience violent crime. For example, a teenager in the US is ten times more likely to experience some sort of assault than a person over 65 years old. In addition, black people in the US are almost twice as likely to experience a violent crime than white people.

Large variations in the prevalence of crimes also exist in different regions of a country, especially property crimes. As is widely known, you're more likely to become a victim of crime in cities than in the countryside, although the types of crime vary and so you have to be cautious about comparisons. For example, not much cattle rustling takes place in New York or London, and not a lot of fraudulent bankers are roaming the Yorkshire moors or Indiana farmland!

Interestingly, violent crimes tend to have the same frequency per head of population – whether in cities, small towns or rural areas – across the UK, which contradicts the general assumption that violence has a higher rate of incidence in the inner cities. Of course, many more people live in inner cities – and more vulnerable people – than in small towns, and so the actual number of violent crimes is much higher. After all, the London Metropolitan police has to deal with about a quarter of all crimes that occur in the UK, but the population they serve accounts for about a third of the people who live in the UK.

Fear of crime and the actual experience of crime aren't always closely related. Fear of crime is often highest in those people who feel vulnerable, such as the infirm and elderly, but in fact this group is the least likely to have directly suffered a crime unless they happen to be in the wrong place at the wrong time.

The effect of local situations on crime

The relative incidence of crimes can be very different in different locations: for example, amongst street gangs in Chicago or Detroit, or vendettas between organised crime groups and within social groups for whom violence is a way of life (as I discuss in Chapter 2). Although these crimes capture the attention of the mass media and raise public concern, the simple fact is that in Western countries the number of crimes reported overall has been dropping steadily for the last 20 years or so.

Over the last decade, a growing number of people think that crime is increasing, but in fact both reported crime and crime surveys show that crime has generally been decreasing.

The murder rate in Oxford in the late 16th century (at the time of William Shakespeare) was many times higher than it's anywhere in the UK today.

Breaking the cycle: Criminals becoming victims and victims becoming criminals

In this section, I want to emphasise an important point that's often missed: many criminals are also victims. So when forensic psychologists are helping prisoners (as I describe in Part V) they have to keep in mind that they're also dealing with people who are likely to have been victims of crime. The typical victim of crime is a young man living in a poor inner city area, possibly with a lone, unemployed parent in rented accommodation. But that's also a description of a typical criminal offender. These young men are likely to have been part of a subculture in which theft isn't unusual and using violence to defend oneself is expected.

I hasten to add that probably the great majority of young people living in these circumstances don't commit crimes; such behaviour is by no means an inevitable consequence of their situation.

The factors that can increase the possibility of a person becoming a victim of crime (for a list, flip to the earlier section 'Identifying the victims') are particularly relevant within a community of criminals, especially within a prison. Therefore, one of the challenges of imprisonment that forensic psychologists who work in prisons (or prison psychologists as they're sometimes called) have to deal with, is to create an environment in which vulnerable individuals don't become victims, with all the traumatic and personally destructive consequences that can entail.

Secondary victims

Many crimes cause a fall-out beyond the imme-diate victim; family, friends and neighbours can all be secondary victims. A criminal event can disturb even passers-by and witnesses. Major criminal events such as the destruction of the Twin Towers in New York (9/11) can cause a trauma that spreads around the world. In New York itself, reports indicate a 25 per cent increase in alcohol consumption after 9/11, a sure sign of an increase in fear and anxiety.

One particularly vulnerable group of people are those who work as street-level sex workers. Of course, people who sell sex on the streets of cities have a lifestyle that's very different from the dangerously romantic image of the film *Pretty Woman*. For most sex workers, prostitution isn't a favoured career choice; the great majority are under pressure from pimps or drug addiction to earn money in the way they do.

Those who work the streets are more vulnerable to assault and homi-cide. Their vulnerability illustrates the circumstances that can combine to increase the risk of suffering crime:

✔ **Dangerous locations:** Sex work is illegal in most places and so has to be carried out away from the relative safety of public settings. This is espe-cially hazardous outdoors without any recourse to others for help.

✔ **Reluctance to talk:** When crimes are committed against sex workers, investigators have difficulty gaining information from the victims or their associates, because of the way revelations about their activities open them up to prosecution. The women are also likely to have been brought into the country illegally so do not have the requisite papers, work permits or visas to stay. Because they may fear deportation to much worse conditions back home they're reluctant to report an assault to the police. Furthermore, their clients are also committing an illegal act that they don't want others to know about, and so they're extremely reluctant to volunteer information to help the police. Identifying clients in the first place is also difficult for detectives.

✔ **Lack of public sympathy:** The general public are less likely to be con-cerned over such victims and so may be unwilling to come forward with information that may help the police.

✔ **Associated drug and alcohol problems:** Many, probably most, street sex workers have alcohol and/or drug dependency, which makes them desperate to obtain money to maintain their addiction. This encourages them to take risks relating to where they go and with whom. If under the influence of drugs or alcohol, they're probably less able to defend them-selves or remember the details to report to the police.

> ✔ **A well-known vulnerability:** Criminals are aware of these vulnerabilities and so may prey on street sex workers, which is why they're the favourite victims of serial killers.

Criminals can also start out as victims. With violent crimes – especially physical and sexual abuse – very often the offender was the direct victim of such assaults within a family or institutional setting when young. Therefore, helping victims as discussed in Part V is often an important way of reducing the cycle of crime from one generation to the next (take a look at the nearby sidebar 'A criminal who started out as a victim').

Establishing who's at risk of repeat victimisation

Many of the conditions that make certain people more at risk of being a victim of a crime than others (check out the earlier section 'Identifying the victims') don't go away after a crime has happened. As a consequence, some people are unfortunate enough to experience repeated crimes over a relatively short period of, say, a year. Yet, although this fact seems obvious, only in the last decade has law enforcement recognised such susceptibility and developed a direct policy for tackling it. This repeat victimisation really comes from criminology studies of general patterns of crime, but forensic psychologists do take the possibility into account when working with offenders or victims.

Studies show that more than one in ten people who suffer a crime, such as burglary, are likely to experience a similar crime within 12 months, if they don't take direct efforts to reduce the risks. In fact, the chances of suffering another similar crime are greatest in the days and weeks immediately following the original crime.

ANECDOTE

A criminal who started out as a victim

Joe Thomson was convicted of 234 crimes in South Auckland, New Zealand, committed over a 12-year period from 1983. These offences included many rapes, incest, abductions and burglaries. When arrested, he described how his earliest memories, from the age of four onwards, were of being sexually abused by his older sisters and cousins. He said his parents were never around, so that he and his siblings were just 'let loose to do what we wanted whenever we wanted'. His parents brought their friends home to rape him, and his sisters had been raped by his parents. He seemed relieved at last to be arrested, although his relief was because he had feared he would get killed during one of his assaults. In the controlled, organised environment of prison, he was a model prisoner.

Efforts by the police and local authorities to reduce the future risk of crime need to take account of the following factors that make people particularly prone to repeat victimisation:

✔ Living in an area where many criminals live or where they visit.

✔ Having chaotic lifestyles or leisure activities that put them at risk of crime, such as spending a lot of time out late at night, getting so drunk that you don't remember where you've been.

✔ Displaying a lack of concern to control the crime, as sometimes happens with theft from shops or petty vandalism.

✔ Crimes that are part of destructive relationships – most notably domestic violence which I examine in Chapter 14 – continue as long as the relationship does, or some outside agent intervenes to stop the violence.

Therefore, reducing repeat victimisation consists of dealing with the context that supports the crime, whether from the locality or from the weakness of the target of crime. This is referred to as *target hardening,* and may be something as simple as making sure that buildings are securely locked or something more complex such as introducing careful stock control in a business. This may not sound like an aspect of forensic psychology. Often it's not, but sometimes a psychologist needs to consider why some people have vulnerable lifestyles or keep taking the sorts of risks that make them open to crime, like not locking doors when they leave their homes.

When the roots of repeat victimisation are within the person's own personality, helping them to understand what they can do to reduce the risk is crucial.

Understanding the Effects of Crimes on Victims

All forms of crime from burglary to rape can have lasting psychological effects on the victims, far beyond any economic or physical consequences. In this section, I take a look at these psychological issues, with which forensic psychologists and the other professional groups who help victims often find themselves working. The emotional effects can influence the victims' behaviour and social lives, including nervousness, anxiety and worry that can last for months or even years.

Viewing burglary as violation

Studies by forensic psychologists, criminologists and others show that after burglaries, many victims feel distress from the violation and intrusion into the place they regard as their private, sacrosanct dwelling. One in five such victims report severe emotional upset that nearly always includes anger and often shock expressed in tears and increased fear of future victimisation. In addition, this distress is frequently accompanied by insomnia.

These effects are strongest when the burglar delves into the most personal parts of the house, such as bedrooms and cupboards, especially when this intrusion also involves ransacking the property and other forms of physical violence.

Some burglary victims compare the violation as having parallels to being raped. Most people see their home as an integral part of how they are and how they present themselves to others, and so when it's abused they feel personally attacked as if the assault were against their body not just their property. Many victims move home so that they aren't reminded of the way the burglar violated them.

Experiencing uncertainty: The worst part is not knowing

Not surprisingly, the experience of suffering property crime, physical assault or rape often induces an increased feeling of vulnerability in victims. The fixed beliefs in the stability of daily routine, free from threat, are eroded and the trust in relationships is jeopardised. This in turn increases the fear of possible future victimisation and a lack of confidence in people and places that had earlier been regarded as unthreatening. In addition, the offender still being at large adds considerably to the victim's anxiety.

In many areas of human activity, stress is partly a product of a lack of control over what a person's trying to do. Not knowing whether an attack or a burglary is likely to recur consequently generates considerable stress.

In the particular case of a crime relating to a family member or friend who disappears, the inability to clarify the emotional relationship to the missing person (for example, whether to mourn the person or not) can cause even more distress, which is why such victims often say that they'd rather know that their loved one is dead than be kept in the dark.

Suffering from the trauma of rape

In this section, I discuss some of the details of how victims respond to the shock of a sexual assault. Two stages are often identified in response to rape:

- **In the hours immediately after the assault:** Victims may experience shock, disbelief, anger and general anxiety, which is likely to be accompanied by confusion and disorganisation in their activities with considerable, general fear.

- **Later on in the days, weeks or months after:** As victims begin to put their life back together, they're likely to feel humiliation, embarrassment and a growing desire for revenge.

Rape victims often feel that they've lost control of social situations and sexual encounters, as well as their autonomy over their intimate relationships. One of the most debilitating psychological aspects is when victims blame themselves in some way for what happened. They may think they gave the wrong signals, through their actions, what they said or the clothes they wore. In some cultures, the tendency to blame the victims can be so strong that they accept their culpability quite inappropriately.

Women in particular often experience rape as life-threatening even in cases where no direct physical or verbal threats were present, which naturally aggravates all the other anxieties associated with unwanted sexual activity. Large variations do exist, though, in how victims react to sexual assaults: some manage to find the ability to pull through and deal with the trauma. Family and social support is very significant in helping victims to cope.

Men who experience rape can suffer particular traumas, whether their assailants are women (as I illustrate in the earlier sidebar 'A criminal who started out as a victim') or men. Men may feel that the attack challenges their identity as men, causing them to feel especially vulnerable and even guilty in some ill-defined way for not being manly enough.

When the victims experience violence, especially including rape and sexual abuse as a child, many more severe effects than those experienced from suffering a property crime are common. These can persist for many years and include:

- Emotional disturbance
- Sleep disorders
- Eating disorders
- Feelings of insecurity
- Low self-esteem
- Difficulties in relating to others

In general, people from minority ethnic communities, lesbians, gays and transsexuals, and the elderly suffer more profoundly from violent crime than others in the population.

Forensic psychologists need to recognise the different situations in which male rape can occur, although of course these situations also have parallels when the victims are women:

- ✔ The victim may be overwhelmed by physical force that he's unable to resist. This can challenge his view of himself as a capable man, whereas women may sometimes accept they're physically weaker than their assailant.

- ✔ A friendly, mildly homosexual encounter may be taken further than the victim wants. Men may feel their heterosexuality has been questioned which they can find deeply hurtful in contrast to women who may have more mildly sexual approaches from men.

- ✔ The victim may be trapped in a situation he can't manage due to substance abuse or unwanted drugs. This of course can also apply to women, but men may be less aware of the risks of getting into such situations.

- ✔ Threats may be used to coerce the victim. Men are more likely to believe they can deal with coercion than women and so feel especially demeaned if they can't.

Surveys show that men are just as likely to report having being assaulted by a partner as women, although women report more frequent assaults and suffer greater injuries. I discuss domestic violence in more detail in Chapter 14.

For details on how the trauma of a violent crime is handled in court, turn to Chapter 11.

Examining the effects of physical abuse on children

Children are especially vulnerable psychologically to the effects of physical and/or sexual abuse, because they're still forming an understanding of who they are and how they can relate to others. At the early stage in their development abuse can have a profound effect on their personalities and create a lack of trust of others and lowered feelings of self-worth. The likely consequences of such abuse are as follows:

- ✔ Beyond the immediate pain and suffering, children are likely to develop medical problems, which can be anything from severe bed-wetting to skin disorders, or extreme anxiety. Young children have less physical capability to cope with physical assault and as a result death can result from a physical injury in some cases, such as blows to the head that may not be regarded as so severe in an adult.

- ✔ Children are likely to express emotional problems through a general level of anger, hostility and anxiety. They may be fearful of adult contact which can also involve an inability to express their feelings.

- ✔ Children can experience physical assault as humiliation and thus have lowered self-esteem.

- ✔ Their relationships with other children may become problematic, expressed as aggression towards others, hyperactivity, truancy, inability to form friendships and poor social skills. Self-destructive behaviour, including excessive risk taking, may also be present.

- ✔ Their inability to be part of a social group or to relate to others can make the educational process very challenging for abused children, with poorer cognitive and language skills being the outcome.

Long-term consequences of child physical abuse are:

- ✔ Possible development of physical disabilities, for example, brain damage or eye damage.

- ✔ A tendency not to get on with others easily, for example, difficulty trusting others within adult relationships or violent relationships.

- ✔ A predisposition to emotional disturbance, feelings of low self-esteem and depression.

- ✔ An increased potential for abusing their own children when they become a parent.

- ✔ Possible development of drug or alcohol abuse.

Identifying and handling traumatic brain injury

Traumatic brain injury, as when part of the brain is damaged, is most often caused by accidents, but it can be the result of violent assault. Such injuries become relevant when forensic psychologists are considering victims, from two points of view:

- ✔ The effects on those victims that may be relevant in trying to help them, such as seeking medical support and medication, or taking account of the way the brain damage has impaired cognitive abilities.

- ✔ The basis that it can provide for understanding how, in some cases, such victims can become criminals, such as changes in their ability to control their emotions or to fully understand the consequences of their actions.

Of course, many possible consequences of injury to the brain can result depending on which part of the brain is injured. In addition, the forensic psychologist needs to recognise that the event may have had a psychological effect in making the person fearful and anxious quite independently of any brain injury. If the injury results from an assault, the psychological consequences that I discuss earlier in this chapter with regard to rape (in the section 'Suffering from the trauma of rape') may be the main cause of any psychological disturbance. Therefore, disentangling the influences of organic brain damage from the emotions associated with the violent crime can often be difficult for anyone trying to help the victim, whether she's a forensic psychologist, a psychiatrist or even the local family doctor.

Children are particularly vulnerable to the effects of brain injury and can display:

✔ Lower levels of self-esteem and ability to cope with challenging circumstances, such as first day at a new school.

✔ Higher levels of loneliness.

✔ Maladaptive behaviour, such as avoiding any problem faced rather than trying to deal with it, like running away from home because of a family row.

✔ Aggressive/antisocial behaviour.

For adults, similar problems may be apparent, but because their involvement in the community at large is more demanding than for children, brain injury can be psychologically debilitating because it reduces the victim's social contact, which may increase feelings of loneliness and related depression. These problems can remain long after the physical consequences of the injury have improved. Social isolation and decreased leisure activities create a renewed dependence on such victims' families to meet these needs.

A very real fear is that these issues increase the likelihood of a person slipping into criminal behaviour (see the earlier section 'Breaking the cycle: Criminals becoming victims and victims becoming criminals').

Consequences of traumatic brain injury that can increase the susceptibility to committing criminal acts are:

✔ Decrease in friendships and social support.

✔ Lack of opportunity for establishing new social contacts and friends.

✔ Reduced leisure activities.

✔ Anxiety and depression for prolonged periods of time.

A particularly important effect of severe brain trauma is the loss of memory, known as *post-traumatic amnesia*. This problem can affect victims, making it difficult for them to help a police inquiry into the nature and cause of the trauma (and is sometimes claimed by offenders as a reason for being unable to give any account of what they did). This memory loss is typically exhibited as a state of confusion or disorientation. Victims may be unable to say their names, where they are or the time or day of the week. (Skip to Chapter 9 to see how forensic psychologists assess whether amnesia is genuine or faked.)

The loss of memories can be those that were formed shortly before the injury. This loss may only exist for an hour or so, or the person may never be able to remember what happened just before the injury. They may also have problems in creating new memories after the injury has taken place. In some cases this inability to form further memories may not develop until several hours after the injury. Awareness of these processes is crucial for any therapy a psychologist may attempt to carry out with a victim. They may not wish to face up to what they experienced or they may genuinely forget it because of the brain trauma. So knowledge of these processes is relevant to everyone who works with victims: police, social workers and the courts.

Criminals' awareness of post-traumatic amnesia can be drawn on as a defence. They can claim they can't remember what happened leading up to the crime or soon after. It can be very difficult to determine if this is genuine memory loss or not (as I make clear in Chapter 9 where I describe how memory loss is assessed). Assessment requires a full understanding of how memory works and what's likely to be forgotten and what not. Forensic psychologists with this special knowledge may be called in to determine if the defendant is malingering or really is a victim of a crime.

Of course, even if he can't remember what happened, the person can still be convicted of the crime. This was the case with John Duffy (which is described in some detail in Chapter 6) who was convicted of murder and rape in 1986. He claimed he had been a victim of an attack, showing a wound to support this, and said that consequently he could not remember anything around the time of the crimes he was accused of. An associate came forward to say Duffy had asked him to attack him in order to provide support for Duffy's denial of any memory, but still for many years Duffy claimed he had no memory of the assaults he was eventually convicted of. A psychotherapist counselled him in prison apparently helping him, after he had been incarcerated for 14 years, to remember that he'd had an associate David Mulcahey, who Duffy claimed, had been the prime mover in carrying out the murders. Mulcahey strongly denied this but forensic evidence taken together with Duffy's memories led to Mulcahey being convicted of murder.

So for a forensic psychologist to disentangle whether a person is a victim or a perpetrator or both does require a detailed understanding of the effects of suffering various sorts of crimes.

Assessing the Psychological Effects of a Crime on a Victim

Psychologists, whether they're general clinical psychologists who provide therapy for many different types of patients with mental health problems, or more specialist forensic psychologists who are helping victims, along with family doctors, psychiatrists and other professionals (even the local priest), may also be called on to assess the extent of the effect of the experience of a crime. This may be done to determine how the therapy should be conducted and to identify the particular problems that the victim needs help with.

But assessment of the victim of a crime may also be carried out to establish exactly what the effects are, so that other forms of help beyond counselling and psychological therapy can be provided. This can include compensation from the state or the culprit or from insurance or other forms of support for disabilities. These assessments often require psychological expertise as well as medical expertise. The forensic psychologist assesses the victim in much the same way as if the person had had an accident. Although crimes generate fears and anxieties that may not be so prevalent as a consequence of accidents, the psychological issues are very similar.

Part of the challenge of making accurate assessments about crime victims is that sometimes the person wants to appear as damaged as possible, perhaps to increase the chance (or amount) of an insurance payment. In addition, in court cases, the victims may be determined to ensure that culprits are seen to have caused deep psychological damage and thus avoid the judge or jury being lenient. Consequently, psychologists assessing the victim have to find ways of determining the true nature of the situation. Psychological processes, however, can further complicate this. Victims may not be fully aware of the extent to which they're trying to reassure themselves that they're really suffering as much as they think they are as a result of the crime.

Here are the main ways in which forensic psychologists assess the experience of a crime victim:

- ✔ Seeking objective information from as wide a range of sources as possible, including medical and employment records and wherever possible interviewing people who knew the victim before and after the critical event, such as family friends and work colleagues.

- ✔ Getting the details of the incident as clear as possible to determine how it may have had any effects.

- ✔ Considering the person's capabilities and emotional tendencies prior to the incident.

- ✔ Assessing the official interviews of the victim in the light of other evidence.

- ✔ Using psychological tests (as I discuss in Chapter 9).

One particular aspect of this last point is to take account of how the victim deals with the interview process itself, sometimes called the *response style*. These responses can display a number of different characteristics:

- ✔ **Malingering,** especially the deliberate fabrication of symptoms or greatly exaggerating them.

- ✔ **Minimisation,** the denial of any symptoms or the reduction in the account of their seriousness.

- ✔ **Distraction,** dealing with questions by going off at a tangent to talk about irrelevant issues, probably indicating an unwillingness to engage directly with the interview procedure.

- ✔ **Lack of effort,** in performing any tasks as part of the assessment; may be due to weariness or frustration but can also indicate other symptoms of which the victim isn't totally aware, notably depression.

- ✔ **Lack of co-operation,** as when the victim refuses to answer questions or gives only minimal answers.

The forensic psychologist uses these response styles to form a view of the disabilities of the victim and the effect of the incident. Alone they don't imply whether the victim's account of the incident's effect is valid or not, but taken together with all the other information the response styles provide a valuable basis to any opinion that the psychologist can offer.

Dealing with post-traumatic stress disorder

I discuss post-traumatic stress disorder (PTSD) in some detail in Chapter 11, where I consider expert testimony in court, because it's one of the most common forms of psychological disturbance used as evidence. Take a look at that chapter for details of the symptoms that comprise PTSD. In this section I focus on identifying and treating PTSD, a common component of any assessment of a victim of a crime or an accident.

To be sure that any incident has given rise to PTSD, whether it's a violent assault or something that looks like an accident, as in the aircraft carrier disaster I mention in the sidebar 'Assessing for PTSD years after the event', the forensic psychologist needs to establish that the symptoms arose close in time to the event. In some cases, PTSD has been diagnosed as many as 30 years after the event (check out the nearby sidebar 'Assessing for PTSD years after the event'), but being sure that the symptoms are really related to the event under such conditions is extremely difficult.

Assessing for PTSD years after the event

The problem of disentangling causes when PTSD is delayed is demonstrated by the Australian disaster in 1964 when an aircraft carrier collided with a destroyer that then sank. Eighty one people drowned. Over 35 years later, hundreds of people claimed PTSD. Assessing these claims required consideration of the individual's psychological state immediately after the disaster and what had happened to that person over the intervening years, particularly identifying any other stressors that may have occurred during this time.

To make matters more complicated, considerable evidence suggests that a person's psychological state and make-up before the traumatic event, taken together with the support and other helpful aspects of his lifestyle (or lack of), can have considerable influence on whether or not PTSD occurs and the form it takes. The emotional reactions that the person is having – anxiety, avoidance of people or places and the other general aspects of PTSD – may have been generated by something other than the particular trauma for which the person is claiming. Or these other experiences may have made a mild shock more significant.

Studies in the US indicate that about half of the population claims to have experienced some sort of serious traumatic event during their lives. If they experience another such event are the effects magnified or has the person developed coping strategies that makes them less vulnerable? The answer is 'yes' or 'no' depending on the person.

If a person is psychologically stable before the event and in a supportive environment after it, that person is very likely to be able to cope with what appear to be serious traumas. A number of examples exist of studies of children who have lived through wars, in Lebanon or Bosnia for instance, who show no signs of PTSD. They were part of warm and loving families and had no psychological problems before the war. These pre-existing circumstances protected them from PTSD.

The various professions that offer help to victims, including clinical and forensic psychologists, draw on a variety of different approaches for treating PTSD and of course people's reactions to events vary enormously. Any help or support for someone suffering from PTSD therefore has to be adjusted to the person (much of the work on this syndrome emerged out of the recognition that soldiers can suffer great traumas). In general, the following activities are involved in treating PTSD:

- ✔ The nature of the problem and what the client particularly wants help with is identified; for example, fear of particular locations, difficulty of being with other people, intimate relationships and so on.

- ✔ Ways of relaxing are explored with the person, perhaps involving forms of self-hypnosis or other techniques widely used throughout psychotherapy.

- ✔ Victims are encouraged to develop ways of relaxing in relation to particular aspects of their problem, perhaps focusing on particular places or occasions or even back to the traumatic event. Various procedures can be used such as: requiring the client to do the 'homework' of trying to deal with some small aspect of the difficult circumstance one tiny step at a time; or guided imagery in which the person thinks carefully about particular stressful circumstances (when calm) and considers how to act effectively in those situations in future.

- ✔ A follow-up is organised as well as addressing the current concerns of the individual to help maintain any improvements in the person's psychological state.

Offering restorative justice

Identifying the traumatic consequences of crime and developing accounts of victims' experiences can imply that they have something close to a medical problem. This approach can lead to them being assigned a clinical label that ignores their unique experiences and ways of dealing with those experiences. They may find themselves being treated as a medical 'case' rather than a person, with expectations of how they should act being influenced by general ideas about those sorts of 'cases' instead of by the individual person's behaviour.

To counteract this problem, many victims are encouraged by those helping them not to think of themselves as victims, but as survivors of something awful. This change in labelling also gives people confidence to take back control of their lives and not allow the offender to carry on exerting an influence over what they do by continuing to give rise to their fears and anxieties.

One way of helping victims feel empowered is by confronting the person who attacked them or stole from them, such as testifying in court or being part of a *restorative justice* process. This approach doesn't focus on the clinical problems, but on the fact that crime involves a relationship between the offender and the victim and this needs to be dealt with. Restorative justice emphasises repairing the harm that has been caused by the crime. Going to the essence of the crime and connecting the offender and the victim together can also have beneficial effects on the criminal.

Restorative justice gives the victim (or survivor) a significant role in the judicial process and that person's suffering is placed centre stage. This differs considerably from most legal systems in which the state punishes the criminal and the victim is just one more witness to provide evidence for the state.

At the heart of restorative justice processes is offenders acknowledging their wrong-doing and apologising for it. Studies show that this humane acceptance is very beneficial to victims and helps them accept the validity of their own suffering and understand more fully the reasons why the crime occurred, which also helps them come to terms with it.

Victims offer the following reasons for requesting a restorative justice procedure:

- ✔ To find out from the offender why he committed the crime in that way with that particular victim.
- ✔ To make the offender understand and accept the effect the crime has had on the victim and to accept and apologise for that effect.
- ✔ To have the opportunity to forgive the offender and thus bring the experience to a resolution.

The restorative justice process can employ many different formats, such as small group meetings, more formal conferences and mediation through a third party. These formats can include support from legal or psychotherapeutic professionals or even ex-offenders. In general, restorative justice follows the process of:

- ✔ **Meeting:** Bringing together all those on whom the crime has impacted to talk about the crime and its consequences.
- ✔ **Recompense:** Exploring how the offender can help to repair the harm caused, including clear indications of remorse, apology and acceptance of the impact of the offence.
- ✔ **Reintegration:** Setting in motion the restoration of victims and offenders as full, positive members of society.
- ✔ **Inclusion:** Ensuring that all those for whom the crime has particular relevance participate in the actions agreed.

Restorative justice isn't a soft option for criminals. Many of them refuse to accept responsibility for their crimes, drawing on the justifications that I discuss in Chapter 2. They also don't want to face their victims or set in motion anything that would redress the damage they have done. In many cases, offenders have preferred to go to prison instead of participating in restorative justice. This problem reveals the central weakness of what's otherwise a good idea: it requires the offender's full and open participation.

When the victim is a whole nation

Forensic psychologists tend to deal with individuals, but unfortunately situations also exist in which large groups of people, possibly even whole nations, suffer crimes. In those cases the principles of forensic psychology are just as relevant for these large numbers of people as they would be for one person. In such tragedies, many thousands, often millions, of victims exist, and each individual may suffer the consequences that I discuss throughout this chapter. In most cases, the poor and dispossessed are the ones that suffer, along with those with limited or no resources for coping. This suffering can readily set in motion the cycle of criminality that I discuss earlier in this chapter in the section 'Breaking the cycle: Criminals becoming victims and victims becoming criminals'. So when countries come through these traumas they sometimes work with forensic psychologists and those who draw on forensic psychology to help heal the nation.

Unsurprisingly, given its traumatic history when generations had their families torn apart by apartheid, South Africa is an example of such problems. Young men and women were born into families in which the father was forced away from home and in which the police and legal system focused on depriving those with the least resources of their rights. Such daily traumas may have predicted that many of them would be unable to relate to others and see criminality as a natural form of existence. The miracle of South Africa as it moved into multiracial democracy is that it didn't explode into a criminal blood-bath. This achievement is due, at least in part, to the social and political processes of reconciliation used to reconstruct the social fabric of that society.

In a form of restorative justice, people from the different sides of the earlier conflict were brought together and an attempt made to balance remorse with forgiveness (the danger being that victims were left feeling as if their suffering wasn't taken seriously).

One interesting finding in this area is that religious institutions play a powerfully positive role, perhaps because they provide individuals with the possibility of reconstructing themselves as members of an ethical, even magnanimous, community guided by civilising principles. They can think of themselves as builders of a new world, rather than sufferers from the misdeeds of others. In other words, they can re-invent their personal narratives so that they do not see themselves as victims who seek revenge but as pioneers creating a born-again country. Like a rape victim who refuses to continue to suffer from fear, individuals in post-conflict societies can use the fundamental forensic psychology idea of the value of taking control of their lives and make the future work for them.

Chapter 8

Preventing Crime: Problems, Processes and Perseverance

In This Chapter

▶ Discovering how difficult preventing crime can be

▶ Examining some ideas for crime prevention

▶ Understanding how psychological insights can combat certain crimes

You may wonder what forensic psychologists have to do with preventing crime. Don't they just help clear up the mess and damage afterwards? In fact, no, because preventing crime is about attempts to influence the actions of individual criminals, and so anything known psychologically about them contributes to more effective crime prevention and reduction. Therefore, when forensic psychologists increase the understanding of criminals and help provide a framework for their rehabilitiation or stop them continuing a life of crime, they're carrying out steps towards preventing future crime.

As I discuss in Chapter 2, the great majority of criminals aren't bizarre, strange individuals – they're people whose psychology can be understood. Making sense of their influences, and how they see the world and opportunities for crime, provides the starting point for prevention.

In this chapter, I focus on those aspects of crime prevention that have a psychological focus: an emphasis on criminals and their actions. I discuss the difficulties involved in preventing crime, some different attempts that have been suggested and tried and the foreseen and unforeseen consequences of these techniques. More specifically, I investigate how psychology can help combat the particular criminal areas of kidnappings, street gangs and organised crime.

Understanding the Difficulties of Preventing Crime

I've never come across a society without crime. One of the first acts of human beings described in the Bible is Cain killing Abel. So you have to face the fact that humans have always committed crime in one form or another, and that the chances of getting rid of it altogether are rather slim. This section looks at the problems involved in preventing crime, how psychological knowledge can help and the fact that society may well have to accept that reducing the crime rate is the best that the authorities can achieve.

Throughout this section, one question about the causes of criminal behaviour arises repeatedly: is committing crime the result of people's inherent characteristics or their social circumstances? (I discuss this subject in more detail in Chapter 2.) Most experts accept that crime results from a mixture of these causes, but the one that people in power believe is *predominantly* responsible is going to be relevant to their thinking about crime prevention techniques and how they use psychological knowledge, insights and approaches.

The prevalence of crime is reflected in the surprising statistic that 34 per cent of the UK male population will have a criminal conviction by the time they're 30. That doesn't mean they've been in prison, just that they've committed a crime and have been caught. This includes a range of different crimes from the most serious to the most trivial. The statistics for the US are more difficult to pin down and are much more disproportionately distributed across different subcultures, but they do seem to be on a par with the UK figures. Obviously, the number of people who commit crimes and don't get caught is much higher. Self-reported criminal activity in anonymous surveys indicate that probably every man and a high proportion of women have broken the law in one way or another by the time they're 30. This can include buying illegal drugs, shop-lifting and more serious crimes like burglary and rape. The figures show that criminality isn't limited to a small subset of the population, although prolific offenders are very rare.

A major challenge is to stop criminals committing more than one crime. A *Recidivist* is the term given to a person who's arrested and convicted again within a given period of time, say, three years. These days, in general terms and very round figures, about two thirds of people convicted of crimes re-offend within three years. Of course, the figures vary a lot depending on the type of crime and the sentence a person gets. People who're locked up for ten years don't re-offend for some time, outside prison at least!

Politicians complain about such high re-offending figures. They put many schemes in place to stop re-offending and sometimes claim success in reducing the recidivism figures. But the truth is that many schemes don't do much better than the general one third reduction, which is what happens if you don't do anything at all. And guess what, in a fascinating book called

The Criminal published in 1901, Havelock Ellis complains about the fact that about two out of every three criminals soon re-offend. In other words, the rates of criminality are remarkably consistent.

Although the number of people who become criminals (or at least who are caught) has been falling over the last two decades, those who do commit crimes are just as likely to re-offend today as was the case 100 years ago.

Preventing crime completely is a tall order. Reducing crime levels and the impact of crime is more feasible.

Keeping pace with the evolution of crime

One of the challenges in preventing crime is that it continues to develop and evolve. For example, one new type of criminal is the offender with information technology skills, who uses the Internet to commit crimes that in the past may have been carried out by door-to-door fraudsters (or farther back in time, highwaymen). Table 8-1 gives some pointers on how changes are opening up ever new areas in which criminals can prosper.

Table 8-1   Developments and Emerging Opportunities for Crime

Developments	*Opportunities for Criminals*
Increased wealth throughout the world (although big differences remain between rich and poor)	More wealth to be stolen or fought over, with plenty of people experiencing injustices
Greater number of portable consumer goods	More, easier-to-steal desirable objects
Information stored and transmitted electronically	Access to confidential, personal information, such as identities and bank accounts without the need for physical contact
Developments in technology	Technology becomes a target as well as a tool for criminality
Easier global travel and more open borders between many countries	Criminals able to move without hindrance and over greater distances
Improved crime prevention	Paradoxically, causes more violent crime in order to overcome protective devices

So new types of criminals are turning to illegal activities and existing criminals are finding their opportunities in different ways. Experts – including forensic psychologists – therefore need to consider whether existing approaches to crime prevention are still relevant or whether the different psychology of today's criminals requires a different set of approaches. For instance, the psychology of the previously mentioned Internet-based thief is going to be quite different to someone prepared to rob a person physically, and so preventing that crime requires a different approach.

Each of the developments in Table 8-1 raises new challenges as to how to prevent or reduce the criminal opportunities and activities. Of course, authorities and citizens still need to make life as hard as possible for potential criminals (the so-called target-hardening that I discuss in the later section 'Making crime more difficult'), but much of this attempted prevention is going to be in cyberspace instead of on the high street.

Despite the changing nature of crime, being alert to the psychological characteristics of offenders and their attitudes to what they're doing (in order to discern their weaknesses) remains central to crime prevention strategies (check out the later section 'Examining Ways to Prevent (or at Least Combat) Crime').

As well as the changes I list in Table 8-1, authorities also need to consider widespread social changes that present new types of criminal behaviour (see Table 8-2).

Table 8-2   Social Changes Relevant to Understanding Criminals

Social Changes	Implications for Criminals
Breakdown of traditional religious and ethical frameworks	Offenders now come from wider areas of society than in the past and from unusual backgrounds
Reduction in the positive influence of family and family discipline across social groups	Criminals' backgrounds are becoming more widely dispersed through social groups
Wider education and availability of better technological skills	The increasing ease of use of many emerging technologies means more people have the skills to abuse them
Increased cultural mix of many cities	Offenders are now drawn from wider ethnic and cultural backgrounds

Pushing to increase the crime rate

Crime is rather like the adaptation of a species when a change in habitat occurs: criminal actions evolve to fit into the new opportunities. Here's just one example. Las Vegas has millions of hotel rooms, each inhabited for a few days by people who may not have stayed in hotels before. Some of these guests aren't as careful in closing their room door as they should be.

As a consequence, a special type of burglar evolved in Las Vegas called the *door-pusher*. These criminals wander around the endless hotel corridors simply pushing on room doors until they find one that's not secured, entering and stealing the belongings. Such burglars are possibly unique to cities with very large numbers of hotels located near to each other.

In many senses, criminals don't change themselves, just their methods (see the nearby sidebar 'Pushing to increase the crime rate'). People who conned vulnerable members of the public 100 years ago – say by selling snake oil as a panacea – now have websites selling equally useless products. Stalkers who used to confront estranged lovers physically or bombard them with endless letters, today threaten via the Internet with streams of e-mails or abuse on Facebook. Perhaps the modern-day equivalent of the boy pickpockets that Charles Dickens portrays in *Oliver Twist* now work at computer terminals stealing through fake websites and fraudulent e-mails.

Asking whether prison works

If authorities believe that some people are inherently criminal, these people have to be discouraged from their errant ways, which can be very difficult in a free society. Often they're imprisoned, which worldwide is a common process for trying to prevent crime.

Clearly, this approach reduces the possibility of people committing crimes for the period that they're in prison – at least on the streets – although they can influence crimes indirectly and of course offend within the prison. But beyond the short-term objective of taking offenders out of circulation, does prison reduce the risk of them re-offending after they're let out?

Although the recidivism figures paint a pessimistic picture of imprisonment – with around two out of every three people re-offending within three years – the prison experience does change some offenders' behaviour permanently.

Viewing prison as just one type of experience, however, is perhaps misleading, because they vary enormously. Some prisons are the boring, violence-ridden places, full of aggressive gangs and drugs, that so delight Hollywood, but many others provide training and support activities that enable people to reconstruct their views of themselves and their lives. These approaches can help offenders back into society, provided that the stigma of imprisonment can be overcome.

Around the world, many other attempts at punishment that can also rehabilitate are in use. Such procedures as electronic tagging, community service orders and various forms of open imprisonment have had mixed success. These approaches seek to reduce the negative effects associated with incarceration, while making clear to individuals that their offending is both unacceptable and unproductive. The challenge is to help offenders deal with the causes of their crimes (perhaps rooted in the social networks and/or their personality characteristics), while simultaneously meting out appropriate punishment, which is an extremely tall order.

Getting tough on the causes of crime

If those in power believe that social settings and upbringing are predominantly responsible for crime, it follows that some possibility of rehabilitation exists and so treatment and support projects may be worthwhile (as I consider in Part V). In this case, authorities are likely to support programmes that help people to be better parents or that try to move children out of the conditions of poverty that foster crime.

As I explore in Chapter 7, many offenders who commit violent crimes have been victims of physical or sexual abuse in the past. Consequently, any reduction in those initial crimes, and efforts to help those who suffer from them, is likely to reduce the number of people in subsequent generations who carry out similar offences.

This last point indicates one of the difficulties in dealing with the causes of crime, however, which is that any positive effects can take decades to appear. In addition, such social programmes are very expensive to put in place and run, and the results are often subjective and hard to prove (at a time when displaying value-for-money public expenditure is crucial).

One area that's often undervalued in reducing crime is education. Many people drift into criminal activity because they haven't received the knowledge and skills from schooling to enable them to find a productive place in society. The reality is that many people in prison have very low levels of educational achievement, often being unable to read or write effectively.

Although academics may argue whether lack of education is the cause or consequence of an involvement in truancy and related criminality, this chicken-and-egg question doesn't matter when the aim is to reduce crime. The important objectives are first to try to keep youngsters in school and second to give offenders the skills to survive legally outside of prison.

REGIONAL TIP-OFF

Tough on crime, but. . .

Tony Blair, the erstwhile British Prime Minister, very famously declared that he was 'tough on crime and tough on the causes of crime'. This statement was a clever attempt to show that although he wasn't going to be lenient with offenders, he understood that considering and dealing with the relevant social issues was necessary as well. As a result, he hedged his bets as to whether he thought the individual or society was responsible for criminal acts – which was probably fair enough as neither one nor the other is the sole cause – but politicians are required to show leadership and such vagueness doesn't help create a clear approach to preventing crime.

Succeeding only in displacing crime

Efforts to prevent or reduce criminal activities often face the difficulty of *displacement,* which is where the crime simply moves to another jurisdiction or no longer shows up in official statistics under previously used headings. Superficially, the crime figures appear to have improved but the overall crime rate (and people's suffering from it) is the same.

Experts have identified the following changes in crime as a result of crime prevention initiatives, all of which contain a psychological element:

- ✔ **Criminals move from one area to another:** for example, muggings stop where CCTV is present but increase away from the cameras.

- ✔ **Criminals change their timing:** for example, office burglaries happen when security guards are away.

- ✔ **Criminals change how they operate:** for example, start to wear hoods to avoid being identified on hidden cameras.

- ✔ **Criminals alter their behaviour:** for example, an improvement in vehicle security reduced the number of cars stolen from the street, but instances of *carjacking* (stealing cars at gunpoint) slightly increased.

- ✔ **Criminals change the nature of their crimes while maintaining the same objectives**: for example, aircraft hijacking is much rarer due to the great increase in security checks of passengers, but terrorists changed their tactics to kidnapping or suicide bombing.

- ✔ **Criminals change their targets:** for example, terrorists move away from attacking highly protected consulates and embassies to striking more vulnerable tourist locations.

Of course, I'm not saying that society shouldn't use all the crime prevention strategies at its disposal, but an understanding of criminal psychology can help to recognise and perhaps anticipate some of the consequences. The fact is that new crime prevention measures change the landscape for criminals and as a result offenders adapt to the new surroundings and take advantage of new opportunities.

Some attempts at crime prevention can in fact increase crime if not handled carefully. For example, a new policy of arresting anyone accused of domestic violence may shame some offenders into less violent behaviour, but others may respond by becoming more defiant, more dangerous and more violent towards their victims.

The possibility of displacement, and of even more serious crimes resulting from attempts at crime prevention, shows the need to understand criminals' psychologies and points of view when trying to change their actions. If due attention is paid and the prevention procedures aren't introduced blindly, research suggests that many new initiatives can be successful in reducing the overall crime rate.

Examining Ways to Prevent (or at Least Combat) Crime

This section covers just a few ways in which authorities try to combat crime: most involve psychology in one way or another and some may be simpler than you'd think.

Understanding the weaknesses of criminals in their use of new technologies opens up new directions for law enforcement. The use of mobile phones is widespread among criminals in South Africa, even those who live in informal settlements (shanty towns). Yet many of these criminals aren't aware of how the police can now use mobile phone networks to locate the offenders. Police have caught serial rapists and murderers through the simple device of calling them on a mobile phone they've stolen from a victim! This is an instance of police using psychology in the battle against crime – or to put it more basically, out-thinking offenders!

Making crime more difficult

The central idea of all attempts to reduce crime, rather than the more optimistic goal of preventing it completely, is to make criminal activity less attractive to the criminal. This reduction can be done in a number of ways:

✔ **Target-hardening:** This is the most common way of thinking about making crimes more difficult to carry out. It can include everything from making sure that people lock their cars, to putting hooks under tables in busy places so that handbags can be hung there and so are less vulnerable to being snatched, right the way through to the concrete slabs outside embassies and airports that stop terrorists from driving car bombs into them. Increased lighting and other design developments that make any nefarious activity easier to see can also be part of this approach.

✔ **Damping:** If it becomes apparent that a particular form of crime is developing, such as a spate of pickpocketing or break-ins to schools, authorities may set in motion attempts at damping the criminal actions. Methods include campaigns to make people more aware of the problem, increased surveillance or even increased direct attempts to arrest the main culprits.

✔ **Zero-tolerance:** This approach seeks to disrupt the development of an individual's criminal career and is based on the assumption that people often start offending by committing minor crimes such as painting graffiti or breaking windows. If they can be made aware early on that their behaviour is unacceptable, and that they risk becoming more heavily involved in the criminal justice system, this awareness may reduce the likelihood of further more serious criminality.

The added benefit of zero-tolerance – if it also includes removing from the streets burnt-out cars, rubbish and other signs that a neighbourhood tolerates antisocial behaviour and criminality – is that it sends a message to would-be criminals that their offences aren't going to be tolerated. This sets in motion a virtuous cycle that produces fewer signs of crime and less attractiveness of the area to possible offenders.

✔ **Gated communities:** This is a direct environmental, or even architectural, approach that seeks to restrict access to potential criminal targets. Gated communities have been established in the richer parts of South American cities for many years and are becoming increasingly popular in the US and a few locations around Europe.

In the UK, attempts have been made to make access to houses more difficult for burglars. For example, the small alleys at the back of houses in layouts such as Victorian terraces are especially conducive to illegal activity. Cutting them off with gates to which only residents have keys (called *alleygating*) removes this problem. The interesting psychological benefit, beyond reducing crime, is that people feel they have more ownership of their area and an enhanced community spirit. This feeds into the virtuous cycle that I note in relation to zero-tolerance above.

In general, research shows that alleygating reduces crime in a particular area. In one circumstance, however, it can increase crime. If persistent burglars live within the area surrounded by the gates, they may not be able to get out easily to offend elsewhere, with a resulting increase in their committing crimes locally!

Ensuring that crime doesn't pay

Many studies of criminals point to the deterrent effect of getting caught. The risk of the punishment isn't what stops them, however, but the challenge and loss of face that comes with being detected. Consequently improvement in policing and detection (to which psychology can contribute, as I discuss in Chapters 5 and 6) is a way of reducing crime.

The problem is that many criminals don't fully understand the risks of being caught, thinking that they're impervious to detection. Also, with police clearing up only around one in ten burglaries, burglars have some cause for holding this assumption. Therefore, increased effectiveness of detection not only brings criminals into the justice system where they can be punished, or helped to see the error of their ways, but also discourages other criminals from taking the risk of getting caught and so can reduce crime.

Disrupting criminal careers

One approach of crime prevention is to work directly with offenders and diminish the likelihood of them committing further crimes, or at least reduce the prevalence of their offending. For much more on the various programmes in place, especially for violent offenders and those who've committed sex crimes, check out the chapters in Part V.

Addressing some of the background contributions to an individual committing criminality can help to reduce or even prevent crime. One obvious example is drug abuse. The expensiveness of high levels of illegal drug use, as well as the way buying and selling these drugs becomes part of criminal activities, doubtless fosters many forms of theft as well as violence. Whether drug addiction itself causes crime is open to debate, but I've certainly spoken to criminals who say that they didn't use illegal drugs until they became involved in property crime that gave them the money to buy the drugs, or were introduced to substance abuse through their association with other criminals.

Alcohol abuse also contributes to many forms of crime, especially outbursts of violence, and so helping people to deal with alcoholism can reduce criminality. This process is very demanding, however, because of peer pressure and the institutionalised popular amusement and even attractiveness associated with drunkenness.

Treating people for alcohol addiction requires helping them to cope with the temptations to have a drink. In prisons where no alcohol is available it is difficult to provide the experiences that will develop those coping mechanisms.

Changing the law

At the risk of stating the obvious, crime is what is proscribed by law. Politicians often ignore the fact that crime can be prevented by changing the law so that certain actions are no longer illegal.

One obvious example is the impact of the prohibition on the manufacture or sale of alcohol. Although best known in 1920s America, many countries have had similar laws in the past and some Islamic countries still have prohibition. Such restrictions generate illegal activity because significant proportions of the population don't regard the activity as criminal. When many people want to do things that they don't regard as wrong, but which the law prohibits, the result is increased criminal activity.

Here is my list of activities that are illegal in many countries, often attracting very severe penalties, but which many people don't think of as wrong. You can probably think of others:

- Adultery
- Exaggerating insurance claims
- Prostitution
- Smoking marijuana
- Smuggling widely-used products, such as cigarettes, to avoid duties
- Tax evasion
- Under-age drinking
- Homosexual acts

Also, of course, many things that are legal for adults are illegal for children. What is a crime if a 14-year-old is involved, isn't for an adult. In most countries this includes many forms of sexual activity as well as buying cigarettes and alcohol.

The psychological message here is that much criminality is the result of people's attitude towards the law and their acceptance of it (or not). As I explore in Chapter 2, many criminals seek to exonerate or minimise their illegal activity but they differ from those people who aren't regarded as criminals within law. In their case there is little distinction existing between them and the population at large.

Of course, most people accept that some form of restriction is necessary on many of these types of activities, otherwise where would the process end? (You may remember the Monty Python sketch in which a pompous 'expert' advocates reducing the number of criminal offences to reduce the crime rate: 'Take arson, for example. Who hasn't at one time or another burnt down some great public building . . . I know I have!')

An important aspect of crime prevention is educating the public to understand the reasons for laws being in place and to accept the consequences of breaking those laws.

Using Psychological Understanding to Combat Specific Types of Crime

In this section I take a look at three very different types of crime and show how psychological knowledge and approaches can be invaluable in combating them: hostage-taking, street gangs and organised crime.

Negotiating in hostage situations

The circumstances in which a person is held hostage can quickly turn into the even more serious crime of murder. The handling of hostage situations therefore requires psychological insight into each particular hostage event and the development of negotiation skills that will enable the least destructive conclusion possible.

Identifying types of hostage-taking and kidnapping

Hostage situations fall into three general groups, each of which requires very different psychological approaches:

- **Siege:** In the UK and US, the most common form of hostage event is one in which a person barricades himself (it's usually a man) in a room or house with a hostage, often a partner, wife or acquaintance. These hostage-takers are often mentally disturbed, depressed or even psychotic, and so any approach needs to appreciate their special way of seeing the world. Occasionally, such hostage-takers may be so mentally disturbed that they even have to discuss their actions with a non-existent, imaginary person before they respond to any law-enforcement suggestions.

  If the offender has a criminal background, he may feel that he has more to lose by giving himself up. Anyone negotiating needs to take that into account by giving him options he may not have considered.

- **Criminal kidnap for ransom:** Kidnapping people for financial gain is very different from a siege in which an angry husband threatens his estranged wife to stop her leaving him. The ransom element creates a negotiation built around threats in which the kidnapper and the negotiator are each trying to control the situation. Threats to harm the victim are used to persuade the authorities to pay up, but the negotiator can offer safe passage or other inducements to the kidnapper. But although a kidnap for ransom may seem like a straightforward business deal, this situation requires a delicate negotiation that recognises that the kidnappers may not be rational businessmen. They may have other reasons for the kidnap than just trying to get money, such as showing the authorities to be fools.

The sad fact is that more often than not hostages in ransom kidnappings are killed, particularly, and tragically, if the hostage is a child. This may be because keeping a child for any length of time is difficult. As a result, attempts to release hostages by using force may be more appropriate than is often thought.

The business plan of gangs that make money frequently out of ransom requires that they hold on to their franchise and keep other gangs out of their territory. Some drug cartels in Mexico, such as the notorious Los Zetas for example, maintain a strong identity and kill people in other gangs who have the temerity to carry out kidnappings in their domain.

Considerable differences exist between countries in how kidnapping and hostage-taking incidents are handled, with pervading attitudes towards criminals influencing how such situations are dealt with. Some authorities strive to avoid loss of life, even of the kidnapper, at all costs. For others, the primary need is to make a stand against such events and the kidnapper is regarded as an outlaw who deserves to die.

In some countries, especially in South America, notably Brazil, people so protect themselves against kidnapping that organised gangs have taken to abducting pet dogs that have to be taken outside for a walk, demanding large ransoms for their release.

✔ **Political:** When the hostage-taking is part of a political act, in which negotiations may concern the release of prisoners or other concessions, the challenges to the authorities are considerable. The constant problem exists that any concessions may be regarded as political weakness and be seen as just encouraging future kidnappings. In addition, the kidnap itself can have symbolic significance and great propaganda value. Consequently some countries refuse to entertain any consideration of negotiating with kidnappers, whereas others do have a history of conceding to political kidnappers' requests.

Dealing with kidnapping

The negotiation process, of course, requires contact with the kidnappers or their agents, which in itself can be difficult to achieve. The kidnappers want to avoid indicating their location and the negotiators have to be sure that the people claiming to be the hostage-takers really are, because many people may attempt to falsely indicate they are the kidnappers when they're not. The film title *Proof of Life* is based on the demand that any negotiator starts with: that the victim is indeed still alive and under the control of the agents with whom negotiations are taking place.

Prevention is better than cure

Obviously, avoiding hostage situations altogether is the best solution. That requires an understanding and awareness of the circumstances under which someone may be abducted, held hostage or kidnapped. Although not possible in sieges with a domestic background, ransom requests and political kidnappings can be tackled in areas where kidnap is virtually an industry and the procedure is well known. In some countries in South America, for instance, networks exist where one group does the actual kidnapping, before the victims are passed on to a sort of wholesaler who keeps them, while a third group does the ransom negotiation. In such circumstances, anyone who's at risk has to have armed guards and live in protected gated communities.

The negotiation is then a struggle for power in which the negotiator tries to convince the kidnappers that they're in control while moving their decision-making in the negotiator's desired direction. Four strategies for doing this have been identified:

- ✔ **Confirmation:** The negotiator acknowledges that the kidnappers have authority over the hostage and in so doing leads them to feel confident that they have room to manoeuvre. For example, the negotiator may say, 'I know you're determined to follow through on this, but I don't want you to do anything that will make matters worse.'

- ✔ **Authorisation:** This strategy puts the negotiator and the hostage-takers together as part of the same group against a third party, such as the political masters or negotiator's superiors. It builds some sort of relationship between the negotiator and kidnappers and makes the latter aware that they're part of a much bigger picture over which neither may have control. The negotiator may say 'I'd like to get you out of here in a car, but my boss won't allow it.'

- ✔ **Complicating:** The negotiator introduces issues that the kidnappers may not have thought of that undermine their assumptions of what's possible. This approach can loosen their belief in what they can achieve. For instance, the negotiator may point out that when outside with the victim they're pray to snipers or may get snarled up in traffic.

- ✔ **Testing:** The negotiator directly challenges the hostage-takers about what they're threatening so that other ways of seeing themselves can surface. The most direct test of this would be to tell the kidnappers that they're clearly not going to harm the hostage if a peaceful solution can be found.

Tackling criminal street gangs

Crime figures show that most members of delinquent street groups are likely to be involved in crime. These youngsters are more likely to have carried knives or even guns and have taken illegal drugs. Some calculations, particularly from the US, suggest that about 5 per cent of gang members account for 25 per cent of crimes committed by youngsters. All this adds to the need to combat illegal gangs and their activities as a direct form of crime prevention.

Gangs provide a clear social role for young people who feel alienated from their family and those around them. A gang is often said to be a substitute family. But gang membership can be more than that in an area in which territories are marked out by rival groups; it becomes a form of protection. Gangs also give status to individuals through direct membership and by the positions individuals can obtain or aspire to within the group.

Therefore, attempts to reduce the impact of gangs need to take into account the psychology involved, subvert these perceived benefits and provide attractive alternatives. Here are some such approaches:

- Provide exciting positive activities for youngsters to participate in.
- Ensure that schools and associated educational activities are safe.
- Provide mentoring for youngsters so that they can relate to individuals whom they admire and who are achieving significance legally.
- Help parents to understand their role and be more effective in it.

Using psychology against criminal networks

Some criminals are part of networks of contacts. For example, to make illegal drugs available the drugs have to be obtained, smuggled across borders, sold on to middle men who then sell them to individuals who sell them on the street or in pubs. This network may involve dozens or even hundreds of people. Undermining this arrangement requires an understanding of how criminal networks operate, which I explore in this section.

Female gangs

As noted throughout this book, men commit the majority of crimes. But although most street gangs still consist of young men, female gang members also exist and carry out the full range of criminal activities. Make no mistake, female gang members aren't just an adjunct to male gangs and some groups of young women have formed their own independent gangs.

When considering how authorities can combat the activities of illegal, criminal networks, I wondered whether they can perhaps subvert the principles of something called *organisational psychology* (a discipline developed to improve the effectiveness of organisations and the satisfaction of their workforce). Could 100 years of such research into *improving* how organisations productively work together be turned on its head to *undermine* organised criminal enterprises? In other words, surely crime prevention can develop a *destructive organisational psychology*. In this section, I suggest some ideas to base this approach on.

Appreciating the difficulties facing illegal networks

Although films and novels often depict criminal networks as being arranged like legitimate companies, such highly structured criminal groups are very unusual. Even the Mafia and the Triads operate very differently from Coca Cola or Microsoft. The reason is that maintaining and managing a criminal organisation is very difficult, something which destructive organisational psychology can take advantage of. Here are some of the problems of setting up an illegal venture:

- Maintaining secret communications is the most difficult part of keeping an illegal organisation active. Communication requires that people contact each other. It helps if they know who they're contacting, and if everything is to be kept secret for fear of it being discovered, communication becomes extremely open to confusion and misinformation.

- Most legitimate organisations inform the market of their products by some form of advertising, which isn't a good idea if you want to keep the police away! Word of mouth is the only way usually open to criminal networks, and it's slow and prone to misunderstanding.

- As criminal networks grow their problems become greater. Their lines of communication become stretched, making it more difficult for communications and contacts to be controlled, as well as giving increased opportunities for mistakes. Furthermore, a larger organisation is likely to have a higher proportion of individuals on the periphery of the network, and these people may have less commitment to it.

- Larger networks demand more complex organisation. Those trying to lead these networks can be pushed beyond what they can cope with. Also, lieutenants and others in less powerful positions may want more of the action and so challenge the positions of the 'bosses'.

- All these above processes create difficulty in maintaining commitment to the illegal organisation, especially if it can't deliver direct financial benefits. Therefore, a strong tendency exists for criminal groups to keep people involved through violence and coercion.

These challenges are the key to how the authorities can destroy or damage criminal networks.

One of the consequences of the difficulty in maintaining an illegal enterprise is that such criminals are rarely formed into neat organisational hierarchies, such as the police, the army or a major corporation. They're more likely to be a loose network of contacts that constantly changes. In fact, even the Mafia in its heyday consisted of many different 'families' that were constantly in competition with each other, with defections from one group to another and no one able to trust anyone.

Understanding the reality of criminal networks helps to give pointers on how they can be undermined, which I describe in the next section.

Nobbling the leader

You may think that taking out the boss is the obvious way to undermine a criminal network. But organisational psychology analysis of these networks indicates this may not always be as effective as you might think.

The network in Figure 8-1 illustrates why the popular idea that a criminal network can be destroyed by taking out 'Mr Big' may be a delusion. Many illegal networks, whether they be dealing in drugs or trafficking human beings, handling stolen goods or setting up fraudulent banking schemes, are constantly changing in a complex ad hoc arrangement of individuals. Even those involved directly in such team activities as bank robberies or hit-and-run crimes aren't likely to keep the same group for every crime. The various members of the gang change depending on contacts and circumstances.

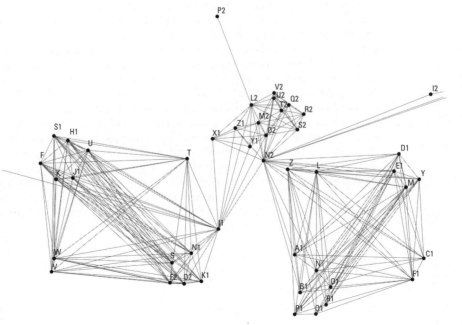

Figure 8-1:
A network of contacts between people involved in staging car accidents to fraudulently claim insurance.

Attacking communication links

The psychological understanding of how groups work (some of which I describe in the earlier section 'Appreciating the difficulties facing illegal networks') can be used to disrupt the activities of organised crime groups. One productive possibility is to gain access to their communication system and use its inherent vulnerability to identify key facts that can lead to investigative actions.

Al-Qaeda was very aware of this possibility and went to great pains to avoid electronic communication that may have given away the location of bin Laden. Nonetheless, to continue to influence his network he had to communicate with his followers. Eventually, one of them used a mobile phone carelessly, enabling the security services to locate the courier and follow him to bin Laden's lair.

Organisational studies show that people on the edge of communication networks may have less commitment to the organisation and be more likely to become dissatisfied with it. Authorities can make use of this insight, because such people may be open to providing information, overtly or inadvertently, that can help law enforcement to undermine the criminals' activities. In addition, criminals often keep people within the crime network through coercion, and so if members feel safe in giving evidence, that can be the key to unravelling the whole illegal organisation.

Getting to the root of the problem

Organised crime can flourish only when it has a home within a community and can't survive without contact with clients or funders: it has to connect to and be part of a group of more or less law-abiding citizens. The psychology of these citizens therefore becomes important. Through fear or ignorance, or an inability to see things happening any other way, the community implicitly or explicitly colludes with the criminals. People in pubs may buy goods that 'fell off the back of a truck'. Pop stars and their fans may buy illegal drugs. Famous footballers may think that forcing themselves sexually on female followers is acceptable, and the victims don't feel able to report the rape. If the local culture accepts illegal activity such as this, it encourages the emergence of organised crime. Therefore, many aspects of organised crime prevention require tackling public awareness of what's being supported by actions that may seem to be only minor violations of the law or not worthy of reporting – for example, making people aware of what's involved in buying diamonds that were illegally obtained or that involved many abuses of human rights to acquire them.

Part III
Measuring the Criminal Mind

The 5th Wave   By Rich Tennant

FORENSIC PSYCHOLOGIST

@RICHTENNANT

In this part . . .

Central to the day-to-day work of many forensic psychologists is the assessment of defendants and offenders. This may be, for example, to see if they are mentally fit enough to stand trial or to determine if there is a high risk of their re-offending if they are let out of prison. Deciding if a person is a psychopath is another example of such assessments. Over the years, a variety of standard procedures, often called psychological tests or instruments, have been developed to ensure the assessments are as objective as possible. To understand what forensic psychologists contribute to assessment, it is useful to understand something of how these measuring instruments are created. In this part, I describe the basics of building psychological assessments and give some examples of what they consist of and the ways in which they are used.

Chapter 9

Measuring, Testing and Assessing the Psychology of Offenders

In This Chapter

▶ Finding out about psychological measurement

▶ Seeing the different forms that assessment can take

▶ Understanding the psychological areas assessed

▶ Hearing how to evaluate psychological assessments

As part of their job, forensic psychologists often need to form a view of someone's psychology – usually a suspect or known offender – and guide that individual directly or advise others on how to deal with the person. Doing so, requires forensic psychologists to be able to assess that individual – for example, the person's ability to understand the legal process well enough to participate effectively, or perhaps diagnosing particular mental or behavioural problems (with the associated implications for how the person should be dealt with and treated).

To accomplish this aim, forensic psychologists use measuring instruments (known generally as 'psychological tests') to assess clients. In this chapter I describe some general psychological test methods, what areas they measure and how to evaluate their effectiveness. The forms of assessment that I consider apply to the general population, but of course are relevant in forensic psychology because criminals are drawn from the general public. (For psychology assessment methods connected specifically to criminals, flip to Chapter 10.)

Introducing Psychological Measurement

People have been exploring ways of assessing psychological characteristics for over 150 years. These efforts produced a variety of psychological *measuring instruments* (assessment procedures, in other words); in essence, standardised processes that have been carefully developed and tested to ensure that they give some consistently useful information. The idea is that trained professionals can use these procedures to come up with more or less the same results. The procedures are hooked into an agreed set of ideas about what's being measured, an agreed theory or set of defined concepts, and how the psychology of the individual is revealed through the use of the particular instruments.

When assessing clients, psychologists use psychological measuring instruments generally known as psychological tests, but more scientifically called *psychometric procedures* (that is, they deal with measurable features). The best known psychological tests are intelligence tests, which assess how a person's intelligence compares with that of people of a similar age, resulting in an *Intelligence Quotient* (IQ). (See the later section 'Standardising psychological tests' for more.)

Loads of other psychological tests exist that can also be of value to legal proceedings, including assessment of various specific intellectual abilities, such as problem solving, educational attainment or particular cognitive skills such as pattern recognition. Some tests are specifically established to diagnose brain damage such as that associated with Alzheimer's. Other tests measure various aspects of personality, such as styles of interpersonal interaction, extraversion or ways of coping with stress.

The central idea behind all psychological assessments is that the result they produce isn't biased by the assessor's particular way of seeing the world; in other words, the result of the assessment must be objective. This requirement is a huge task and not always fully achieved, but the processes of assessment are constructed to be as free from personal bias as possible. After all, if two psychologists assess the IQ or personality of the same individual and come up with totally different answers, no one would have faith that what they're doing is scientific, objective and therefore useful in any way.

In this chapter, I consider general psychological tests because criminals are members of the overall population and understanding them requires knowing what sort of people they are, as it would for anyone else. Therefore, to help offenders and understand more fully their circumstances, it's important to assess their general psychological characteristics. Intelligence level, personality and any indications of mental disorder can all be crucial for determining the nature of a person's involvement in crime as well as how the law courts should treat them, as I discuss in more detail in Chapters 3 and 11.

Getting to Grips with Psychological Measurement Methods

Psychological tests take many different forms and aren't restricted to 'box-ticking' questionnaires. The easiest way to think about the differences between different tests is in terms of what the respondents are asked to do. Are they just answering questions or being asked to complete a task? Is the psychologist listening to what they say or observing what they do? In this section, I describe just a few methods to give you more of an idea of what psychological assessment is like.

Thousands of psychological assessment possibilities exist and many major organisations are devoted to developing and selling them.

In Table 9-1, I give an overview of general psychological assessment procedures. (Procedures developed specifically for use with offenders are discussed in Chapter 10.)

Table 9-1	Summary of Personality Assessment Procedures
Projective procedures (see the later section 'Saying what you see: Projective techniques'):	**Rorschach inkblot test:** Accounts of what's seen in ambiguous images are interpreted to indicate aspects of their subconscious mind.
	Thematic Apperception Test (TAT): Stories told about ambiguous pictures are interpreted to indicate the underlying needs and motivations that characterise a person.
	Szondi test: A curious test in which the respondent indicates which drawing of a face is preferred. The drawings are of people with various mental illnesses and so on. The selection is meant to indicate the testee's mental state. This isn't used much these days, but I mention it because of its novelty.

(continued)

Table 9-1 (continued)

Objective questionnaire style tests (see the later section 'Standardising psychological tests'):	**Minnesota Multiphasic Personality Inventory (MMPI):** A wide-ranging exploration of personality, through answering whether nearly 600 questions are true or false.
	Millon Clinical Mulitaxial Inventory (MCMI): An assessment of mental illness developed using people in psychiatric hospitals who already have diagnoses for mental problems.
	Personality Assessment Inventory (PAI): Consists of 344 questions developed to assess a person's problems in a way that can aid treatment planning; takes about an hour to complete.
Measures of intellect/cognition:	**Wechsler Adult Intelligence Scale (WAIS):** This is the standard test used to measure intelligence. It has gone through many revisions and spawned many variants, including versions for special populations such as children.
	Trail Making Tests A and B: A simple test to administer that assesses how quickly a person can carry out visual tasks such as joining up numbers in sequence; used to diagnose various forms of dementia.
	Luria-Nebraska Neurophysiological Battery: Consists of 269 items (that can take a couple of hours to complete) covering many aspects of brain functioning; used to assess the nature and extent of any brain damage.

Talking with people: Interview protocols

Sometimes the assessment takes the form of talking to the person to be assessed and listening carefully to their account of themselves and their experiences. Such interviews are more than an informal chat although, even if done properly, the experience can feel like that to the person being interviewed. These interviews are usually based on a standard framework that's often called a *protocol*, which can be thought of as a fixed agenda for the meeting with the client.

The protocol varies according to the purpose of the assessment, for example whether the person is being assessed for competence to stand trial or risk of future offending (as I discuss in Chapter 11), but in general the following issues are explored:

- ✔ Early upbringing and family relationships.

- ✔ Education and educational achievement.

- ✔ Personal relationships, especially any intimate relationships.

- ✔ Work experience.

- ✔ Offending history.

- ✔ Any medical or psychiatric history of relevance.

Much of the gleaned information relies on a personal account from the interviewee, which is open to bias and can be self-serving, especially if the answers are directly relevant to the charges against a defendant. The possibility of malingering also exists (something I cover in Chapter 10). The forensic psychologist therefore tries to validate the related information against any available records, such as medical, prison or earlier police reports. In serious cases, the psychologist may also interview the defendant's family and associates. They, of course, function as essential informants if the focus of the interview is deceased (such as when determining the cause of an apparent suicide), a procedure known as a *psychological autopsy* (turn to Chapter 11 for more info on this process).

As well as the verbal answers, the psychologist also carefully observes the way the respondent behaves in the interview, because doing so can reveal something of the person's way of dealing with other people (and offer indicators of deception as I mention in Chapter 5).

The open nature of the interview is open to distortion by an offender wanting to hide personal aspects, or to bias by the interviewer in interpreting what's said. For this reason, many psychologists prefer to use more structured procedures such as the ones I discuss in the following three sections.

Saying what you see: Projective techniques

Projective techniques have their origins in Freudian ideas of the unconscious and consist of presenting ambiguous images for the client to interpret. The idea is that when people interpret such images they 'project' onto it their unconscious desires and feelings, and so reveal aspects of themselves that they may be trying to hide or are even unaware of.

Finding meaning in blots

The Rorschach inkblot test (and no, not everyone sees a butterfly!) has its origins in the parlour game of 'Blotto' that was very popular a hundred years ago. The game consists of giving meaning to indeterminate smudged blots, providing a hilarious evening of entertainment in the days before TV game-shows.

The best known projective test is the Rorschach inkblot test: a standard set of symmetrical smudges, initially produced by folding an inkblot into a piece of paper. Respondents have to describe what they see in the ambiguous image. Some of the blots are monochrome, others coloured. The psychologist carefully records everything that's said. This record is analysed by considering which part of the blot was mentioned, any themes in what the respondent described seeing, and any references to colours or movement in the image.

Another commonly used projective procedure is the Thematic Apperception Test (TAT), in which a set of ambiguous pictures is presented and the respondent is asked to tell a story that each picture illustrates. The pictures may include, for example, a young man sitting on a bed with a woman sitting on the other side of the bed with her back to him, or a young boy on his own with a violin. The themes of the stories created are considered in relation to what they reveal about the needs or desires of the respondent. For example, are the man and woman described as just having had riotous sex, or as a couple who've been married for many years and no longer talk to each other? Is the boy described as aspiring to being a concert soloist or as being sad because he can never afford his own violin?

In all projective techniques, the idea is that respondents reveal something about their unconscious or hidden desires and thoughts through the way they interpret the images. Detailed scoring procedures analyse the responses. A simplified example is that someone describing sex and violence in the images may be thought to be revealing the significance of this aspect in their life. By contrast, a person building an interpretation around future aspirations may be assumed to have a mature and forward-looking approach to life.

Many challenges exist to the scientific value of projective techniques. The problem is that if the test is measuring unconscious aspects of the individuals, that they may not even be aware of themselves, what suitable external criteria can be used against which to test the test? The issues that the tester claims are being revealed may never become manifest because, after all, they're unconscious. An ensuing problem is how anyone can know whether the test is revealing anything other than the tester's speculations about the person being tested.

Even more challenging is deciding what aspects of the answers to use to generate a sense of what the responses mean. When the given response is very open-ended, such as telling a TAT story or interpreting an inkblot, a real possibility exists that different testers (or even the same tester on different occasions) may identify different aspects of the comments as being important. For example, should the tester give emphasis to the specific part of the inkblot that's mentioned (for example, the movement or colour) or focus on the content of the meaning? In addition, with what population or sample should the responses be compared to determine whether they're unusual or significant?

Despite these problems, the Rorschach inkblot test is still very popular and used widely to give court assessments. Psychologists like the idea that an offender can't know what answers are expected and that any extreme attempts to distort the responses may well be detectable. Also, American psychologist John E. Exner claims to have developed a procedure to overcome challenges to the subjective nature of the Rorschach by providing a precise process for interpreting responses that's supported by computing technology. A major weakness in this more precise approach, though, is that not every tester follows it, and so courts may be ignorant of the consequences of such negligence on the part of the tester.

Assessing intelligence and skills through performance

Intelligence tests require respondents to complete a number of tasks, usually examining aspects such as verbal skills, mathematical skills and spatial skills. Their distinct quality is that firm right or wrong answers are involved, and so respondents can be assessed on the number of correct answers they give in each area being tested, in turn allowing the comparison of intelligence across each of the areas. If a great disparity results, perhaps it indicates some neurological problem, disturbances in educational background or other aspect of the person that requires more intensive examination.

Psychologists can use simple forms of intelligence tests to estimate brain damage and intellectual competence. Even discovering whether a person has a clear idea of the date, day and time can be a useful indicator, especially if the test is combined with simple arithmetic tasks such as subtracting, say, seven from a series of numbers.

Short-term memory is also a useful pointer to severe mental problems, and psychologists can test for this problem by mentioning three objects and then asking a few minutes later what they were. Psychologists can also incorporate motor movements into such assessments, such as those that were once used to test how drunk a driver was before 'breathalysers' became common – for example, touching the nose with a finger or grabbing the left ear with the right hand (close your eyes and try these tasks yourself after a few drinks!).

Many psychologists carry with them specially designed blocks of different shapes and colours and other test equipment, such as components of pictures, which are parts of standard testing procedures. These kits have been developed to explore particular aspects of a person's abilities and are often used in conjunction with neurological measurements such as brain scans.

Standardising psychological tests

The most structured and fixed of psychological assessment methods are known as *standardised* tests. The standardisation process consists of having the test completed initially by hundreds of people, sometimes thousands, in order to create a starting point for comparison. Their responses are then analysed in relation to each other and to other external criteria.

The classical illustration is the development of IQ tests. The number of correct answers given by children of each age is calculated, so that any given child can be compared with others of the same age. To make a child's score on the test easily interpretable, the average score for each age group is set at 100, so that a score of 59, as in Daryl Atkins's case that I describe in the nearby sidebar, can be seen as far below average. The statistics allow the precise calculation that less than 1 in 100 of the population has an IQ of 59 or below. A value this low has been found to be typical of people who can't really take advantage of most schooling and are generally regarded as unable to make a lot of sense of what goes on around them. (I talk more about IQs in the later section 'Achieving precision: The need for norms'.)

Standardised measuring instruments provide the backbone to a lot of forensic psychology activity, not least because the courts are more comfortable with a view based on a standard procedure that many professionals agree is appropriate. Tests also provide a standardised framework for describing a person, thus making the preparation of a report much easier than searching afresh for relevant and appropriate terms.

A standardised psychological test widely used in the forensic context, especially in the US, is the Minnesota Multiphasic Personality Inventory (MMPI). This test comes in a number of versions, but the standard form consists of 567 statements which respondents have to decide are true or false as regards themselves. The MMPI takes between 60 and 90 minutes to complete and features statements such as:

- My daily life is full of things that keep me engrossed.
- There often seems to be a lump in my throat.
- I enjoy detective stories.
- Once in a while I think of things too bad to speak about.
- My sex life is pleasing.

ANECDOTE

Taking IQ into account

This case illustrates the highly significant role that a psychological assessment of the defendant can play (whether a person lives or dies), as well as the ethical and professional challenges faced by any psychologist giving evidence in court (expert evidence is given to assist the court in its decision, whether the expert agrees with that decision or not).

In August 1996, Daryl Atkins was sentenced to death in Virginia, USA, for shooting Eric Nesbitt as part of a robbery. Before the death sentence was carried out, a psychologist was required to assess Atkins, and he determined that Atkins had an IQ of 59. This result categorised him as what is known as learning-disabled in the UK. This result was used as the basis for an appeal under the Eighth Amendment to the American Constitution, which disallows punishment that is 'cruel and unusual'. The Supreme Court upheld this appeal and accepted that people with such low IQs aren't mentally sound enough to be executed.

Forensic psychologists then apply a complex and highly developed scoring system to the answers in order to indicate a wider range of potential problems the person may have, including schizophrenia, hypochondria, depression, and the sort of psychopathy (something I describe in Chapter 10) that relates to disrespect for society's rules.

The test also includes measures of whether the respondent is faking good or faking bad, or generally lying, but as with all attempts to tell how honest respondents are being, considerable debate remains about the validity of these measures. The MMPI's detailed range of questions is probably one reason why it's so often used as the basis for forensic evidence despite continuing discussion of its effectiveness.

Identifying the Different Aspects That Measurement Methods Assess

In this section, I look at the different areas of psychological functioning that the methods from the earlier section 'Getting to Grips with Psychological Measurement Methods' typically assess. Most of the methods can investigate all the following areas, but clearly some are better suited than others to certain aspects. The details that follow relate to the general population as well as to offenders, who are after all from the general population! (For a description of assessment methods specifically and directly related to forensic issues, turn to Chapter 10.)

Aptitude tests

Loads of tests are tuned to determining a person's skills and talents. They tend to focus on specific tasks that are relevant to particular jobs, such as making sense of diagrams or having a relevant vocabulary or numeracy skills. They're rarely relevant in forensic settings and so I don't discuss these any further. I suppose they could be of significance in an employment tribunal where a person complained of unfair dismissal, but I've never heard of them being used in that situation.

Thinking ability: Cognitive tests

Mental ability and *cognition* (that is, the ways a person thinks and how effective it is) is such a significant part of human functioning that many tests have been developed to explore different aspects of it. The ubiquitous intelligence test is only one of the many examples of cognitive tests that exist. In general they explore three aspects of intellectual performance:

- ✔ **Attention:** Some forms of mental disturbance can have a direct influence on the ability to attend to specific tasks, or the readiness with which a person can be distracted from concentrating.

- ✔ **Memory:** Many different aspects of memory can be assessed. I discuss the nature of memory in Chapter 4 (because an interview really relies on getting someone to remember), but that tends to be longer-term memory. With some mental conditions, short-term, or immediate memory, can fail, something that gets more common as people get older.

- ✔ **Reasoning:** People's ability to draw logical conclusions from presented information or to formulate reasonable concepts about things is an indication of both their intellectual ability and mental state. These tests can consist, for example, of a set of differently shaped and coloured blocks that have to be assigned to sensible groups. I still remember, as a student, carrying out this test with a person suffering from dementia. All she was able to do was make pictures with them. I don't know how she felt, but it left me traumatised trying to write a report about her.

Discerning a person's personality

In this context *personality* is the enduring aspect of people (and not how charismatic they are or how much 'personality' they have). Personality has been measured for many years by asking people questions about what they like to do and how they act in various situations.

Such assessments can include questions along the lines of 'do other people include you in their activities?', or 'would you rather go to a party or stay at home and read a book?' These questionnaires (often known as *inventories*) are then analysed to determine people's scores on a number of different aspects (called *dimensions*) of their personalities, in order to give a profile of scores across the various dimensions.

In general, most psychologists agree that it's useful to recognise five major aspects of personality, known as the Big Five:

- **Agreeableness:** Kind and warm, sensitive and trusting; being affable and tolerant.

- **Conscientiousness:** Dependable, systematic and punctual; being well-organised and wanting to achieve.

- **Extraversion:** Outgoing and talkative; enjoying social situations.

- **Neuroticism:** Moody and temperamental; anxious and irritable.

- **Openness:** Creative and original of thought; being open to new ideas.

A number of personality questionnaires measure these five dimensions: some are very short and easy to complete and freely available over the Internet. Take a look at www.outofservice.com/bigfive/.

Personality tests can be helpful in many forensic settings because they give you a systematic overview of the person you are dealing with. This can help with treatment or deciding what activities will be helpful to a person as reviewed in Part V.

One major criticism of personality inventories is that they really tell you only what you'd find out from a casual meeting with someone – they reveal what the person wants you to know. To understand people's innermost thoughts and feelings, you'd need to spend more time with them and talk with them more intensively.

Discovering beliefs: Attitude scales

By *attitudes,* psychologists mean people's thoughts, feelings or intended actions towards some person, object or situation. As with so many other areas of psychology, questionnaires are the most frequent way of assessing people's attitudes. Such questionnaires can be developed for specific purposes, such as attitudes towards religion, and also explore belief systems, a common one being the beliefs that people hold about the conditions under which rape occurs, called *rape myths.* So, for example, knowing what a convicted rapist's attitudes are towards the conditions under which rape occurs can be a crucial starting point in helping him to change his behaviour. (Have a look at the whole process of treating sex offenders in Chapter 15 if you want some more details on how this works.)

Over a century ago William James, one of the founders of modern psychology, said, 'Because of its ease of use the questionnaire is the bane of modern society.'

Classifying mental disorders

The classification of mental disorders is fraught with difficulties because they don't line up as distinct diseases like measles or tuberculosis. Therefore, procedures for assessing what mental problems a person has are often used only in combination with a careful clinical interview and information from other sources. However, some major organisations have carried out brave, if somewhat controversial, attempts at the classification of mental disturbances.

Two approaches to classification dominate these considerations:

- ✔ **Diagnostic and Statistical Manual of Mental Disorders,** which is produced and regularly revised by the American Psychiatric Association. Having reached a revised text version of its fourth edition, it's known as DSM-IV-TR. Check out the nearby sidebar 'The five DSM axes of mental disorders' for more details.

- ✔ **International Statistical Classification of Diseases and Related Health Problems: Mental Disorders,** compiled by the World Health Organisation (WHO), and now in its tenth edition and hence known as ICD-10.

These classification schemes are widely drawn on, especially in legal proceedings, when the mental state of a defendant can be a crucial issue to determine, despite their authors being at pains to warn against their use in court. They are, nonetheless, used in this way because they give a framework (or useful shorthand) for typifying bundles of a person's features.

Fitting individuals into the classifications on offer can sometimes feel like packing smoke into boxes. The classifications deal with complex and changing aspects of how people interact with others and live their lives; they don't identify particular bacteria or damage to distinct parts of the brain.

Different questionnaires have been developed to help in the assignment of people to the different diagnostic categories (including the MCMI and PAI ones listed in the earlier Table 9-1).

All the authorities who produced these classification schemes emphasise that the DSM and ICD systems are guidelines that can be used only by clinically trained individuals. They aren't 'cookbooks' to be followed without carefully guided experience. This salutary warning indicates that diagnosis of these mental disorders is more of a craft than an objective scientific procedure.

The five DSM axes of mental disorders

DSM identifies what it calls five 'axes' of mental disorders, each containing descriptions or definitions of particular mental problems. Forensic psychologists most frequently draw on axes I and II:

✔ **Axis I:** These are the disorders that bring people into a mental health clinic, such as major mental problems like schizophrenia, drug addiction and other forms of substance abuse disorders. They also include severe depression, anxiety disorders, bipolar disorder (which used to be called 'manic-depression'). The conditions typically identified in children such as attention deficit hyperactivity disorder (ADHD) and autism spectrum disorders are axis I as well. Eating disorders, notably anorexia nervosa and bulimia nervosa also belong in this axis.

✔ **Axis II:** These are the aspects of personality and intellectual disabilities. This includes being paranoid, schizoid and the other personality disorders that I consider in Chapter 10.

✔ **Axis III:** Acute medical conditions and physical disorders.

✔ **Axis IV:** Psychosocial and environmental factors that contribute to the disorder.

✔ **Axis V:** Global assessment of functioning, which includes how the person copes with the challenges of daily life.

Testing the Tests

Obviously, experts need to know how effective the different psychological tests are, because they vary enormously. To this end, a number of characteristics of tests have been identified that give an indication of their qualities. Understanding a test's good and bad points is essential because it helps you to evaluate how valuable a test is likely to be and what weight you can put on its results.

Imagine a ruler that's made out of very flexible elastic for measuring length, which gives you a different result every time you use it for measuring the same piece of metal – that's not a measuring tool you're going to trust again.

Aiming for test reliability

The most basic quality any assessment instrument must have is a high degree of reliability.

Reliability is the likelihood that carrying out the same test under very similar conditions, on more than one occasion, gives the same results.

The establishment of reliability is more difficult for psychological measurements than for measures of physical objects, but broadly the same process is used – the test is given under similar conditions to the same people on different occasions to see how close the measurements are to each other. Of course people change more than a lump of wood does and they may even learn something from carrying out the test the first time; and so various ways around this have been devised, such as having two very similar tests administered at the same time.

In general, perfect reliability is never expected. A measure that varies between 0.0 and 1.0 is used to assess reliability. Anything above 0.9 is regarded as excellent, but tests that achieve around 0.8 are in common use, even reliabilities as low as 0.6 aren't unusual.

Evaluating a test's validity

A test can be very reliable and produce consistent results (see the preceding section) and yet still not really measure what it claims to measure. For example, a thermometer gives you a reliable measure of temperature, but isn't very accurate if you used it to measure altitude! The problem with testing psychological characteristics is that (unlike physical objects) determining what you're actually measuring isn't easy. A measure that claims to be assessing how authoritarian people are, for example, may just be measuring their conventionality.

The degree to which a test measures what it claims to measure is known as its *validity*.

You can evaluate a test's validity in two broad ways. One is the simple process of seeing what it does, called *face validity*. If the test asks questions that can be right or wrong, it's measuring intelligence or some aspect of general knowledge. If it asks about your feelings towards religion, it's measuring attitudes towards religion. If it asks about your drinking habits, it's probably picking up something relevant to alcoholism.

But face validity can be misleading. For example, measuring instruments that look as if they're of great relevance to criminality can turn out to be quite invalid. An interesting illustration of this problem is that many people assume that a lack of sophistication in moral reasoning is the hallmark of a criminal, but until this is proven this belief is merely a hypothesis. Many tests show that criminals can have their own moral perspective, which you may not share, but it's not necessarily less sophisticated than yours.

Therefore, a second way to evaluate a test's validity is known as *construct validity*. What ideas or 'constructs' is the test claiming to measure? This can be examined by comparing results using it with results from associated procedures that have similar constructs. For example, intelligence tests are supposed to give some indication of how well a person does at school or college, and so the results can be compared with examination marks. A perfect relationship isn't expected because many other things can interfere with how well you do at school besides your intelligence, but at least some reasonable relationship indicates whether the test does what it says on the tin. An IQ test wouldn't be of academic interest, if the scores people obtained on it didn't relate reasonably closely to a person's educational achievements.

To take a more extreme example, if serial criminals didn't on average have higher psychopathy scores than people who lead blameless lives, you wouldn't take the measure of psychopathy (that I describe in Chapter 10) very seriously.

Measuring validity by comparison with other assessments is a bit of a chicken and egg problem. In the early stages of the development of a test, its relationship to other measures raises questions about its additional value. Only over time, as the test becomes more widely used, does a history of associations build up to show its utility in a variety of different situations.

The tests listed in the earlier Table 9-1 (with the exception of the peculiar Szondi test) have been used over many years in many different situations. Consequently, plenty of examples exist of how useful they've been as well as illustrations of what they assess beyond the face validity of the test items themselves.

Standing up over time: Test robustness

Although you don't find test robustness listed in textbooks on psychological tests, I think that it's the attribute that leads to tests being used instead of being left on the shelf. By *test robustness,* I mean how easy they are to use and how difficult to misuse. Can they really stand up to being used in many different situations by many hundreds of different sorts of people without the results being compromised?

Although thousands of psychological tests have been developed over the last century or more, relatively few are in very wide use. These tests have demonstrated reliability, validity and robustness and are the ones that people have found most useful.

Achieving precision: The need for norms

Achieving precision in something as subjective and fluid as a person's psychology is clearly problematic. With, for example, temperature, you can define fixed points for the benchmarks of measurement, such as when water freezes or boils. Variations have obvious meanings and have well understood implications. But how do you weigh how intelligent, extrovert or psychotic a person is? Faced with these questions, psychologists came up with a deceptively simple answer – compare the person's results on the test with others in the relevant population.

The distribution of scores achieved on a test by a population of people who've taken it's called the *norms* for a test.

This process of comparing an individual's scores with norms is what makes these measuring instruments different from the sorts of informal questionnaires found in magazines, where journalists create arbitrary score values and give interpretations. The use of norms also distinguishes these measuring instruments from public opinion polls in which the interest is solely in the proportion of a given population who agree with a specified opinion.

The determination of the norms for a test, and the establishment of how scores vary from the average for a particular population, is known as the *standardisation* of a test. I describe this aspect in more detail in the earlier section 'Standardising psychological tests', where I illustrate how IQ norms were used in the defence of Daryl Atkins. IQ measures are a good example of standardised psychological tests because they're so highly developed and widely used. Indeed, many of the principles of their use, especially the calibration of scores by comparison with norms, are applied to many other forms of psychological measurement.

To understand the applicability and utility of any psychological measurement, therefore, you need to know what norms are being used to calibrate it. Unlike IQ measures, some tests aren't calibrated against the average for a relevant population but by comparison with one or more subgroups. This comparison may be done, for example, by establishing the scores that people diagnosed with particular mental illnesses get, or people who've done well in particular jobs. Those comparison scores provide benchmarks for assessing other people.

The appropriateness of a given test's norms and how well their validity is established is a crucial aspect of their value. In particular, norms may not be appropriate in places different from where the test was originally developed. For instance, an indicator of psychopathy developed in the USA may have little value in countries with very different cultures, such as India, Nigeria, or Russia. Until the test is translated and standardised in those different contexts, its use may be counterproductive.

Creating and Giving Psychological Tests

Not just anyone can invent a psychological test or administer it. Creating such measuring instruments isn't the same as a journalist thinking up questions for a magazine to indicate 'how good you are in bed'! Nor are psychological tests like opinion poll surveys in which you're asked a single question such as, 'Would you vote for the president if he stood again?' from which percentages across representative samples are used to test the public mood.

Anyone giving a psychological test has to know something about how it was developed and how the results can be interpreted. The test has to be given under special conditions that relate to its intended use and the background to the test. A major industry is involved in creating tests and standardising them, and then setting up training courses for people who want to use the tests.

Very broadly, three categories of test exist that determine who can administer them:

✓ Tests that can be used by anyone with a little background knowledge, such as general attitude surveys.

✓ Tests that require some university qualification in psychology, such as general personality measures.

✓ Tests that require specific training in their use and application. All the tests listed in the earlier Table 9-1 are of this kind. Some tests may require intensive training over many months, whereas others may require only a few days training.

For important tests that require considerable expertise, people have to achieve a special licence to be allowed to administer them, which is usually awarded when certain standards are achieved on the training course. For these tests people are only allowed to administer them if they have an up-to-date certificate.

Training in the application and administration of a psychological assessment, at the very least covers the following points

✓ **Choosing the appropriate test for the purpose at hand:** This requires an understanding of any psychological theory that underpins the test and the situations in which it has been used that reveal its validity.

✓ **Understanding how to administer the test:** Often very specific procedures apply that the tester is required to carry out for the test to maintain its reliability and validity.

✔ **Knowing how to score the test:** The way in which answers are combined to derive scores may not be a simple addition, but different answers may get different weights in various ways. So the training explains how this is done, including the different aspects of the test that can be derived separately. For instance, in the intelligence test respondents may get different scores for verbal, numerical and spatial intelligence.

✔ **Writing reports:** How the report of the test should be prepared and what headings are to be distinct for each test.

✔ **Recognising the sorts of ethical and professional issues,** such as those I describe in Chapter 17, which include abiding by aspects of confidentiality and how and what the person being assessed should be told.

Chapter 10

Diagnosing Evil: Measuring the Criminal Mind

. . . .

In This Chapter

▶ Addressing the difficulties of assessing an offender's psychology

▶ Assessing psychopathy

▶ Determining the risk of future offending

. . . .

*O*ver the years, psychologists have developed many assessment methods specifically to describe the psychology of offenders. Most commonly, these procedures assess the risk of the individual committing another crime in the near or distant future. Other tests have been developed to explore the sexual attitudes and preferences of an individual, or an offender's competency to understand the trial process. But dealing with offenders is a difficult area.

Forensic psychologists nearly always use these procedures alongside an in-depth interview. The tests provide a way to describe important psychological aspects of a criminal and compare those characteristics with other known offenders and the population at large. Also, these tests are of value in looking back to the original offence and helping to understand those aspects of the person that contributed to the crime occurring. The results of these assessment procedures can therefore be of great significance in the life of offenders.

Uncovering Possible Malingering

One of the crucial challenges when assessing an offender, which isn't usually a concern with other people, is whether the person is telling the truth. This may be lying about the events surrounding the crime that I discuss in Chapter 5, but in this section, I consider the use of psychological tests in discerning whether an offender is lying about his mental state.

The use of the polygraph and other aspects of lie detection that I discuss in Chapter 5 are relevant to many aspects of crime, especially in determining whether offenders' reports of their actions are truthful, but a quite different set of requirements emerges when a suspect claims to have some sort of mental disturbance.

As I mention in Chapter 1, one strand of forensic psychology grew out of the defence that a person was so mentally disturbed that he didn't understand what he was doing or that it was wrong. As lawyers put it, the defendant didn't have *mens rea*. Therefore, a strong defence can be that a person was, in common language, 'mad' or 'insane' (although as I discuss in Chapter 11 the law does not define insanity the way common language does) at the time he carried out the criminal actions, which clearly gives an incentive for criminals to malinger.

Malingering is a way of giving information that deliberately fabricates or grossly exaggerates symptoms. Malingerers may also feign symptoms, whether physical, such as a limp, or psychological, such as pretending to hear voices.

Defendants often think that they can have the trial postponed or stopped altogether if they're thought to be mentally ill, or at the very least receive a shorter sentence. Malingering isn't limited to criminal cases. A person claiming compensation for injuries resulting from a car accident or an incident at work – especially when these injuries are difficult to observe as in a psychological disorder – may also be motivated to exaggerate or fake symptoms.

As a consequence, any assessment of mental state needs to take account of the possibility that a mental illness is being invented or faked in some way. Forensic psychologists often use special procedures to establish how honest any claims of mental illness may be. The most common such method is an intensive clinical interview. In this, the person is asked in a relaxed atmosphere to talk about his life and any mental issues that have affected him. The interviewer isn't only listening carefully to the content of what's being said, but also to the way in which the account is being given. Some indications of possible malingering are:

- Dramatic or exaggerated presentation of the experiences or symptoms.
- Overly careful or deliberate recounting of what has happened.
- Inconsistency in what's described compared with what's known about the claimed psychological problems.
- Reporting only well-known aspects of a recognised psychological syndrome, such as hearing voices.

ANECDOTE

Malingering goes to Hollywood

One exotic illustration of how a criminal can mislead experts about his mental state is the case of the malingering Kenneth Bianchi, who pretended to have 'multiple personalities' (Chapter 11 has more details). And because Hollywood loves a battle of wits between a clever criminal and a psychologist, a movie was based on the case called *Primal Fear,* in which Richard Gear plays the hoodwinked attorney just as Bianchi initially fooled psychiatrists.

You can't use these aspects definitively to determine malingering, but they can be an indication that a more systematic examination is necessary using standardised tests (which I define in Chapter 9).

Evaluating reported symptoms

One of the most highly regarded standardised procedures for assessing malingering is the Structured Interview of Reported Symptoms (SIRS). The latest version has 172 items and takes about half an hour to complete. Some of the questions are subtly repeated to check consistency in responses. The following issues illustrate some aspects of how the SIRS procedure works:

- ✔ If rare symptoms are described that are known to occur in less than one out of every ten patients, the tester's suspicions are aroused. Claims about a lot of these rare symptoms are a useful indicator of some sort of malingering.

- ✔ Claiming a large number of symptoms has to be treated with caution. Severely mentally ill patients typically have rather few symptoms and malingerers tend to over-egg the pudding.

- ✔ If an offender claims a lot of well known 'obvious' symptoms but few less obvious ones, the tester may suspect malingering.

- ✔ The claim of really odd, very unlikely, symptoms is also a pointer to faking. Preposterous symptoms are extremely rare and if a person claims to have a lot of them, the tester will question the individual's honesty.

- ✔ The tester carefully examines whether the reported symptoms are consistent with each other and with observations available from other people. For example, someone claiming to be very depressed who has a healthy appetite may well be faking, as is a person claiming he's suffering from tremors that no one has ever seen.

Testing memory

Memories are highly malleable and subject to being distorted. One understandable problem, therefore, is determining whether someone genuinely believes the memories even if the events didn't happen (as I describe in Chapter 4). A different problem arises, however, when a suspect claims not to remember what happened. Such amnesia or other forms of memory loss may be relevant to claims of brain injury or the inability to give an account of what happened in a crime for which the person is accused.

Various procedures have been developed to assess memory impairment. One of the most widely used is the Test of Memory Malingering (TOMM). This test was developed by comparing how people with known brain injuries perform against what's typical of responses from the population at large. The person with an unusually low score, but a pattern of responses that doesn't relate to known brain injuries, may be thought to be feigning the memory problems.

This clever test appears to be an ordinary test of memory that seems more difficult than it actually is. So it has the paradoxical benefit that if the person being tested gets an exceedingly low score, the individual's likely to be trying to pull the wool. But someone who gets a high score also doesn't have the claimed memory problem. Getting the appropriate score and pattern of answers that do relate to genuine memory problems is difficult to feign without knowing the inner workings of the test.

Exploring Cognitive Distortions, Justifications and Sexual Deviance

One of the challenging features of many offenders, is that they see other people and their own actions in distorted and sometimes warped ways. Their thoughts don't follow a logic that non-offenders would think appropriate (as I discuss in Chapter 2).

A particularly challenging group of criminals in this regard are those convicted of sexual offences, whether the crime is the abuse of children, rape or other criminal sexual activities. These criminals' activities and experiences are caught up with particular ways of thinking about sex, including the sort of sometimes bizarre fantasies they have (that can shape their desires) and how they justify their actions. A child molester, for example, may claim that his 4-year-old victim wore suggestive clothing and so seduced him, or that because his wife wouldn't accept his sexual advances, raping his daughter was acceptable.

Such individuals tend to think about their offending in ways that the great majority of people would think was very odd and irrational. These cognitive distortions contribute to them justifying the crime to themselves and anyone else who asks them about it. They don't think of what they've done as wrong. Their justifications shape their criminal activity. Therefore, psychologists developed special procedures to explore these aspects of offenders' thoughts and attitudes. These tests allow the clinician to develop a profile of the offender's sexual orientation and psychology that's of value in developing treatment programmes (as I discuss in Chapter 15), and predicting whether the individual is likely to continue to be dangerous to other people. In some cases these assessments can be used in court to form a view of the accused and the nature of their crime, as in the later sidebar 'Psychosexual tests in action'.

One widely used assessment of a person's psychosexual characteristics is the Multiphasic Sex Inventory, which consists of 300 questions describing aspects of a person. Respondents have to indicate whether the questions are true or false for themselves. The test takes about an hour and a half to complete and is analysed under a number of different headings that provide the profile of scores. These analysed areas include:

- The person's normal sex drives and interests, to determine whether the respondent is telling the truth or trying to present what sounds like normal behaviour – in other words, what the respondent believes the tester thinks is acceptable.

- An obsession with sex, giving it a prominence that goes beyond normal adult interest.

- Any attempt to deny involvement in illegal sexual activity, or an unwillingness to accept that certain sexual behaviours are inappropriate.

- Any justifications that may be offered for sexual offending, including minimising the seriousness of an offence or its consequences for the victim.

- Any sexual fantasies and the role they play in the offender's actions, including the exploration of the stages an offender may go through from fantasy to justification, and then on to planning and carrying out the assault.

- Any *paraphilias,* which are unusual objects or situations that cause sexual arousal, such a shoe-fetish, bondage, making obscene phone calls or voyeurism.

- Any sexual dysfunction, such as physical disabilities, impotence or premature ejaculation.

- Any knowledge and beliefs about sexual matters.

ANECDOTE

Psychosexual tests in action

A 20-year-old man was accused of raping and killing a young woman he'd met at a nightclub and taken back to her house. The police called in an FBI agent to comment on whether the assault was part of a sexually deviant fantasy. The agent looked at the crime scene photographs and autopsy report and said that the killing was sexually sadistic: in other words, the offender had got sexual excitement from the killing. This assessment implied that the offender was extremely dangerous. In the particular jurisdiction the person would have had to spend perhaps 12 years in prison if found guilty of murder but much longer, twenty or thirty years, if the killing was thought to be part of sexually sadistic fantasies. Indeed, he may have been regarded as so dangerous that he would never be let out of prison.

I was called in by the defence to establish whether the individual was a deviant, sexually sadistic person. I interviewed him carefully, exploring his life history and giving him a standardised test of his sexual fantasies. From the results, I formed the view that he came from a background in which outbursts of violence were to be expected, but that he had no deviant sexual fantasies or experiences. Therefore, I argued that the FBI report was mistaken and the offender wasn't a sexual killer. On the basis of my report, the prosecution withdrew the FBI report from the court and the defendant admitted to the murder. He was given a life sentence, which meant he would spend a minimum of ten years in prison.

Examining the Inability to Relate: Psychopathy

A crucial aspect of assessing the psychology of offenders connects to their personality, that is, their enduring characteristics and the broad way in which they relate to other people and deal with the world. (Flip to Chapter 9 for a fuller discussion on personality.)

REMEMBER

Some people's personality is so unusual that they're regarded as being 'disordered' in some way (which is different from the person having a mental illness). Of course, not all such people necessarily commit crimes. They may just be regarded as strange and perhaps quite distressed about why, as they see it, other people don't relate to them effectively.

The nearby sidebar 'Some personality disorders as listed in DSM' contains a few labels given to different types of personality disorders in the Diagnostic and Statistical Manual (DSM) of the American Psychiatric Association (which I describe in more detail in Chapter 9).

The type of personality disorder particularly relevant to criminality, and which has found its way into popular discourse and court use, is *psychopathic disorder* or *psychopathy*. People with this label are lucid and coherent with no signs of any learning disability or psychotic symptoms. Some of them can be superficially charming and are intelligent enough to be very plausible on first acquaintance. They don't hear voices or think that they're commanded by forces beyond their power. Yet over and over again, they abuse people, lie without any compunction or remorse, can be unpredictably violent and seem unable to relate effectively to others over any extended period.

Labels such as psychopath, psychopathy and antisocial personality disorder aren't medical diagnoses that can be linked to a bacterium or even a very specific brain disorder – they're summary descriptions of the person in question. Some experts have even commented that these labels are moral judgements masquerading as medical explanations. The labels 'personality disorder' and 'psychopath' are useful as condensed descriptions of some rather difficult, and often nasty, people.

Getting to grips with psychopathy

Instead of requiring the offender to fill in a questionnaire, psychologists use checklists when assessing a person's level of *psychopathy* for the reason that a psychopath can be expected to lie. In addition, the person is interviewed and his associates also questioned, so that a number of pointers can be indicated on the special checklist in section 'The psychopathy checklist' later in this chapter. The scores the person gets are then used to decide whether an individual is a psychopath or not.

Some personality disorders as listed in DSM

Here are just some of the personality disorders that DSM specifies:

- **Paranoid:** Sees other people as generally demeaning and threatening and untrustworthy.

- **Schizoid:** Solitary, indifferent to others; limited emotional expression or experiences.

- **Borderline:** Rapid mood changes, intense anger, impulsive, self-mutilations; fears abandonment.

- **Histrionic:** Great excess of emotional reactions, although often superficial; seeks attention.

- **Narcissistic:** Extremely self-important, feels entitled to admiration from others; very upset when criticised.

- **Antisocial:** Displays irresponsibility and behaviour disorders, at least from the age of 15, including fights, defaulting on debts, recklessness and lack of remorse.

Various forms of criminality often reflect an aspect of psychopathic individuals' lifestyles. If they commit crimes they understand what they're doing and that it's illegal. But these same aspects of their personality have been cited in court to claim that, although not mentally ill, they are mentally disturbed and that this should be taken into account during any legal proceedings.

The term *psychopath* itself is hotly debated. It is not part of any formal list of medical diagnoses. The DSM that I discuss in Chapter 9 prefers the term *anti-social personality disorder.* In the US some people prefer to talk about *sociopaths.* But it's such a useful way of summarising particular bundles of characteristics that clinicians still like to use it, drawing on the psychopathy checklist that you can jump to later in the chapter.

The term *psychopathic disorder* isn't a medical diagnosis, but a legal term under English and Welsh law that refers to a 'persistent disorder or disability of the mind', not that far removed from the McNaughton rule that first emerged over 150 years ago and which I discuss in Chapter 1. Thus, some debate exists as to which of the psychiatric diagnoses of personality disorder listed in the earlier sidebar 'Some personality disorders as listed in DSM' are closest to the legal definition of psychopathic disorder, and whether any of them relates to the popular conception of a psychopath.

After you've met someone who you know has committed horrific violent crimes, and yet can be charming and helpful, continuing to believe in the Hollywood stereotype of the psychopath (that I describe in the nearby sidebar 'Beyond the Hollywood stereotypes') becomes difficult. Without doubt, though, some people seem pleasant and plausible in one situation but can quickly turn to viciousness, and some people can never connect with others and are constantly, from an early age, at war with those with whom they come into contact.

Not all psychopaths end up as vicious criminals. Some experienced businessmen and politicians would probably get a diagnosis of psychopath if they were clinically assessed. For example, Bernard Madoff who defrauded thousands of investors out of billions of dollars had many of the characteristics of the Type 1 psychopath as listed later in this chapter.

The psychopathy checklist

The many ideas surrounding the notion of the 'psychopath' led Robert Hare to develop a standard checklist that can be used to measure the degree to which a person exhibits psychopathic traits. It consists of 20 items that can be given a score of 0 if they don't exist and a score of 2 if they do, with a score of 1 for the possibility that they exist. These scores are then added up. In general a score higher than 30 is taken to indicate a full-blown psychopath.

Beyond the Hollywood stereotypes

The Hollywood psychopath is inevitably a merciless serial killer, often some sort of cross between Dracula and Frankenstein's monster! Films from the silent 1920s cinema, such as *The Cabinet of Dr Caligari* to the more recent *Kalifornia* and *No Country for Old Men*, never really provide any psychological insights into the actions of the monsters who are the anti-heroes of their dramas – they're presented as pure evil. The rather more psychologically interesting films such as *Psycho* or *The Boston Strangler* do provide explanations for the nastiness of their villains (drawn from a simplistic use of the outdated theories of Sigmund Freud), but still present their anti-heroes as alien individuals who can appear unthreatening but deep down are malevolent.

A further refinement is that two different styles of psychopath can be identified from the scores:

- ✔ **Type 1 psychopaths:** These people have superficial charm, but are pathological liars, callous, remorseless and manipulative. The clearest fictional example of this sort of psychopath is Tom Ripley, who has the central role in many of Patricia Highsmith's amoral novels.

- ✔ **Type 2 psychopaths:** These people are more obviously criminal, impulsive and irresponsible, with a history of juvenile delinquency, antisocial tendencies, early behavioural problems and whose lives are chronically unstable.

These types are captured in the following items in Hare's checklist:

- ✔ **Selfish, callous psychopathy (Type 1):**
  - Glibly, but superficially, charming
  - Grandiose feeling of self-importance
  - Pathological liar – lies even when no need to exists
  - Manipulates others; cunning
  - Lacks remorse or any feelings of guilt
  - Doesn't really feel strongly about anything
  - Lacks empathy
  - Doesn't accept responsibility for own actions

✔ **Deviant psychopathy (Type 2):**

- Easily bored, needs excitement
- Feeds off other people
- No realistic, long-term goals
- Impulsive
- Irresponsible
- Lack of control over actions
- Behavioural problems in childhood
- Juvenile delinquency
- Different types of offending
- Abuses any conditions set by the courts

Perhaps not surprisingly, both styles of psychopathy are also related to:

✔ Promiscuous sexual behaviour

✔ Many short-term relationships

Assessing the Risk of Future Offending

A vital area of forensic psychological assessment is the determination of how likely a person is to re-offend and whether he's likely to be violent in the near or distant future. This form of assessment is very common when deciding the court's sentence and whether, after undergoing some sort of treatment, a person should be allowed back into the community. This process is called *risk assessment* and relates to the risk that a person may be a danger to themselves or other people.

Dangerousness covers everything from the possibility of attempting suicide to being abusive to a neighbour. A high probability exists that many offenders will continue to offend, but that isn't a reason under most legal systems for keeping them locked up. The issue in risk assessment is whether any indications exist that the person will be seriously dangerous.

Predicting the risk of future offending is, well, risky. The process can never be foolproof for the simple reason that predicting what a person may experience and the unfolding circumstances of their future life is impossible.

Forensic psychologists usually take into account three general aspects when predicting the risk of an offender's future dangerousness:

- **Dynamic factors:** Those characteristics of the individual that can, potentially, be changed through experience or direct intervention, including the person's attitudes and compliance with treatment, his views of his crimes and indicators of mental illness.

- **Static factors:** These are a person's aspects that aren't open to change, including previous history of violence, age and ethnicity, previous relationships and education and employment experience.

- **Protective factors:** Some aspects of a person and his circumstances can reduce the risk of future violence, including a supportive social network, a feeling of responsibility for a family, or a satisfying job.

Appraising sexual violence risk

A number of standardised procedures have been developed for use in assessing the risk of future violence, especially of further sexual offending. A well-known instrument is the Structured Assessment of Risk and Need (SARN). In addition to evaluating static and dynamic factors (see the preceding section), it also examines issues relevant to formulating treatment programmes for individuals. The SARN covers the following issues:

- **Sexual interests:**

  - Pre-occupation with sex and related activities.

  - Sexual preferences for children and pre-pubescent individuals over adults.

  - Sexual violence – preference for coerced rather than consensual sex.

  - Sexual deviance of relevance – other aspects of original offences that were socially deviant.

- **Distorted attitudes:**

  - Regarding male dominance as a significant part of sexual relations.

  - The man's entitlement to sexual activity as he desires it.

  - Minimising the seriousness of sexual activity with children.

  - Justification of rape.

  - Viewing women as corrupting or exploitive.

✔ **Social and emotional aspects:**

- Feeling lonely and inadequate.

- Preferring emotional intimacy with children.

- Suspicious, angry and vengeful.

- Lack of intimate relationships as an adult.

✔ **Self-management:**

- Impulsive and irresponsible.

- Difficulty in dealing with challenges.

- Uncontrolled outbursts of emotion.

Women, of course, can also have distorted attitudes and beliefs about sexuality and violence, but the great majority of assessments in these are carried out with men.

Many of the aspects that are evaluated in the SARN reflect aspects of personality disorder that are also explored in other protocols. The main difference from assessing a person using the SARN and, for example, Hare's Psychopathy Checklist (that I describe in the earlier section 'Using the psychopathy checklist'), is that the checklist assigns a person to a particular *personality type,* whereas the SARN gives a profile of the psychology of the individual in various areas of his functioning. By combining this with what is known about the person and his circumstances, forensic psychologists can make predictions of future risk and the appropriate forms of treatment.

Working with the young: Juvenile Sexual Offender Protocol

Youngsters who become involved in violence and especially sexual assaults pose a particular risk-assessment challenge for the authorities. They may not be regarded as having *mens rea* (knowing what they're doing) and so the law may not allow them to be imprisoned as a form of punishment, but instead recommends treatment. Although greater potential may exist for successfully treating juveniles than for adults who are already set in their ways, research has established that young people who find their way into any form of illegal activity have an increased risk of drifting into a life of crime (and so present a risk to the public). For this reason, any successful interventions early in an offender's development can be of great significance.

Forensic psychologists have given a lot of attention to assessing the nature of the risk of re-offending by juveniles. A typical example of a number of developed procedures is the Juvenile Sex Offender Assessment Protocol (J-SOAP), which is designed for use with 12 to 18-year-olds. It draws on as much objective information as possible, so that the personal, subjective judgement of the assessor is kept to a minimum.

J-SOAP covers the four following crucial aspects of the offender:

- **Adjustment in the community:** These are the protective factors that I discuss earlier in this section, including the stability of the current living situation and experience of schooling. Other positive support systems are also of relevance.

- **Antisocial activity:** This focuses on what I refer to as static factors earlier in this section: the variety of offences for which the offender was arrested before the age of 16, but also the inconsistency of experience of caregivers.

- **Effects of intervention:** An exploration of any lack of empathy for victims or remorse for crimes is considered in relation to any treatment the offender may have received. This aspect relates to the possibility of the personality disorder of psychopathy that I discuss in the earlier section 'Examining the Inability to Relate: Psychopathy'.

- **Sexual offence history:** This includes the number of offences for which the youngster has been convicted, including the extent to which he has himself been a victim. His preoccupation with sexual activity is also assessed.

Part IV
Viewing Psychology in Court

"As a forensic psychologist, it's my opinion that the defendant is not a risk to the public. Any more passive-aggressive questions?"

In this part . . .

Forensic psychology started off as a service to the courts around the 1900s. That is still a central part of the area, although probably more forensic psychologists these days work in other settings. As in other areas their contribution to the legal process has broadened out. What started as assessment of defendants to determine if they had the mental capability to deal with the legal process, has reached out into considerations of jury selection (most notably in the US) and advising attorneys on how to ask questions. Many of these contributions to the work of the courts raises challenging issues about what is the appropriate due process, and whether psychologists are over-stepping the mark by these contributions. By getting a fuller understanding of these issues in this part, you will be in a better position to join in this important debate.

Chapter 11

Giving Guidance in Legal Proceedings

As I mention in Chapter 1, the 'forensic' part of forensic psychology indicates a professional activity that provides guidance to the courts. So, although the current reach of forensic psychologists extends well beyond the courts into many secure settings such as prisons, a common activity is offering guidance to legal proceedings. Traditionally, this activity started with comments on the reliability of testimony (often dealing with the erratic nature of memory that I explore in Chapter 4), but it soon blossomed to include comments on the mental state of defendants.

Some forensic psychologists become associated with particular points of view and consequently offer opinions solely for the prosecution or for the defence. However, as in all other areas of expert evidence, the legal process forces the development of standard procedures in order to reach conclusions. Over time, frequently challenged evidence disappears from the courts and accepted procedures become better established.

In this chapter, I explore some of these standard procedures, including: issues of competency; what constitutes insanity in criminal cases; what to do about people after they're convicted (especially assessing how dangerous they're likely to be); how to form an opinion about someone's mental state at the time of their death after the death; and ways in which forensic psyhcologists can contribute to civil court cases.

Come on in!

Although psychologists had been popping up in courts around the world for over 100 years, only in 1962 did a US court formally accept that a psychologist (that is, someone without medical training, as opposed to a psychiatrist – I explain the differences between these professions in detail in Chapter 1) could testify about mental health issues. This decision rectified a situation in which many formal assessments about mental health were made by psychologists trained in the use of the tests outlined in Chapter 9, rather than medical doctors or psychiatrists. A psychiatrist or medical doctor then reported these procedures in court. It makes much more sense for the person who gave the test to report on the results than someone else doing it second hand.

Assessing Insanity Pleas in Court

Forensic psychologists may be called as expert court witnesses to provide testimony concerning a defendant's claim of insanity. Other professionals, especially psychiatrists are likely to be called as well. Whether it's a psychiatrist or a psychologist will vary from place to place, depending sometimes on who happens to be available.

Forensic psychologists face certain particular problems when giving evidence in court arising from the fact that they're assessing a person rather than an object. Crucially, as a court expert, the forensic psychologist is a privileged witness who's allowed to offer an opinion rather than just the facts as he knows them.

Legal casebooks are full of defendants who exhibit the most bizarre behaviour even when giving evidence in court (behaviour that most people would agree indicates that they're obviously mad) but who are still found guilty and whom the courts don't classify as insane. I touch on this subject briefly in Chapter 2, but because it's the starting point for a lot of forensic psychology advice to the courts, I examine the issue more closely in this section.

Forensic psychologists may be required to provide some sort of psychological assessment of the defendant at three broad stages in the legal process:

✔ **Before the trial,** when issues of the person's competence to stand trial are considered.

✔ **During the trial,** when the issue of the defendant's mental state at the time of the crime may be significant.

✔ **Prior to sentencing,** when the convicted person's likelihood of changing, and particularly how dangerous he is, can be crucial to determining what form of sentencing is applied.

A court of law isn't really interested in whether a person charged with murder, robbery, arson or any other crime thinks that he's Napoleon, that computer hackers are controlling his mind or that he has to rid the planet of aliens masquerading as traffic wardens. The concern of the legal system is whether the person had 'a guilty mind', or to use the Latin phrase that I introduce in Chapter 1, *mens rea*. In other words, did the defendant know at the time he committed the crime that what he was doing was wrong; did he know that he was doing it; and did he have voluntary control over his actions. If he didn't, he can offer the court the 'insanity defence': the plea of 'not guilty by reason of insanity'. Establishing this in reality, however, turns out to be a lot trickier than you may expect.

Contrary to popular belief, people claiming that they're not guilty by reason of insanity is extremely rare. Only about 1 in 100 serious cases in the US involve a person making this plea, and on average just 1 in 4 of those are successful.

Claiming diminished responsibility

Many people have tried to define insanity in legally acceptable ways. In fact, a sign of a civilised society is that it doesn't want to find a person guilty only on what he did but also based on his intentions. But probing into anyone's mind is extremely difficult and doing so in a way that fits the requirements of legal advocates is even more challenging. For this reason, continuous debate rages about the legal definition of insanity, with the variations very briefly summarised in the nearby 'A very brief history of defining insanity' sidebar.

A very brief history of defining insanity

The legal definition of insanity has varied over the centuries as the understanding of mental illness has changed:

18th century: 'The Wild Beast' test was the idea that for a person to be regarded as insane in law the person would be acting like a brute or infant, completely unaware of what he was doing, with no memory of it or understanding of its implications.

19th century: The McNaughton rules that I mention in Chapter 1 were the start of the modern concept that the person can suffer from a 'disease of the mind', causing him not to understand the nature of what he did and that it was wrong.

20th century: Modifications made include: weakening the 'understanding' requirement to 'lack substantial capacity to appreciate' that what he did was wrong; putting emphasis on a person's inability to control his actions; and the defendant needing to prove that he's insane with clear and convincing evidence, rather than the prosecution demonstrating that he's sane beyond reasonable doubt. In some jurisdictions, the verdict of 'guilty but mentally ill' was introduced in addition to 'not guilty by reason of insanity'. The intention was to allow the person to be assigned to a treatment programme and when/if that was successful to be moved to a normal prison.

With the developed understanding during the middle of the 20th century that mental illness can take many forms, a further refinement was added to legal codes in many countries. In the US, the new term was *diminished capacity;* in the UK, *diminished responsibility.*

The result was to weaken the requirement that the accused had *mens rea.* If a person pleads diminished responsibility, he can claim that he didn't intend to commit the crime although he accepts he did it. In murder cases, he may be charged with the lesser crime of manslaughter or its equivalent and so get a lesser sentence. Defendants and their lawyers can draw upon a number of different mental disorders to support the claim of diminished responsibility:

- ✔ **Amnesia** is when the accused claims that he can't remember significant events to an extent that's far more severe than normal forgetfulness, particularly if this is related to some physical or intense psychological trauma. Amnesia is particularly difficult to validate because a person can so readily claim to have forgotten something. Claims of amnesia occur in quite a few murder cases.

- ✔ **Automatism** is the condition in which actions occur involuntarily and quite possibly without the person even being aware that he's doing them. The clearest examples are those in which a person is violent during his sleep without ever waking up. Automatism is a recognised clinical condition and so if assessed by a competent clinician, which is usually a psychiatrist but can be a forensic psychologist, is rather more difficult to fake than might be expected.

- ✔ **Dissociative identity disorder,** otherwise known as multiple personality disorder, is the condition reflected in Robert Louis Stevenson's famous tale *Dr Jekyll and Mr Hyde.* Kenneth Bianchi claimed that he had an involuntary switch to a different identity, but he was discovered to be faking and was convicted of being the Hillside Strangler (see the later sidebar 'Tricking the trickster').

- ✔ **Intoxication** can be used as a defence, especially if the person can demonstrate that he wasn't aware of the possible impact of imbibing so much alcohol or other drugs in increasing the risk of committing the crime, and especially if he can demonstrate that his drinks were spiked. Just being drunk when committing a crime may attract a more severe punishment, but if the defendant can show he had not intended to get drunk this could be a mitigating circumstance.

- ✔ **Personality disorder** is a catch-all increasingly being used to claim diminished responsibility. The defendant is presented to the court as having an enduring set of characteristics that causes his behaviour to be pervasively and inflexibly antisocial. Because of this condition, he can't fully control his actions and so isn't fully responsible for them. I discuss aspects of this disorder in more detail in Chapter 10.

STRANGE BUT TRUE

The Twinkie defence!

Dan White was accused of shooting the mayor of San Francisco, George Moscone, and city supervisor, Harvey Milk, in 1978. As part of their defence, his lawyers claimed that White suffered from manic-depression (now called bipolar disorder) and that his condition was made much worse when he binged on soft drinks and junk foods. Although Twinkies (an American sugary sponge cake bar) weren't named in the proceedings, the tongue-in-cheek term of the Twinkie defence caught on (to indicate an improbable defence). White was convicted of 'involuntary manslaughter' due to diminished capacity, rather than murder.

This defence could never have happened in Britain . . . because Twinkies aren't for sale in the UK. Perhaps you can think of an equivalent sugary defence!

Making sense of madness

If you're a bit confused about the legal definition of insanity and diminished responsibility, don't worry . . . you're in good company! Intense debate continues to rage between experts about most of the issues I mention in the preceding section. Even more importantly, juries are often confused as well. Studies indicate that juries are often reluctant to accept an insanity defence, whereas judges are more inclined to do so. This tension puts pressure on the forensic psychologist or other expert witnesses to be able to provide an objective report that the court finds acceptable.

One of the difficulties faced when forming an opinion about someone's mental state at the time of crime, is that it's a retrospective examination of the psychological condition of the person months or even years earlier. Necessarily, this assessment relies on the account that a person, or people who know him, gives about his thoughts and emotions at that time.

Exposing malingering

One of the most important aspects of any assessment of a defendant is to determine if the symptoms he describes are genuine (which is somewhat different from detecting attempted deception that I discuss in Chapter 5). If he does not have the symptoms or is faking them in some way it's known as 'malingering'. In this case, the forensic psychologist isn't evaluating the truthfulness of what the person says, but whether the mental state of the individual and related experiences indicate some psychological condition or relevance to the trial. Some standardised tests (that I mention in Chapter 9) have been developed for determining this malingering. A carefully structured clinical interview has also been shown to be very useful. More informally, malingering may be indicated by:

✔ Exaggerated and dramatic account of symptoms.

✔ Unusual carefulness and deliberateness in answering questions.

✔ A mix of symptoms that's inconsistent with known diagnoses.

✔ General inconsistency in what's said.

✔ Presentation of only the most well-known and obvious symptoms.

Realising he'd been caught out, Bianchi agreed to testify against his cousin Angelo Buono who was charged with him, but he still got multiple life sentences (though not one for each personality!).

Assessing insanity

Besides the determination of malingering that I discuss in the preceding section, surprisingly little standardisation exists in assessing a person's mental state at the time of the crime. The clinician has to determine as best as possible what dysfunctions were present in intellectual, emotional and behavioural aspects of the defendant at that key time when the crime happened, and how those disturbances relate to the criminal act.

These assessments are usually made on as wide a range of information as possible, not just a carefully structured interview of the person concerned. This information usually includes:

✔ Employment records

✔ Medical records

✔ Police reports

✔ Previous psychological tests (as I discuss in Chapters 9 and 10)

✔ Witness statements

The aim is to determine whether a consistent pattern of actions and reports about the defendant exists that's in accord with his own account of his experiences.

Examining Issues of Competency

As well as having to testify in connection to a person's plea of 'not guilty by reason of insanity' or 'diminished responsibility' as I discuss in the preceding section, a far more common form of assessment that may be made, is whether the person has the mental and emotional ability to stand trial. This idea of the *competence* of the defendant is based on the ethical requirement that no person should be subjected to a trial if he doesn't at the time:

✔ Have the ability to interact effectively with his lawyers.

✔ Have the capability of understanding the legal proceedings of which he's a part.

ANECDOTE

Tricking the trickster

When Kenneth Bianchi was charged with a series of rapes and murders across Los Angeles in 1977 and 1978, which led to him being called 'The Hillside Strangler', he offered as part of his defence that he should be regarded as insane because he had multiple personality disorder, saying that his other identity 'Steve Walker' had done the killing.

Two experts originally believed him, but the police were suspicious because Steve Walker was the name of the student that Bianchi had used to fraudulently obtain a college certificate so that he could practise psychology; also, in interviews, he kept on referring to Steve as 'he' rather than 'I'. The police called in Marin Orne who'd done many studies of how people behave when pretending to be hypnotised. Orne set about hypnotising Bianchi and decided that he was faking it. To test this suspicion further, Orne purposely mislead Bianchi into thinking that people with multiple personalities usually have more than one extra personality. Bianchi unwittingly fell for Orne's trick, soon generating a new personality, Bill, and a couple of others.

This competency requirement applies throughout the legal process even before the person is charged, and can occur during police searches, eyewitness line-ups, police interviews and so on, and also after the trial for parole hearings and during appeals. Of particular importance is the situation in which the person pleads guilty (which happens, perhaps surprisingly, in the great majority of cases). The court must be confident that the person does understand the implications of such a plea. The same is true if the person decides to waive constitutional rights, such as the right to trial by jury. The person who does this must know what he's doing, have the intellectual capacity to understand what it means and be clear that he has made that decision.

The assessment of competency can therefore relate to many aspects of the legal process. A forensic psychologist may explore a person's mental state at the time of the crime while deciding his competence to stand trial, but many professionals frown on this combination of assessments because of the room for confusing rather different issues.

A number of standardised procedures (which I explain in Chapter 9) are used to assess competence, although many practitioners still rely on carefully organised interviews. The assessment instruments include standard measures of intellectual ability, notably intelligence tests, as well as broader assessments of personality that may indicate some form of mental disorder. They may also include direct tests for malingering as I mention in the preceding section or lying as I discuss in Chapter 5.

More specific tests have been devised that explore a person's understanding of what goes on in court. They include their ability to make sense of the legal process and how a verdict is reached; their capacity to distinguish what's relevant from what's not and their understanding of the implications of pleading guilty or not guilty. Crucially important, also, is their ability to makes sense of their own legal predicament. These tests of competency, for example, ask the person what the jury actually does. Another version gives defendants a brief fictional vignette of a case and asks them to answer questions about what happens and why.

About one out of every five people referred for a competency evaluation is eventually found to be not competent enough to undertake the legal process. These people tend to be those who:

- ✔ Have a history of institutional treatment.

- ✔ Are diagnosed with a mental disorder, typically schizophrenia and/or other psychotic symptoms (although some authorities try to dissuade practitioners from using such diagnoses because a jury, and even a judge, may misinterpret it by thinking it means a split personality rather than a lack of contact with reality).

- ✔ Are found to lack competence in the formal forensic mental health assessment of their cognitive and related abilities.

Considering children's competency

In general, courts don't have a firm view on how old a person must be before he's competent to give evidence or stand trial. The age has varied considerably over time and differs between jurisdictions. If any doubt exists, the child is assessed to demonstrate his ability:

- ✔ To accurately perceive, recall and share facts.
- ✔ To distinguish truth from lies.
- ✔ To understand that he must tell the truth.

Restoring someone's competence

If a defendant isn't declared competent to stand trial, the assessment moves into another gear and is required to indicate whether the defendant can be helped to become competent in some way and, if so, how long this process may take. After all, the court wants to bring the person to justice. If an expert says that the person is probably never going to be fit to plead, or at least in the foreseeable future, the court has to decide whether to drop the charges or commit the defendant to some sort of institution. This detainment can become a form of endless imprisonment, even though most jurisdictions require a regular review of the person's condition, often by some sort of mental health tribunal at which psychologists are often present, to assess whether he's now able to deal with the criminal trial.

People assigned by the courts to a mental health institution or some other setting, because for example they aren't competent to stand trial without the requirement for treatment, can be incarcerated for much longer than they would be if they were found guilty of a crime. An assessment of 'not guilty by reason of insanity' can have the same outcome. For this reason, some defence lawyers may try to avoid an assessment of incompetence, or insanity, so that their clients are released sooner.

In order to enable defendants to cope with the court process, they may be given medication. This can mislead the jury into thinking that the calm, quiet person they see listening to the evidence is exhibiting behaviour that would be the same without that medication. Therefore, legal debate exists about whether enabling the person to be competent before the court is actually helping his case or whether it's better to try and get treatment, so that what the court sees is a person whose actions aren't being controlled by medication.

Assessing competency for execution

In the USA, 38 states have the death penalty. But under US law a person can only be executed for a crime if at the time of his execution he has the mental state to understand the reason for the execution and its implications. This situation generates challenges for forensic psychologists and psychiatrists who may be uncomfortable with the whole idea of executing people who have committed certain crimes. As a result, many professionals refuse to take part in the competency assessment of a person who may be executed for his crimes.

Assessing whether a convicted person, on death row, is competent to be executed is a challenging task. The American constitution doesn't allow the execution of a person who's not aware of the punishment he's about to receive or why he has to undergo it. The inability may be because of intellectual deficit, such as very low intelligence, or extreme mental illness that gives him little contact with reality.

Giving the court an opinion that will influence whether a person lives or dies is an extremely onerous task. If done properly it will be based on:

- Detailed interviews with the convicted person.

- Formal psychological assessment (using one of the personality inventories I describe in Chapter 9).

- Interviews with death row prison staff.

- Observation of the person in his cell.

- Interviews of his family, friends and any spiritual advisor.

- Review of any legal, military or health records available.

- Consideration of any letter in support of clemency.

Getting Controversial: Examining Syndromes in Court

One controversial area of psychological guidance to the courts revolves around giving expert testimony on why the actions of key individuals, usually victims or defendants, aren't what would normally be expected. Unusual or difficult to comprehend behaviour is problematical for the courts to digest, partly because judges believe that they know a lot about human beings and that juries should be allowed to draw on their own experience to make sense of what they're told.

Consequently, if a standardised test can be used to support a psychological conclusion, it adds an extra level of expertise beyond that available to the court from personal experience. Similarly, if a particular behaviour can be presented as a sort of medical diagnosis, it may also be more acceptable and carry more 'weight' than mere 'professional opinion'.

For this reason, a burgeoning number of psychological 'syndromes' to explain behaviour have found their way into legal proceedings. In medical terms, a *syndrome* is a cluster of symptoms that occur together in some meaningful way and are usually kick-started by an identifiable event.

Many lawyers and psychologists are uncomfortable with presenting patterns of behaviour in this way, as if they were some sort of distinct disease like measles or tuberculosis with little or no individual variation, when in fact large differences exist between people in how they behave.

But this reluctance hasn't stopped such behavioural syndromes from becoming part of the vocabulary of forensic psychologists.

Post-traumatic stress disorder

The most common psychological syndrome to be used in evidence is *post-traumatic stress disorder* (PTSD). This syndrome has a long and chequered history, with its origins residing partly in the 'shell-shock' recognised during the First World War and what was called 'battle fatigue' during the Second World War. (A similar phenomenon was identified in the American Civil War called 'soldier's heart'.) As a distinct clinical diagnosis, it gained strength after the Vietnam war when the difficulties so many veterans had in returning to civilian life were recognised.

Initially, all these extreme reactions to the experience of battle were dismissed by those in authority as cowardice or a weak personality. During the First World War, some soldiers were even shot for cowardice or desertion who'd now be recognised as suffering from PTSD. Indeed many of them have been posthumously exonerated. Today's clinical understanding of the effects of severe trauma has helped to produce a more enlightened understanding of what people experience in the heat of war, but this work has also provided a framework for evaluating the psychological impact of many other traumatic situations.

Some estimates suggest that as many as one in ten of the population suffer PTSD during their lives. For example, if you're involved in a driving accident and thereafter are reluctant to drive again and are hyper-cautious when on the roads (responding with a sudden surge of anxiety whenever you become aware of squealing tyres), you have the basis of at least a mild form of PTSD. If these symptoms last for two or three weeks, they may well be labelled *acute stress disorder*.

The diagnosis of PTSD requires a number of distinct components:

- ✔ A clear cause of a traumatic event that can be regarded as beyond normal human experience, particularly if it involves intense fear, helplessness or horror.

- ✔ Psychological consequences of the trauma shown to have lasted for longer than a month and to include upsetting memories or flashbacks or distressing dreams, or some mixture of these symptoms.

- ✔ The need to avoid anything associated with the trauma, such as places or people, or even with some of the memories.

- ✔ An increased sensitivity to potential threats, especially from anything linked to the cause of the trauma, with associated anxiety and anguish, often indicated through sleep disturbance.

If some aspects of each of these four constituents are present, PTSD is diagnosed. The number, intensity and longevity of the symptoms are drawn on to indicate the severity of the disorder.

PTSD has been accepted in US courts as a form of mental illness and thus can be used as mitigating circumstances for a violent attack.

The New Jersey Superior Court accepted that a violent attack by a war veteran on a police officer was a product of a flashback in which the police officer was mistaken for an enemy combatant.

PTSD and insanity pleas

The use of PTSD as part of an insanity plea was used controversially in a Canadian court decision in a case of a sexual assault of a child. The defendant claimed that he had PTSD as the result of an incident while on a peace-keeping mission in Bosnia. He'd interrupted a sexual assault on a child by killing the attacker. He argued in court that the assault of which he was accused was the result of a re-enactment of that event in Bosnia. The judge accepted that

he was insane at the time of the crime, being unable to appreciate the nature of what he was doing.

Many experts are concerned about this extension of PTSD to be an insanity defence in crimes of intimate violence. The extent of blackouts and memory loss as part of PTSD, as in so many other areas of memory, are extremely difficult to validate.

The main use of PTSD is in accident claims, where it provides a well-tried and clear set of criteria for assessing the psychological impact of the accident. This can contribute to decisions about compensation or even consideration of the punishment if someone had caused the accident. However, even this apparently obvious application is open to question. Considerable evidence suggests that the impact of any trauma depends on the psychological well-being of the person who suffers the event before it occurs. Also, the experiences after the trauma, such as social support or loss of employment, can have an impact on the development of PTSD. Most problematic is the clear indication that PTSD may be more long-lasting and severe if ongoing litigation is involved in which it could play a role, as would be the case if a person is seeking compensation.

Battered woman syndrome

When a woman brings a charge of assault against her husband or partner, claiming that he frequently battered her, the defence may assert that the wife stayed with her husband over many years and so the assaults can't have been as bad as she claims. Consequently, opposing lawyers sometimes use the *battered woman syndrome* to explain why a woman suffers extensive physical abuse over a period of time and yet still fails to leave the relationship, even when the abuser is absent or asleep.

The characteristics of the syndrome revolve around the idea that the victim is taught by the offender to become helpless. *Learned helplessness* is a phenomena first observed in animals that were unable to escape from electric shocks in unpleasant experiments. They eventually stop trying to avoid the shocks and just lie there listlessly. This passivity in relation to unavoidable, random abuse has since been found in many individuals.

As well as this feeling of helplessness, women suffering from battered woman syndrome also display the following associated behaviours:

- ✔ Development of ways of surviving (for example, through appeasement rather than escaping).

- ✔ Low self-esteem.

- ✔ Depression.

- ✔ Self-blame (the victim mistakenly believes the abuse is her fault and that she can do something to stop it happening in the future).

- ✔ A genuine fear for her life or her children's welfare.

The abuse may well have psychological blackmail components too, such as telling the victim that her children will be taken from her if she reports the violence. All this abuse is often supported by an irrational belief that the perpetrator is all-powerful and all-knowing.

An important aspect of battered woman syndrome is that a cycle of abuse evolves: tension builds up, the assault occurs and then the offender is contrite and remorseful; tension increases again, another assault takes place and so on. This cycle can occur many times before the victim reports what's happening and tries to get help from the authorities.

The acceptability of this syndrome, as for all the others described in this section, is dependent on the jurisdiction and the particular judge. In some states and areas of the UK there are general guidelines to judges as to which syndromes are acceptable as mitigating evidence. However, because they are not illnesses caused by a bacterium that can be seen under a microscope, but patterns of behaviour that are interpreted by experts, there will always be debates in any legal proceedings as to whether the syndrome is relevant to a particular case.

Some experts regard battered woman syndrome as a form of PTSD (check out the preceding section).

Parental alienation syndrome

In child custody cases in the US and Canada, usually as part of divorce proceedings, lawyers have identified cases in which a child exhibits extreme reactions against one parent. Dr Richard Gardner named this behaviour *parental alienation syndrome,* which he describes as 'a parental campaign of unjustified disparagement against another loving parent'. This is usually inferred from various reports available to the court, especially what any children involved say or do.

The crucial aspects of this syndrome are:

- A lack of any apparent basis for the child's hostility to the parent.
- An active programme of one parent influencing the child's opinion.
- The generation of strong negative opinions by the child in the dispute.

Assessment of the existence of this syndrome is based on evaluating the child's behaviour across the following areas:

- Negative acts or statements towards the victimised parent.
- Criticisms based on absurd generalisations.
- Polarised emotions towards the parents.
- Claims that the reactions are the child's own ideas.
- Total loyalty to the parent carrying out the disparagement.
- No remorse for cruelty towards the victimised parent.
- Imagined or rehearsed scenarios.
- Extension of negative emotions to those associated with the victimised parent.

A central difficulty in accepting the existence of parental alienation syndrome in any particular case is that, although it claims to be a comment on the child's state of mind, it's really a way of indicating that the alienating parent is doing something pathological, that is, 'brainwashing' the child. As a consequence it's highly suspect. It has not found its way into any of the diagnostic lists that I described in Chapter 10, such as DSM. Even though many experts have challenged whether this really is a scientifically valid syndrome, parental alienation syndrome has found its way into civil proceedings as a way of challenging children's claims of physical or sexual abuse.

Premenstrual stress syndrome

Many syndromes that courts accept relate directly to women's actions, often to help juries understand the apparently surprising behaviour of female victims (such as in the behaviour of abused wives that I describe in the earlier section 'Battered woman syndrome').

These women-behaviour-based syndromes generate lively debate as to whether they're forms of misogyny in disguise and/or not really established medical conditions.

One such syndrome is premenstrual stress (PMS), (sometimes called Premenstrual Tension or PMT) in which women at a particular stage of the menstrual cycle may be more emotionally vulnerable and suffer a mixture of physical and psychological deficits. PMS has been accepted as a form of temporary insanity in a number of jurisdictions and also used as a defence in violent assaults (and even a few murder cases).

Although some evidence exists for monthly mood swings in males, this can't be related so directly to major physiological changes. As a result, women have access to a legal defence that's unavailable to men. Therefore, one of the basic tenets of the law, that all are equal before it, isn't followed through by the acceptance of this defence.

Rape trauma syndrome

Rape trauma syndrome (RTS) is typically associated with women rape victims but is potentially applicable to men. RTS has parallels to PTSD (see the earlier section 'Post-traumatic stress disorder'), although its emphasis is rather different and less clearly defined. The use of RTS in court is to clarify why a rape victim delays reporting the assault, the claim being that this delay indicates some doubt about her role in the rape, even possibly blaming herself. This delay is claimed to be part of the psychological effects of the trauma of the attack, which often include depression, suicidal thoughts and general fear and anxiety.

An important point about all the psychological consequences of various stressors and traumas that result from rape is that they can also result from events that don't involve obvious, extreme violence. Fear and profound psychological insult can be as traumatic, or even more so, as vicious physical aggression. Many studies show that stress relates to a lack, or loss, of personal control. As a consequence, situations that take the feelings of control away from the individual can have a significant impact on feelings of self-worth and the ability to be in charge of one's life.

Munchausen syndrome by proxy

Munchausen syndrome is where a person displays a relentless determination to obtain medical treatment from self-inflicted injuries or non-existent symptoms. *Munchausen syndrome by proxy* is a related behaviour, a very curious form of child abuse in which a parent (nearly always the mother) forces medical attention on her child frequently over an extended period of time without anything medical being wrong with the child at all. The child is used as a surrogate (or proxy) and may have to endure falsely reported symptoms (perhaps by adding substances to the child's excreta to distort the laboratory tests) or even injuries or illnesses induced by the parent (such as starving the child or giving it toxic injections) in order to gain medical attention.

Experts don't agree on the reasons for Munchausen syndrome by proxy behaviour, but the following characteristics have been identified as common to those diagnosed with this syndrome:

✔ Mother is highly involved with her child and father is emotionally distant.

✔ The parent is emotionally empty, unable to feel for other people, and lonely.

✔ The parent experienced childhood emotional, physical or sexual abuse.

✔ The parent appears as an ideal, very concerned parent.

✔ The parent is over-protective of the child.

✔ The parent is obsessed with the child's illness.

As these characteristics indicate, the parent can often be very convincing. As a result, in the cases of reporting false symptoms, sometimes the modifications of samples sent to the laboratory may be the first indicator that something non-medical is wrong with the child because the test results are so unusual.

The sorts of false symptoms reported by the parent commonly include:

✔ Asthma/allergies

✔ Diarrhoea

✔ Failures to thrive, such as claims of not putting on weight

✔ Infections

✔ Seizures

✔ Vomiting

Some vets report that a family pet may also be a 'proxy'; owners deliberately hurt a pet in order to get sympathy and medical attention.

The term Munchausen comes from the 18th-century German soldier and politician Baron von Münchausen, who was renowned for inventing incredible stories about his travels and military exploits.

Making Judgements for Risk Assessment

At different stages through the legal process, before, during or after the trial, a forensic psychologist may be called upon to assess how dangerous the defendant is likely to be in any future situation. This process is called *risk assessment* and includes the possibility that he may harm himself or others through violence or sexual assaults.

Risk assessment is becoming a major and extremely challenging task in many different settings. In general, recommendations are based on reviews of static, relatively unchanging factors alongside more dynamic risk factors that are potentially open to change.

The static risk factors tend to be historical, such as:

- ✔ Previous violence
- ✔ Employment problems
- ✔ Clear evidence of psychopathy
- ✔ Substance abuse

The dynamic factors are more directly psychological issues:

- ✔ Lack of insight
- ✔ Impulsivity
- ✔ Unfeasible plans for the future
- ✔ Social support and how the individual dealt with any previous forms of remedial intervention
- ✔ Potential stressors

In order to illustrate how risk assessment works, I compare two different offenders:

- ✔ A married man in his mid-30s who pleads guilty to sexually abusing his teenage daughter since she was the age of 4.
- ✔ A single young man in his early 20s who's convicted of having sex with an under-age boy a few years younger than himself, who he'd just met in a local park.

According to some standard risk assessment procedures, the young man has a much higher risk of future offending than the married man. The reason is that statistics show that a married man, aged over 25 years old, who abuses a female family member is less likely to offend again than someone not in a cohabiting relationship, who offends against a male stranger. This difference may come as some surprise, but it's based on studies using these assessment procedures and following up how accurately they do predict what happens later.

Although such risk assessment procedures have a strong logic to them, and studies show that they're generally accurate, they're far from being foolproof. One reason for this is that, although it may be possible to characterise an individual, characterising and predicting the situations in which that person may find themselves is much more difficult. Also, for many people who must be assessed, little reliable background information is available.

Courts may use risk assessments in the following circumstances:

- ✔ If a decision needs to be made for involuntary committal to a hospital or other institution, this can't be made only on the grounds of mental illness. The person must also exhibit impending danger to themselves or others.

- ✔ If an expert becomes aware that a person has the potential to be violent towards a specific person, they must provide a report that warns of this possibility.

- ✔ If the person poses a serious risk of future criminal conduct, a risk assessment report can contribute to deciding on preventative detention.

- ✔ To assess how dangerous a person is who's been convicted of predatory sexually violent behaviour, and to provide background information as regards sentencing and the form of institutional commitment.

The general principle for risk assessment is that the more recently a person has been violent in the past, the more likely he is to be violent in the near future. Consequently, risk assessment is more likely to predict with accuracy whether a person will be violent in the next 48 hours, or even 14 days, than over a longer period such as 48 months or 14 years.

Psychological Autopsy

When the cause of a person's death is equivocal – for example, some doubt exists as to whether someone committed suicide, suffered an accident or was murdered – a forensic psychologist may be asked to establish the characteristics of the deceased in order to throw light on what happened. In other words, an autopsy is conducted but on the person's psychology and not his body. This task is called a *psychological autopsy* (or if you want a term that sounds more sophisticated *reconstructive psychological evaluation*).

The psychological autopsy process consists of trying to build a picture of the dead person's thoughts and feelings leading up to their death, as well as a detailed examination of exactly how the fatality happened. The psychologist uses documents (such as letters, diaries, blogs or e-mails) the deceased left behind as well as interviews with people who knew the person.

The resulting reports can provide important information in murder trials where the defence is that the deceased committed suicide, but also in contested wills or other circumstances in which the mental state of the deceased is of significance.

Equivocal death analysis

One important example of the confusions that can surround inferences about a dead person is the examination of the explosion in the gun turret on the US Navy battleship USS Ohio in 1989, which killed 47 of the turret's crew. FBI agents carried out what they called an equivocal death analysis of the incident and those in the turret room. They concluded that one of the crew members, Clayton Hartwig, had exploded the gun in an act of suicide. Subsequently, the American Psychological Association set up a special working-party to review what the FBI had done and the related evidence. The party was critical of the FBI report and not all the members supported the view that Hartwig had committed suicide. A further detailed technical examination of the turret concluded that an accidental over-ram of the gun had occurred, which caused it to explode. Subsequent inquiries in turn challenged this conclusion, which shows just how complex the examination of equivocal deaths can be.

Another term sometimes used is *equivocal death analysis,* but this usually refers to an examination carried out by law enforcement agents rather than forensic psychologists. Equivocal death analysis is particularly prevalent in military situations where the complexity and dangerousness of what's going on, sometimes aggravated by 'the fog of war', can raise many important questions about how someone died. I describe one notorious example in the sidebar 'Equivocal death analysis'.

Conducting a psychological autopsy is fraught with difficulties, not least because the person who could answer many of the key questions is dead! In addition, if a murder inquiry is in progress, legal hurdles may be put in the way of interviewing all the people who have some knowledge of the dead person (and, of course, the prosecution and defence are likely to have access to different sets of witnesses, who may hold opposing views). If suicide is an issue, the people close to the dead person may be unwilling to give full and frank information (they may feel some guilt if the person killed himself and so be keen to support belief in some other cause that exonerates them).

Conducting psychological autopsies into possible suicides

In order to help explain a psychological autopsy, in this section I discuss the various aspects that have to be considered in order to produce a report on a suicide. The psychological processes considered when examining the possibility of suicide draw on four dominant processes: stressors, exposure, availability of lethal agents and psychopathology.

Stressors

An important consideration in any fatality is the circumstances surrounding the event, in particular any indication of the stressors that the deceased may have suffered. Studies show that people who attempt suicide often experienced significant life stressors in the four weeks prior to the attempt. The weakness in these studies, however, is the lack of careful exploration of people with similar stressors who don't attempt suicide, or of the surrounding social and family circumstances that may consistently be associated with the stressors. Without such knowledge, the pre-existence of stressors in an examination of an equivocal death may be given too much weight.

Exposure

Police inquiries, as well as more systematic studies, suggest that teenage suicides in particular may be more likely after direct exposure to another suicide through family or friends, or indirect exposure from media coverage. If, for instance, the person had been consistently brooding on the event, a safe assumption is that at the very least it focused their thoughts. Such intense analysis may also provide ideas about the actual mechanics for carrying out their suicide.

Studies indicate that the latter situation sometimes seems to be the case when what may be considered 'unorthodox' means of suicide are used, such as setting fire to oneself or laying one's head on a railway track. Enough examples exist of minor 'epidemics' of suicides following initial, widely publicised incidents using the same method to support the contention that some individuals decide *how* to commit suicide from these exemplars.

A particularly disturbing illustration of this sort of 'copycat' suicide is exhibited by the spree killers I mention in Chapter 6. These people almost invariably end up being killed or killing themselves as part of their killing spree. Evidence suggests that some increase in this sort of suicide occurs when a similar event is highly publicised, such as the Columbine school shootings in the US.

A morbid fascination with a suicide event can certainly be taken as indication that the deceased had at least considered the implications of taking their own life. And if the experience of the suicide was more direct – or the deceased thought in some way that the original suicide was positively regarded or in some senses 'heroic' – it can be considered to have had the effect of 'validating' the planned action.

Inevitably, however, the simple extrapolation from a deceased having had exposure to another's suicide and their own subsequent death involves many difficulties. You have to be cautious about assuming that a suicide, or suspicious death, imitates a related event in some way. For a start, you need to be sure that the deceased was aware of the example they're supposed to have imitated! And if no other evidence exists – say in a suicide note or comments before death – that the deceased admired the original suicide (or saw the act as appropriate in some way), the idea of a person replicating the event has less strength.

Availability of lethal agents

No, lethal agents doesn't refer to those dubious characters who represent highly-paid footballers! In this case, *lethal agents* are the means by which people can kill themselves.

Many experts believe that ready and easy access to a quick cause of death, the most notably being a firearm, increases the risk of suicide. Such access would certainly be expected to reduce the number of cases in which a person survives a suicide attempt, because failure is simply less likely. The chances of a person being discovered before the effects of an overdose become fatal, or of not taking enough pills, don't apply when the pulling of a gun trigger is all that's needed.

In fact, you will find it difficult in the UK to buy some pills in a bottle if taking lots of those pills would kill you. Instead, you have to buy them in one of those blister packs that takes some doing to open. There does seem to be evidence that people who want to kill themselves by taking lots of pills often can't be bothered to fight with lots of blister packs!

It's an open question as to whether the mere availability of ready-to-use fire-arms, or any other lethal agent, is a strong indication that an equivocal death is suicide. Many suicides are carried out with remarkably limited means and lots of people live their lives in the presence of highly lethal agents without ever thinking about suicide.

Psychopathology

One of the major assumptions made in guiding an equivocal death investigation is that any evidence of prior *psychopathology* (which is some form of mental illness or other psychological disturbance) can be taken as an indicator of the probability that a person took their own life. Because this area of interest is such a natural part of psychiatric assessment, the various structured protocols that have been developed to elicit indications of mental illness (that I describe in Chapter 9) have been adapted for use with surviving parents and family in an attempt to complete a psychological autopsy as if the deceased is present.

Signs of depression, or previous acts of self-harm, provide support for suicide as opposed to accidental death – even if no direct signs of depression in the deceased are available. Many studies also show that if close relatives have had mental problems, then it's important to consider whether there's the possibility of early stage depression developing or unrecognised aspects of mental disturbance, in the person whose death is equivocal.

What to make of a diagnosis of schizophrenia or personality disorder, however, is more difficult. Where a severe psychosis is apparent, the borderline between accidental and intentional self-destruction is wide and vague. Was the person lucid enough at the time to be aware of the *full* consequence of their actions? Even though the person had expressed a desire to commit suicide, were they *fully* cognisant of what that meant?

An extreme, but useful, example of the difficulties of using information on psychopathology in an equivocal death investigation, is any case referred to as 'suicide by cop'. In such situations, a person creates a confrontation with the police that inevitably leads to being gunned down in a shoot-out.

British police officers may well be aware that the person they're surrounding in a siege is potentially suicidal and therefore try to avoid giving him the opportunity to get them to execute him. In some US jurisdictions, however, fewer qualms may exist, or at least, less understanding of the possible psychopathology of the offender they're trying to disarm.

The 'suicide by cop' scenario illustrates the intense complexities involved in this area. The individual may even see himself as heroic and look to the agents of the state to enshrine his heroism. After all, many acts of suicide, across a variety of different cultures, are typically regarded as heroic, often involving some confrontation with the state or a designated enemy, whether it be biblical heroes such as Samson, Second World War kamikaze pilots or present day 'suicide bombers'.

Contesting wills

A special aspect of the psychological autopsy is the consideration of whether a person was competent to make a will when he did so – *testamentary capacity* is the legal term used in the US. Most jurisdictions don't set very high standards for achieving this competence, requiring only that the person knew:

- ✔ He was making a will.
- ✔ The extent and nature of his property.
- ✔ Who (or perhaps what) was to receive his property.
- ✔ How his property was being divided.

A psychological assessment would consider appropriate indicators by obtaining information from records, and from those who knew the person, ascertaining whether drugs, mental illness, or physical or emotional trauma may have so influenced his state of mind that he wasn't appropriately competent at the time he prepared and signed his will.

ANECDOTE

When eccentric people die

Howard Hughes, the famous millionaire, who had been a recluse for most of his later years, gave rise to the need for a psychological assessment of his mental capacity because of challenges to his will. Raymond Fowler, a past president of the American Psychological association, carried out a psychological autopsy on Hughes and concluded that 'psychological problems, numerous head injuries and drug misuse had changed a vibrant millionaire into an emaciated recluse'. The possibly psychotic basis of his reclusiveness, rather than mere eccentricity, posed challenges to the probity of his estate. The many millions of dollars he left were divided up between dozens of relatives and other causes.

Providing Expert Testimony in Civil Proceedings

An increasing variety of situations outside of criminal proceedings requires some sort of psychological assessment to be drawn on to reach a legal decision. I have already mentioned some of these earlier in the chapter, but for tidiness here are some legal circumstances in which a psychologist's report may be used in civil proceedings:

✔ **Child custody cases** in which the parents as well as the children and their relationships are evaluated. This assessment can include recommendations of the conditions under which children should visit a parent or other guardian.

Expert evidence can be crucial where there are issues of credibility regarding allegations of abuse or concerns over the child's evidence in such child custody issues.

✔ **Civil rights claims** where the psychologist may comment on gender or racial stereotyping.

✔ **Claims of breach of contract,** where the psychologist may comment on the traumatic effect of the breach.

✔ **Sexual harassment,** where counselling or advice to a company may be part of the outcome of the case as well as assessment of the parties involved.

REGIONAL TIP-OFF

In the state of Oregon, a mentally competent adult with less than 6 months to live may ask his physician to prescribe medication that would hasten death. An expert, such as a psychologist, may be called upon to advise on whether the individual is mentally competent to make this decision.

Examining the capacity to consent to treatment

In some jurisdictions, mentally disturbed individuals have to agree to any treatment they're given. This situation, in turn, requires a test of the decision-making competence of the patient in relation to their ability to:

- State a choice.
- Understand relevant information.
- Appreciate the nature of their own situation.
- Reason with the information provided.

As with many other attempts to provide standard procedures, these tests of competence have generated much debate about whether a test that seems sensible for one person (say, a white young woman) would be equally relevant for someone from a different generation and ethnic background.

For much more on this subject, flip to the earlier section 'Examining Issues of Competency'.

Assessing for compensation

In a range of situations (from possible negligence on the part of an employer to that of another person in a car accident), civil courts or similar settings may need to assess whether a person has suffered an injury at the hands of others and if so, the degree of that injury. Although physical injury has long been accepted as a basis for claiming compensation, in recent years courts in many countries have been willing to accept evidence of psychological or emotional damage as well.

Many of the assessments carried out for such claims are of a highly specialised kind, relying on neurological tests, exploring brain damage or other physiological defects. Beyond these examinations, many of the issues that I mention earlier in this chapter in relation to mental state at the time of a crime are relevant. Any evidence of chronic mental health problems that predate the injury would be considered to throw light on what the consequence of the trauma was and what may be an enduring aspect on the person.

A crucial part of the assessment is an attempt to predict the longevity of any injury and its future consequences. This task is especially difficult with psychological examinations because the very fact that a compensation claim is pending may cause stress-related symptoms. The psychologist also needs to be alert to various forms of faking, as I discuss in the earlier section 'Exposing malingering'. Where significant financial gain is feasible, various forms of fraud are always possible.

Detailing a Forensic Psychologist's Report

Forensic psychologists' reports that are the main form of contribution to criminal or civil proceedings need to have the following properties:

- ✔ Distinguish clearly between established facts and the inferences which are derived from those facts.
- ✔ Address all the issues raised by the legal representatives in their letter of instruction.
- ✔ Keep close to the reason for the report, but avoid bias or pressure to give a particular opinion.
- ✔ Limit information to what's necessary.
- ✔ Minimise the use of specialist jargon.
- ✔ Be alert to any prejudicial information.
- ✔ Avoid direct comment on the ultimate question.

Chapter 12

Making Sense in Court: Psychological Aspects of the Legal Processes

*M*any of the forensic psychology activities that I describe in this book revolve around assessing the mental state of offenders, or the practice of *clinical* psychologists who work with mentally ill or disturbed people. But this chapter is a little different in that it focuses on the psychology of people without problems, who aren't criminals. It covers the ways in which forensic psychologists illuminate court processes by drawing on the psychology of judges, lawyers and jurors and how they interact with each other (that is, the practice of *social* psychology). In particular, the presence of people without legal training (the jury) taking an active role in court proceedings raises many interesting questions for psychologists.

In this chapter, therefore, I explore the legal processes themselves and the attitudes and behaviour of juries, lawyers and of course expert psychologists, in order to throw light on the thought processes and behaviour of the people involved in this most curious of human institutions.

Uncovering Psychology in the Courts

The adversarial legal process consists of judges and juries hearing witnesses being questioned and the prosecution and defence lawyers offering their account of the evidence (I describe this process and other legal systems in detail in Chapter 3). All this activity takes place within a long-established framework, which many legal experts have developed and studied. And yet, in all English-speaking countries and many other democracies, a central role is taken by ordinary people because they make crucial decisions as part of a jury. These juries operate in different ways in different countries, but for the present chapter I focus on the sorts of juries that you will find in the US, UK, Australia and Canada.

The jury is an unusual (even unnatural) but fascinating social group. It consists of people who don't know each other and yet have to come to momentous decisions within legal constraints that are novel to them.

The power of the interpersonal processes that are active when a jury debates the evidence is brilliantly illustrated in the classic film *12 Angry Men,* in which Henry Fonda's character eventually persuades all 11 other jurors to change their minds. And yet in general, the forms of influence that people exert on each other in the jury room are poorly understood because of the secrecy of their deliberations as they interpret the evidence.

The 12-person jury we take for granted in English-speaking countries is not the same around the world. Juries can have many different mixes of people. For example, some juries in France consist of 9 ordinary people and 3 judges!

Of course, judges and lawyers also have to make sense of the available evidence and decide how to present it to the jury, or whether to present it all. To do so, they draw on psychological ideas about how people deal with evidence and how information can be presented to put their case in the strongest light.

Examining existing legal rituals

Over many hundreds of years, the trial procedure in courts developed into a standard practice with many associated rituals. These rituals make plenty of psychological assumptions about how seriously everyone involved takes the legal proceedings, and how readily they accept the power and legitimacy of the courts. For this reason, although many of these assumptions haven't been scientifically tested, it's extremely valuable to consider what the assumptions are, and the psychological sense they make.

The rituals are enshrined in the physical layout of most courts. This has changed over the years and varies from one place to another. US courts tend to have a more informal layout than in the UK, and courts that deal with families usually deliberately try to break down many of the formal barriers inherent in traditional layouts. But it's useful to be aware of the symbolic significance of the traditional layout, because that reveals the symbolic and psychological significance of the various actors in the court proceedings.

In the traditional layout the sitting judge has the highest seat, usually in the centre of the court, in order to reflect the position's supreme importance and high status (and ensure that the person can see everything going on!). Below the judge is likely to be a clerk to the court (who looks after proceedings) and often a stenographer or someone else who's recording the whole proceedings.

The rest of the layout also represents the significance of the other individuals in the legal process. If it's a court that has a jury, they will typically be to one side, on benches slightly lower than the judge, or in their own boxed area. In the Crown Courts in the UK (where the most serious crimes are tried), the accused stands in what's known as the *dock* at a separate location, with direct access to the holding cells. Interestingly, in the US, the accused may often sit with his attorney, which gives them an opportunity to communicate during the trial, an arrangement not so feasible in most UK Crown Courts.

The descriptions of courts and juries in this chapter relate to the courts that deal with the most serious crimes. In most countries the great majority of crimes, as many as 97%, are dealt with in courts that do not have juries, but have only one judge – or, in the UK, three people who aren't qualified lawyers, known as magistrates – who makes the legal decision. (More details are given in Chapter 3.)

Each witness stands, alone and in turn, often in a *witness box,* to show that the person in that location is playing a significant role on which the court is focussed. In front of the judge, in the main body of the court, there are seats or benches for the lawyers and behind them for the solicitors who advise them. The area for the public is behind the lawyers, because justice in a democracy 'must be seen to be done'. In courts that hold trials of public significance, special benches are set aside for reporters.

Many constraints are placed on how the proceedings are conducted. Witnesses aren't usually allowed in court until they give their evidence, so that they aren't influenced by the evidence of other witnesses. The defendant is brought into the court after everyone else has assembled, except for the judge, who enters last. When the judge comes in, everyone stands as a sign of respect. In all criminal courts the judges and often the lawyers wear some sort of distinguishing costume, usually a gown. In the UK they also wear wigs, whose length and style relates to their seniority. Like any costume, this distinguishes the key players from the general mass of people and demonstrates that they're playing a special role.

Getting to grips with legal definitions

Loads of technical terms are used for all the different jobs associated with legal professions. Just about anyone with a legal qualification can be called a *lawyer.* An *advocate,* though, is someone who speaks on behalf of another person. Advocacy is usually taken to mean the ability to support someone else's case, and so in US courts the person who presents the case for or against the charge is known as an advocate.

In the UK and British Commonwealth countries, a select group of lawyers are allowed to be advocates in the higher courts, known as *barristers, or counsels.* Junior and senior counsels work in most significant cases, but don't expect the juniors to wear shorts and chew gum; the term simply means that the person is an assistant to the senior counsel who manages the prosecution or defence case in court.

By legal definition, *attorneys* are people who can act on behalf of others, but the term is most common in the US. In the UK, people who help others with legal matters are called *solicitors.* They can't present cases in a higher court, but appoint barristers to do so for their clients. In English-speaking legal systems, judges are typically selected from among experienced barristers or advocates, which is why they're often quite elderly, although this is changing now that they have to retire at 70. In other jurisdictions, such as France and Spain, being a judge is a direct career choice with its own training, and so they're much more likely to be young, and yes, female. In some of the lower courts, the person presiding over the court is known as a *magistrate,* which is the term used in France and other countries for the person who English speakers call the *judge.* (The French TV serial *Spiral (Engrenages)* is an excellent illustration of how the French legal system works, and shows the magistrate sometimes assisting with the investigation of crimes, which could not really happen in the UK.) The terms magistrate and judge are interchangeable for the issues that I explore in this book.

This whole dramatic layout exists to demonstrate the seriousness of the proceedings and create a psychological impact on all involved. You know you're not in a place of casual conversation, where any sort of informal behaviour is acceptable. Many judges and lawyers believe that the rituals and setting increase the likelihood that the truth is going to be revealed in court. They think that the power of the legal ceremony influences people to take the whole situation extremely seriously and so be honest.

These processes can be very daunting for people who don't experience them daily and can cause considerable confusion as to what's considered appropriate behaviour and what is being discussed (flip to the later section 'Comprehending the legal rituals and terms' for more).

Understanding the court process: Order of ceremony

Besides the symbolic rituals and layout of the court that I describe in the preceding section, legal proceedings under the English-speaking, adversarial system, and most other systems, also follow a standard process – an *order of ceremony*. You need to have some idea of this process to understand the various psychological issues that arise along the way:

1. **The judge and lawyers discuss what evidence can be acceptably introduced and how the trial is going to proceed** *before* **the jury is brought in.** This part is known as the *voir dire*, which is derived from the Latin meaning to 'tell the truth'. In particular there's a discussion of what evidence is going to be allowed and which experts will be called. The judge makes the final decision but there's often a lot of give and take between the opposing lawyers at this stage. In the US, it's also the opportunity for lawyers to object to particular jurors in the process of jury selection (see the later section 'Getting the Desired Jury' for more on this practice).

2. **The jury is selected and swears an oath to act honourably.**

3. **The judge explains its task to the jury.**

4. **The prosecution counsel presents a summary of the case and the evidence that is to be brought, followed by the defence counsel's summary of the evidence and the issues to be aware of.**

5. **The prosecution calls its witnesses to give evidence. The sequence is as follows:**

   - The prosecution counsel questions the witness.

   - The defence counsel *cross-examines* the witness (check out the later section 'Cross-Examining the Psychology of Cross-Examination').

   - The prosecution counsel is allowed a few more questions for clarification.

6. **The defence calls its witnesses to give evidence, following the same sequence of questioning as in step 5.**

7. **The prosecution and defence counsels present their closing arguments.**

8. **The judge instructs the jury on what it needs to consider.** This stage often includes a recounting of the key points in the evidence and, for example, whether the jury needs to decide whether a key witness was telling the truth or not. The judge also draws the jury's attention to key points of law, such as the need for the defendant to have intended to commit the crime, especially for a verdict of murder.

9. **The jury is sent to the private jury room, where the members deliberate on what they've heard without any contact with people outside.** When they've reached a decision, they return to the court and the person chosen by the jury to represent its view, *the foreman,* reports the jury's conclusion to the judge.

At every stage of this unfolding process, the lawyers have to determine how best to present the information and arguments to the judge and especially to the jury (if there's one). The jury in turn has to make sense of all that's going on and come to an informed decision. Psychological factors are relevant at every stage, and I explore some of the key ones in the following sections.

Delving Into Jury Psychology

A joke goes as follows: a jury is a group of 12 men and women who have to decide whether the defence or prosecution has the best lawyer! This somewhat cynical take on court procedures is useful in drawing attention to the huge power of how evidence is presented in court, and the significance of the skills of the lawyers in laying the case before the jury.

People used to assume that judges were able to ensure that jury members knew what they were doing, how to respond to the legal processes and make sense of the legal arguments with only limited guidance. Over the last 50 years or so, however, various studies show that juries don't necessarily act in the logical, informed way that the law assumed. For this reason, psychologists started demonstrating to lawyers and judges the problems that members of the jury face and how best to inform them. I discuss some of these psychological issues in this section.

Facing decision time: How juries act and make decisions

In the legal systems that put great store by jury decisions, the jury members are kept protected from any outside influence. Their deliberations are secret and they aren't allowed to tell anyone what went on in the jury room. This secrecy makes it extremely difficult to study jury decision-making in real trials or to determine how individual members reach their conclusions. From necessity, what's known about jury decision-making comes from indirect sources (which has to be treated with some caution) and from more general examinations of the relationships between personal characteristics and legally relevant decisions.

One way of studying jury decision-making is to get a group of people together to simulate a jury (called a *mock jury*). Court proceedings can then be presented to the members and they're observed coming to a decision. The main concern is to discover what makes the members more likely to decide in favour of guilt or innocence. Of course, one large problem here is that the same pressures don't exist on these people as in a real case. For example, no one's going to be imprisoned for a long time and members of the jury don't get into legal hot-water for misbehaving. So there aren't the same pressures on them to do the right thing as there would be in a real court. Unsurprisingly, such results are far from a clear reflection of what happens in real-life practice, and in fact tend to show that juries are rather more able to deal with the complexities of the legal process than may be expected.

How juries decide the verdict is psychologically fascinating. Research shows that in fact jurors do what anyone does when hearing about a crime. They try to work out the most plausible storyline that accounts for the facts; that is, they produce a cause-and-effect sequence that accords with their understanding of how events can occur. This sequence draws on assumptions about the evidence presented, judgements about the defendant and about how and why such crimes happen.

The development of a plausible story by jurors often goes through three phases:

1. **The jury members individually construct various possible plots that tie together the evidence as it's presented.** The extent to which the evidence is covered by any proposed narrative is used to select from among the different stories on offer. The possible plots are also examined in terms of how internally consistent they are, how well the facts agree with each other and how they fit into the narrative. All these aspects are checked against the juror's understanding of how things typically happen – how plausible they are.

2. **The jury members evaluate various storylines against the instructions given by the judge.** This step includes the key legal issues and the different types of verdict available.

3. **The jury members select the verdict that most closely matches with the most plausible cause-and-effect narrative sequence of actions.** The result is a lengthy discussion or even a hung jury, one on which no overall agreement can be reached between all or most of the members of the jury. This is because no close match emerges, or members of the jury disagree with each other on the most plausible story or how well it fits the facts or implies a verdict.

The contrast effect

An interesting phenomenon found with jury decision is the *contrast effect,* which applies to many human judgements. If you're offered a very expensive pair of shoes and then a cheaper pair that are still expensive you're likely to think that the second pair is more reasonably priced than if you're offered a very cheap pair and then the moderately expensive pair, which then seem very expensive. In other words, people's judgements tend to be relative.

The contrast effect is found in studies of people making decisions about guilt or innocence in simulated legal decisions. If a rape case is presented followed by a vandalism case, a greater chance exists of the vandalism case receiving a guilty verdict; if the vandalism case is presented first, it has a lower probability of leading to a conviction.

Of course this effect is most powerful if the jury, or the judge even, is dealing with a series of cases one after another. Their idea of 'seriousness' is influenced by what it's compared with. That's one reason why there are guidelines on what crimes should receive what sentences to try and make sentencing less influenced by these sorts of psychological effects.

Comprehending the legal rituals and terms

The legal profession all over the world delights in its own vocabulary. The esoteric labels for the different participants in court (check out the earlier sidebar 'Getting to grips with legal definitions') are only the tip of legal jargon. Even everyday terms such as *insanity* take on special meanings in law (as I discuss in Chapter 3). Concepts such as *mens rea,* that I describe in Chapter 1 and refer to throughout this book, and many other legal terms, are used in court and jurors need to understand them.

A jury is deliberately a random sample of local people who consequently have a great mix of education and intellectual ability. This situation raises questions about how well juries really understand what's going on in court and the instructions they're given. Studies in the US, mainly with mock juries (described earlier), indicate that as few as half the instructions given to a jury by the judge may actually be understood by the jury.

The sorts of issues that juries often struggle with or don't understand include:

- ✔ The notion of *the burden of proof*, and especially the idea in criminal cases of *beyond reasonable doubt*. These terms turn out to be somewhat ambiguous and jurors may have difficulty in agreeing on what they mean.

- ✔ The requirement of *intent* before a person can be convicted of murder.

✔ The fact that physical injury doesn't need to be present for an assault charge and the difference between *burglary* and *robbery* (the latter incorporates assault or the threat of it; check out Chapter 6 for more info).

✔ The aspects of a crime that make it particularly heinous (known as *aggravation*) or that help explain the defendant's actions and reduce the implications of its seriousness (called *mitigation*).

Such confusions and misunderstandings can have serious consequences. Research shows that the impact of legal jargon increases the likelihood of a defendant being found guilty when the charges are presented in archaic legal language. Jurors are less likely to find the defendant guilty when the instructions are translated into everyday language.

Other matters also make things difficult for jury members and so put psychological pressures on them:

✔ How complex the trial is, especially if it lasts more than six months. In these cases, jurors can have great difficulty in understanding the judge's instructions.

✔ Low educational achievement of jurors. Not surprisingly, people of a higher educational level can make more sense of what's going on in court.

✔ Willingness (or not) of specific jurors to accept authority and adhere to the instructions given because of aspects of their personality. People concerned to present a good impression are more likely to follow instructions.

✔ Pre-existing beliefs about how courts work and what goes on within them. These ideas often draw on fictional accounts and also reduce a juror's ability to act in accordance with real legal frameworks. Such jury members may act on what they believe is common sense far more readily than observing the niceties of legal requirements.

Various attempts have been made to help lawyers and judges work more effectively with juries, including:

✔ Carefully analysing the instructions to juries to take account of the educational level required to make sense of them.

✔ Giving written instructions to jurors.

✔ Presenting instructions to jurors before they hear the evidence.

✔ Repeating instructions to the jury.

✔ Providing special verdict forms for the jury to complete.

✔ Supplying diagrams and illustrations that lead the jury step by step through the evidence to reach a decision.

Animated, computer-based illustrations have even been tried, for example, to help a jury understand what forms of self-defence are legally acceptable. But the power of legal precedence and accepted rituals puts a strong break on the acceptance of such innovations. In addition, the legal problem exists that, if instructions to juries differ from accepted practice, the way is opened for an appeal.

Also, research isn't clear that any of the attempts listed inevitably improve jurors' understanding of what they need to do and how they should reach a verdict, because every case has unique qualities and what may be helpful in one case may hinder in another. Most experts believe, however, that a lot of room still exists to improve how juries are helped to reach decisions.

Dealing with inadmissible evidence

At an early stage of the court process, an attempt is made to decide what evidence the jury is to be allowed to hear (see my earlier description of the *voir dire* stage). Most typically, information about a defendant's previous crimes is kept out of court by the defence (if at all possible, although in the UK, changes in the law are making this more difficult for the defence to do). Their argument is that the person should be tried only for the crime currently before the court, and not for previous misdemeanours. The defence claims that facts about previous offences will *prejudice* the jurors, that is, lead them to make decisions in advance of, and probably ignoring, crucial facts of the case.

The influence of such prejudicial information is certainly very powerful. I carried out a simple study in which a set of actions were described that were ambiguous and could perhaps imply a crime (or not). I had two sets of instructions, which differed only in one simple aspect. In one condition the protagonist was described as having just come out of prison, in the other he was described as just coming home from work. People were given just one description and asked whether the person was guilty or not. An overwhelmingly larger number of people decided that the protagonist was guilty when a hint was included that he'd been in jail. Although they were not aware of it, people used the information about the protagonist's criminal background to reduce the ambiguity in the direction of criminality.

A similar problem may arise (that may lead to a jury giving a guilty verdict) when a person is tried for a number of similar crimes all together. The reason may be to save time and money, but as you'd expect, if a person is charged with a string of offences the jury is likely to be rather suspicious about him and more likely to convict. For this reason again intense debate takes place, before the court proceedings begin in front of the jury, as to whether cases are sufficiently linked to warrant being presented together.

Another problem is when jurors are at risk of finding out evidence that the judge decides isn't admissible in court. In the US, this evidence often comes from newspaper reports before or around the time of the trial. (In recent cases in the UK this has been from Googling details on smartphones!) In the UK and many other countries, after a person is charged with an offence the offence becomes *sub judice,* meaning that it's now in the hands of the justice system and no one can mention anything that may influence potential jury members (which before selection can be almost any member of the general public). With its stronger commitment to a free press, the US doesn't have such strict *sub judice* rules.

The judge instructs jurors to put all emotional concerns out of their minds and to review the facts as objectively as possible based on the way they've been determined in court. They're also told to ignore anything they've heard about the case except the evidence they hear in court, and yet when jury decision-making is looked at closely, research often finds that jurors are unable to ignore what they may have heard or to only pay attention to the facts as presented in court.

Making sense of the evidence

Particular challenges arise for a jury when it has to consider scientific or technical evidence. The following matters are examples of the sort of things juries can have difficulty dealing with:

- ✔ **The probability of an occurrence.** For instance, if an expert says that 1 out of 100 cases would randomly produce the results found in this particular case, members of the jury may not be able to determine whether this means the results found are so unusual that they could have just happened by chance, or are so unusual that they have to be significant for the case. By contrast, eyewitnesses stating with confidence that they saw the defendant at the crime scene may be taken as strong evidence, even though (as I discuss in Chapter 4) such a confident assertion may sometimes have little validity.

- ✔ **Large amounts of information.** If a lot of information is available, especially when that information is complex scientific information, jurors may feel well-informed but then find it very difficult to disentangle the different aspects of that information and come to a conclusion.

- ✔ **Requirement for a control group.** Often, jurors aren't aware of the need for some sort of comparison against which to assess any scientific conclusion (what scientists call a *control* group of people or objects to whom the procedure hasn't been applied). For instance, being informed that a particular chemical was found in people who'd died would only be suspicious if the chemical wasn't found in people who hadn't died.

Cross-Examining the Psychology of Cross-Examination

In this section, I examine the psychology involved in the questioning of witnesses in court.

Setting questions and giving answers

The legal process relies heavily on the questioning of witnesses. How well the lawyers asking questions understand the issues at hand is therefore central to how a case unfolds in court. If the lawyer goes off in a direction that the witness (whether an expert or not) thinks is misleading, getting back to what the witness considers crucial to understanding the matter at hand can be extremely difficult.

The whole legal process therefore depends on how effective the question and answer sessions are from which the evidence is drawn. This arrangement gives the lawyers considerable power in how evidence is presented to the judge and jury. They can guide the sequence in which information is presented and thus how readily it may be believed.

As a university teacher I'm used to giving lectures on topics, using illustrations wherever possible. I was surprised, therefore, the first time I gave evidence in court and discovered that I wasn't expected to give a talk explaining my opinion and the reasons for it. Instead, the barrister led me through a series of questions as a way of revealing who I was and my opinion. Courts are rarely designed to allow easy presentation of illustrations and so most of what's explained comes in answers to questions. This means that it's difficult to develop elaborate explanations of subtle issues, and, as I describe in the following sections, the way the material is presented is open to strong influence from how the lawyers want to show it.

Avoiding leading questions

The rules of what's acceptable in court are shaped to avoid unfair bias in questioning that can influence answers unfairly. The most significant of these rules is the avoidance of *leading questions*. For example, a lawyer asking a witness, 'Did you see a red car?' is normally considered improper, because the question assumes that a car was involved and that it was red. A more acceptable question would be, 'Did you see any vehicles?'.

The assumption is that leading questions imply facts and may therefore influence a jury even if no evidence exists for those facts. They may also encourage witnesses to give positive answers because of the intimidating pressure of the legal rituals (which I discuss in the earlier section 'Examining existing legal rituals').

These assumptions about leading questions are valid and can be taken a stage further by building implicit suggestions into questions. In one study, when people were asked to estimate the speed of a vehicle, they gave much higher estimates when the question mentioned the cars 'smashing' into each other than when the phrasing was 'contacting' each other. Witnesses are also more likely to report seeing broken glass when the word 'smash' is used, even though none was present. This research relates to the easy influencing of memory that I explore in Chapter 4.

Although leading questions are improper when lawyers are questioning witnesses from their own side (for example, the prosecutor questioning prosecution witnesses), such questions may be tolerated, indeed may be explicitly permitted in some jurisdictions, during cross-examination of the opposition's witnesses, sometimes causing distress and confusion in the witness.

Variations on leading questions are also acceptable in the forms I discuss in the following list. Certain aspects of these questions, however, raise problems because although they may seem innocent enough they may implicitly distort the given answers or mislead the jury. These types of questions include:

- ✔ **Directed questions.** 'What colour cap was he wearing?' is a question that assumes he was wearing a cap. In addition, it doesn't deal with anything else he was wearing and so draws attention to only one aspect of the clothing. Witnesses are likely to be comfortable with such questions, because they can appear supportive and encouraging, and so are more willing to answer them confidently even when their memories are less than clear.

- ✔ **Directed choices.** When lawyers offer a set of options, this approach can distort the jury's perception of what's at issue as well as putting witnesses in a position where they can seem unhelpful or awkward if they don't choose one of the options. 'Would you say the wounds caused death or were serious?' is a question that requires strong conviction to answer by saying that the wounds were neither, and yet the jury has already been led to believe that, at the very least, they were serious.

- ✔ **Short questions.** The legal ritual often supports the use of short questions, especially those containing two sharply contrasting parts, such as, 'Would you say this was a dangerous action or not?' Such questions imply that a simple answer must exist to such a simple question. Expert witnesses may want to quibble around being given such a simplistic choice, but any attempt to develop a more subtle answer, for example along the lines of, 'It all depends on what you mean by dangerous,' can be seen as pedantic and unhelpful. Short questions therefore give the lawyer much more control over how the evidence is revealed to the court than may seem apparent at first sight. The lawyer can guide the direction in which the witness unfurls the facts without the jury necessarily being aware of what's happening.

✔ **Casting doubt.** Because the law in criminal cases requires that the decision is beyond reasonable doubt, any suggestion of doubt can be used, especially by the defence, to raise questions in the minds of the jurors. The most prevalent way of doing this is to ask whether some alternative is possible such as, 'Is it possible these injuries occurred when paramedics examined the body?' Such a question can force experts or other witnesses into making categorical assertions or seeming wishy-washy if they admit to some doubt. If doubt exists, further questioning can give weight by asking whether this isn't a 'reasonable' assumption.

✔ **Facts or opinions?** Courts allow only expert witnesses to give opinions (as I discuss in Chapter 11); other witnesses are supposed to limit themselves to the facts. So if a lawyer can imply a witness is offering an opinion and not facts, this can persuade the jury not to take what the witness says seriously. The problem is that no simple division exists between facts and opinion when people are drawing on their memories. 'Can you be sure the car was red?' leads to the possibility that what the witness is saying isn't a hard and fast fact, but an opinion of what's likely to be the case.

✔ **Exchanges.** The question-and-answer sequence is the essence of giving evidence in court. Although this approach can appear to be a cumbersome way of informing people of the facts as the witness sees them, it gives the lawyer the possibility of setting up a rhythm of questions and answers that can corner unsuspecting witnesses into revealing weaknesses in their evidence.

ANECDOTE

Here's an example from my own experience of giving evidence to challenge the opinion of another expert, whom I call Reverend Q:

Barrister: Is it true Professor Canter that you invited Reverend Q to give a presentation at a conference you organised?

Me: Yes.

Barrister: Is it also the case that you give lectures on Reverend Q's work on your postgraduate course?

Me: Yes.

Barrister: Yet you're now telling the court that his work is of no value.

The barrister was clearly expecting me to be flustered by this sequence of events and to give some less than convincing answer. However, I saw his trap coming and answered:

Me: Yes. I think it's important for my students to see poor science so that they can distinguish it from work to be trusted!

Getting the Desired Jury: How Psychologists Can Help

One area in which forensic psychology expertise can directly help is in giving guidance on how to select a jury, as I describe in this section. The use of juries in courts is to ensure that anyone accused of a crime is judged by people similar to him from his community, the assumption being that they understand his way of life and are able to make sense of his actions. The belief is that members of a jury will make honest, objective judgements of the facts presented to them.

Various legal systems, however, accept that if a juror holds prejudices that are relevant to crucial issues in the case, that person can't make unbiased decisions on that case. For example, if a juror thought that female doctors can't ever be trusted, they should not be allowed to sit on a jury in any case involving a female doctor. Therefore, legal systems allow challenges to the presence of individual members of the jury on the grounds that they'd be biased. This bias can be the simple matter of the juror knowing the defendant.

In the UK, requests by the defence or prosecution to challenge any member of the jury are very rare and have to be based on clear legal issues, but in the US the possibility of challenging the presence of one or more people on the jury is accepted in many states. This objection may even be allowed without the need for any explicit or distinctly legal reason. This can become a major aspect of the court procedure in the US, requiring hundreds of jurors being asked to attend court for possible jury service (as happened in the trial of O.J. Simpson for murder).

Psychologists can offer some general principles on jury selection, such as older people being more willing to convict someone. Another suggestion is that people who have had previous experience of a trial are more likely to support a conviction. However, no strong evidence exists for any simple relationship between the characteristics of people and the decisions they'll make after they've heard the evidence and discussed it with other jury members. Even unexpected findings (for one such phenomenon, check out the later sidebar 'The black sheep effect') can confound any simple assumptions about a jury.

No coaching allowed

A personal experience illustrates how cautious UK barristers are about any form of 'coaching' or interaction with a witness. Some years ago I gave evidence about tape recordings, the transcripts of which were read out in court. On the first day I gave evidence it emerged that two of the recordings were very similar. Overnight I realised that I'd inadvertently recorded the same material twice, but the transcribers hadn't produced identical versions, which is why the material read in court wasn't absolutely identical. I was to continue to give my evidence the next day, so I tried to speak to the barrister before the court proceedings began to explain the error. But he gently told me that he couldn't speak to me while I was still giving evidence. So the court never heard why there were two very similar transcripts!

About the only aspect of a juror's characteristics that does predict an above-chance probability that the person is more likely to convict someone, is the person's attitude towards the legal system. The more confident people are in the processes of law, the more likely they're to convict.

The ploys described in the following section for preparing witnesses, and other forms of 'scientific' advice on how attorneys should behave, are totally unacceptable in many jurisdictions outside the US. Therefore much of the information in this section relates only to the US.

Selecting juries for scientific trials

A particular challenge to the judge and lawyer as well as for juries, is how they deal with scientific and technical information in areas about which they may have had no formal training. In the US, where legal practice allows extensive selection of jury members, issues arise of how to select a jury that's most likely to give the desired verdict (from both sides' point of view). As a consequence, a special area of expertise has grown up to advise attorneys on how to do this, which inevitably raises ethical as well as legal and psychological questions (check out the later sidebar, 'The Runaway Jury').

The possibility of jury selection improving the chances of each side giving the verdict wanted, spurred on the study of how jurors make decisions. This information has been included in the commercial practice of providing guidance, usually to the defence, on the selection of juries and has become known as *scientific jury selection*. Employing this expertise is often very expensive and is usually only used in very high-profile cases, such as the trial of

O.J. Simpson. In order to decide whether someone available for the jury is going to be acceptable, the attorney can question the person or even use standard questionnaires such as the Juror Bias Scale. This form has 17 questions, such as 'Anyone who runs from the police is probably guilty' and 'Too often juries do not convict someone who's guilty out of sympathy' that people have to indicate whether they agree or disagree with. The scale indicates whether the person is likely to be more inclined to support the defence or the prosecution.

For those cases in which the jury is required to determine the sentence after a person is convicted, or levels of compensation in civil proceedings, the significance of a juror's pre-existing attitudes is particularly important. In the US this issue comes to a head, especially when a jury is required to decide whether a convicted murderer should be executed. A person opposed to the death penalty in principle is often excluded from such a jury.

Coaching witnesses

One of the contributions that psychologists have made to major cases in the US is *witness preparation*, that is, coaching witnesses by reviewing what they're going to say and how they'll say it. The aim is to improve their effectiveness in convincing the jury. This is much more common in the US and is somewhat frowned on in the UK (see the 'No coaching allowed' anecdote earlier).

The black sheep effect

You may think that jurors would be more lenient to defendants of their own ethnicity, but in fact studies show the opposite may be the case. This tendency is called *the black sheep effect*. The jurors think that the defendant has let down their ethnic group and so should be treated more harshly. Clearly this research has implications for jury selection. Jury selection assisted by psychologists can also be part of a broader range of psychological support, the most intensive of which is the creation of a *shadow jury*. This consists of employing a group of people who closely match the actual jury in terms of age, ethnicity and socio-economic status. This parallel jury then listens to exactly the same evidence as the real jury but is available for comment and discussion on the sense that evidence is making to them. The attorneys can then modify how they present subsequent information to the jury.

Witness preparation involves educating the witnesses in courtroom procedures and reviewing their previous statements, for example to the police, to ensure that no contradictions are included. If this preparation involves some form of rehearsal, it increases the witness's confidence and fluency in court, which in turn is likely to increase the credibility of the witness. Witness preparation further ensures that the attorney is totally familiar with what the witness knows and is likely to say.

The Runaway Jury

The various psychological interventions of coaching witnesses, studying jury decision-making, using shadow juries and developing questioning strategies add up to a great deal of potential interference with how a court works. This problem is delightfully illustrated in the book by John Grisham called *The Runaway Jury* (made into a film starring Gene Hackman). In the movie, every possible psychological device is employed by the attorney to get the jury to accept his arguments. However, the plot twist is that a member of the jury is even more sophisticated than the attorney and gets the opposite decision. This clever narrative device illustrates how problematic any attempt is to shape activities in court.

The Runaway Jury also draws attention to the ethical and legal dilemmas created by introducing psychological expertise into how the court processes should run. Not least is the fact that the experts providing such services are usually very expensive (although free online advice is increasingly becoming available). As a result, rich defendants are more likely to use them, especially a major corporation (which is the defendant in the John Grisham book), instead of ordinary folk who can't afford the cost of such advice. Another concern is that the advice can drift into distorting the evidence presented and how the legal procedure unfolds in ways that undermine basic principles of the law, notably that it should be objective and its processes openly transparent.

Part V
Helping and Treating Offenders

The 5th Wave   By Rich Tennant

"Mike! It's Dr. Presky. I'm a psychologist. If you come out now we can probably blame a lot of this on your mother."

In this part . . .

The most important way to reduce crime is to stop it happening in the first place, or if someone does commit a crime to set in motion some intervention that will reduce the chances of him or her doing it again. Psychologists are very active in both working with families to lower the probability that their children will become criminal and providing interventions with offenders that are aimed at helping them out of future criminality. Violent and sexual crimes are the ones most obviously open to some form of treatment programmes. Illustrations of how they work and the principles on which they are based is dealt with in this part.

Chapter 13

Intervening to Rehabilitate Offenders

....

In This Chapter

▶ Looking at the psychological effects of imprisonment

▶ Discovering different approaches to treatment

▶ Hearing about the challenges of treatment

....

*I*n this chapter, I explore the psychological issues surrounding punishment and rehabilitation of offenders. I examine the use of imprisonment and ways in which incarceration is helpful or otherwise. I also describe using psychological treatment programmes *(interventions)* with prisoners, some effective and others less so, and the associated challenges. Although there are many difficulties in providing successful interventions, some do have benefits and reduce re-offending.

A very large proportion of convicted offenders don't go to prison. They have to attend probation sessions and carry out services in the community or suffer other forms of sentencing, such as a curfew (electronic tagging). Many of the interventions that I mention in this chapter are relevant to people in prison and those that aren't, although delivering the therapy to offenders who aren't in the controlled environment of the prison can be very difficult.

Examining the Challenges of Imprisonment

The sentence that a convicted criminal receives has a number of possible objectives, including:

✔ Retribution for wrongdoing.

✔ Removal of the offender from society so that he can't commit further crimes while in prison.

> ✔ Deterrent to discourage others from comitting similar crimes in the future.
>
> ✔ Rehabilitation to encourage the offender to desist from his criminal ways.

For the widest possible benefit to both prisoners and the general public, the last point is perhaps the most important of all.

The overall objective of prisons is seen as combining *reformation* with punishment, which is why they can be called *'reformatories'* or in the US *correctional* establishments. Yet this view raises questions about how successful prison really is in changing people for the better, and whether other more effective ways exist of enabling offenders to find their way onto the straight and narrow, as I examine in this section.

Investigating the effectiveness of prison

A major form of criminal sentence these days is to serve time in prison, with debate revolving around how long a person's sentence needs to be for any given crime. However, a strong case exists for using alternatives to prison because the experience of prison can be so destructive. For this reason, different forms of punishment, such as service in the community or in special secure units (including the therapeutic communities that I describe in the later section 'Treating in therapeutic communities') are increasingly being used in the judicial system.

Prison was introduced as a major form of punishment relatively recently, about 150 years ago. (This is not to be confused with the medieval practice of throwing people in dungeons or locking them in the Tower of London. They were not legal punishments as such but ways of keeping awkward people out of circulation.) Its increased use in the 19th century drew on the idea that crime was a product of association with other criminals. The notion was that if a person was separated from other criminals and given the Bible to study, he'd mend his ways. Physical exercise, such as walking on a treadmill or around an exercise yard, was allowed, but all imprisonment was, in effect, solitary confinement.

This system was soon found to be very debilitating to prisoners (see the nearby sidebar 'Isolating a prisoner') and expensive to manage. As a result, the authorities quickly changed it to today's prison system in which inmates are allowed to mix with each other (known in UK prison jargon as *association*), and required to participate in any work activities that are available. Prisons now often aim to provide something to replace the traditional sewing of mail bags, however, so that the work provides both a sense of achievement for individuals and a social context in which habits of working productively with others can be developed. If possible, the work also gives the inmates skills that they can use in legitimate jobs on release.

REGIONAL TIP-OFF

Banning cruel punishment

Throughout history, societies have used many different forms of punishment, including physical assault, such as whipping or binding with chains, and different types of execution, as well as fines, being forced to join the army or navy, or being transported to the Americas or Australia.

In most countries, the more vicious forms of punishment have been stopped and both the US and Europe have special constitutional requirements that disallow torture, demeaning or unusual forms of punishment.

In the US, the eighth amendment to the constitution forbids excessive fines or cruel and unusual punishments.

The European Convention on Human Rights, article 3, states that 'No one shall be subjected to torture or to inhuman or degrading treatment or punishment'.

Education is another positive area of prisons. Many offenders failed in school and can barely read or write or do elementary arithmetic. Crime may have been the only way they could survive with these disadvantages. When prison provides the opportunities that school never did, it can make a difference to their lives, although of course it can also enable them to commit more sophisticated crimes!

Training in prison is also useful, especially with younger offenders. Giving a person a trade qualification can open up job opportunities that were never available to them before. Although setting up training facilities is demanding for prisons, where it's done it can be very effective.

Asking whether prison can make offenders worse

Prison can cause distinct, debilitating, psychological effects on inmates, including:

- ✔ **Feelings of worthlessness and low self-esteem** including depression. Incarceration denies people their basic right to privacy and forces them to relinquish control over everyday features of their daily lives that other people take for granted. They may live in a small, sometimes extremely confined and poorly lit and ventilated cell and may have little or no say in choosing the person with whom they have to share that space. In addition, they have no option over when they get up or go to bed, when or what they eat, when they shower or use the toilet or exercise. These degrading circumstances continually remind them of their stigmatised existence. In some cases, prisoners can come to believe that they deserve the degradation and stigma to which they've been subjected while imprisoned.

✔ **Becoming institutionalised:** Prison is a 'total institution' in which every aspect of the inmates' lives is controlled, as I describe in the preceding point. Prisons withdraw much of the inmates' independence or right to decide for themselves. This situation can be difficult for prisoners to cope with initially, but on release causes problems when trying to re-adjust. People can become institutionalised and passively accept everything the regime requires them to do. Consequently, they can have difficulty taking any active role themselves in the future.

✔ **Anger with specific individuals and with 'the system':** They may believe that certain prison officers or other inmates have caused them harm, whether or not that is the case, as well as feeling that the whole legal process and incarceration is unfair and something to be challenged.

✔ **Hyper-vigilance, interpersonal distrust and suspicion** become natural in prison, because after all it's full of criminals, many of whom have a history of violence. Some male prisoners learn to project a 'hard man' image believing that unless they do they're likely to be dominated and exploited. They don't tolerate anything they think is an insult, no matter how trivial. This can get them into trouble in prison as well as on release.

✔ **Emotional over-control, alienation and psychological distancing** are consequences of the potential threats prisoners may see all around them. Prisoners who develop this unrevealing and impenetrable 'prison mask', risk creating an enduring and unbridgeable distance between themselves and other people.

✔ **Social withdrawal and isolation** is part of the process whereby prisoners protect themselves. They hide behind a cloak of social invisibility and become as low-key and discretely detached from others as possible. In extreme cases, this behaviour can make prisoners seem to be clinically depressed.

✔ **Accepting the exploitative and extreme values of prison life** such as agreeing to the unwritten prisoner code of conduct or risk repercussions. This can include not reporting any assaults they have experienced or that they know about and relying on any gang hierarchy for guidance on what they should do. This can tie them into a criminal subculture that is difficult to shake off once outside prison.

Isolating a prisoner

Today, solitary confinement in prison occurs for one of two main reasons: the prisoner's own protection (for example, for abusers of young children who are likely to be picked on and attacked by other prisoners) or for punishment and control (for example, if a person breaks important prison rules, violently attacks another prisoner or smashes up his cell in anger).

Solitary confinement can be extremely debilitating for some people, especially if the prisoner has no contact at all with others, but in some progressive prisons it's used as an opportunity to help a prisoner to calm down and then to open up to one-to-one counselling in a controlled environment. Most jurisdictions have legal limits on how long a person can be kept in solitary confinement as a punishment.

Spending 23 hours a day in a cell with nothing to do can be soul-destroying for anyone. For a person who has difficulty in reading and never had his awareness of possibilities broadened through effective education, it can be extremely destructive.

All these aspects cause difficulties when working on psychological issues with prisoners. The central challenge is expressed clearly by a very experienced prison psychologist, Kevin Rogers, who told me:

> *Prison culture looks down on any sign of weakness and susceptibility, and discourages the expression of sincere emotions or familiarity. Some prisoners embrace this in a way which encourages a keen investment in one's reputation for toughness, and promotes an attitude towards others in which even apparently irrelevant verbal abuse, disrespect, or physical infringements must be responded to speedily and intuitively, often with decisive force. In some cases, the failure to take advantage of weakness is often seen as a symbol of weakness itself and viewed as provocation for manipulation. In male prisons, it may encourage a type of hypermasculinity in which power and control are overestimated as critical parts of one's identity.*

These consequences of imprisonment make exploring any psychological problems an inmate may have extremely difficult, especially any aspects of themselves that may indicate weakness or require them to acknowledge and explore their emotional reactions. Offenders can be particularly reluctant to seek any help with their difficulties or even recognise that they have any problems in dealing with other people that need addressing.

A further aspect that makes psychological help so difficult within a total institution is that a high percentage of prisoners have experienced some form of childhood abuse, which featured similar qualities of coercive strictness and psychological and possibly physical insult. The callous nature of prison existence may seem to some prisoners as just 'business as usual' – that's what their world is like, inside or outside prison. Imprisonment just reminds them of what made them feel so unworthy initially, which may have been part of the reason for the criminality that brought them to prison in the first place.

Specialising in working in prisons

Psychologists who spend their careers working in prisons, sometimes call themselves *correctional psychologists,* and have their own associations such as the American Association for Correctional Psychologists (AACP), which has hundreds of members.

The bulk of British psychologists working in prisons and secure units would look to the Division of Forensic Psychology of the British Psychological Society, but they're regulated, like all professional psychologists by the Health Professions Council. But they refer to themselves as *prison psychologists* or even just *applied psychologists.*

Some psychologists provide guidance to the institution rather than individual prisoners, to help prisons work as organisations that contribute to reforming their inmates. This work can include helping to select or train staff or to set in motion various programmes of work with offenders. Sometimes such work is very challenging because the institutions have an ingrained set of attitudes and a culture that's fundamentally punitive and not informed by any understanding of the causes and processes that underpin criminality.

In certain crisis situations, such as a prisoner taking someone hostage, psychologists may help to negotiate and deal with the situation as I discuss in Chapter 8.

Investigating Some Approaches to Treatment

Although all offenders are subject to the pressures of institutionalisation that I describe in the preceding section, and respond in different psychological ways and to varying degrees, some prisoners are much more vulnerable to these pressures and the overall pains of imprisonment than others. These inmates include the mentally ill and those who aren't very bright, often being learning disabled and having been passed over in their schooling, as well as those held in solitary confinement because of their inability to cope with prison (flip to the earlier sidebar 'Isolating a prisoner' for more on this issue).

Psychologists often treat these specific difficulties on an individual basis, usually in a one-to-one format using cognitive behavioural therapy (see the later 'Getting it together: Group or one-to-one programmes' and 'Using cognitive behavioural methods' sections respectively) over an agreed time span and number of sessions. Ideally, prison staff monitor changes in mood or behaviour that the vulnerable inmate suffers, and reports them to psychologists on a regular timescale with interventions amended accordingly.

In this section, I focus on the opportunity that incarceration provides for psychologists to work directly with inmates, providing various programmes that may be thought of as forms of 'treatment'.

Except in a small subset of offenders, I'm not implying that people commit crimes because they're 'ill'. I use the word *treatment* to describe many different forms of intervention with convicted criminals.

These programmes are also provided for people on probation and outside prison in therapeutic communities and various forms of secure units and other settings. The authorities increasingly realise, that locking a person away in a highly controlled setting provides an opportunity for psychological interactions with offenders that can produce changes in their future behaviour.

Working with offenders

Psychologists work with convicted offenders in relation to the following broad tasks that connect to three different stages of the offender's life:

- ✔ **Past:** Helping offenders to deal with problems that may have been a direct cause of the actions that produced the offence, such as inability to manage their own aggression, drug and/or alcohol addiction or longer-term problems, such as mental illness or personality disorder.

- ✔ **Present:** Counselling to assist offenders to cope with their current circumstances, for example reducing the risk of suicide in prison or helping people who've recently been given a life sentence.

- ✔ **Future:** Trying to determine what risks individuals pose to themselves and others and the most appropriate way of managing those risks (I discuss risk assessment further in Chapter 10). These assessments may relate to managing these individuals within a specific institution or determining the risks of releasing them into the wider community.

Assessing effectively: Horses for courses

For any work with offenders to be effective, it needs to start with some form of assessment (just as a doctor diagnoses a patient's problem to decide on the most appropriate form of treatment). Many reasons for criminal behaviour exist, and so a careful analysis of each individual's circumstances can help to guide the process of intervention.

In a psychological context, one specific cause – such as a mental abnormality or a particular experience (such as sexual abuse as a child) – is very unlikely to explain criminal behaviour, although these aspects can be important contributing factors. Instead, assessment includes forming a broader understanding of an individual and his life and all relevant aspects. Assessment takes on board the fact that plenty of people suffer particular traumas and yet don't commit crimes, and so understanding the full context out of which a person's offending grows is important.

Most of the psychological measurement procedures that I mention in chapters 9 and 10, also play a part in getting a grip on an offender's particular problems. In some cases, the assessment may just be an induction interview, explaining how the prison works and what's expected of the prisoner. But in more forward-thinking prisons, an assessment takes place of two distinct aspects of the inmate:

- ✔ **Issues directly relevant to the person's criminality,** such as substance abuse, attitude to employment and their background in crime.

- ✔ **Broader issues of the person for which they may need help,** such as depression, low self-esteem or any mental health problems. Even day-to-day problems such as the difficulty of finding a place to live may be important to note so that they can be dealt with before release.

One standard measurement procedure, developed by psychologists and gaining in popularity, used for assessing offenders when they first arrive in prison is the *Level of Service Inventory*. This procedure consists of 54 questions that explore ten aspects relevant to determining how a person should be dealt with in prison and the forms of intervention that are likely to be most relevant. The inventory covers a person's:

- ✔ Criminal history and experiences.

- ✔ Educational and any employment history.

- ✔ Financial aspects.

- ✔ Family/marital issues, including upbringing and family background.

- ✔ Accommodation history and experiences.

- ✔ Leisure/recreation preferences.

- ✔ Companions, such as friends and criminal associates.

- ✔ Alcohol/drug problems.

- ✔ Emotional/personal issues, including personality characteristics.

- ✔ Attitudes/orientation, especially towards criminality.

Modifying behaviour

Some approaches – known as *behaviour modification* – sought to change prisoners' actions directly. They were very fashionable in the 1960s and derived from the idea that human and animal behaviour is directly shaped by the associated pattern of rewards and punishments.

The idea involved providing or withdrawing rewards for acceptable behaviour. For example, a prisoner was given access to the prison gym or store only if he had no disciplinary violations over a given time period.

Although some such programmes produced initial successes, they eventually lost favour, mainly because they produced no long-term benefit. People behaved well for the rewards but after they were withdrawn their actions reverted to earlier patterns.

The great mistake of the behaviour modification approach was to forget that human beings, unlike animals, can think about their actions and their implications. They make sense of what's happening and use that to guide how they behave. Although most people are aware of this every day, sad to say it took psychological experiments to convince psychologists. One benefit, however, was that this awareness gave rise to a therapy that combines actions with thoughts – cognitive behavioural therapy.

Getting people together

Much of the therapeutic work in prisons is carried out in groups, typically of 6 to 12 individuals. The purpose of such group work is to enhance the power of therapy by enabling people to share experiences and to learn from each other's attempts to deal with their problems.

For people who have difficulty relating to and trusting others, which is a common problem for inmates, as I describe in the earlier section 'Asking whether prison can make people worse', such group sessions can be very demanding and, if managed properly, have a powerful effect. They're also much more cost-effective to run than one-to-one therapeutic sessions.

Using cognitive behavioural methods

Cognitive behavioural therapy (CBT) focuses on challenging unwanted thinking patterns and emotional and behavioural reactions that are learned over a long period of time. The aim is to identify the thinking that causes unhelpful or unproductive feelings and behaviours and discover how to replace them with more positive ones. CBT helps prisoners to make sense of potentially destructive experiences by breaking them down into smaller parts, as follows:

✔ A situation (problem, event or difficult circumstance) gives rise to:

- Thoughts
- Emotions
- Physical feelings

✔ With consequent:

- Actions.

    Each area affects the others. How an offender thinks about a problem can influence how he feels and also alter what he does about it.

Figure 13-1 shows how different thoughts, feelings and actions feed on each other producing a positive, productive circle or a negative, destructive one.

Figure 13-1:
The cycle
of thoughts,
feelings and
actions that
is dealt with
in Cognitive
Behavioural
Therapy.

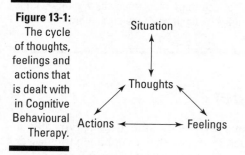

This vicious circle can make someone feel worse and is likely to give rise to other situations that produce even worse feelings. The person's beliefs can also be distorted during this process, leading to unrealistic and uncomfortable thoughts about themselves. The added distress can make a person more jumpy and ready to interpret things in extreme and unhelpful ways.

Here's an example of how this process works in practice. A prisoner is expecting a visit from his partner who promised to arrive by 2 p.m. At 2:15 p.m., he's escorted to the visits room and she's not there. Table 13-1 contains some helpful and unhelpful responses that he may feel.

Table 13-1	An Example of CBT Being Used with a Prisoner	
	Helpful	*Unhelpful*
Thoughts	Perhaps she's missed the bus; she won't be long.	She's left me and doesn't want to tell me.
Feelings	Happy, positive, in high spirits.	Angry, upset, jealous.

	Helpful	*Unhelpful*
Physical	None; feel comfortable.	Stomach cramps, low energy, feel sick.
Action	Wait quietly, get a coffee and chat with prison staff.	Go back to the wing, telephone, accusing her of being unfaithful.

It's explained to the prisoner that if he goes back to his cell feeling depressed, he may become moody and brood on what has happened. This reaction would make him feel worse. If he doesn't do this, he has the chance to correct any mis-understandings about what his partner thinks of him and what he thinks of her.

A great deal of skill is involved in providing CBT and setting up effective pro-grammes. In general, these programmes only work if they:

✔ **Use methods that take account of how participants come to under-stand what they're told.** For example, some people learn by active involvement and others from reflecting on what they have to learn. Some want to see immediately the practical implications of what they're learning, whereas some may want fully to understand the ideas behind what they're being taught.

✔ **Address specific factors associated with offending in a clearly planned way,** instead of the programme being general explorations of unaccept-able behaviour.

✔ **Are delivered as designed.** This requirement may be more difficult than it seems, because staff and inmates get moved around and pressures from other areas – such as attendance at court – can interfere with participation. The staff in a prison may offer the programme without adequate training.

Four different styles of learning that are relevant to providing CBT interven-tions with offenders are:

✔ **Activists** learn best by:

- Being offered new experiences.

- Trying 'here and now' activities.

- Exploring a range of diverse activities.

- Experiencing high visibility of themselves and the activities.

- Being allowed to generate ideas without limits.

- Being thrown in at the deep end.

- Being involved with other people.

- Being allowed to 'have a go'.

✔ **Reflectors** learn best by:

- Being allowed to observe and think about what they do.
- Standing back from events.
- Having time to think and prepare.
- Doing their own research.
- Producing reports.
- Being enabled to exchange views in a protected environment.
- Operating to their own deadlines.

✔ **Theorists** learn best by:

- Being offered interesting theories.
- Being given time to explore ideas.
- Having the opportunity to question.
- Being intellectually stretched.
- Facing structured situations with a clear purpose.
- Reading about logical ideas/concepts.
- Analysing success or failure.
- Participating in complex situations.

✔ **Pragmatists** learn best by:

- Dealing with links between the topic and their job.
- Trying things out and receiving feedback.
- Following models provided.
- Being shown techniques applicable to their job.
- Implementing what they've learned.
- Understanding that the activity has validity outside of the situation.
- Concentrating on practical issues.

Employing rational-emotive therapy

Some therapists put more emphasis on thought processes and their implications for emotional responses than on the action component that I describe in the preceding section. This emphasis on rational thought processes is a dominant aspect of *rational-emotive therapy* (RET), which is distinct from CBT. One central concept is that some thoughts are irrational and if the person can appreciate their illogicality and act on this realisation, problems caused by those thoughts can be reduced.

Three programmes based on CBT

Enhanced Thinking Skills (ETS) is the programme most frequently used in the UK, with over 40,000 offenders having completed it within British prisons over the past 12 years.

ETS, which consists of 20 group sessions of 40 hours in total, is based on the idea that much antisocial behaviour stems from offenders' inability to do what they want in acceptable ways because they lack effective ways of thinking about themselves, others and their actions. These problems aren't due to low intelligence or educational attainment, although they may contribute, but to styles of thinking and attitudes that lead to antisocial behaviour.

The course explores:

✔ Impulse control

✔ Flexible thinking

✔ Social perspective taking

✔ Values/moral reasoning

✔ Logical reasoning

✔ Inter-personal problem solving

Another popular programme is *Chromis* (no one seems quite sure why it's called this!), a complex and intensive one that aims to reduce violence in high-risk offenders whose level or combination of psychopathic traits disrupts their ability to accept treatment and change. Chromis is specifically designed to meet the needs of highly psychopathic individuals and provides participants with the skills to reduce and manage their risk of offending. In other words, it recognises the chronic problems these individuals have in generating acceptable behaviour and explores ways of managing it and reducing it, while accepting that getting rid of it altogether may not be possible.

Prison Addressing Substance Related Offending (PASRO) is a cognitive behavioural group work programme designed to address drug dependence and related offending. The programme targets offenders who are dependent on one or more drugs or on a combination of drugs and alcohol.

For example, a person who thinks that failure at a given task is an indication that they're no good at all would be regarded as irrational and a possible contributor to depression and low self-esteem. By examining with the client why that illogical link has been made can help to reduce the power of this thought. Another example, particularly relevant in the criminal context, is the belief of some men that being domineering towards a female partner is essential to being a 'real man'. Considerations of the origins and implications of this belief may in some cases help an offender to stop his violence.

The application of RET with prison populations, however, has a lot of problems. For instance, considerable discussion revolves around what is an irrational belief and what isn't. Also, people often have great reluctance in rejecting a viewpoint that they've held for many years, and which the community they belong to believes is obvious and logical.

Treating in therapeutic communities

As I note in the earlier section 'Asking whether prison can make people worse', prisons aren't very effective environments in which to carry out therapeutic interventions with inmates. Therefore, from time to time attempts have been made to create communities for offenders that counteract the prison culture that can maintain criminal behaviour. A central part of this approach is to remove the strongly hierarchical, coercive nature of prisons and open up decision-making to all those involved. For that reason, these communities are often referred to as *democratic therapeutic communities.* The residents in these communities are usually selected by those already there, or at least by a subset elected by the community. (Yes, the prisoners are involved in deciding which new inmates should be allowed to join their community.) The community also decides when a person can be discharged. Any new member also has to be clear what they're signing up to, which includes an acceptance of a range of aspects that are alien to a prison environment and are often psychologically demanding to deal with. For example:

- ✔ **Democratisation** is embraced with gusto. All major decisions relating to the community are made jointly by all its members, including staff and residents. Residents are expected to take an active role in this process.

- ✔ **Communalism** takes the democratic process a stage further. Open and free communication between everyone is encouraged, with no secrets between people.

- ✔ **Permissiveness** means that although people must obey the rules of the community, low-level misbehaviour is considered for its reasons and for ways to ensure it doesn't re-occur, instead of being a reason for punishment or ejection from the community.

- ✔ **Reality confrontation** requires that residents have to face up to their 'true colours'. They can't hide behind denial, withdrawal from contact with others or distortion of the facts to suit themselves (see the later 'Dealing with denial' section for more information).

- ✔ **Group therapy and group sessions** are used to deal with the problems that originally led people to be sentenced; these sessions can follow various therapeutic principles.

- ✔ **Community meetings** are how the community makes decisions and manages its affairs.

The environment of a therapeutic community is an intensely social one in which every aspect of every day is regarded as some form of therapeutic intervention. Unsurprisingly, many offenders can't tolerate those conditions and prefer to spend their time quietly in prison. The communication demands of these communities also means that they tend to attract and select the more capable and articulate offenders.

When treatment goes wrong

In the late 1980s, a novel form of therapeutic community was set up in the US especially for people diagnosed as psychopathic. Its activities were built around 80 hours of therapy each week, and as a result virtually no time was left for leisure, opportunities for training or for development of useful skills. The programme also included two weeks in a self-contained chamber where food and drink was provided from pipes in the walls. Along the way the inmates were made to use a variety of psychotropic drugs, such as LSD. People were expected to participate for two whole years and weren't allowed out until they showed that they had complied with what the 'treatment' was expected to achieve.

Perhaps not surprisingly, people identified as psychopaths before they joined this community were in fact more dangerous and disturbed when they left than before they entered.

The success of therapeutic communities usually relies on a charismatic leader who can keep the highly charged atmosphere in a positively supportive state rather than it imploding. Any success they have seems to depend on offenders spending at least a year or longer as members. This length of time allows people to move through various reactions to the therapeutic community experience, such as hostility and depression, before they can benefit from the new perspectives on themselves and others.

The change in lifestyle that's so central to participating in a therapeutic community is particularly useful for people whose problems centre on substance abuse. For this reason, these communities are often a framework for those institutions that provide rehabilitation for celebrities whose careers are being destroyed by their drug addiction or alcoholism.

Therapeutic communities, however, are very expensive to run (which is why they work well for the addicted rich and famous). They require special buildings and many dedicated staff. Impoverished prison systems rarely have the resources to maintain such institutions, despite any benefits they may have.

Deciding what interventions work

In the UK and elsewhere, a concerted effort has been made to evaluate various forms of intervention, which is much more difficult than you may think.

One crucial question is what criterion of success to use. Some experts prefer to look at whether a person's attitudes or behaviour in prison have changed subsequent to participation in an intervention. The problem with this approach, however, is that offenders may just discover how to adopt a therapeutic vocabulary to describe their actions and get to know what sort of opinions they're supposed to express, without ever fully embracing the attitudes involved. This problem leads to the possibility that their behaviour changes back to their criminal ways when they leave the institution.

Other evaluations focus on offending activity after the intervention. But again, the question arises of what exactly should be monitored – reduction in criminal activity or total cessation? And over what time period? Should it cover serious crimes, arrests or all illegal activity?

The possibility also exists that interventions make offenders more aware of the risks of getting caught, and so they don't reduce their criminality but merely their coming to the attention of the police. They learn how to talk their way out of situations where they're challenged about their crimes or even just learn more in the group sessions about how others got away with their offending.

A somewhat different approach to considering these interventions with offenders, is to make sure that at least they're professionally conducted and follow appropriate guidelines so that programmes are as effective as possible. This approach led to the accreditation of programmes in the UK to ensure that required standards are maintained as follows:

- **A clear model of change:** An explicit model is necessary to explain how the programme intends to bring about relevant change in offenders; that is, specifying how it's going to do this and what's achieved at each stage of the programme. The model must describe why this combination of targets and methods is likely to work with the offenders selected.

- **Selection of offenders:** Clear specification is required of the types of offender for whom the programme is intended and the methods used to select them. The programme has to identify the characteristics of the offenders selected, such as the nature of their offences that the programme is tackling, risk, motivation, learning style, gender and race. The programme must have ways for dealing with offenders who have started and are then found to be unsuitable.

- **Targeting a range of dynamic risk factors:** A range of risk factors known to be associated with re-offending must be addressed in an integrated manner within the programme. The programme needs to focus overtly on the factors that are open to change – the dynamic risk factors I consider in Chapter 10.

- **Effective methods:** Evidence needs to show that the treatment methods used are likely to have an impact on the targeted dynamic risk factors. For example, CBT methods work well with most types of offenders, including sex offenders (check out the earlier section 'Using cognitive behavioural methods'). Structured therapeutic communities are helpful in changing the lifestyle of people with drug or alcohol addictions or other patterns of antisocial behaviour (see the earlier section 'Treating in therapeutic communities').

✔ **Skills orientated:** The programme needs to facilitate the learning of skills that support involvement in legitimate pursuits, including literacy, numeracy and general problem solving, as well as how to find work and make and keep relationships.

✔ **Sequencing, intensity and duration:** Length of programme needs to match risk. The amount of treatment provided must be linked to the needs of programme participants, with the introduction of different treatment components timed so that they complement each other. Offenders with a high-fixed risk (for example, they have a history of antisocial behaviour) need programmes long enough to change established attitudes and habits. For lower-risk offenders, a shorter programme may be sufficient.

✔ **Engagement and motivation:** The programme must be structured to maximise the engagement of participants and to sustain their motivation throughout. Staff need to be positively committed to the programme.

✔ **Continuity of programmes and services:** Clear links are necessary between the programme and the overall management of the offender, both during a prison sentence and in the context of community supervision. Relevant information needs to be shared. Key agencies concerned with protection of the public are to be kept informed, to aid work with victims and to monitor offenders.

✔ **Maintaining integrity:** Provision is needed to monitor how well the programme functions, as well as a system to modify aspects of it that don't perform as expected.

✔ **Ongoing evaluation:** Provision needs to be built into the programme to evaluate its efficacy. Checks must be done to ensure that staff are properly selected, trained and supervised and that the programme is run as intended. Given the challenges of carrying out therapeutic treatment in prisons, this list of ten requirements for effective interventions is a very tall order indeed, and they're unlikely all to be achieved all the time. But at least these points give targets to aim for. If they aren't achieved, people shouldn't be surprised that the relevant interventions fail to reach their goal of reducing re-offending.

Acknowledging the Challenges to Treatment

When a person walks into a doctor's consulting room and asks for treatment, the only limits are those that come from the doctor's professional situation and what the patient needs. Psychological interventions with convicted criminals, in contrast, are constrained by legal, confidentiality and institutional factors.

The legal complexities of treatment for inmates

A convicted rapist was coming to the end of his sentence and the authorities, understandably, feared he may offend again on his release. Therefore, they required him to undergo a programme (of the sort that I consider in Chapter 15) that they hoped would reduce that risk. This programme required him to talk about all the crimes that he'd committed so that a full understanding was obtained of his actions and their causes. He challenged this request, saying that this requirement may mean that he'd mention crimes he hadn't been convicted for and thus was against his human rights not to incriminate himself. This challenge went through various legal considerations, but in the end the courts decided that he had no such right to refuse treatment in this case.

Facing up to legal constraints

In democracies and other open societies persons convicted of a crime still have the same human rights as anyone else. Their liberty may be restricted or they may be required to fulfil community service, but beyond that in theory they have access to the full assistance of the law. As a result, they can claim legal support for certain aspects of their activities that aren't compatible with obtaining appropriate treatment to help reduce the likelihood of their re-offending.

Like everyone else, prisoners have the right to refuse medical intervention as long as such refusal doesn't cause anyone else harm. For example, inmates with a very infectious disease, such as tuberculosis, may not be allowed to continue to associate with others in prison unless they accept treatment to cure the disease. But the situation becomes more complicated in relation to psychological interventions. These interventions may open up legal implications that confound the possibility of treatment.

The prison environment may compromise the professional requirement known as *informed consent,* which demands that any interaction with a professional, especially in therapy, is based on the patient willingly accepting the treatment and knowing the implications of that treatment. But in a prison, coercion often takes place (as I note in the nearby sidebar 'The legal complexities of treatment for inmates'). The requirement to attend treatment may be implicitly or explicitly associated with how the person is dealt with in prison, such as the privileges they're allowed or their opportunities for parole.

Handling constraints of confidentiality

A sacrosanct necessity of privacy and confidentiality exists in conversations between therapist and client, which can be compromised by legal necessities. For instance, when the client is an offender, the person may reveal incriminating information relating to past or intended criminal activity. And yet this sort of information is precisely what a therapist needs to work with.

Dealing with denial

You may be surprised how many people in prison claim to be innocent! I regularly get letters from prisoners who claim that they were wrongly convicted, asking my help to reveal the truth. Whether they really are innocent or not, a problem clearly exists when setting up any treatment scheme to help them if they deny any wrongdoing. Of course, many people who claim to be innocent simply refuse to enrol on any sort of therapeutic programme, but where individuals are required to attend a programme, and strong evidence exists that they were at least some way involved in the crime, dealing with their denial can be a very important part of a therapeutic intervention.

This problem can be dealt with by exploring the reasons why the inmate thinks he was convicted and then considering various interpretations of his actions that may have convinced others of his guilt. This process can be harrowing for all concerned, but at the very least may enable the offender to see his actions from other people's points of view and so consider the circumstances that he needs to avoid in the future.

Needing to work around institutional constraints

Providing treatment programmes in prison can be problematic because of conflicting demands from the institution, including:

- ✔ Prisoner's sentence is too short to complete any designated programme and so they refuse to start it.

- ✔ Disciplinary activity, for the individual or an area of the prison, may not allow them out of their cell to attend a session.

- ✔ Staffing levels or other management issues can mean that no one is available to supervise the prisoner's movements or the area where the programme is being carried out.

- ✔ Other commitments, such as court attendance, visits or demands of a job within the prison can prevent them from attending.

The great majority of prisoners, especially those serving short (six months or less) prison terms will never be assessed or seen by psychologists (unless they do something really bizarre or bad) because the system can't cope with the logistics and the staff aren't available to carry out the work.

Chapter 14

Dealing with Violence

· ·

In This Chapter

▶ Distinguishing two different types of violence

▶ Determining the risks of further violent behaviour

▶ Discussing the difficulties of treating violent offenders

▶ Dealing with the offence of stalking

· ·

Although fortunately not the most common of offences, crimes involving violence are the ones that cause people most anguish. As a result, psychologists have devoted a great deal of attention to trying to work out why people are violent towards each other and what processes may help offenders to reduce their violent aggression.

One central area of research is risk assessment: the challenge of predicting whether a person is likely to be violent again in the future. Psychologists have developed ways of making these predictions that are quite effective if used carefully.

As well as examining risk assessment for violent offenders, in this chapter I also distinguish two basic types of violence, describe treatment programmes for anger management and take a closer look at one particular, often violent, offence – stalking.

Investigating Two Different Sorts of Violence

Many different types of violence exist as well as many different circumstances in which it can occur. In this section, I describe how psychologists distinguish between two general forms that differ in one crucial aspect:

✔ **Instrumental violence** is physical aggression to achieve a particular purpose. This type is the calculated violence (or threat of it) that's used to control other people and make them do what the offender wants – perhaps to obtain money, for example, or to make them carry out acts they wouldn't otherwise do.

Organised crime often keeps people within its networks by the use of this sort of violence.

People who use violence in a calculated way are less likely to be responsive to treatment programmes that focus on anger management and alternative ways of expressing fierce emotions.

✔ **Expressive, emotional or anger-promoted violence** is the explosive aggression that comes from a lack of impulse control in which someone feels the need to hit out when challenged or frustrated. These hostile individuals are likely to act on their urges in other ways, for instance by substance abuse, casual volatile relationships and other aspects of personality disorder.

This group of expressively violent people are the ones most open to some sort of psychological help with their impulsive aggression, although their openness to treatment is by no means certain.

Programmes to treat violent individuals need to explore what type of violence a person exhibited in the past in order to ensure that any treatment offered is appropriate. Working out what type of violence someone indulges in isn't always easy, however, because in some subgroups wearing your emotions (especially your anger) openly is a way of exerting control. In such cases, what may seem to be expressive violence may in fact be instrumental – the person gets a reputation for having 'a short fuse', which gives him a power that he wouldn't otherwise possess.

Considering some reasons for violent behaviour

When thinking about violent behaviour (and particularly ways to reduce or manage it), you need to keep in mind several features of violent events, as follows:

✔ Particular situations that may trigger violence, such as confrontations.

✔ Beliefs, such as the need to defend oneself against any insult.

✔ Emotional states, such as anger or depression.

✔ Personal goals that are seen to be assisted by violence.

✔ Inability to cope with threats or frustration in a non-aggressive way.

✔ Possibility of brain damage.

✔ Impulsivity and emotional extremes.

✔ Substances that reduce inhibitions, notably alcohol.

✔ Availability of weapons.

Examining the situations in which violence occurs

Violence occurs in a variety of different situations. The psychological implications of violence vary depending on the particular situation, which always need to be closely considered:

✔ **Brawls:** These commonly emerge out of interpersonal conflicts between people in competition over some person or resource. They can also be fuelled by struggles for power within particular subgroups. The sometimes ritualistic threats between different gangs can spill over into violent gang fights as well.

Sometimes, all the people involved display a similar degree of aggression. In these cases, the 'victim' and the 'aggressor' is an accident of timing or the use of a weapon, and things could have easily gone the other way.

✔ **Domestic violence:** Sadly, violence takes place between those who share an intimate relationship in many different types of circumstances. This can be the consequence of one partner, typically the man, being a violent individual who expresses his anger, jealousy or frustration only in an aggressive way. His violence can also be coercive, as a way of trying to control aspects of the relationship, such as when the woman indicates she wants to leave him (check out the following section 'Predicting domestic violence' for more on this subject).

Situations do occur in which the woman is the violent partner. Most commonly any violence from the woman is in self-defence, but aggressive women sometimes initiate violence. This event can be so unexpected that male victims of such aggression can have difficulty getting law enforcement to take it seriously.

✔ **Criminal coercion:** The use of violence as part of criminal activity (*instrumental violence*) can include street muggings, bank robberies, aggravated burglaries and sexual assaults. In such cases, criminals choose to be violent or not. Some bank robbers, for example, insist that they ensure that the people in the bank are so afraid of them that the thieves don't have to assault them physically. (At least, this is their claim for why they carry a gun.) Many burglars take care only to break into a house if they're sure they won't need to confront the occupants. In contrast, other offenders may delight in being physically threatening and seek confrontation.

Don't think of instrumental aggression as merely a logical choice for criminals: such behaviour is also an aspect of their personalities and a way of interacting with other people.

Predicting domestic violence

The Spousal Assault Risk Assessment Guide (SARA) is a standard set of 20 items that provide a checklist developed specifically to predict the likelihood of violence against family members or others. Tribunals and review boards use SARA when making decisions about individual cases.

The guide consists of four scales:

- ✓ **Spousal assault history:** Considering violence that has occurred within the family in the past and the circumstances in which that happened.
- ✓ **Criminal history:** The amount and nature of previous crimes the individual has committed.
- ✓ **Alleged/Most recent offence:** Careful consideration of the activities that brought the person to notice for the review.
- ✓ **Psychosocial adjustment:** Examination of how the person has related to others in a variety of situations and any indications of particular personality problems.

Clinicians using SARA are encouraged to also use their judgements to augment the results of the scale.

ANECDOTE

The association of domestic violence, harassment and murder

The sportsman and media star O.J. Simpson divorced Nicole Brown in 1992. In 1994, Nicole and her friend, Ron Goldman, were found murdered. O.J. was charged with the murders. It emerged during his trial that he'd been violent to Nicole on several occasions. The police were called out to their home at least nine times and in 1989 he'd been convicted of spousal assault. For several months after the couple separated, O.J. waited outside her new home, called her to persuade her that they needed to work things out, brought her flowers and left them on her doorstep, and went to neighbourhood restaurants they'd previously used in the hope of seeing her.

O.J. Simpson was eventually acquitted of the murder charges but was ordered, in the subsequent civil case in 1997, to pay $33.5 million to the relatives of Nicole Brown and Ron Goldman. He subsequently wrote a book called *If I Did It*, which somewhat ambiguously implies that he may well have committed the murders.

This illustrates how violence can build up from a failed relationship with many occurrences over time and be the end result of stalking that I discuss later in 'Managing Stalking'.

Assessing the Risk of Future Violence

The legal and therapeutic processes contain many aspects that seek to determine whether a person is dangerous. The concept of 'dangerousness', however, is rather difficult to define, because it implies an all or nothing categorisation, and so instead experts consider the *probability* that a person may be violent in the future. As a result, risk assessment has become a very common activity for forensic psychologists.

(I mention risk assessment as it relates to general re-offending briefly in Chapter 10, but such assessments are so fundamental to dealing with violent offenders that I consider the subject in more detail in this chapter.)

Forensic psychologists can be requested to produce predictions of the risk of future violence at many stages in the legal process:

- During bail hearings, to decide whether a person be allowed out on bail or kept imprisoned awaiting trial.

- During sentencing, to influence where an offender may be sent to serve his sentence, or whether to place him on probation or send him to prison.

- During decisions about what treatment programme to offer a person or whether to insist he takes part in one.

- During decisions about release, or whether a person is eligible for parole from prison or other institutions.

Using risk predictors of possible future violence

The risk of violence is higher for each of the following aspects:

- If the person's a man (need I say more?).

- People with any previous history of violence or serious criminality.

- People who experienced physical abuse as a child.

- People who live in an area with high levels of crime and violence.

- People with a history of substance abuse and dependence.

- People with a personality or adjustment disorder, such as those I discuss in Chapter 10 (people with other mental disorders, such as schizophrenia, are typically *less* likely to be violent in the community).

✔ Psychiatric patients who have hallucinations of voices commanding violent acts.

✔ People reporting violent thoughts and imagining violence in the future.

✔ People found to have a high degree of anger.

The risk of future violence, however, can be greatly reduced if any of a number of things happen to a person to change how they see the world and themselves. These *protective factors* include getting a satisfying job, forming a caring relationship and having children. Certain sorts of mental illness, for example, in which a person suffers from delusions, can turn the person in on themselves so much that they're not a danger to others, but may be a danger to themselves.

The details of a person's previous offences are very important. If the violence erupted against particular targets or in certain situations, understanding them and the person's views about them can be helpful in predicting future violence and in setting up any therapeutic treatment.

One particularly important predictor of violence is when an offender has a specific target in mind. If he's angry or vengeful towards a particular person, and is willing to mention that fact, the forensic psychologist needs to take his statement very seriously. Plenty of examples exist where released offenders said that they'd take violent revenge and did exactly that.

Understanding the risks of risk assessment

If, as a forensic psychologist, you're asked to say whether a person is dangerous, a lot of pressure is on you to say, 'Well, yes, I suppose so.' After all, the individual's name hasn't been pulled out of a hat at random, so some background applies to make people suspicious. And if you say that the person is dangerous, people accept that and the person is kept under observation, or even lock and key, which may reduce the risk of him being violent. On the one hand, if he's violent, you can say, 'I told you so,' and on the other hand, if you say, 'he's a nice chap, I'm sure we won't have any trouble with him,' and later he acts violently then you look like an idiot and someone else suffers.

The risk of the risk assessment being wrong is therefore much greater if you say that no risk exists than if you say risk does exist.

Therefore, experts are very cautious when making risk assessments, and tend to err on the side of saying that the person does present a risk. Studies of how often people have been violent when it was predicted they would be have shown that far fewer were violent than was predicted. This either supports the notion that experts were over-cautious or that a prediction of violence is a good way to reduce the chance of people being violent in the future!

Standardised risk assessment procedures

A number of standard procedures have been developed for assessing risk and are now widely used. Here are brief details of two of them:

The *Historical/Clinical/Risk Management Scale* (HCR-20) is particularly useful for considering people with psychiatric or personality disorders. It contains 20 questions relating to:

- ✔ The person's background and previous experiences (historical)

- ✔ The person's attitudes to others and violence as well as any indication of mental disorder (clinical)

- ✔ External risk factors such as housing situation and family support (risk)

The *Violence Risk Appraisal Guide* (VRAG) aims to predict whether a person will be violent if released into the community over a number of years. It covers 12 issues, including:

- ✔ Alcohol abuse

- ✔ Elementary school maladjustment

- ✔ Present mental condition, especially any indications of psychosis or psychopathy

This guide assigns a person to one of nine categories, with category 1 indicating a very low likelihood of future violence and category 9 indicating an almost certain probability of violence within the following seven years.

Keeping people locked up to protect the reputation of experts is a serious matter, which is why recent moves have been made towards using objective assessment procedures like those I describe in the sidebar 'Standardised risk assessment procedures'. Even though they aren't foolproof, at least the basis of the decision can be seen to be honest and independent of the expert's subjective opinion.

Appreciating the difficulties of risk assessment

People with a propensity for violence are some of the most difficult individuals to deal with as regards providing therapy or treatment, and they're very likely to refuse to participate in any assessment procedure. However, the procedures listed in the nearby sidebar 'Standardised risk assessment procedures' can be completed without the person answering questions, by drawing on records of their behaviour and talking to those who've dealt with them. Such an approach, however, isn't ideal and any lack of co-operation and the consequent necessary degree of speculation involved needs to be made clear in any reports.

Considering Some Approaches to Treatment

In this section, I take a look at some treatment programmes for violent offenders that address anger issues and help to re-orientate unhelpful personal narratives. As I state in the preceding section, people with violent histories are often reluctant to participate in any assessment process and are well-known for being very challenging when trying to carry out treatment with them. Compared with other offenders they are:

- ✔ Less determined or motivated to participate in any treatment programme.
- ✔ More resistant to what is being suggested in the programme.
- ✔ More likely to be uncooperative in taking part.
- ✔ Have a higher rate of dropping out of treatment.
- ✔ Less likely to show any effects of treatment.

One particularly tricky problem that has arisen in recent years, is that some prisoners from certain religious groups consider that talking about their previous offences is against their religion and so refuse to participate.

Managing anger

Treatment programmes aimed at helping people manage their violent angry outbursts typically work on certain key assumptions. The main assumption is that, although the person's emotional reactions may be difficult to alter, they can be trained to be in command of those reactions. The idea is that these people shouldn't let these strong emotions get the better of them which can result in a violent outburst.

The programmes deal with aspects of violent anger that are open to change taking into account the dynamic risk factors that I mention in Chapter 10. These changeable factors include attitudes and associated ways of thinking about the individual's interactions with others. More static, unchangeable aspects of the person, such as their criminal history, although predictive of future violence, aren't a suitable focus for treatment.

Such treatment interventions often include:

- ✔ Showing the offenders how to relax.
- ✔ Getting them used to stress without allowing it to take over their whole feelings.

This latter aspect includes getting them to recognise when their physiological arousal is building up, and how they can take account of their emotions and focus their attention in a more productive direction.

In addition to finding out how to deal with stress and anger, psychologists question offenders' beliefs that underlie their anger. This process includes examining how they interpret certain situations or people as hostile and looking closely at the consequences of their aggression.

The programmes therefore combine both a direct examination of the actions and feelings that give rise to violence, as well as challenges to thinking patterns that support their aggressive behaviour. The central objective is to persuade the participants in the programme that their way of acting and reacting in the past hasn't been productive for themselves or others. The idea is to make them accept that even if they believe they were right to feel and act the way they did, it didn't help them or other people, and so other ways of behaving would make them more successful.

The following sections provide details on two specific treatment programmes used in UK prisons within the area of anger management.

Controlling Anger and Learning to Manage It (CALM)

The CALM programme is aimed at people for whom anger and associated violence is a factor in current or previous offending. It isn't intended for those whose aggression is only apparent when in prison or other institutions. So although actions in the institution provide useful information about the person's problems, he's only allowed on the programme if he committed an offence involving the expression of anger or another intense emotion (and therefore excludes calculated aggression).

The programme was developed specifically to meet the needs of offenders in managing emotions associated with the occurrence of aggression and antisocial behaviour. It uses a cognitive-behavioural approach to teach offenders skills in managing anger and other emotions.

CALM consists of 24 two-hour sessions, with groups of two to eight people, in which various stages of emotional response are examined and productive ways of dealing with them explored. The treatment is developed to teach and promote a lasting change of inappropriate and unproductive thought and behaviour patterns by the use of:

- ✔ **Personal assignments,** a sort of homework to experience what's covered in the group.

- ✔ **Modelling,** in which individuals discover appropriate and inappropriate reactions.

✔ **Role-play,** to experience within the supportive context of the group how violent reactions can unfold and be calmed.

✔ **Teamwork,** learning to work with others, accepting and providing support.

✔ **Self- and peer-evaluation** of progress through the course of sessions.

The CALM programme is regarded as so successful that UK courts routinely order that an offender convicted of repeated assaults is required to participate in it, if he is thought safe to serve a sentence in the community.

Cognitive Self Change Programme (CSCP)

This programme targets high-risk violent offenders and includes group and individual sessions. It equips prisoners with skills to help them control their violence and avoid re-conviction. CSCP is aimed at offenders with a history of violent behaviour and is suitable for those whose violence is emotional and/ or calculated.

The programme runs over six to eight months with two, two-and-a-half-hour sessions each week. It consists of acquiring and demonstrating the ability to perform four skills:

✔ Paying attention to what and how offenders think in potentially violent situations.

✔ Recognising when thoughts and feelings are leading an offender towards committing a violent or criminal action.

✔ Cultivating new thinking that leads away from violence and crime, and that they feel is an acceptable way to think.

✔ Practising using these new ways of thinking in real-life situations.

Participants also have to prepare a Thinking Report in which they report objectively the thoughts and feelings they experienced during the commission of past offences.

After a person finishes the CSCP, in some jurisdictions they're encouraged to move onto the Making Choices Programme, which helps them to make sense of how they came to offend. It teaches them to recognise points in their life where they could have made a different choice and gives them skills to get a better outlook on life, and to think about positive aspects of themselves and their activities.

They're helped to manage their emotions and situations better and improve their relationships, as well as live a life free from crime. At the end of the programme they're asked to prepare a 'safety plan' that identifies particular situations in which they may have been prone to violence in the past. They have to prepare details of what they'll do in those situations to ensure that they don't act violently.

ANECDOTE

The dangers of a destructive narrative

When 33-year-old Gavin Hall described in court how he fed his 3-year-old daughter anti-depressants to make her drowsy before smoth-ering her, he said that the two of them were just like 'Romeo and Juliet'. This statement showed how in his depressed state (which he said was brought on by his wife's infidelity) he drew on a well-known storyline to explain his actions to himself.

Reconstructing personal narratives

One innovative way of helping violent offenders to change their way of deal-ing with others is to help them reconstruct their personal narratives. The idea is that all people see themselves as living out some sort of story built around the roles they lead, for example, being a supportive parent, conscien-tious shopkeeper or gifted choirmaster.

These roles and their associated narratives evolve out of the individual's experiences and interactions with other people. They're supported by memo-ries, especially of key episodes and points in a person's history that signified changes to the unfolding plot (that is, their life story).

Many violent offenders see themselves as part of a *destructive narrative* in which their identity is defined by hitting out and other acts of violence (check out the nearby sidebar 'The dangers of a destructive narrative'). They tend to think about and perhaps focus on past events that validate this view of themselves. This allows psychologists to get them to reconsider key epi-sodes in their lives and interpret them in a new way in order to give them a different way of seeing themselves. The offenders are encouraged to recon-struct a more positive personal narrative, in which the violent character they had thought themselves to be no longer plays a role.

Managing Stalking

Stalking doesn't always include violence, but it certainly generates a fear of violence and can lead in extreme cases to murder. *Stalking* consists of unwanted attention over a period of time that gives rise to fear by the targeted person; in about half of reported cases some physical act of aggression occurs.

Because of a number of high-profile cases that did lead to assaults, some countries introduced laws that make stalking a specific crime. The essence of the crime is that the targeted person is fearful because of the attentions of another person. In other words, it is harassment rather than 'stalking' that's been made illegal.

In the UK this was The Protection from Harassment Act 1997. This is routinely used against stalkers in England and Wales. The general prohibition against harassment does not require the law to define the behaviours which constitute stalking. If named actions were made illegal, stalkers will just find other ways of harassing their victims.

Here are some typical stalking behaviours (most illustrated by O.J. Simpson as I describe earlier in this section):

✔ Very high degree of inappropriate intimacy

✔ Contact through various media, especially over the Internet *(cyberstalking)*

✔ Attempts at face-to-face contact

✔ Overt or covert surveillance

✔ Invasion of personal property

✔ Intimidation and harassment

✔ Threats and attempts at coercion

✔ Direct aggression

Stalking can cover a great range of actions and continue over a long period of time . . . sometimes many years. There are cases that have lasted for 20, 30 or even 40 years! It may include sending many different messages, by phone, letter or e-mail, unwanted presents or directly watching the person targeted, even entering their house and stealing personal objects. Celebrities aren't the only people who are stalked, although they're particularly vulnerable to this sort of unwanted attention. But most stalking occurs when the victim has had some sort of prior relationship with the stalker, intimate or not. Some estimates indicate that as many as one in four women have had some form of continuous harassment from another person during their life. Men can also suffer, with more than one in ten experiencing this type of harassment. Companies or other organisations can also become the target of stalkers who bombard their executives and managers with various missives.

The following aspects of stalking relate to the stalker's potential to become violent:

✔ Threats

✔ Substance abuse by the stalker

✔ Earlier intimate relationship with the victim

✔ Personality disorder in the stalker

✔ History of violent behaviour

People who have a severe mental disorder (psychosis) are less likely to be violent stalkers than those who don't suffer from this problem, although those who are psychotic are more likely to stalk people with whom they have had no contact.

Stalkers are typically men in their 40s known to have some established problem of relating to other people. They can be 'serial stalkers', moving on from one target to the next.

Stalking isn't to be confused with the sort of adulation that can come from a fan. Even a person as lacking in celebrity as myself gets the odd letter or other contact from time to time, out of the blue, from someone with whom I've had no prior contact at all, who wants to indicate his or her admiration for my work.

Such behaviour is quite different from the secretary who phoned me at home over 100 times a day, demanding I continue her employment after her contract ended. Only after I got a court order to have her desist, under the Protection from Harassment Act that I mentioned earlier, was I able to hear the phone ringing without immediate anxiety.

Trying to explain stalking

Different psychological processes seem to shape different forms of stalking:

✔ **Obsessional stalkers,** who are the most common, tend to emerge out of the breakdown of an existing relationship. The stalker feels demeaned and helpless and seeks to increase his self-esteem by demoralising and creating anxiety and fear in the former spouse. This behaviour is often a continuation of domestic violence by another means, wanting to control the victim even though she has left him. If the stalker thinks that she's trying to remove herself even further from his attempts to control her, he may become even more violent. This type of stalking is most likely to lead to murder.

✔ **Love-obsession stalking** is where the target is a casual acquaintance such as a co-worker or neighbour, or even a celebrity who the stalker has never met, with whom the person desires to establish an intimate relationship. This obsession can also grow out of low self-esteem and depression. The stalker believes that he'll be more significant if he establishes a relationship with his desired target. He's likely to re-interpret any response, no matter how negative, as some indication of a desire for a relationship. Or he may resort to violence to gain attention from the victim. The most well-known example of this type of stalker is John Hinckley who shot President Ronald Reagan in the belief that it would make the actress Jodie Foster love him.

✔ **Erotomania** is a delusional state where the stalker believes that an intimate relationship with the victim already exists. These people usually have a serious mental illness such as schizophrenia, and aren't able to tell reality from the confused world in which they live. They're erratic and greatly troubling to their victims but are typically more danger to themselves than anyone else. Margaret Ray was such a woman. For about ten years she believed herself to be the wife of David Letterman, the talk show host, even thinking she had born his children. She broke into his property on many occasions, was arrested driving his car and sent him flowers and sweets. She eventually killed herself.

✔ **Vengeance stalkers** don't want to form a relationship with their target. They want to change the behaviour of others or just get revenge for what they regard as an insult, and damage the person or organisation that has caused them hurt. However, what turns their behaviour into stalking is its obsessional quality, with a great deal of activity over a long period of time. If the stalker has some intellectual capability he can become a great expert on the target and ferret out many details that can be used against them, which can be enormously intrusive and disturbing. The stalker gains a feeling of significance and self-worth in the reactions he manages to achieve from his victim.

✔ **Political stalkers** may consider themselves to be heroes who're taking on the might of an organisation. Their constant challenge to individuals or groups whose activities or opinions they dislike gives them a sense of achievement, and supports their view of themselves as involved in a just cause. They'd never consider themselves as being in the same class as the other stalkers listed, but their incessant activity beyond the bounds of acceptable political debate and action, marks them out as disturbed individuals whose behaviour owes more to their particular psychology than to the opinions they espouse.

Asking the question: Do stalkers ever stop?

The great challenge of dealing with stalkers is that often they refuse to accept that they're doing anything wrong. They may see themselves as just like any other infatuated fan, or a lover whose target really wants to reciprocate, or a person on a mission to avenge wrongdoing or stop unacceptable activity. Almost invariably, stalkers have some background of relationship problems and in some cases are clearly mentally ill. These factors all come together to make stopping their stalking behaviour very difficult without addressing the more fundamental aspects of their personality, that lead them to use stalking as a way of dealing with their challenges and frustrations.

The key to getting the stalking to stop is by the victim not giving any indication at all that the stalker exists, or that his actions have any significance. The overt and psychological objective of stalking is to obtain some reaction from the victim: perhaps an indication of the desire for a relationship, new or continued, or to show that the victim is suffering. If the stalkers can't have that effect they may move on to other targets.

Of course, ignoring constant pressure from stalkers is extremely difficult and victims may be tempted to try and reason with them, which is in fact almost universally pointless. The stalker simply re-interprets the contact as he wants and it usually fuels his actions.

Unfortunately, a nil response can also lead to more aggressive and/or intrusive actions. In that case, the use of harassment laws to get a court order may be the only way forward. In some cases they succeed in getting the stalker to desist. The stalker may find another 'love object' to attend to.

Police intervention such as arrest and conviction has to be handled very sensitively, because it can make matters considerably worse, antagonising the stalker and causing even more violent actions. But if combined with some removal of access to the victim, such intervention may be of help.

Sadly, removing the possibility of contact with the victim may require the target to move away totally from any area to which the stalker has access. This requires hiding the new location from anyone who may have contact with the stalker, which can be enormously disturbing and still leave the victim with the fear that the stalker may discover their new whereabouts.

Chapter 15

Treating Sexual Offenders

· ·

In This Chapter

▶ Introducing the forms of sexual assault

▶ Assessing sex offenders and their deviance

▶ Looking at some approaches to treatment

▶ Investigating child abuse within the family

· ·

Sexual assault is particularly disturbing because it violates the most intimate aspects of the victim. Sexual crimes also raise fundamental challenges around attitudes held by various subgroups or within different cultures. Such problems are illustrated by the stark fact that in Western developed countries, until quite recently the law didn't recognise rape in marriage. Even today, many countries in the world don't accept that a husband's sexual assault of his wife is against the law.

In addition, male victims of rape in many countries still have difficulty getting the crime against them taken seriously. As has recently been widely publicised, certain institutions, such as the Catholic Church or children's hostels, have hidden from public view – or even implicitly condoned – the sexual abuse of children.

These examples go to show that probably more than any other crime, sexual assault is embedded in a set of norms and accepted values that are part of local customs and ways of life.

Awareness is growing, however, that these crimes have to be dealt with and that sexual offenders may benefit from special forms of treatment. As with all such interventions, the starting point is a careful assessment to diagnose the individual's particular problems as well as the need for a prognosis, which amounts to a prediction of the likelihood of them offending again (in other words, risk assessment).

In this chapter, I give a brief introduction to the different types of sexual assault and their associated psychological aspects, and I examine ways of assessing the perpetrators. I also discuss several treatment programmes and focus more closely on a particularly widespread and yet problematic area – child sexual abuse within the family.

Defining Sexual Offences and Offenders

Sexual offending is probably the crime with the most connected psychological issues, because it involves behaviour, attitudes and aspects of the offender's personality and ways of relating to other people. Unsurprisingly, therefore, sexual crimes are the ones that forensic psychologists have studied the most.

Many different types of sexual offences and offenders exist and being aware of this large variation is important, because different types of offence require different forms of treatment (check out Table 15-1).

Table 15-1	Varieties of Sexual Offence	
Type	*Activity*	*Psychological Features*
Child abuse	Can take many forms; within the family or with strangers. Can be violent or seductive.	Main sexual interest is children (Paedophilia)
		Absence of preferred partner
Rape	Adult male or female	Thinks has right to sex (denies lack of consent)
		Angry wish to demean victim
		Extreme desire for sexual gratification
		Sadism
Sexual murder	Usually female victim, often part of series of crimes	Kills victim so she cannot testify
		Sexually aroused by violence
		Wishes for sex with corpse (Necrophilia)
Child pornography	Usually downloading (or creating) images of children involved in sexual activity. N.B. Ownership of sexual images of children is illegal, but not of adults in most countries. The fundamental crime is creating the images; without their uptake by 'customers' who acquire the images they would never be created.	Sexual preference for children. Often do not wish to have direct contact, sometimes is preparation for direct contact.

In addition to the criminal sexual offences in Table 15-1, a variety of sexual activities *(paraphilias)* are generally regarded as being sexually deviant. Some of these are clearly illegal and others less so (see Table 15-2). In fact many paraphilias can be part of fantasy explorations between consenting adults. In some cases they shape or cause a person to become involved in the illegal activities listed in Table 15-2 or other crimes that these desires engender.

Table 15-2	Selection of Paraphilias
Label	*Description*
Exhibitionism	Exposing genitals to a stranger, sometimes while masturbating, but with no attempt at direct physical contact.
Fetishism	A wide range of non-living things, such as boots, or female underwear can be used to provide sexual arousal while holding, smelling or the partner wearing.
Frotteurism	Getting sexual excitement from rubbing against a non-willing, or even unaware, person – usually in a crowd.
Sexual masochism	Sexual arousal from being humiliated, beaten, bound or being made to suffer, either self-inflicted or from a partner.
Sexual sadism	The physical or psychological suffering of a victim by domination or torture creates sexual excitement.
Transvestite fetishism	Heterosexuals who become aroused by cross-dressing as a woman. People who do not get aroused by cross-dressing may be considered as transvestites but not fetishistic. Not to be confused with transsexualism in which the person wishes to acquire the anatomical characteristics of a person of the opposite sex. So neither being a transvestite or a transsexual is regarded as a paraphilia if it does not relate to a person's sexual arousal.
Voyeurism	Gaining sexual excitement by watching people, usually without their knowing, who are naked, undressing or having sex.
Piquerism	Obtaining sexual pleasure from inserting sharp objects, such as pins or knives into a victim.

Assessing Sexual Offenders

In order to provide the most effective treatment *(intervention)* for offenders, psychologists explore their characteristics and aspects of their background relevant to their crimes. As with the assessment of violent offenders (which I discuss in Chapter 14), such assessments deal with static and dynamic factors:

> ✔ **Static factors** relate to the fixed aspects of a person, who they are and their offending history. These factors are most useful in estimating the probability that a person may re-offend in the future.
>
> ✔ **Dynamic factors** relate to the person's interests, attitudes and personality. These factors are particularly useful in determining appropriate treatment programmes, as I describe in the later section, 'Treating Sexual Offenders'.

In this section, I examine the assessment of sexual offenders, including risk assessment, and take a closer look at particular issues surrounding rape.

Considering the risk of future offending

A number of standard procedures have been developed for assessing the risk of future sexual offending, almost invariably used with male offenders even though women do commit sexual assaults, which is a crucial aspect of any consideration of what to do with a convicted offender. I summarise two of the most widely used in this section.

Static-2002

This procedure deals with those aspects of a person not open to change, essentially their offending history:

- ✔ Age at which to be released.
- ✔ Number of times previously sentenced for sexual offences.
- ✔ Any arrests as a juvenile for sexual offence with an adult conviction.
- ✔ High rate of sexual offending.
- ✔ Any convictions for non-contact sexual offences.
- ✔ Any male victims.
- ✔ Two or more victims under the age of 12.
- ✔ Any strangers as victims.
- ✔ Any breach of conditional release.
- ✔ Any convictions for non-sexual offences.

Sex Offender Risk Appraisal Guide (SORAG)

This procedure pays more attention to offenders' characteristics and the violence in their background:

- ✔ Indications of psychopathy.
- ✔ Behavioural problems at school.

✔ Diagnosis of personality disorder.

✔ Age at time of most recent offence.

✔ Evidence of mental disorder.

✔ Alcohol problems.

✔ Long-term intimate relationships (especially lack of them).

✔ Violent criminal history.

✔ Deviant sexual preferences.

Risk assessments, of course, aren't foolproof. They give only general probability estimates that are based on samples drawn from the past of people who have been assessed and then followed up. Broadly speaking, these assessments predict correctly whether or not the offender will offend in the future in 60 to 70 per cent of cases. They don't get it right in all cases, because they can't take account of individual circumstances, such as a person losing a job, which may increase the risk, or finding a caring partner, which can reduce the risk.

Looking into the role of fantasies

Assessing offenders' fantasies is crucial to being able to assess these people effectively. Some sex offenders do seem to have particularly deviant fantasies and a strong desire to act on them. It has also been claimed that some sexual crimes are carried out in order to feed a fantasy. The proposal is that the person commits the offence in order to be able to draw on the experience for later private sexual gratification.

Although attempts to control offenders' fantasies haven't been successful in reducing the likelihood of their re-offending, identifying and assessing what the fantasies are, can be useful in setting up other forms of intervention. The plethysmograph that I describe in the nearby sidebar 'The penile plethysmograph' has been found to be helpful in this regard.

A lot of normal, acceptable sexual contact between caring partners involves some sort of fantasy, about the context of the activity, the person involved or the activities associated with it. In a surprisingly high proportion of cases, these fantasies can include thinking about activities that may be considered paraphilias (flip to the earlier Table 15-2) or even violently deviant. Consequently, sexual fantasies in and of themselves can't be regarded as the reason for sexual assaults.

The penile plethysmograph

Sex offenders may not be willing to indicate their sexual preferences, especially if they're deviant; or they may not recognise their own reactions clearly. Therefore, a procedure to find out what their preferences are is sometimes used to examine these preferences directly. These procedures are sometimes known as *phallometric* measures because they measure blood flow in the phallus directly.

The person is placed in a quiet room and shown various sexual images, played sounds of sexual activity, or both. While receiving these images, his various physiological reactions are measured, which typically include heart rate, sweating rate and penile engorgement measured through a cuff placed over the penis (known as a penile plethysmograph). By recording reactions to different sorts of sexual activity, deviant and non-deviant, psychologists or psychiatrists can ascertain the person's predilections. Of course, this doesn't prove that a person is going to act out the indicated desires.

In general this approach is useful for identifying people who are especially sexually attracted to children, but its wider use is open to debate.

Reviewing the dynamic aspects of sexual offending

When assessing sex offenders, psychologists carry out a careful examination of their ways of relating to other people and their ways of making sense of the world that may be open to change. A procedure widely used, particularly in the UK, for determining the possibility of change is the Structured Assessment of Risk and Need (SARN), which explores a number of areas:

✔ **Sexual interests** examines preoccupations with sex and any particular sexual interests, such as preference for sexual activity with children, or desire for coerced sex with adults.

✔ **Distorted attitudes** explores whether the person thinks that the male needs to be dominant in sex (and on other occasions) or whether the person believes that women are deceptive or corruptive.

Views of women causing themselves to be raped, and related myths about sexual assaults, are also considered (for more details, see the following section 'Inquiring into the motives for rape'). Any beliefs that minimise or justify sexual activity with unwilling partners or children are an important aspect of this area.

✔ **Sexual and emotional functioning** considers whether the person has low self-esteem and sees his actions as not really under his own control but in the hands of fate. Whether this feeling is linked to feelings of loneliness and preferred emotional intimacy with children rather than adults, is also important. These attributes can also be associated with a general suspiciousness and anger that doesn't recognise anyone else's point of view.

✔ **Self-management** deals with a person's failure to solve the problems he faces with any responsibility. Impulsivity and uncontrolled outbursts of emotion are monitored. Any dysfunctional impulses the person has, need to be considered and how they may have contributed to his offending.

Inquiring into the motives for rape

Psychological assessments of sexual offenders and rapists focus on the aspects of the person that contribute to him carrying out sexual assaults. They indicate enduring features of his lifestyle as well as attitudes and beliefs.

Many of the dynamic (changeable) components exist in men who don't rape and would never consider doing so, and so psychologists need to explore a little more deeply the explanations that rapists give for carrying out sexual assaults.

The various reasons that offenders offer for raping tend to overlap and usually have their roots in rape myths (as I describe in the later 'Rape myths' section), as well as limited empathy for the victims. These allow rape to be used as a weapon in many wars, harnessing propensities in some men to try and destroy a population regarded as 'the enemy'. Some people even suggest that rape is an inevitable product of male dominance in society, a requirement for men to demonstrate their masculinity. This 'feminist' view of rape sees such crimes as part of a general picture in which men attempt to keep women in fear as a means of maintaining control over them.

The idea that all men are potential rapists is taken a stage further by a curious group who call themselves 'socio-biologists'. They claim that rape offers an evolutionary advantage for men who can't have sex any other way to pass on their genes. This bizarre notion doesn't explain why homosexual rape happens or why women may be involved in rape. Nor does it explain why some men in established sexual relationships still sexually assault other women.

Rape myths

One argument is that many people, mainly men, in Western societies hold views about rape that are conducive to sexual assault. Psychologists have even developed a 'Rape-Myth Acceptance Scale' that asks people if they agree or disagree with such statements as:

✔ 'If a drunken woman has sex with a stranger, she's asking for other men to have sex with her too.'

✔ 'It is a woman's own fault if she is involved in some mild sexual activity and she lets it get out of hand.'

✔ 'A woman who snubs men deserves to be taught a lesson.'

✔ 'Women unconsciously want to be raped.'

Men who agree with many such statements would be expected to be more willing to participate in sexual assaults. Their attitudes are seen as drawing on a set of views prevalent in the subculture of which they're a part. Certainly, men who share these attitudes and who end up in treatment programmes sometimes have great difficulty recognising that what they did was rape. I remember one such man saying eventually, 'Oh. If that's rape, I've done it quite often.'

Sadism as an explanation of rape

Although sadism is regarded as a paraphilia (see Table 15-2), it's sometimes given as an explanation of rape when the person wants to be coercive in their sadistic activity. Those men (and some women) who get sexual gratification from hurting others and obtaining sex violently force their victims, because of the pleasure they get from doing so.

These people are, fortunately, extremely rare, but they do make the headlines when they act on their disturbing impulses. They're likely to attack strangers and become serial offenders. They prepare for and plan their attacks, possibly getting some gratification from anticipating what they're going to do.

Anger in rape

Some men develop a feeling for revenge against women, sometimes particular women or a type of woman. Their victims become substitutes for the people the rapist is angry with. Their anger may be fuelled by alcohol or drugs and explode when a particular possibility occurs. The sex is a way of insulting the victim and so is likely to be violently aggressive.

No deviant fantasy is usually involved here as is likely to be the case with the sadistic rapist.

Opportunity

Men who lack any sort of empathy or concern for the feelings of others, may select victims simply because they spot the opportunity for forcing them to have sex. These men are often talked of as 'sexual predators', accosting a woman in a bar and then assaulting her if she refuses to have sex. Their violence is used to control the women, as opposed to playing any role in deviant fantasies or desires. They just want sex and then to get away. They may even mistakenly think that after they start carrying out their sexual activity, the woman enjoys the act and wants to participate.

As with so many violent crimes, alcohol or drugs can remove the person's inhibitions, reducing their ability to control themselves. Even if that isn't really the case, perpetrators may use alcohol as an excuse, as in: 'It was the drink that made me do it.'

Power

Some men see rape as a way of demonstrating their power over women, usually a result of their own feelings of inadequacy and insecurity. These men are strongly influenced by the cognitive distortions and rape myths that I discuss earlier in this section and in Chapter 14. They think of sexual conquest as an important way of demonstrating their control and significance. These views may be magnified by constant brooding on sex and developing fantasies of control and sexual prowess.

Managing and Helping the Sex Offender

The preceding section contains several possible explanations for rape, some more convincing than others. But the fact is that the great majority of men don't carry out sexual assaults and indeed find the whole idea abhorrent. Therefore, explanations that relate directly to an offender's particular background, upbringing and related attitudes and personality characteristics are the most useful areas to investigate and so these form the basis of most treatment programmes.

The question of whether and how to treat (or indeed simply manage) sex offenders is a difficult issue. In this section, I examine some of the difficulties involved and describe some approaches to treatment currently in use around the world.

Investigating the complexities of treating psychopaths

Unfortunately, little evidence exists that any of the therapeutic interventions that I describe in the later section 'Appraising some sex offender treatment programmes' are particularly effective. They may help in some cases but for many sex offenders they're irrelevant or have little impact. As an extreme example of the difficulties involved, in this section I illustrate the complexity of the processes that need to be explored when dealing with serious serial rapists and sexual murderers.

Fred West was guilty of killing at least 10 young women and probably considerably more over a 20-year period without ever being caught. He and his wife Rose sexually and physically abused these young women before killing them and burying them in the garden of their house in Gloucester, UK under their notorious patio. What would a forensic psychology assessment have revealed of Fred West if one had been carried out before he killed himself in prison?

The first and most obvious point was that West was virtually illiterate and probably learning disabled. The police assigned an *appropriate adult* to be with him throughout their interviews with him when he was initially arrested on suspicion of murder. The law requires such a person to be present if the possibility exists that the suspect may not fully understand what's happening to him and the legal process. The fear was that West wasn't able to fully understand the implications of the situation he was in and what he'd done.

Indications that this was the case are located in his comments. When told that a body had been found under his patio, he said that the police should be careful how they put the paving back. His further request, after the fact that he'd committed murder had become plain, that he should now be allowed home may have been dark irony, but was more likely to be part of his lack of awareness of just how serious the situation was.

If a psychologist were able to get West to talk about his upbringing, she'd probably become quickly aware of how sexualised it was. West wrote a sort of memoir before he killed himself and although this document seems to be intended as a portrayal of the innocent loving life he lived, he does indicate in passing that his father had sex with West's daughter and that sexual activity in general was a prevalent part of family life.

The crucial point is that West doesn't seem to recognise the destructive quality of all the sexual activity within the family, taking it much more for granted than the very great majority of people would.

In addition to his acceptance of untrammelled sexual gratification quite early on, in his teens he raped a young woman but managed to avoid being convicted of the crime. The stage was thus set for a continuation of this predatory activity. His patterns of behaviour and attitudes were ingrained within a view of himself that was shaped in part by the way his parents and others in his family treated him. Possibly, his only feeling of being at all significant came when he was sexually violent.

But even these precursors in parental role models, deep-seated attitudes and a limited understanding of the consequences of his actions may not have turned him into a serial killer. Only when he got together with Rose, who had a background in crime and prostitution, was he encouraged to take his depredations further. Together, they created an environment that made sexual violence and murder a way of life.

Appraising some sex offender treatment programmes

Treating sex offenders needs to be broadly based, dealing with the many different aspects of their thoughts, feelings and actions that contribute to their offending. This process involves intensive and frequent contact with offenders in a supportive and open context, which can be very difficult to achieve in a prison. Also, many sex offenders don't want to participate in such activities.

The general disgust that other prisoners have for sex offenders can make their experience of prison particularly damaging and dangerous. As a result, many prison systems organise prisons so that sex offenders are kept away from other prisoners. Certain prisons or wings of prisons even contain only people convicted of sex offences. Of course, this approach can be counterproductive because these individuals then mix with each other and help to validate each other's sexual preferences, including teaching each other how to avoid detection.

Those offenders willing to participate in treatment programmes may discover how to 'fake being good'. They master the vocabulary of therapy and know what to say without ever totally accepting the new attitudes and behaviours that society requires of them. But providing some form of treatment is better than leaving these people to rot in prison, or letting them back in the community with no hope of rehabilitation.

The 'good-lives' approach

Many sexual offenders come from dysfunctional families and have themselves experienced various forms of abuse. They've often been told that they're worthless and their criminal offending may well emerge out of a mixture of doing to others what's been done to them, as well as attempts to gain some feeling of significance.

In recognition of the extent to which offending can grow out of habits, and beliefs embedded in destructive and personal processes, one approach to therapy emerging in recent years emphasises enabling offenders to develop the skills to achieve a 'good life' in an acceptable way. Thus, instead of focusing on the reduction of the risks of re-offending, this more humanitarian approach deals directly with helping to achieve positive aspects of life.

Central to this approach is the proposal that everyone, offender or not, seeks a number of primary features in their lives:

- Autonomy
- Community
- Creativity
- Freedom from stress
- Friendship
- Happiness
- Health
- Knowledge
- Mastery of experiences, and
- Meaning in life

The 'good-lives' treatment approach therefore works with offenders to determine how they can achieve this range of positive outcomes in an acceptable and productive way. This aim is a tall order for people imprisoned because of despicable actions, which they themselves may abhor, but with appropriate guidance the approach at least offers an optimistic way of helping offenders.

The 'risk-needs-responsivity' approach

This is a down-to-earth approach to intervention with offenders and deals directly with the issues that their offences reveal:

- **The more at risk of re-offending a person is (as indicated by the assessments that I mention in the earlier section 'Assessing Sexual Offenders'), the more intensive the treatment needs to be.** This process includes longer sessions over a longer period of time that deal more exhaustively with the cognitive and emotional aspects of the person's offending.

- **Treatment focuses as directly as possible on the needs revealed in the assessment of the individual.** This approach deals with the dynamic risk factors that may be open to change, including attitudes and beliefs as well as sexual preferences.

- **None of the above aspects of the treatment programme can work without a degree of responsiveness from the offender and the therapist.** The programme requires the offender to be willing to participate and the therapist to be able to adjust the way the programme is delivered to suit the individual. This approach can include aspects of learning styles as I describe in Chapter 13, as well as adjustments that take into account the subculture and belief systems of the offender.

Sex Offender Treatment Programmes (SOTP)

A detailed programme for treating sex offenders is in wide use across prisons in the UK. I summarise this one to show how such treatment programmes unfold with inmates. SOTP emphasises teaching offenders how to understand and control their thinking, feelings and behaviour. A range of programmes are available to teach a person how to adjust the activities in which he participates to suit his particular risks, needs and priorities:

- ✔ **Core programme:** The treatment goals of this programme include:
  - Helping offenders develop an understanding of how and why sexual offences are committed.
  - Increasing awareness of the harm to victims of the offences.
  - Developing meaningful life goals as part of a plan to prevent relapse.

- ✔ **Extended programme:** This one is for high-risk offenders and covers:
  - Dysfunctional thinking styles.
  - Emotion management.
  - Offence-related sexual fantasies.
  - Intimacy skills.
  - Detailed consideration of how to develop adequate plans for relapse prevention.

- ✔ **Adapted programme:** Although the goals of this programme are similar to the core programme, the methods are adjusted to suit learning-disabled sex offenders across all risk levels. An adapted programme is designed to:
  - Increase sexual knowledge.
  - Modify offence-justifying thinking.
  - Develop the ability to recognise feelings in themselves and others.
  - Gain an understanding of victim harm.
  - Develop relapse prevention skills.

- ✔ **Rolling programme:** This programme covers the same topics as the core programme but with more emphasis on relationship skills and dealing with feelings of loneliness and abandonment.

- ✔ **Booster programme:** This option is designed to provide an opportunity for offenders to refresh their learning in treatment and to prepare for additional relapse prevention and release work.

✔ **Healthy relationships programme:** Especially aimed at offenders who are at risk of being violent to intimate female partners, it targets:

- Attitudes and beliefs that condone domestic violence.

- Poor emotional control.

- Deficits in social skills.

- Anger or other reasons for offending.

Taking a more direct approach: Chemical castration

On the assumption that sex offending is a product of heightened sexual proclivity and uncontrollable libido, from time to time special medication has been administered to persistent sex offenders in order to reduce their sexual desires and greatly reduce their libido. This procedure has had some success in very specific cases.

However, if the sexual assault arises from anger, power or feelings of revenge (issues that I discuss in the earlier section 'Inquiring into the reasons for rape'), this sort of 'castration' can in fact lead to the offender becoming violent and much more dangerous.

Dealing with Child Sexual Abuse in the Family

Around one out of ten adults report that they experienced some sort of abusive sexual contact as a child. The prevalence for women is somewhat higher than for men. The sexual abuse of children most commonly occurs within the family, although the perpetrators are also likely to carry out sexual assaults on people who aren't family members. The great majority of abusers are men, but as many as 1 in 20 are female.

Examining child abuse in the family

The disturbing fact is that many children are abused within the home and family and suffer sexual and/or physical assaults a number of times, often by different people and over many years. This abuse typically occurs within an abusive family that is able to hide what they are doing from the authorities so that the child's disclosure of the abuse to teachers, social services or others is ignored. In contrast, a one-off assault by someone the child has little or no prior relationship with is more likely to be acknowledged by the child's carers and dealt with quickly, reducing its impact and ensuring that it doesn't happen again.

All types of abuse and neglect of children can leave their mark in many different ways:

- Aggressive behaviour
- Antisocial activity
- Emotional instability
- Mental illness
- Self-harm
- Sexual assaults on others
- Sexual dysfunctions
- Substance abuse
- Symptoms of post-traumatic stress

Unsurprisingly, given the far-reaching effects on the individual that such childhood abuse can cause, as many as three out of every four young people in prison have been abused and/or neglected when they were children. However, the resilience of young children is shown by the fact that as few as one in ten sexually abused boys goes on to commit sexual assaults later. The ones that do are usually the children who suffered multiple and varied assaults and neglect. Girls who are sexually abused are quite likely to become violent in later life.

Sexual child abuse is frequently associated with violence within the family, especially towards the child's mother. Therefore, any consideration of sexual abuse needs to take into account the possibility of many other forms of dysfunctional activity within the home. Abuse of alcohol and drugs is to be expected as part of this pattern as well as a generally coercive and violent atmosphere. Relatives such as uncles, brothers or cousins may also be party to extended sexual abuse.

Some good news is that many children survive physical and sexual abuse remarkably well, although others are psychologically and often physically scarred for life. Many factors influence how severe the effect is on the child:

- Whether the abuse involves direct contact or verbal abuse and a climate of acceptance of sex and violence.
- The particular developmental stage of the child when maltreated.
- The duration and frequency of the abuse.
- How violently any victim resistance was dealt with.

✔ Whether an abuse of trust is involved, because of the close relationship between the child and the perpetrator.

✔ If the child was listened to when telling about the abuse.

✔ How helpful the support was from teachers, social services, police or psychologists.

Preventing child abuse in the family

Attempts to deal with sexual abuse within the family operate at three levels:

✔ **Primary prevention** is aimed at the whole population and includes public awareness campaigns that emphasise zero tolerance. Useful programmes within schools also deal with bullying and explain the difference between good and bad secrets to encourage children to report abuse. However, these aren't as effective as dealing directly with women and children to increase their self-esteem and empower them to disclose their concerns.

✔ **Secondary preventions** are services targeted at families that are deemed to be at risk or in need of further support. This approach is most effective when it consists of a number of different agencies working together, including special child protection units within the police, social services, education and health authorities and probation services. Co-ordinating these different agencies in the interest of children at risk can be a complex and daunting task though.

✔ **Tertiary prevention** is the most common strategy and has some of the qualities of closing the stable door after the horse has bolted. It's a reaction to the discovery of abuse within a family, setting in motion procedures to prevent it happening again and to punish and/or treat the perpetrator.

This strategy has to deal with possibilities of false allegations and the need to get a clear and full account of what has been going on. It also has to manage the problems that arise from removing the perpetrator from a family, who may be the only breadwinner, and protecting the victims from reprisals by the perpetrator. The offender is likely to eventually be released from custody and so the challenge arises of how to manage his return into the community.

The treatment of offenders as I describe in the earlier section 'Appraising some sex offender treatment programmes', is perhaps the most effective way of protecting children. If the risks of a person re-offending are low enough for that person to be managed within the community, a greater chance exists of his eventual rehabilitation. Without treatment, he's more likely to re-offend.

Autobiography of an abused person

Gypsy Boy is a remarkably candid and detailed account written by Mikey Walsh about the violence and sexual abuse he experienced as a child over many years. This abuse included regular beatings by his father and frequent sexual assaults by his uncle. When he tried to tell his father about the latter, he was just beaten again.

A number of such autobiographies exist by people who survived such distressing childhoods. They illustrate the abuse of trust and unwillingness of anyone to listen to their cries for help. But what's remarkable about all these books is that the authors invariably manage to survive their appalling childhood and seem to be able to lead healthy, well-balanced adult lives. This process is often a consequence of finding one or two caring people who believe their stories and support them, and eventually protect them enough for them to create a productive life for themselves. Publishing their stories undoubtedly helps their therapeutic process as well.

Evidence suggests that of those who participate in extensive treatment programmes, the majority, if not all, do improve their behaviour to a significant degree.

REGIONAL TIP-OFF

Sadly, such programmes aren't widely available throughout the world. They tend to be found only in Western Europe, Australasia and North America. In some countries, the victim is the one punished, with the assumption that the child brought the abuse on herself. In Eastern Europe, for example, the authorities are more likely to put the child into an institution than to prosecute or treat the offender. This misguided approach leaves the offender at large to assault others and can expose the child to abuse in the institution, increasing the probability that the child in turn becomes an abuser.

Chapter 16

Working with Juvenile Offenders

The truth is that young people commit a majority of crimes (as I note in Chapter 2) and youngsters who commit a series of crimes are likely to develop into adult offenders if they aren't helped in some way. Understanding and dealing with young offenders is therefore a crucial basis for reducing crime now and in the future. In the great majority of cases, children and young adults become involved in crime because of their family circumstances, and so the most effective procedures aimed at reducing juvenile offending are the ones based on working with families.

The various treatment interventions that I review throughout this chapter have been shown time and again to be more effective than institutionalisation. But early intervention to reduce the chance of serious offending occurring is even better. Positive parenting programmes and targeted interventions of children at risk are more powerful and in the end much more cost-effective than prison. The earlier a child reveals serious problematic behaviour, the worse the risk is for future criminality unless interventions are carried out to help the child.

Most offending behaviour occurs in adolescence, when people's identity begins to settle down as they explore what they can do and who they are. This crucial period is when minor legal infringements can be a passing phase or more seriously the start of a criminal career. What subsequently happens often depends on how the minor crimes are dealt with. Stopping adolescent misdemeanours from becoming a habit of offending is therefore a major focus of many interventions with children and their families.

In this chapter, I investigate the main elements that can cause youth crime as well as some protective factors that reduce the risk of youngsters becoming offenders. I also examine the central role of parenting and the family, and as an extreme case of youth crime, I take a look at school shootings, particularly in the US.

Understanding the Cycle of Youth Crime

Half or more of prisoners reveal that they committed antisocial behaviour as youngsters, typically in their mid-teens. Their early delinquency set in motion a pattern of behaviour that became a criminal lifestyle because it wasn't stopped; how this process can happen is my subject in this section. Crucially, these antisocial activities tend to be learned, condoned or in some way influenced by the family or institution in which the youngster grows up.

Therefore, children who become habitual criminals are likely to have children who also become offenders and so the cycle continues (check out Figure 16-1). Anything that can be done to break this cycle is consequently not only of value for the individuals concerned, but also for future generations and their victims.

Despite all the evidence showing that youth offending is rooted in the domestic circumstances of the child, and considering the ways in which the school and community can help to reduce any debilitating impact that results from those circumstances, a surprisingly high number of youngsters in many countries are still incarcerated. Taking them away from criminal backgrounds may have some simple-minded appeal, but two-thirds of incarcerated young offenders re-offend within a year of their release. And they're the ones who are caught! Surely many others, when separated from non-deviant friends and people who could care for them, find out how to avoid detection while in prison.

Locking youngsters up does nothing to deal with their difficulties in relating to other people, their low self-esteem and all the criminal habits they've developed to help them cope with their often difficult lives.

Committing antisocial behaviour can lead to adult criminality

A child who exhibits three or more of the following attributes is at risk of becoming seriously antisocial as an adult:

- ✔ Breaking into buildings or cars.
- ✔ Cruelty to animals.

✔ Cruelty to people, especially vulnerable people.

✔ Deliberate fire-setting.

✔ Destroying property, his own or others.

✔ Frequent truancy.

✔ Habitual lying.

✔ Running away from home overnight more than once.

✔ Stealing more than once.

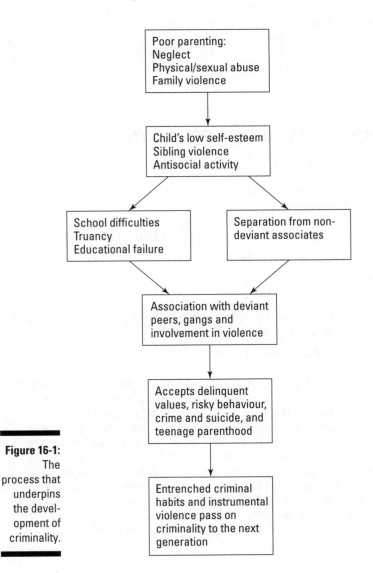

Figure 16-1:
The process that underpins the development of criminality.

Although a family's attitudes and behaviour are crucial for the development (or otherwise) of criminality in young people, the social and economic circumstances a child experiences can make matters better or worse. Children from large families with a low income, or with unemployed parents or who live in poor housing, are more at risk of becoming criminals. If the family unit has been broken in a distressing way through a messy divorce and a stepparent who doesn't really relate to the child, this situation can also increase the prevalence of antisocial behaviour in the child.

When one or more members of a child's family have been convicted of a crime, the probability increases of the child also drifting into criminality. This probability goes up further if the child isn't particularly bright and if schooling fails to deal with the problem and ignores the child. This situation can also result in the youngster leaving school early and so being even less equipped to gain an honest living. Some children don't engage with school but are shrewd enough to become effective criminals.

Examining causes of antisocial behaviour within the family

Research has established a number of aspects of family life as being at the root of delinquent behaviour:

- ✔ Little involvement by the parents in the lives of their children.
- ✔ Poor communication within the family.
- ✔ Little feelings of attachment to each other and the related lack of family cohesion.
- ✔ Erratic discipline, which can be too harsh or too permissive, and which often varies from one parent to the other.
- ✔ High levels of conflict at home framed in anger.

Sometimes, people (perhaps the parents) claim that a child 'got in with the wrong crowd'; in other words, the child's friends and associates led him astray and so are to blame. But in fact a dysfunctional family life aggravates this process. When the relationship between the parents and child is poor – for example, with little interaction between them and when the interaction that does exist doesn't support the child and is full of conflict – it increases the child's search for significance among other children. In addition, the aggressive style of interaction characteristic of such families is mirrored in the child's interaction with peers, so that other children who aren't comfortable with that behaviour reject the child. He then drifts into contact with deviant children and by this route can find his way into drug and alcohol abuse, theft and violent offending.

Dealing with delinquency

As I describe in Chapter 2, males are most likely to commit crimes. Research reveals that boys who get involved in crime do so at a younger age than girls and their crimes include violence much more often than girls.

The high number of youngsters who carry out some sort of criminal activity is surprising. For example, Sweden isn't known for its high crime rate, but in one recent survey over half the boys questioned admitted theft and only slightly fewer girls. Also, about one in five boys reported committing a violent offence, but less than one in ten girls.

In the US, gang culture is an important aspect of youth offending. Among 17-year-olds, about 1 out of every 12 declares that they're in a gang; almost one in five reports having sold drugs and carried a gun. These young gang members appear to be responsible for a high proportion of violent and non-violent offences in the US.

Youthful offending therefore appears to be rather common, but only a small minority of people who commit some sort of offence as youngsters go on to be criminals as adults. It is those who commit a number of offences who are most likely to drift into a criminal career. The task for the authorities is to distinguish between those juvenile delinquents who are on a path to serious crime and those who're exhibiting youthful exuberance and impulsivity. Often the difference lies in the family's reactions to the youngster's misdemeanours, as I emphasise throughout this chapter.

When thinking of children as criminals, the legal requirement of *mens rea* (the child knew what he was doing and that it was wrong; see Chapter 1 for more) has to be taken into account. This may mean the child can't be tried at all or that, in very serious crimes, they have to go through a process that is very similar to what adults experience, but then *mens rea* becomes a crucial part of the trial and can be difficult to establish with a young person. The individual may not be able to express thoughts or feelings clearly, or even to have an effective understanding of what has gone on, and may be confused by the questioning process.

Many jurisdictions therefore have a blanket assumption that children below a specific age can't be regarded as being responsible for their actions. The curious fact is that this age of criminal responsibility varies considerably from place to place (and some countries don't bother to specify any age at all). Some countries have ages that vary (the US age ranges from 6 to 12 years old across different states and Iran shows its sexist attitudes by using 9 years old for girls and 15 years old for boys).

Here are some ages of criminal responsibility in a few countries, from lowest to highest:

- 7 years old: India
- 8 years old: Kenya
- 10 years old: England and Wales
- 11 years old: Turkey
- 12 years old: Scotland, Israel and Japan
- 13 years old: France
- 14 years old: Austria and China
- 15 years old: Sweden
- 16 years old: Portugal
- 17 years old: Poland
- 18 years old: Belgium and Brazil

Focusing on a distinct group: Child sex offenders

Child offenders who commit sexual offences – such as sexual harassment, child molestation and rape – are a separate group of young criminals. Youngsters in their mid- to late teens or younger commit perhaps as many as one in four of these sorts of crimes.

A young person gets a life sentence

In 1999, Kathleen Grossett-Tate was babysitting 6-year-old Tiffany Eunick along with her 12-year-old son Lionel Tate. Not long after Kathleen went upstairs to rest, leaving the two children alone together, Lionel disturbed her to say that Tiffany had stopped breathing. She was indeed dead. He said that he'd been showing her 'professional wrestling moves' – he was about four times larger than Tiffany.

The prosecution claimed that Tiffany's injuries were so brutal that they couldn't have occurred as Lionel claimed. He was convicted and became the youngest person in the US to be sentenced to death. He won an appeal against the conviction on the grounds that his competency to stand trial hadn't been assessed for his initial trial. However, his subsequent criminal activity, including holding up a pizza delivery man with a gun, led to him being sentenced to 30 years in prison in May 2006.

Boot camp failure

One approach to trying to rehabilitate juvenile offenders, favoured by many conservative politicians, is known as the 'Boot Camp'. This idea follows the model of basic training in the military. The youngsters assigned to these places are forced to live a highly regimented life. They get up early each morning and have plenty of drills and exercise with harsh discipline, rigid codes of dress and frequent admonishments to ensure that they follow camp rules.

The idea is that these children simply need some firm authority and a healthy lifestyle to refrain from antisocial behaviour and criminality. However, studies of the effects of these regimes show that, although most inmates obey the rules while in the boot camp, these institutions have no lasting effect. They don't deal with the underlying psychological problems that lead to delinquency in the first place. All society ends up with is fitter, more athletic criminals!

Male and female juvenile sex offenders tend to be rather different from other sorts of young offenders. They often exhibit sexually abusive behaviour at a young age; some of their victims are male and they often have had a number of different victims. Lack of social skills can be an important aspect of their offending, as well as low intelligence, but a family history of sexual abuse is also often present.

Don't confuse these sexually abusive children with youngsters taking part in natural childhood explorations of sexuality. The 'I'll show you mine if you show me yours' games of early childhood can be healthy if limited and under control, and not turned into some desperate secret that then produces tremendous adult disapproval. Discovering what's private and what's for public display is a natural part of child development that needs to be handled sensitively.

The heightened sexuality of so much in adult life these days, and the increasing acceptance of sexually suggestive clothing for young girls, must be having an effect on how children under the age of puberty see the world. Displays of conjugal activity that would never have found their way into a Hollywood film 50 years ago, now seem par for the course. Whilst not making sexual activity seem secret and forbidden is a healthy aim, getting the balance right, especially when considering receptive young minds, is a challenge that all parents have to face.

Looking into the criminal careers of young offenders

Not all young offenders set out on a criminal career in the same way. This has been demonstrated by a major study carried out over many years by David Farrington and his colleagues at Cambridge University. They followed youngsters from their early years to see which of them became involved in crime, how they did, and why. Their different journeys to becoming adult criminals help to clarify the nature of their criminal behaviour and the likely progress it may follow:

- **Early-starter persistent offenders:** The teachers of these youngsters often recognise when they are 8, 9 or 10 years old that the child is already on a path to criminality. By the age of ten, a few children already show serious signs of deviance (as I describe in the earlier section 'Committing childhood antisocial behaviour is indicative of later criminality'). If not helped, these children go on to extensive criminal careers and may spend a large portion of their lives in prison.

- **Offences limited to adolescence:** Some youngsters drift into deviant peer groups in their mid-teens and their criminal activity fades as they move into their mid-20s, being limited to trivial crimes (mainly drug-related). They become isolated from their criminal friends and find a non-criminal lifestyle through work and entering into a caring relationship and starting a family.

- **Serious offenders of limited duration:** A crucial period exists in people's mid-20s when some can become involved in serious crimes. This period can even include murder despite them having no previous history of significant violence. This behaviour seems to be part of what may be called a late adolescence, in which the person is trying to make sense of who he is. Often, these people are capable but for some reason failed at school. By their early 30s, they may have 'found themselves' and dropped out of criminality, ended up in prison or committed suicide.

Recognising Protective Factors: The Good News

Of course, the great majority of children from vulnerable backgrounds don't become criminals, because many things can protect youngsters from the potential impact of debilitating circumstances. For example, they may be poor but well cared for by their parents, or a step-parent is delighted to take on a supportive parenting role. Even if these cases don't apply, children may find someone who cares for them outside their immediate family, such as a grandparent or teacher. They may discover success in some areas, such as sport or music, which gives them a feeling of healthy self-esteem and provides opportunities that take them away from delinquency and deviant friends. Inherent personality aspects that include lower impulsivity and more self-reliance can also reduce the impact of negative environmental factors.

These protective factors can be enhanced by various activities set up specifically to generate contact with people whom the child senses care about them, and who engender feelings of self-confidence and achievement. Examples include after-school programmes of positive activities. The Scouts is an obvious example but other activities such as youth clubs, sports organisations and orchestras or bands, or mentoring projects in which an adult gets to know and support the child on a one-to-one basis, have all been found to help children who may be vulnerable to avoid drifting into criminality. Trained foster carers are a more intensive and highly effective way of taking mentoring a step further.

Working with parents and families on such things as literacy skills or with reading schemes, also helps to give the child some feelings of achievement. Tackling school truancy directly and tackling why a school is excluding pupils also provide positive support that can counteract youngsters' potentially destructive experiences.

Keeping Things in the Family: The Central Importance of the Home

The most effective treatments to reduce delinquency and later criminality are those that work with the whole family (as I describe in this section). Importantly, these approaches keep the child in question at home and in the community, so that any interventions are integrated into their daily life. As a result, they avoid the many problems associated with institutionalising the child, including any deviant changes in behaviour that have occurred in the institution being transferred to the world outside.

Family-oriented approaches see the child as being part of a system of activities, feelings and attitudes. For this reason they're often called *systemic* therapies. They don't explore only the troubled individual's characteristics and problems, but also the dynamics within the family and any problems that parents and siblings may be facing.

Parenting wisely

In this section, I take a look at two approaches to improving parenting of problem children.

Donald, a US psychologist, takes a very direct approach to dealing with problem behaviour in children. He claims that what's needed is 'wise parenting'. He sees this idea as being based on such a clear set of principles that it can be understood and learnt initially from a CD-ROM, which therapists can use as the basis of their training.

A central idea behind *wise parenting* is that many of the problems the family face, can be re-interpreted to form the basis of positive productive activity rather than negative disturbing concerns. For example, if fights between the children are seen as a problem, parents can instead think of them as being a product of jealousy, boredom or a desire for attention. Dealing with conflicts as signs of such issues allows parents to deal with them effectively, as opposed to just shouting at the children and making matters worse. The other central principle of 'wise parenting' comes from the significant work of the psychologist B.F. Skinner, which was mainly conducted on pigeons, but nonetheless provides a simple and direct piece of guidance for many aspects of human behaviour.

Skinner's central notion is that punishment doesn't make people behave better, it just suppresses the actions that are punished. In order to get people to do the right thing they need support and encouragement for any steps they take along the way towards doing what's required. An illustration is that if a child is regularly late for school, shouting at the child is less likely to have an impact than finding out the stages that lead to lateness, such as going to sleep so late that he's difficult to rouse in the morning. Encouraging the child to go to bed earlier, and rewarding him for that, even if initially this approach doesn't lead to him being on time at school, is a step in the right direction.

Here's a very brief summary of the stages in the wise parenting process to show how these principles can be put into practice. Essentially four stages take place in each meeting with the family:

1. **Building rapport and trust with the family by relating to their daily concerns and experiences.**

2. **Establishing goals of what the family wants to achieve.**

3. **Reviewing any successes in achieving initial changes, however small, so that the family begins to feel that the process is having some effect.**

4. **Identifying parenting skills that can be developed and tried out between sessions with the therapist.**

These stages are repeated at every meeting with ever more intensive consideration of the goals and problems the family is facing, as well as developing the skills needed to achieve the goals. These skills include both the ability to make sense of the behaviour of the children and the parents, and the social skills of managing conflict and dealing with heightened emotions.

Of particular importance in wise parenting is helping the family as well as their children to make effective use of schooling, including:

- ✔ Minimising criticism of school work and increasing the children's confidence in what they're doing at school.
- ✔ Setting in motion good homework habits around a regular, co-operative routine.
- ✔ Setting clear limits on what's acceptable, which are agreed within the family.
- ✔ Communicating effectively with teachers.

To illustrate, here's an example that demonstrates family therapy in practice in the case of delinquent behaviour.

Sixteen-year-old Laurence was referred for family therapy by the juvenile court after being convicted of theft for the third time. He was known to be active in a gang and getting involved in fights after school. But the court thought that a greater chance of his rehabilitation existed outside of an institution. His stepfather was disabled and looked after the house and his mother had a full-time job in a nearby factory. His sister, Louise, was 14-years-old and seemed to avoid getting into any trouble.

Over three weekly meetings, family therapists established that little listening was taking place within the family, and a readiness existed to blame each other. Small problems weren't resolved so that they blew up into major rows. Laurence dealt with this situation by running out of the house. Louise kept in her stepfather's good books, being obviously his favourite, by reporting on Laurence's misdemeanours. No effective monitoring was undertaken of either child's behaviour even though the parents complained about this problem.

Over the following five weeks, the therapists dealt with the family's resistance to talking and listening to each other. They pointed out that the parent's lack of consistent support for appropriate behaviour in the children reflected their own experiences when they were growing up. The parents were told that Laurence obtained feelings of significance and respect from his friends that he didn't get at home. Each of these debilitating actions identified within the family was examined to show that a positive side existed if they were used only to encourage good behaviour rather than punish bad. For example, Louise reporting on Laurence was presented as wanting parental approval, but she could also achieve that approval by reporting any good things Laurence did.

After the family began to accept the re-examination of what was going on they were trained in various skills to help them communicate and deal with anger and conflict. They were encouraged to rehearse these skills in the presence of the therapist and then to try them out as 'homework' before the next therapy session. Follow-up sessions a couple of months later showed that far less conflict was occurring in the family and that they had the capability to resolve future difficulties.

Bringing all the groups together: Multisystemic therapy

Working with the family is central to any treatment programme, but psychologists can't focus on the family in isolation. *Multisystemic* is a technical term for an approach to helping juvenile delinquents that works with all the groups of relevance – friends and associates, family, school and broader aspects of the society with which the individual has contact. Multisystemic therapy has a number of key principles:

- ✓ **Understanding the context:** This is the need to assess how the identified problems relate to the family, friends, school and community of which the child is a part. Determining the ways in which any successes with the child interact with these contexts is also important.

- ✓ **Concentrating on strengths and other positive aspects of the people and their circumstances:** Effective and capable aspects of the child and what he has access to can set in motion important changes. The strengths in the family provide opportunities that the family already knows how to use – building feelings of hope, identifying protective factors (see the earlier section 'Recognising Protective Factors: The Good News' for more), decreasing frustration by emphasising problem solving, and enhancing caregivers' confidence.

- ✓ **Taking responsibility by all those involved:** Interventions are designed to promote responsible behaviour and decrease irresponsible actions, not only by the child at the core of concerns, but also by all family members.

- ✓ **Focusing on the here and now and what can be done about it:** Actions are sought that can be taken immediately, targeting specific and well-defined problems. Such interventions enable participants to track the progress of the treatment and provide clear criteria to measure success. Family members are encouraged to work actively towards clearly defined goals. This focus contrasts with traditional approaches that spend a lot of time looking into the past and assessing its impact. Examining what can be done now with a view to future implications is a different strategy.

- ✓ **Unpacking the sequence of actions that gives rise to problems:** Unwanted behaviour typically emerges out of a sequence of events. This sequence needs to be identified and interventions introduced that target specific aspects within and between the various aspects of the adolescent's life – family, teachers, friends, home, school and community.

✔ **Ensuring that interventions are appropriate to the stage in development:** Children of the same age may be at different levels of maturity. Any interventions therefore need to fit the child's developmental needs. This requirement stresses building the adolescent's ability to get along well with peers and acquiring academic and vocational skills that promote a successful transition to adulthood.

✔ **Encouraging continuous effort:** Interventions require daily or weekly effort by family members so that the youth and family have frequent opportunities to demonstrate their commitment. Advantages of intensive and multifaceted efforts to change include more rapid problem resolution, earlier identification of when interventions need fine-tuning, continuous evaluation of outcomes, more frequent corrective interventions, more opportunities for family members to experience success and giving the family power to orchestrate their own changes.

✔ **Evaluating and being accountable:** Intervention effectiveness is evaluated continuously from multiple perspectives with support in place to help overcome barriers to successful outcomes. Everything possible is done to avoid blaming the family for any lack of progress. Responsibility for positive treatment outcomes is placed on the team supporting the therapy.

✔ **Working towards positive accounts now and in the future:** All interventions are designed to enable the family and those associated with the child to be effective and successful in producing positive outcomes. The family must be able to maintain any gains during therapy after the support team withdraws.

Of course all of this is a tall order and very expensive, especially if many different agencies and well-qualified experts are involved. But it is a lot cheaper than dealing with the consequences of crime, keeping offenders in prison, and all the fall-out effects within society.

Going Back to School: Investigating School Shootings

An especially disturbing example of juvenile violence is when killing occurs in schools. The horrific shooting of many students in one spree – as in Columbine High School in Colorado in 1999 where two boys in their midteens killed 12 students and a teacher, and Jokela High School, Finland in which an 18 year old killed nine people in 2007 – capture the headlines around the world. Although these events are very rare they do seem to emerge in spates after a particularly bloody incident, particularly in the US.

The destructiveness of these rampages doubtless owes something to the availability of firearms to youngsters, but as in spree killings committed by adults (that I mention in Chapter 6), school shootings almost invariably end in the death of the perpetrator(s). Therefore, they have to be considered as a form of extremely violent suicide and their roots are likely to be very similar to the roots of many suicides – despair, anger with those around and a desire to leave the world in some significant manner that sends a message.

In response to understandable concerns about school shootings, the US Secret Service prepared a summary in 2000 of what's known about school shooters to help identify them and reduce the risk of these events occurring.

As with all such attempts to summarise a complex psychological issue, with many variations between individuals, the summary provided by the US Secret Service isn't to be used without careful consideration of particular persons and their context. The vast majority of youngsters who experience insult and isolation from others, don't get hold of guns and seek to kill their school mates.

The summary the US Secret Service provided includes the following indications:

- Someone is likely to have been told about the intention to carry out the attack. In three out of four incidents, the attacker(s) told a friend or sibling of the plans. This shows the sorts of thought processes growing out of personal narratives that I discuss for other violent offenders in Chapters 14 and 15.

- A plan of attack nearly always exists; they're rarely impulsive acts, which means that careful surveillance can reveal aspects of this preparation.

- These spree killers have easy access to often high-powered weapons. In most cases they get the guns from their own home or a relative. This shows that the family context, as with all young offenders, is relevant.

- Often some explicit or implicit support from friends or schoolmates is present for the idea of the attack, if not for the actual shootings. So the power of the peer group in influencing youngsters is present here as in delinquent behaviour that I discuss earlier in this section.

- Although no characteristic 'profile' for the typical school shooter exists, because they differ from each other in many ways, many of the perpetrators have experienced bullying and harassment.

- If they can be spotted and interpreted, early warning signs are often present that the individual is in need of help. This can be talk of suicide or general anger, as described for violent offenders in Chapter 14.

Part VI
The Part of Tens

The 5th Wave   By Rich Tennant

CULINARY FORENSIC PSYCHOLOGIST

"Whoever committed this meat loaf clearly suffers from an 'edible complex.'"

In this part . . .

Forensic psychology is a professional activity, constrained by legal and ethical boundaries. The activity itself is carried out by people who go through many years of training. This part gives some examples of the stages in becoming a forensic psychologist and the principles that its practitioners are bound by. Examples of cases that illustrate some of the matters that I discuss earlier in this book are also given, as well as indications of the emerging areas that forensic psychologists are moving into. This part draws heavily in my own experiences over the last quarter of a century training forensic psychologists and providing consultancy in many different legal situations.

Chapter 17

Ten Professional Requirements for Forensic Psychologists

In This Chapter

▶ Putting the legal demands of the court first

▶ Remaining unfazed by external pressures

▶ Maintaining professional standards

F orensic psychologists in fiction are often portrayed as gung-ho characters who totally ignore the ethical and legal constraints of the profession – no doubt the everyday realities are likely to slow the story down. But if you employ or have to challenge a forensic psychologist, you need to make sure that they're following the rules and not stepping outside their professional remit. Or, if you're an aspiring forensic psychologist, you need to be aware of the scope and boundaries of professional practice. In this chapter, I look at some central rules and principles guiding the work of forensic psychologists.

Providing Evidence for the Court, Not the Client

You may think that he who pays the piper calls the tune, and that if you're hiring a forensic psychologist as an expert then he is accountable to you. But as with many aspects of the legal world, the one who foots the bill doesn't necessarily have control over the proceedings.

In the UK, a defendant can pay for an expert out of his own pocket or from legal aid – the expert can also be employed by The Crown (the State) or in civil cases, by the plaintiff.

In such cases, the legal requirement is that the expert is a neutral advisor to the court and not a servant of whoever's paying the bill.

Contrary to what you see in TV courtroom dramas and films, and from reports of legal cases, the expert is there to serve the court, even though attorneys may try their utmost to make sure that the expert gives the necessary evidence to support their case.

This has a curious result that I have experienced in a number of cases I have advised on, and colleagues have reported similar events. The attorneys will ask for a report for which (eventually) I will get paid, but then it will not be presented in court because the attorney does not think it will help his client. I am doing my job of producing a report for the court. But the attorney does not want the judges or jury to see my report so I am thanked for my services. What I have written is quietly filed away.

Getting Ethical Approval for Research

Before starting on a piece of research, the forensic psychologist writes a research proposal. Most Western countries require any research proposals for any discipline to be vetted by *ethical committees*, but particularly if the research deals with people or animals. These committees are made up of people experienced in the type of research, but who are often also members of the public or representatives of client groups.

Ethical committees have many areas of concern, including the need to obtain:

- ✔ **Informed consent:** Making sure that anyone taking part in the research knows the purpose of the research and how it affects them. Whenever you take part in a study, you're asked to sign a consent form to show that you fully understand and agree with the objectives of the research.

- ✔ **Privacy:** Making sure that the results of the study and the records kept of what people say or do have suitable levels of confidentiality and anonymity. Ensuring privacy is so that people's responses can never be used for purposes other than the research, and that people can't be embarrassed or otherwise discomforted by what they said or did in the research process. Maintaining privacy includes destroying the records of the raw information collected when the research is over.

- ✔ **Safety:** Making sure that no one is physically or psychologically hurt or abused during the research.

Following Codes of Practice

Members of a professional body usually work within a well-established code of practice (rules) of the organisation. Codes of practice can be comprehensive and detailed. For example, the codes of practice of the American Psychological Association form a substantial tome. Other professional bodies around the world have similar though less extensive lists of dos and don'ts (usually more don'ts than dos).

Codes of practice relate to a wide range of matters, from the need to declare 'conflicts of interest' – for example, a commercial interest in the results of an experiment – to avoiding compromising relationships with clients (even though fictional forensic psychologists can't seem to help falling in love with suspects!). Keeping up-to-date with developments in the relevant subject areas, called *continuing professional development* (CPD), is a requirement that is usually included.

Avoiding the Ultimate Question

I talk about what the court expects of the experts in the section 'Providing Evidence for the Court, not the Client'. But experts also have to bear in mind a crucial issue that may be a little surprising – being careful not to steal the court's thunder. Stating an opinion can be particularly problematic for forensic psychologists because their evidence isn't usually the hard evidence that, for example, forensic scientists may offer.

Forensic psychologists are commenting directly on the character of the accused, the mental state of the defendant or the reliability of testimony, or other aspects of the person involved. Therefore, they're dealing directly with the opinions that the judge or jury form of the defendant.

Experts can all too easily slip into offering an opinion that implies guilt or innocence. The expert's statement can appear as an indirect, corroborative opinion, such as stating that a key witness couldn't possibly have remembered what they claim to remember, or the statement can be more direct, such as whether the defendant has the intellect or skills to carry out the crime. If the jury accepts the expert's opinion, that amounts to the expert making the crucial decision about guilt.

Therefore, experts in court have to be cautious about how their opinions are expressed. This situation is well understood in forensic science, when experts say, for example, that the blow to the head is 'consistent with that produced by a blunt instrument', even though everyone knows a piece of lead pipe is at the heart of the case. For forensic psychologists, however, avoiding the direct implication of their opinions may be more difficult. But if forensic psychologists sail close to the 'ultimate question' of innocence or guilt, such as saying 'what is known about memory is incompatible with the claims of the witness', the judge is likely to keep such opinions away from the jury in order that the trial is truly a trial by jury and not a trial by expert.

The judge reviews the evidence to be presented to the jury and other legal aspects of the case in what's known as the *voir dire* (an investigation, in the course of the trial, into the truth or admissibility of evidence about to be given without the jury present). If the judge considers that the forensic psychologist's opinion is something the jury may be able to form a view on without expert advice, or that the expert advice may be too close to the ultimate question, the forensic psychologist's statement isn't allowed. As I mention earlier (in the section 'Providing evidence for the court not the client'), the judge will also be careful to ensure the expert is offering an objective opinion supported by professional expertise and is not just a 'hired gun'.

Working Within Your Area of Competence

Despite what crime-drama psychologists get up to on TV – interrogating suspects in dark alleys and impatiently charging into dangerous locations in front of armed police – in real life, codes of practice emphasise the importance of the professionals having the necessary skills, training and qualifications to practise particular aspects of their profession. The professional needs to know what areas are outside of his competency, even though many people may assume he can operate in those areas.

Competency in carrying out the job may seem obvious – the thought of having a leg amputated by a heart surgeon is scary – but within forensic psychology the precise boundaries of someone's competence for a particular case can be subtle. Even if forensic psychologists themselves are clear where their competence lies, the people who employ them may not be, introducing pressures that aren't always easy to avoid. Lawyers in particular often have a limited understanding of the precise nature of forensic psychology, and the different skills that different aspects of forensic psychology require, how it differs from psychiatry and what the various specialisms are within the different professions.

Once, despite being clearly listed as a forensic psychologist, I was asked by an attorney to carry out an examination of a rape victim to determine if an assault had taken place. I have no medical qualifications and therefore have never been trained in how to carry out a medical examination.

This extreme example serves to illustrate how readily experts can be drawn into areas in which, well, they're just not expert. In such situations, I take the opportunity to point out to the legal profession the difference between the disciplines and the different qualifications needed to be competent to carry out the job.

A subtle example is when a forensic psychologist is giving advice to a family court on the likelihood of abuse occurring if a child is returned to their parents. The advice may be based on talking to the child and careful examination of the parents, their background and any offence history. During the course of the proceedings, the forensic psychologist is asked whether the information from certain witnesses is likely to be accurate. However tempted the forensic psychologist is in wanting to assist the court, if he hasn't studied the work on witness testimony or had the opportunity to examine carefully the claims of the witness, he has to acknowledge that offering an opinion on the matter is beyond his competence.

Submitting to Peer Review

How can busy professionals be sure that they're conforming to their code of practice (check out the earlier section 'Following Codes of Practice') and staying within the bounds of appropriate competence? The answer is to do as the contestants do on the quiz show *Who Wants to be a Millionaire* and 'phone a friend' – consulting with colleagues is a practice called *peer review*.

Peer review involves a set of experts in the same field, but not directly involved in your work, considering what you're proposing or writing and evaluating your work in the light of what they know and understand.

Peer review is standard practice for evaluating research grant applications and is at the heart of the work of ethical committees (discussed in the section 'Getting Ethical Approval for Research'). The process is also used for assessing research work being submitted for publication in academic and professional journals.

Of course, peer review isn't a foolproof system and is open to misuse. Most notably, peer review can be conservative and stifle innovation, for example, when established experts feel that the proposal threatens their own livelihood or are just uncomfortable with the proposal's implications.

Nonetheless, peer review greatly reduces the possibility of professional abuse by making sure that individuals in the profession don't drift into areas of activity in which they risk being incompetent, or worse. The process limits the impact of arrogance and egotism and can save experts from being inappropriately self-confident.

Also, peer review looks at the emotional and personal consequences of being involved with the horrors of forensic cases and can help forensic psychologists deal with the possible traumas of the cases that they're considering in detail.

Of course the peer review process needs to take into account the confidentiality central to any reports prepared (see the later section on 'respect for confidentiality'). Reports for the court are confidential until the judge agrees that they can be made public.

Having a Duty of Care

Forensic psychologists deal with people and how a person is thinking and behaving. Unlike the forensic scientist examining fibres or carrying out autopsies on dead bodies, forensic psychologists are talking to people and making use of what the person is saying. Thus codes of practice draw attention to the special duty of psychologists to take care in avoiding harming people with whom they're interacting.

Determining the boundaries of the duty of care can be testing for forensic psychologists, because their paymaster or client may not be the person they're dealing with directly or whose life they're influencing (I describe the complex relationship between the professional and the hirer in the section 'Providing Evidence for the Court, Not the Client'). For example, while talking to a defendant to determine his sexual fantasies, the forensic psychologist has to avoid doing so in a way that may be disturbing or upsetting.

An illustration of the duty of determining the boundaries of care, is the case in which a forensic psychologist was guiding an undercover police operation. A woman police officer was directed to try to get a confession from a suspect that she was deliberately befriending. The suspect turned out to be completely innocent but he was greatly disturbed by the whole experience, which included spending 11 months in prison. Also, the woman police officer suffered mental distress as a result of the event. The forensic psychologist appears to have failed in carrying out his duty of care in guiding the police operation. In this particular case, no inquiry ever established failure, but the suspect and the police officer were awarded substantial sums of money in recompense for the harm they were suffering, a tacit acknowledgement that something had gone badly wrong.

Respecting Confidentiality

In some informal professional discussions between colleagues, one may mention to the other the sorts of problems her clients had in very general terms, perhaps because these problems were particularly interesting. But professionals will always be careful never, ever to mention a client's name.

Nor will they mention any details that would allow their colleague to guess who the client was, where he or she worked or anything else that related to the client's identity. You could meet her clients in many social or professional situations, but would not have the slightest idea that they had ever had psychological advice or had any private concerns. That is the essence of confidentiality. The identity of people with whom the psychologist has professional interaction is protected, as are the details of their condition.

Maintaining confidentiality is hugely important. Forensic psychologists have to protect the identity of persons with whom they interact professionally, together with the details of the person's situation, condition or problem.

In the legal context, confidentiality is vital because of the adversarial nature of the procedure; the prosecutor and the defendant prepare their arguments in secret until they can present their cases in court. Thus the knowledge that one side is using a forensic psychologist, with some prospect of their opponents guessing why, can weaken the whole process. Even the fact that a forensic psychologist was employed but their report not used can provide ammunition.

The information that comes out during the course of forming an expert opinion also has to be kept confidential. Such information may be of use to criminals or others who have an axe to grind with a client. People can take advantage of the fact that a forensic psychologist is involved in the case.

This situation is especially true in cases where psychologists give advice to criminal investigations. It is usually best that there is no public indication that a psychologist is involved at all. Particularly in cases involving a lot of public interest, the psychologists can come under a great deal of unwanted pressure to reveal their opinions if people discover that the police have consulted them. The identities of psychologists who advise police investigations are therefore usually kept secret.

Professional Humility

Some years ago, I coined the term *professional humility* to draw attention to the fact that no single professional discipline has all the answers. The need always exists to work with others and learn from their insights.

Forensic psychologists may sometimes think that they hold the answers to a case just because they're dealing directly with the key people involved, and exploring and finding out what the criminal felt or thought, and why he's behaving the way he is. But that can be misleadingly arrogant.

Everyone involved in the case has a useful perspective and everyone needs to recognise that they see only a part of the picture.

Telling the Truth

You may think that the need to tell the truth in a court of law is stating the obvious, but forensic psychology is such a complex and growing area, having many challenges and demands, that I believe stressing the need for honesty is important.

Unfortunately, forensic psychologists may sometimes be tempted to take short cuts or give in to the pressures from clients, lawyers, the press or the police to provide the answers or opinions most wanted. Material can even be presented to the forensic psychologist in ways that are subtly biased to suggest the desired answer or, in some cases, the people commissioning the psychologists may omit crucial information to try and influence the opinion she forms. Psychologists, just like all the other advisors to the courts or investigations, therefore have to be alert to what background information they are given and whether it may be biased in any way.

On one occasion, I was asked to comment on a suspicious death, being told that, 'We found the wife dead on the bed and the husband says he was away in Aberdeen at the time.' Clearly, by phrasing the information in this way the person wanted an opinion that incriminated the husband. I had to step back from this nudge by trying to build up a picture of the circumstances of the death that made no assumptions about guilt. In other words, I had to tell the truth as I saw it.

Chapter 18

Ten Stages in Becoming a Professional Forensic Psychologist

*O*ne of the things that makes forensic psychology so fascinating is the overlap of the austere academic discipline of psychology with the law in its many manifestations, and the range of contexts in which the profession can be applied.

Although the professional position of the forensic psychologist is just getting a foothold in the US, it's well established and protected in the UK and Australia. In these countries, controls exist on who can call themselves a forensic psychologist and the qualifications a person needs in order to practise.

The profession attracts loads of capable people who work in a wide range of different settings, not just prisons and mental hospitals. The various techniques, approaches and applications that I describe throughout this book provide plenty of work for the forensic psychologist, but getting into the profession is highly competitive, although this chapter can certainly help. Here I describe ten stages that a forensic psychologist goes through before they can practise as a professional.

Although you can read the following ten sections as a logical sequence, please don't see the process as an inevitable route. For example, I became involved in forensic psychology after 25 years as an applied psychologist, and a number of my students moved into the profession from the police. People from backgrounds not directly related to psychology or the law have also become professionals in this area after experience in other contexts. When such people qualify, they often bring fresh perspectives and new insights not immediately available to people who follow the more traditional routes.

Thinking about the Profession While at School

If you're at school and have a definite long-term goal of becoming a professional forensic psychologist, remember that the field is ever more competitive and so the most important aspect is to do well in whatever subjects you're working on. But of course studying subjects relevant to psychology is a good idea: for example, biology, mathematics, philosophy and geography.

Personally, I don't think that studying psychology at school is a great idea if you want to go on to be a psychologist professionally. I'm sure many of my colleagues will howl their disagreement, but my view is that in order to convert psychology into a subject that can be digested by teenagers it needs to be made less problematic than it really is, dumbed-down even. As a consequence, a lot of material presented in school as reasonably clear-cut has to be questioned later at university and so needs to be 'unlearned'. Better, therefore, is to get a good grounding in other subjects that psychology feeds on than to start on a subject that can become your life's obsession. I don't mean to suggest, however, that you don't read any psychology books before going to university. You're reading this one and I certainly approve of that!

School students' ideas of topics or professions are likely to change as they mature and gain a wider experience of the world. In addition, forensic psychology is evolving and changing and takes on many different forms in many different situations. For these reasons, having in mind only one fixed career choice can be a mistake. Many other possibilities may become attractive, and a wider education allows you to take advantage of new opportunities as they arise.

Studying at University

Forensic psychology isn't usually a first (undergraduate) degree in any country, and so your choice of university and degree may be best based on opportunity, location and other interests rather than any particular focus on this area of psychology.

Of course, a degree in psychology is the most direct route towards becoming a forensic psychologist. Generally, any good university qualification in psychology is a sound basis for further professional development; it doesn't have to be a focused psychology degree. Many other university qualifications may be acceptable for the academic step. Sometimes, some form of 'topping up' of a first degree as a preparation for subsequent high-level study is advisable if psychology wasn't the dominant part of the first qualification.

As with the selection of subjects to study at school (see the preceding section), I counsel against focusing on forensic psychology as a major part of a first degree. Again, achieving a high standard in a highly regarded university is much more important than the specific topics that you study. However, as the big wide world beckons, a good idea is to start getting a taste for future professional prospects. Seize on any options at university that give you a feel for what different areas of psychology deal with in practice, because they can open up the vista to possible careers.

When choosing a university, many try to attract students by indicating that they offer courses that have plenty of bits and pieces of popular subjects (such as forensic psychology or, heaven forbid, 'offender profiling'). In fact, the people teaching those subjects are often only a chapter ahead of the students using the book for the course. They may have no direct knowledge of the topics and give a bowdlerised version of them. Carry out a quick search on the Internet of who the lecturers are on any particular course. Find out what they've published to get an indication of what they're likely to be expert in and able to offer.

For most serious university degrees, you need to do some sort of project towards the end of the course. This point is where you need to focus on something relevant to your later career. Not only do such projects help you explore in some depth a topic that's relevant to your later ambitions (and therefore gain a better flavour of what that field is like), but also they provide a topic for future job or course applications and interviews, showing both some expertise in and commitment to the chosen profession.

Getting Direct Work Experience

Although forensic psychology work experience after graduating is a definite advantage, it isn't essential to being accepted onto postgraduate courses that provide the thorough training necessary to become a professional (see the next section 'Gaining a Master's Qualification').

Perhaps this is fortunate because getting such direct work experience is difficult. The number of people looking for such opportunities is so great that finding somewhere to provide you with practical activity is challenging. Part of the problem is that at this stage people looking for professional experience don't have much in the way of skills to offer beyond what they've learned as an undergraduate.

Here are some of the many values, however, that derive from practical involvement in real work of relevance to forensic psychology:

- ✔ Seeing what the real working day is like, with its challenges and demands.
- ✔ Getting to understand how the law works in practice, with its delays, tedium, confusions and frustrations.
- ✔ Appreciating the different areas of activity, including those for which further qualifications aren't necessary and those for which they're essential.
- ✔ Finding out about the sorts of people involved in this area, clients and staff, and whether you want to spend your professional career with them.
- ✔ Opening up possible job opportunities for the future.

You can achieve such practical experience in many different settings; you don't need to 'shadow' an established professional psychologist. As long as the placement has contact with the legal process and a link with psychologists, your experience is going to be worthwhile. Therefore, consider the following possibilities:

- ✔ Assisting a lawyer who deals with criminal cases.
- ✔ Being part of rehabilitation projects for ex-prisoners.
- ✔ Working as a volunteer for the Victim Support service.
- ✔ Joining a prison's 'prison visitor' scheme that involves meeting with prisoners and hearing their accounts of their experiences.
- ✔ Taking advantage of what some police forces offer to be a community officer; you don't have the powers or responsibilities of a fully-fledged officer, but the role provides help in many law enforcement activities.
- ✔ Helping out with a forensic psychology research project can help you discover something of the area and perhaps get a foot in the door for future training or employment.
- ✔ Supporting the work of a forensic psychologist, though such opportunities are few and far between (professionals usually take on people with higher-level qualifications, see the next section 'Gaining a Master's Qualification'). If such an opportunity does arise, seize it: even simply photocopying, filing, printing out reports and sorting out websites is useful. Any contact provides insights into the work and organisation.

In all these areas, bear in mind the legal, professional and ethical considerations that I discuss in Chapter 17.

Gaining a Master's Qualification

The first serious step that commits you to developing a career as a forensic psychologist is obtaining a postgraduate qualification. The nature of this qualification varies considerably around the world, however: in some countries, it's a 2-year period of study whereas in others a Master's is more of a doctorate qualification, spread over at least three years (see the later section 'Striving for a Doctorate'). It varies a little from state to state in the US but is typically part of a Doctoral level training. A useful starting point for finding out about such courses, especially in the US, is www.forensicpsychology.net/.

Master's qualifications are intensive taught courses, often including some practical experience. They open up the range of topics that forensic psychology covers and allow in-depth study of many of them. A project is usually required that allows the development of research skills and the opportunity to make a contribution to the development of the discipline.

Master's courses are usually accredited by a national or state organisation as a crucial step to achieving a recognised qualification. These organisations typically provide a framework of the minimum requirements of topics that the course needs to cover. This book covers the range of issues that I'd expect to be included in any Master's course in forensic psychology (different universities may have different emphases that are worth exploring, such as ones that relate broadly to the contexts in which forensic psychologists operate):

 ✔ Giving evidence, as an expert in court, on fitness to plead, *mens rea* and so on (the sort of things I discuss in Chapter 11).

 ✔ Working with offenders in prison, as I describe especially in Chapters 13, 14 and 15.

 ✔ Contributing to the investigative process that I introduce in Chapter 6 (a handful of places around the world emphasise this).

 ✔ Providing an emphasis on the psychology of the court process that I outline in Chapter 12 (a few places in the US do this).

 ✔ Working with extremely disturbed individuals who've committed very serious crimes, in secure treatment centres or 'special hospitals', or in the US 'correctional establishments'.

Becoming an Intern

Opportunities for working as an intern within a forensic psychology setting usually open up during a Master's course or immediately afterwards (see the preceding section), because people have developed the crucial skills, internalised the professional ethics and established stronger contacts. These internships have all the advantages of getting experience that I mention earlier in this chapter (in 'Getting Direct Work Experience'), but now the person is much more part of the team rather than a lowly assistant. Many organisations survive because of the help given by people at this stage in their careers.

These internships are supervised by an experienced, qualified professional, and the supervised professional practice may cover a defined set of professional activities, so that the intern gets some contact with the major aspects of the discipline. Log books and other forms of assessment and recording of the experience are also a normal aspect of this professional training.

An internship can be just another way of gaining experience (and earning some money), whilst more direct opportunities for developing professional skills emerge. But for this experience to count as a formal step towards becoming a qualified forensic psychologist it needs to be properly supervised. I deal with that next.

Being Supervised

Usually, you need to undertake a 2-year period of supervised professional practice after your Master's or Doctorate course before being regarded as a qualified forensic psychologist. So, after three years of an undergraduate degree, typically two years on a Master's course and then these two years, seven years in total is needed for you to be able to stand up in court as a qualified forensic psychologist, or to get many of the jobs that advertise for a 'qualified forensic psychologist'.

All established forensic psychologists see part of their role as giving guidance and support to those who aspire to emulate them. Such available support can include supervising, giving lectures as part of university courses and participating in research projects. Any well-established forensic psychology department in a university has a network of contacts for gaining supervision.

Striving for a Doctorate

A doctorate (PhD, DPhil, DClin Psych etc) is nearly always awarded for making 'a contribution to knowledge'. This contribution is based on a major research project that takes about three years to complete and write up as a significant document. The topic of research is agreed between a supervisor (or supervisory team) and the student. These topics vary enormously and go into the chosen area in great depth. So, people who complete a Doctorate often become world experts in the topic of their thesis. In forensic psychology these will often be carried out whilst employed in professional practice. They can deal with any topic that is covered in the rest of this book, but will usually relate to the particular area of forensic psychology in which the person is engaged.

Various places are emerging that offer 'professional doctorates' that have a little less emphasis on contributing to knowledge. They have more concern with developing professional skills and understanding. In the future, these 3-year qualifications are likely to replace the Master's degree.

Deciding to Specialise

As your professional experience develops and particular opportunities emerge, you may well begin to specialise in some particular area of activity: perhaps a special set of patients, such as those with severe mental disorders or alcohol problems; or specific areas, such as giving evidence of malingering or suggestibility.

These specialisms often emerge from research activity, notably at the PhD level (see the previous section), but can also be a consequence of particular prior experiences. For example, I became involved in human rights cases about prison conditions because of my earlier work as a psychologist working in a school of architecture. People get known for their special expertise and therefore get asked to work on cases that involve this activity. In turn, their experience and understanding increase, which strengthens the contribution they can make.

Flying Solo

After a few years within a professional framework, people gain the experience and confidence to work completely independently, which isn't necessarily an entirely good thing to do. Many of the ethical and professional issues that I discuss in Chapter 17 imply the need to keep in contact with other experts.

Indeed, many professional bodies require 'Continuing Professional Development' (CPD) to maintain registration as a professional, in order to ensure that individuals keep up-to-date with developments in their field, particularly their own specialisms. People can also enhance their skills by attending various courses, for example, on some new method of assessment.

Attaining Guru-Like Status

Many doors open after a person becomes established in the energetic, rapidly developing discipline of forensic psychology. Many senior members of the forensic psychology profession move into important administrative posts. They may continue to contribute to popular understanding and the development of the science and profession, or they may do equally important administrative duties in offices. Such people can become deans in universities, advisors to prison administrators or even significant people in government departments, helping to shape policy and inform professional practice at national and international levels.

With my tongue somewhat in my cheek, a few forensic psychologists make such significant contributions to the profession that they become gurus. These people are regarded as having special wisdom and deep experience that they can pass on to others. In the modern world, such people can be bombarded with e-mails asking for assistance or even (amazingly/amusingly) asked to sign photographs of themselves to be made into wedding presents. Forensic psychologists can also be asked for help in apparent miscarriages of justice (or even plain weird approaches that have no obvious rhyme or reason).

Sadly, such fame often owes more to the person being drawn on by the broadcast and printed media for comments, than through any substantial contribution to the development of the science or the profession. That, however, is changing as more people with professional and scientific qualifications become the gatekeepers for the mass media. Any person with some degree of popular recognition for their contributions to the profession has to steer a course between overexposure and the inevitable trivialisation of the discipline, and ensuring that some sensible account of the established science is used in popular accounts, such as writing *Forensic Psychology For Dummies!*

Chapter 19

Ten Emerging Areas of Forensic Psychology

In This Chapter

▶ Investigating new areas connected to forensic psychology

▶ Contributing to court proceedings in innovative ways

▶ Helping with some big decisions

*F*orensic psychology is a growing, evolving profession. Much of the concern with crime, law enforcement and the legal system is to do directly with individuals. So understanding their psychology and experiences is an inevitable part of what legal processes have to deal with. As a result, plenty of nooks and crannies exist in which the discipline can get a foothold and spread its roots and branches from there into other areas.

In this chapter, I describe ten emerging areas of forensic psychology that point to intriguing new directions to which forensic psychology is contributing.

Dealing with Human Rights Cases

With the emergence of Human Rights legislation in Europe and its long-standing presence in the US, a growing number of cases have arisen in which a person claims that they have been treated to unacceptable punishment, as I mention in Chapter 13. These claims often relate to prison conditions, especially in relation to shared cells and the lack of availability of appropriate sanitation. Other cases relate to solitary confinement and its use over longer periods than is ethically acceptable.

When these cases are brought to court, the difficult task arises of sorting out the general effects of imprisonment from the specific conditions that are the basis of the appeal: plus, of course, the individuals bringing these claims are offenders. The initial assumption is likely to be that they aren't providing the whole truth and may even be distorting the account of their experiences. When these individuals have been assigned the label 'psychopath', then the assumption may be made that they're pathological liars and that their testimony shouldn't be accepted at all.

Forensic psychology can contribute to the legal process in these cases by drawing on psychology studies about the way prisoners make use of, and experience, their cells and other aspects of the prison they are in.

This contribution is illustrated by the judge's summing up in an appeal by a Mr Napier that the conditions he experienced were inhumane. I gave evidence in relation to Mr Napier's appeal. In quoting from my evidence the judge noted the following areas:

> *Within the cell, the lack of opportunity to create appropriate 'places' for activities, most notably the lack of a distinct place of excretion and associated washing facilities.*
>
> *The sharing of the cell, causing the lack of possibility for creating a 'personal space' and distinct area or 'territory' for his own activities. . .*
>
> *The pressure of overcrowding and lack of enough facilities, on the landing and in the block, on the opportunities there might otherwise have been for hygiene, recreation and 'psychological release'.*
>
> *The arbitrariness yet excessive control of the regime over the minutiae of daily activities.*
>
> *The impact of Mr Napier's eczema on his ability to make use of coping strategies that may have alleviated the brutalising quality of his incarceration.*
>
> *The uncertainties associated with being on remand.*

In my opinion, these conditions interact to create circumstances that in total are more debilitating and dehumanising than could reasonably be expected for imprisonment . . . that view is consistent with the impact that the conditions did, in fact, have upon the petitioner.

Rebutting Pseudo-Science

Psychology is embedded in strong scientific traditions, and so psychologists can bring many basic principles of how to evaluate conclusions from studies of human activity and experience to legal considerations. Curiously the courts, especially in the UK, have no clear way of determining what expertise is allowable – it depends on the particular judges and the circumstances of the case. Therefore, from time to time, individuals are allowed to offer opinions as experts, even though the basis of their expertise is open to challenge. I have experience of such people claiming that some text or transcription of an interview is (or isn't) the words of a particular person. For example, they assert that a transcript of a confession isn't the words of the person who's reputed to have confessed; or that an anonymous, offensive letter was written by an identified individual. These claims of authorship, or lack of it, are invariably based on the details of the particular text in question.

Any scientist will insist that some sort of comparison or control material is required in order to show that the conclusions would not be equally applicable to any text, and so can't be claimed as definitive for the material under study.

By carrying out studies with control material, I've been able to show that the results the 'experts' claimed were virtually random. They'd plucked out of a hat the results that suited their case, but could just as readily have found results that led to the opposite conclusion. (If you want some more background on the study of language in the forensic context skip to the section' Examining Documents to Help Solve Crimes' in Chapter 5.)

Providing Evidence in Mitigation

In the evolving complexity of legal processes, people are increasingly charged with rather subtle crimes, such as intending to carry out a terrorist attack or being willing to help in the distribution of illegal drugs. These crimes come close to what George Orwell in his book *1984* called 'thought crimes'. The defendant may not have carried out a physical act that was criminal, but in fact suggested to others they should do something criminal, or even indicated that they were preparing for criminal activity.

This situation generates court cases in which the utterances of the individual aren't in doubt and the prosecution can clearly present the person's apparent intentions. The defence is to offer some evidence of mitigating circumstances that relates to the personality and interpersonal style of the defendant, something that forensic psychology can help with.

In some cases, this defence consists of demonstrating that the person is highly suggestible. Various procedures assess 'suggestibility' and are used in courts around the world. Suggestibility is particularly powerful when people confess to a crime because they feel they had to accept what was put before them, even though they weren't physically guilty of carrying out the crime.

In other cases, the argument may propose that the defendant's desire to be accepted by others and be 'one of the lads' made him particularly vulnerable to social pressures, and so led him to make statements that he didn't fully understand or endorse. The effects of these arguments hardly ever lead to an acquittal, but can help with a reduction in sentence.

Helping to Combat Workplace Violence and Harassment

Increasingly, companies are treating the possibility of workplace violence and harassment as serious matters that require planning and procedures to reduce incidents, and to deal with them if they occur. Although this area draws mainly on organisational psychology, forensic psychology can contribute to the central issues:

✔ Screening potential employees, using psychological assessments to ensure that they don't have characteristics that may make them likely to be violent or particularly vulnerable to harassment.

✔ Helping to produce workplace risk audits that review the policies, procedures and design features that are in place to reduce the likelihood of violence and harassment.

✔ Assessing the risks of various forms of threats and having in place processes for dealing with them if they arise.

✔ Reducing the impact of any violence or harassment that does occur, such as through counselling those involved and reviewing procedures to limit the possibility of it re-occurring.

Working on Corporate Liability

In the US, one area of forensic psychology and criminology that is growing rapidly relates to the legal duty that business owners have 'to exercise reasonable care that will prevent criminal attacks that could be anticipated'. Considering the possibility of offences against customers within retail or other premises, such as schools, restaurants and workplaces, draws on the understanding of criminal patterns of behaviour (the realm of criminologists) as well as on the forensic psychology of offending. Cases brought by shoppers mugged in a shopping mall have therefore opened up a broad area of professional consultancy to support or challenge their claims.

Experts offering evidence in these cases have to deal with a number of issues:

- Demonstrating good practice and whether the key incident revealed that such levels were achieved or not.

- Deciding on some clear and close link between any failure of the business to achieve appropriate standards and the offence that occurred.

- Assessing the degree of damage to the victim. In some cases, this can be adjusted in relation to the assumed portion of the damage that was the consequence of the business's failure.

Analysing Probity

If you are in a tough business negotiation, say another company wants to buy you out but you don't want to sell, then besides the work your accountants may do, you'll want answers about the sorts of people you are dealing with. Giving a psychological analysis of these people can therefore be very helpful.

I coined the term 'probity profiling' (because it considers the decency and integrity of the people being examined) to describe this sort of consultancy which I've provided on a few occasions and can see it's an area of psychological expertise that is growing. Because the character of the person is being examined, especially for any traits that may indicate weaknesses or possible dishonesty, the process draws on many ideas from forensic psychology, such as indications that the person may minimise the significance of risk-taking or have difficulty relating effectively to others.

When I've carried out probity profiling of an individual for large companies, understandably, I haven't been allowed to interview that person directly. Such an interview may suggest a lack of trust, or may be refused as irrelevant to the negotiations. So the analysis has to be carried out at a distance, not unlike the 'psychological autopsy' that I describe in Chapter 11. Available records of the person have to be examined. This is much easier with Internet searches. I've even found family photographs and other personal details on the Web that are very helpful in understanding a person I've never met, and probably never will.

Committing People to Institutions

Sometimes people need to be committed to a hospital or other institution for their own protection or to safeguard others. A medical professional takes this decision and in many countries the court process isn't required. Notoriously, totalitarian regimes use the process as a way of locking dissidents away without the trouble of a legal process.

In recent years, many jurisdictions have enacted much clearer criteria for the operation of such draconian measures, putting more emphasis on the professional assessment of the individual being committed. Some key principles are emerging that forensic psychologists will draw on, if asked to contribute to such an assessment:

✔ The person must demonstrate some clear mental illness.

✔ The person has to be demonstrably incompetent in making decisions about treatment or medication.

✔ Clear evidence is needed that without further treatment or medication the person would become even more disabled and/or their condition worsen considerably.

✔ Substantial probability is needed that without appropriate treatment the person's condition would so deteriorate that they'd suffer severe psychological or physical harm that would result in an inability to function independently outside of an institution.

Ending One's Life

People have debated the right (or otherwise) to end one's own life since the time of the ancient Greeks, but in the last few years the possibility of medically assisted suicide and euthanasia raises many questions that require assessments residing at the heart of forensic psychology. These assessments can relate to an individual's active requests for end-of-life procedures, passive refusals to have life-sustaining treatment or actions by relatives to terminate life-support systems. In all cases, the central issue is the competence of an individual to make such a significant decision.

Assessments of competence need to go beyond the natural logic or rationality of any termination request. They have to incorporate an understanding of the individual and the context of the person's request, by asking questions such as:

✔ Are there any indications of mental illness or other psychological disorders that would cloud judgement?

✔ Does depression influence judgement and, for instance, minimise the prospect for recovery?

✔ How does the decision accord with previous expressed preferences and attitudes?

✔ If the person has changed his views from previously held ones, what gave rise to that change and how plausible is it?

✔ Is there any indication of pressure from others or desire to respond to the concern of others?

✔ Are there any impairments in the person's ability to communicate or express a viewpoint so that decisions can be delayed until the person can express a view?

Assessing the Impact of Child Abuse

As legal processes around the world accept more readily the prevalence of child abuse when reported by adults about their earlier experiences, a particularly demanding requirement emerges: to determine the extent of damage the victim suffered, even though the abuse may have happened 30 years previously or longer. Such assessments are carried out to establish compensation as well as any therapeutic interventions.

As well as detecting any malingering or symptom exaggeration by the victim (something I consider for offenders in Chapter 10), a mixture of other matters need to be examined:

✔ Comparison with other related youngsters who weren't abused.

✔ Similarities and differences in the victim before and after the alleged abuse.

✔ Particular consideration of cognitive and emotional functioning especially in school; matters such as impairment of attention or social alienation can be important.

✔ Corroborative information from associates and other family members.

✔ Any post-traumatic symptoms.

✔ Behaviour of the victim that relates directly to the presence of the perpetrator.

Linking Criminal Cases

If a court can be convinced that a series of crimes is the work of one individual, those crimes can be tried together because of what's called *similar fact evidence.* This phrase means that evidence that convicts a person in one case, implicitly convicts him for the others. Taken together, this approach can greatly strengthen the prosecution of an individual. The courts are therefore very concerned that similar fact evidence is extremely strong so that innocent people aren't convicted because of conjecture.

The aspects of linking cases in an investigation that I describe in Chapter 6 are also relevant for the courts, but are applied much more stringently when used as evidence. They require that distinct aspects of the actions in crimes exist, or some definite features of the culprit that are so specific that they can be characteristic of only one individual. The parallels to fingerprinting and DNA evidence are clear, but in those cases science has established that the fingerprint and DNA of each person is unique – the same can't be said for patterns of behaviour.

In order to establish that the actions in a series of crimes are distinctive enough to have been produced by a particular person, information needs to be obtained about the prevalence of those actions, singly and in combination. The expert can then use these 'base-rates' to assess how different the behaviour is from what typically happens in similar crimes. Sometimes (although much more often in fiction than in reality), a criminal does something in each of a series of crimes that's so unique that it's regarded as a sort of 'signature'.

Certainly, some serial murderers have left something distinct, like a playing card at each murder scene, or burglars who always bought a new jemmy to open windows with thus leaving new marks each time. But evidence of these signature actions is unlikely to be found at every crime scene for a serial offender. Therefore, more complex searches for distinctive aspects of patterns of behaviour have to be carried out if the case for similar fact evidence is to be established in court.

Chapter 20

Ten Cases in Which Forensic Psychology Was Crucial

In This Chapter

▶ Illustrating forensic psychology in action

▶ Showing how the contribution can be powerfully simple

▶ Setting up experiments to test particular legal issues

Psychology makes the clearest and most direct contribution to the legal process when it relates to specific cases. Although forensic psychologists do much more than just give evidence in court, the cases that I describe in this chapter reveal the many different ways in which psychologists contribute to court decisions affecting the lives of individuals.

I was personally involved in a couple of these cases. I include these because sorting out the complexity of a legal case, and summarising key aspects of it in a few paragraphs, can be very difficult if one isn't actively involved in the process.

Considering the Effects of Media Accounts

One of the earliest uses of modern psychology in court is still relevant today, and it concerns the influence of accounts in the press of matters relating to an ongoing trial. This event happened in 1896, and so nothing much has changed!

Baron Albert von Schrenk-Nortzing was a German physician who devoted a lot of his time to examining psychics and related paranormal phenomena. As part of these studies, he became aware of the ways in which memory can be distorted by events that intervene between the things remembered and the recall of those events. This subject would be an active area of psychological research a century later (as I discuss in Chapter 4), but at the time such a claim was a challenge to conventional views of how memory operated. The Baron pointed out that his finding was particularly important when evaluating the reports of witnesses.

In a case of great public interest, a man from Munich was accused of murdering three women. Then, as now, press coverage of the case was widespread and speculation abounded about what had happened and who was involved.

The Baron argued in court that witnesses were likely to have confused their actual memory of what had happened and what they'd seen with ideas they may have gleaned from the newspaper accounts. He even coined a rather grand term for this effect, calling it *retroactive memory falsification*. However, the court disregarded the Baron's evidence and the defendant was found guilty.

Legal systems in many countries now acknowledge that reports and comments about events and especially about suspects can influence juries. Therefore, laws forbid comments to be broadcast or published that may influence them. These *sub judice* laws make it illegal to comment on a court case before it's completed. Straightforward reports of what happens in court are allowed but, for example, speculation on the character of the accused would be regarded as 'contempt of court'.

This law only applies, however, after a person has been charged with a crime and the court proceedings have started. In the US, the freedom of the press is regarded more highly than the possibility of distorting a jury's memory and so the *sub judice* rules are much more lenient. Consequently, cases still occur today for which the Baron's opinion would be relevant.

Determining Whether a Convicted Murderer Is Telling the Truth

Hugo Münsterberg was a highly regarded psychologist in the US at the turn of the 20th century. He was aware of the many contributions that scientific, experimentally-based psychology could make to legal processes and wrote popular articles and academic accounts of his work for the courts. He introduced many of the issues that forensic psychologists still deal with over 100 years later, including false confessions, distortions in eyewitness testimony and determination of lying. At the time, however, he wasn't taken very seriously.

In 1908, he published a controversial book called *On the Witness Stand*, in which he describes his experiences of providing evidence in court cases. The book advocated much more use of psychological scientific cases in legal proceedings, but many years passed before evidence from psychologists became accepted in court. Indeed, many of his recommendations have still to be taken up.

One example of his account, in his own words, illustrates how innovative his thinking was. In this case, one convicted murderer was giving evidence against another and Münsterberg was seeking to determine whether this man, who claimed that he'd become religious and was now telling the truth, was lying.

Münsterberg first made sure that the witness believed in the powers of the psychologist:

> *I told the witness directly that I had come to examine his mind and find out what was really at the bottom of his heart . . . I began with some simple psychological tricks . . . which were naturally unknown and somewhat uncanny to the witness . . . and soon he was entirely under the spell of the belief that I had some special scientific powers.*

> *Then I began with a real experiment. I told him that I should call at first fifty words, and each time, when he heard a word, he was to name to me as quickly as possible the first thing which came to his mind on the hearing of the word . . . My first word was 'river,' he associated 'water'; then 'ox,' he said 'yoke'; 'mountain,' he said 'hill'; 'tobacco,' he said 'pipe.' All the interest thus seemed to belong to the choice of the words, and he saw that I wrote his answers down. But the fact is that I did something else also; I measured in fractions of a second the time between my calling the word and his giving a reply. Between his hearing of the word 'river' and his speaking the word 'water,' eight-tenths of a second passed; between 'ox' – 'yoke,' six-tenths; between 'tobacco' – 'pipe,' eight-tenths. On the whole, seven to eight-tenths of a second was the very short standard time for those associations which represented familiar ideas.*

> *Now, there were mixed in among the fifty words many which had direct relation to his criminal career and to his professed religious conversion – for instance, the words confession, revolver, religion, heaven, jury, death, Bible, pardon, railroad, blood, jail, prayer, and some names of his victims and of his alleged accomplices. Let us not forget that he was fully under the belief that I had a special power to discover from his spoken words the real tendencies of his mind. If he had had anything to hide, he would have been constantly on the lookout that no treacherous word should slip in . . . and yet, however quickly he might have done it, it would have taken at least one or two seconds more; and he would have used the longer time the more freely, as he had no reason to suspect that time played any part in the experiment.*

But the results show the very remarkable fact that the dangerous words brought, on the whole, no retardation of the associative process . . . Even the names of his accomplices and of his victims awoke associations in less than nine-tenths of a second. The fact that these associations were produced by the witness in the minimum time, which made deliberation impossible, while he was convinced that the words would unveil his real mind, is strong evidence indeed that this man did not want consciously to hide anything, and that he himself really believed his confession.

This quote shows Münsterberg using the psychological procedure of measuring reaction time to determine how much the witness needed to think about his answers before uttering them. Münsterberg thought that the longer the reaction time the more the person was trying to develop in his mind an appropriate answer. If he gave a very quick answer then he was not trying to invent anything at all and so his answers could be trusted. Like any good scientist Münsterberg also made sure he had some comparison figures for the individual in question under neutral conditions. Psychologists still use similar explorations today, but with much more sophisticated equipment. However, I've not heard of this being used as an assessment of the trustworthiness of a witness in court.

Recreating Events to Test a Claim's Validity

Professor Lionel Haward is primarily responsible for establishing the use of psychological evidence in UK courts. In the first major book in the UK on the work of forensic psychologists, published in 1981, he describes many of the cases for which he appeared in court.

One case that illustrates his approach of setting up studies specifically to test the validity of claims in a case, relates to a road accident in which a 14-year-old boy was knocked down by a car as he turned from a farm track onto a country road on his bicycle.

The defence of the driver related in part to the suggestion that the boy was of low intelligence and, as a consequence, had been guilty of 'contributory negligence'. In other words, the accident was to a certain extent the boy's own fault because he hadn't been cycling sensibly. Professor Haward therefore tackled this claim directly:

1. **He established the boy's intellectual ability prior to the accident.** This process wasn't simple because the boy had suffered severe head injuries from the accident, and so Haward had to consult his school records and other information.

2. **He selected two groups of cyclists.** One group had the measured intelligence of the boy before the accident and the other had average intelligence. The boys rode their cycles through a puddle containing fluorescein dye so that their precise wheel tracks showed up on the road. Each set of cyclists then rode, one at a time, into a road from a junction similar to the one where the accident took place.

3. **He carefully measured the tyre tracks and evaluated the route taken to determine how dangerous the taking of the curve had been.** The crucial issue was how close the cycles kept to the side of the road or how likely they were to swerve into the middle, which was much more risky.

The results showed that cyclists of low intelligence were no more likely to take the corner in a risky curve than riders of normal intelligence. In addition, the average curve followed by the cyclists was compared with the line the victim had taken to show that his behaviour was normal. This allowed the court to dismiss the claim of contributory negligence.

Haward used the process of setting up specific experiments to test aspects of claims in many cases. In doing this he was following directly in the footsteps of Münsterberg and the Baron that I mention earlier. The same sort of thing is still done today in some cases, as I did in relation to the case described later: 'Examining the Role of Implicit Influence in the Lockerbie Bomber Case'.

Forcing Drugs to Make a Defendant Fit to Stand Trial

Charles Thomas Sell was a St Louis dentist long known to suffer from delusions. Although he hadn't been convicted of any crimes, in 1997 he was charged with over 60 cases of fraud. Psychiatric examination determined that his mental state was such that he wasn't fit to stand trial. The courts sent him to a mental institution with the plan that he'd get enough treatment to become competent enough to face the charges. However, while in hospital Sell refused to accept any medication that would influence his mental state. Prosecutors requested that the law require him to be forced to take the medication so that he'd become fit to stand trial.

This case was a *cause celebre* and a number of professional organisations submitted reports offering opinions on what should happen, including the American Psychological Association. These reports provided detailed guidance on the conditions under which various medical interventions are ethically acceptable.

The resulting guidelines have since found their way into various statutes. They include the recognition that any administered medications that influence a person's thought processes are matters over which the individual should have an influence. Furthermore, the courts need to be aware that such drugs are liable to influence other aspects of a person's behaviour that can modify how someone seems in court. Therefore, courts need to be extremely careful before requiring coercive treatment with drugs to make a person competent to appear before a judge and jury. All other less invasive methods should be considered first.

In a protracted set of legal judgements, the parties eventually agreed that it was probably appropriate for Charles Sell to be given medication involuntarily.

By then, however, he'd spent longer incarcerated than he would've done if he'd been found guilty of the original charges, and the case was dropped!

Investigating a Honey-Trap Gone Wrong

The young model Rachel Nickell was murdered while walking her dog with her 2-year-old son on Wimbledon Common in South London in July 1992. A couple of months later the police decided that Colin Stagg was the likely culprit. He came to their notice through lonely-hearts correspondence he had carried out with a woman, who thought it was rather odd.

The police set about trying to get Stagg to admit to the murder using what's often called a *honey-trap*. A woman police officer, 'Lizzie', pretended to be part of the lonely-hearts' circle and opened up correspondence with Stagg. Her activities were guided by a person with some forensic psychology background who'd generated a 'profile' of the killer that he thought fitted Colin Stagg.

Over six months, Lizzie corresponded with Stagg and met him a few times. Using pointers provided by the psychologist, she got as close as she could to offering Colin sexual favours if he admitted to the murder of Rachel Nickell. He never did admit that, but seemed to mention some aspects of the case that the police thought indicated knowledge that only the culprit would know. Armed with this and the willingness of the psychologist to give evidence that Stagg fitted the profile of the killer, the police charged Colin and took him to court.

As part of his defence, I and a number of colleagues examined closely the transcripts of all the interactions between Lizzie and Colin. We saw quite clearly that a concerted effort had been made to use various well-known psychological persuasion techniques to get a confession from Stagg, and that any claim that he fitted some sort of 'profile' of the killer was speculative in the extreme.

When the case eventually came to court, after Stagg had been in prison for 11 months, at the earliest stage of the trial the Judge, Mr Justice Ognall, commented on the 'honey-trap' activity saying: 'I am afraid this behaviour betrays not merely an excess of zeal but a substantial attempt to incriminate a suspect by positive and deceptive conduct of the grossest kind'.

He threw the case out and Colin Stagg walked free.

Some years later, a quite different man was convicted of the murder. While the police were focusing on Colin Stagg, the man carried out a very similar murder. In other words, the obsession with honey-trapping Stagg enabled the real killer to go free and kill another young woman.

In January 2007, Colin Stagg was awarded £250,000 in damages. Lizzie also received a substantial sum in payment for the trauma she received from her participation in the fiasco.

Profiling Howard Hughes

When the eccentric billionaire Howard Hughes died in 1976, people expressed the concern that he'd been so reclusive and generally odd in his later years that he hadn't been competent to make an appropriate will. The then president of the American Psychological Association, Raymond Fowler, was called in to review what was known about Howard Hughes and offer an opinion on his mental state and competence towards the end of his life. Dr Fowler was thus asked to perform a *psychological autopsy* (something that I describe in Chapter 11).

Fowler obtained a vast amount of material about Hughes, which he studied over a number of years: material included Hughes's diary and those of people close to him; business memoranda; articles in newspapers; interviews with Hughes; and letters he'd written or others had written to him or about him.

Dr Fowler's conclusion was that Howard Hughes was a deeply disturbed man when he died. This mental disturbance had been evident from his earliest days, but developed into a very serious obsessive-compulsive disorder. At no time, however, had he been psychotic and totally out of touch with reality. He always knew what he was doing and had logical, if rather misinformed, reasons for doing what he did.

After extensive legal battles the will was generally accepted and many relatives of Hughes received payouts as well as a number of good causes.

Evaluating a Suicide Note

On 4 June 1992, Paula Gilfoyle, who was eight and a half months pregnant, was found hanging in her garage in the northwest of England. Her husband, Eddie Gilfoyle, found a suicide note in Paula's handwriting, which he showed to the police. Initially the event was assumed to be a suicide, although Paula had told her friends how she was looking forward to having the baby and had made many arrangements in preparation.

A few days later, friends of Paula told the police that she'd told them that Eddie got her to write the suicide note because, they said, she'd told them her husband claimed to be doing a course for which he required a simulated suicide note!

If you think that this story is all rather odd, I agree with you. Certainly what one person says another person said (called *hearsay evidence*) isn't usually allowed into court. It wasn't allowed as evidence in this case, but it did form the background gossip that informed how the police went about the investigation.

Eddie denies any wrongdoing, but was convicted of the murder and after serving many years in prison was released on parole. Along the way, he appealed against the verdict. I was asked to consider the possibility that the crucial suicide note, which Paula had written, had been dictated by Eddie.

I discovered that Eddie and Paula were working different shifts and so had been leaving notes for each other. In addition, two other notes came to light that appeared to be precursors to the suicide note. In total, 11 communications existed from Paula to Eddie in the months leading up to the suicide. By examining the narrative that these notes implied, it was plausible that Paula had been contemplating leaving Eddie and then thinking about ending her life over a long period of time, but hiding this from others. Other studies I subsequently did on genuine and simulated suicide notes also supported the idea that Paula had written the suicide note herself.

Although the solicitors commented on the thoroughness of my report, the appeal judges refused to accept it as evidence. They claimed that my report provided no indication that Paula had been mentally disturbed and amounted to a form of 'profiling', which was unacceptable. (This unacceptability of 'profiling' was partly a consequence of the disastrous honey-trap case that I describe in the earlier section 'Investigating a Honey-Trap Gone Wrong'.) The judges made this decision, even though the analysis I carried out hadn't been done for the original court proceedings when Eddie was tried and convicted. So this was legally 'new' evidence which, if it had been available at the original trial, may have swayed the jury. Very recently, a box has been found in which Paula had locked away her private papers. These show she sometimes hid important feelings from those close to her, supporting the view that the happy face she presented to others before her death may not have been an indication of her true state of mind.

Researching False Confessions

A few hours after two weak, elderly women were found battered to death in 1987 in their home in the South of England, a local 17-year-old was arrested and questioned intensively for over 14 hours. Eventually, he said things that the police took as incriminating him in the murders and associated sexual assaults and theft. This case is one of hundreds that Professor Ghisli Gudjonsson (see Chapter 5, 'Dealing with false confessions'), a British forensic psychologist, studied that provide a clear example of a 'false confession'. He examined cases, like this one, in which it was clear from later evidence that the suspect had confessed even though he didn't commit the crime and tried to establish what it was that led to the confession.

In this case, the youth initially repeatedly denied any involvement in the murder or even being in the house. Yet after five different officers took turns in questioning him, telling him that witnesses had seen him near the victims' house around the time of the murder, and repeatedly challenging his account of what he'd done and where he'd been, the teenager became very distressed, shaking and sobbing. Eventually, he admitted being near the house and agreed with the incriminating claims made by the police.

The next day, however, after he'd rested, he again denied any guilt. For a year, he was kept in custody but throughout all that time he maintained his innocence. He said he'd offered self-incriminating agreement to the claims put to him because the police kept questioning in such a way that he felt they'd never stop. He felt very tired and just wanted the interrogation to end. He became frightened of what they may do to him and so eventually gave in and told them what he thought they wanted to hear.

A year later, another man was charged with the murders and pleaded guilty. He had his guilt corroborated with other evidence, and was convicted.

Because of these cases and the intensive research that Professor Gudjonsson and his colleagues carried out over many years, courts around the world are much more cautious about accepting confessions as indications of guilt. The most extreme example of this situation is in India where a confession isn't accepted by the courts, unless it's given in court to a judge with no police officers present.

Examining the Role of Implicit Influence in the Lockerbie Bomber Case

On 21 December 1988, Pan Am flight 103 blew up over Lockerbie in Scotland killing all 243 passengers and 16 crew members. The police investigation identified clothing that had been with the bomb and believed that it came from a shop in Malta, where the shopkeeper at the time was Anthony Gauci.

Police approached Gauci about a year after the bomb exploded to see whether he was able to remember selling the clothing and who'd bought it. By the time the investigators questioned Anthony Gauci, they were sure that the person who put the bomb on flight 103 was Abdelbaset al-Megrahi. They therefore presented Gauci with various sets of photographs, some of which included a picture of al-Megrahi, to see whether Gauci was able to identify the customer from a year earlier. When Gauci did indeed select al-Megrahi from the set of photographs, apparently the police threw a party to celebrate.

The investigation and the identification of al-Megrahi was much more involved and complicated than I can indicate in a couple of paragraphs. But even this brief summary reveals reasonable doubts that a shopkeeper could remember who'd bought what clothes many months earlier. The possibility has to be considered that the police, even inadvertently, influenced Gauci's judgements because they were so keen to get identification in this internationally significant case.

As part of a major study that I was asked to carry out in preparation for an appeal al-Megrahi wanted to make against his conviction, I set up an experiment to see whether people can be indirectly influenced to select a picture without being aware of it. In this experiment, two different sets of administrators were each given similar instructions. They were asked to show the set of pictures that Gauci had been shown to a number of different people and ask them to guess who the Lockerbie bomber in the set was.

One crucial difference existed in the instructions given to the administrators. One set were told which picture was al-Megrahi, but they were instructed not to tell anyone that. The other set of administrators weren't given this simple piece of information.

The results found that the administrators who didn't know who the 'target' picture was never had the photograph selected. Whereas those who 'knew', had the target selected in about a third of cases, much more than would happen by chance. This result showed that implicit influence (known as an *experimenter effect*) is likely to have been very powerful in this case.

Al-Megrahi was diagnosed with terminal cancer and released from prison on compassionate grounds, and his appeal dropped.

Identifying Ritual Murders in South Africa

Brigadier Gerard Labuschange is an unusual forensic psychologist. He's a qualified clinical psychologist but leads an Investigative Psychology Unit within the South African Police Service. Therefore, uniquely, he carries out investigations as well as providing psychological evidence in court. He thus brings a rarely found systematic, scientific approach to his detective work as well as psychological insights.

He has been particularly interested in distinguishing a particular type of murder, which is usually only found in Africa, from other forms of murder. These murders are ones that happen because body parts of the victim are used in traditional African medicine. People outside of the culture that supports this type of murder have difficulty understanding just how powerful such long-established belief systems can be.

The brigadier's gruesome task is to distinguish mutilations found on a murdered victim from those that may be the result of some psychotic, bizarre sexual or other mentally disturbed feature. This job requires understanding the belief systems involved that sustain this sort of murder and the sorts of victims (often children), that are considered appropriate for providing the necessary anatomical component. This understanding goes beyond the knowledge that a physician who carried out an autopsy would have. It requires psychological awareness that can recognise that the killer isn't mentally disturbed at all, but totally accepts the attitudes and beliefs that support these horrible crimes.

Index

• S •

FOR DUMMIES®

Making Everything Easier!™

UK editions

BUSINESS

Bookkeeping
Jane Kelly
Paul Barrow, MBA
Lita Epstein, MBA
978-0-470-97626-5

Persuasion & Influence
Elizabeth Kuhnke
978-0-470-74737-7

Starting & Running a Business ALL-IN-ONE
Colin Barrow
978-1-119-97527-4

REFERENCE

British Politics
Julian Knight
978-0-470-68637-9

DIY
Jeff Howell
978-0-470-97450-6

Dad's Guide to Pregnancy
Dr Roger Henderson
Matthew M.F. Miller
Sharon Perkins
978-1-119-97660-8

HOBBIES

Growing Your Own Fruit & Veg
Geoff Stebbings
978-0-470-69960-7

Keeping Chickens
Pammy Riggs
Kimberly Willis
Rob Ludlow
978-1-119-99417-6

Beekeeping
David Wiscombe
Howland Blackiston
978-1-119-97250-1

Asperger's Syndrome For Dummies
978-0-470-66087-4

Basic Maths For Dummies
978-1-119-97452-9

Body Language For Dummies, 2nd Edition
978-1-119-95351-7

Boosting Self-Esteem For Dummies
978-0-470-74193-1

British Sign Language For Dummies
978-0-470-69477-0

Cricket For Dummies
978-0-470-03454-5

Diabetes For Dummies, 3rd Edition
978-0-470-97711-8

Electronics For Dummies
978-0-470-68178-7

English Grammar For Dummies
978-0-470-05752-0

Flirting For Dummies
978-0-470-74259-4

IBS For Dummies
978-0-470-51737-6

Improving Your Relationship For Dummies
978-0-470-68472-6

ITIL For Dummies
978-1-119-95013-4

Management For Dummies, 2nd Edition
978-0-470-97769-9

Neuro-linguistic Programming For Dummies, 2nd Edition
978-0-470-66543-5

Nutrition For Dummies, 2nd Edition
978-0-470-97276-2

Organic Gardening For Dummies
978-1-119-97706-3

Available wherever books are sold. For more information or to order direct go to www.wiley.com or call +44 (0) 1243 843291

11–37870

UK editions

SELF-HELP

Cognitive Behavioural Therapy For Dummies
978-0-470-66541-1

Creative Visualization For Dummies
978-1-119-99264-6

Mindfulness For Dummies
978-0-470-66086-7

Origami Kit For Dummies
978-0-470-75857-1

Overcoming Depression For Dummies
978-0-470-69430-5

Positive Psychology For Dummies
978-0-470-72136-0

PRINCE2 For Dummies, 2009 Edition
978-0-470-71025-8

Project Management For Dummies
978-0-470-71119-4

Psychometric Tests For Dummies
978-0-470-75366-8

Renting Out Your Property For Dummies, 3rd Edition
978-1-119-97640-0

Ruby Union For Dummies, 3rd Edition
978-1-119-99092-5

STUDENTS

Philosophy For Dummies
978-0-470-68820-5

Student Cookbook For Dummies
978-0-470-974711-7

Sociology For Dummies
978-1-119-99134-2

Sage One For Dummies
978-1-119-95236-7

Self-Hypnosis For Dummies
978-0-470-66073-7

Storing and Preserving Garden Produce For Dummies
978-1-119-95156-8

Study Skills For Dummies
978-0-470-74047-7

Teaching English as a Foreign Language For Dummies
978-0-470-74576-2

Time Management For Dummies
978-0-470-77765-7

Training Your Brain For Dummies
978-0-470-97449-0

Work-Life Balance For Dummies
978-0-470-71380-8

HISTORY

The Tudors For Dummies
978-0-470-68792-5

Medieval History For Dummies
978-0-470-74783-4

British History For Dummies
978-0-470-97819-1

11-37870

FOR DUMMIES®

Making Everything Easier!™

LANGUAGES

Spanish For Dummies
978-0-470-68815-1
UK Edition

French For Dummies
978-1-118-00464-7

Polish For Dummies
978-1-119-97959-3
UK Edition

Art For Dummies
978-0-7645-5104-8

Bass Guitar For Dummies, 2nd Edition
978-0-470-53961-3

Criminology For Dummies
978-0-470-39696-4

Currency Trading For Dummies, 2nd Edition
978-0-470-01851-4

Drawing For Dummies, 2nd Edition
978-0-470-61842-4

Forensics For Dummies
978-0-7645-5580-0

German For Dummies
978-0-470-90101-4

Guitar For Dummies, 2nd Edition
978-0-7645-9904-0

Hinduism For Dummies
978-0-470-87858-3

Index Investing For Dummies
978-0-470-29406-2

Knitting For Dummies, 2nd Edition
978-0-470-28747-7

Music Theory For Dummies, 2nd Edition
978-1-118-09550-8

Piano For Dummies, 2nd Edition
978-0-470-49644-2

Physics For Dummies, 2nd Edition
978-0-470-90324-7

Schizophrenia For Dummies
978-0-470-25927-6

Sex For Dummies, 3rd Edition
978-0-470-04523-7

Solar Power Your Home For Dummies, 2nd Edition
978-0-470-59678-4

The Titanic For Dummies
978-1-118-17766-2

MUSIC

Ukulele For Dummies
978-0-470-97799-6
UK Edition

Guitar Chords For Dummies
978-0-470-66603-6
Lay-flat, UK Edition

DJing For Dummies
978-0-470-66372-1
UK Edition

SCIENCE AND MATHS

Biology For Dummies
978-0-470-59875-7

Algebra I For Dummies
978-0-470-55964-2

Genetics For Dummies
978-0-470-55174-5

11-37870

FOR DUMMIES®

Making Everything Easier!™

COMPUTER BASICS

978-0-470-57829-2

978-0-470-61454-9

978-0-470-49743-2

DIGITAL PHOTOGRAPHY

978-0-470-25074-7

978-0-470-76878-5

978-1-118-00472-2

MICROSOFT OFFICE 2010

978-0-470-48998-7

978-0-470-58302-9

978-0-470-48953-6

Access 2010 For Dummies
978-0-470-49747-0

Android Application Development For Dummies
978-0-470-77018-4

AutoCAD 2011 For Dummies
978-0-470-59539-8

C++ For Dummies, 6th Edition
978-0-470-31726-6

Computers For Seniors For Dummies, 2nd Edition
978-0-470-53483-0

Dreamweaver CS5 For Dummies
978-0-470-61076-3

iPad 2 For Dummies, 3rd Edition
978-1-118-17679-5

Macs For Dummies, 11th Edition
978-0-470-87868-2

Mac OS X Snow Leopard For Dummies
978-0-470-43543-4

Photoshop CS5 For Dummies
978-0-470-61078-7

Photoshop Elements 10 For Dummies
978-1-118-10742-3

Search Engine Optimization For Dummies, 4th Edition
978-0-470-88104-0

The Internet For Dummies, 13th Edition
978-1-118-09614-7

Visual Studio 2010 All-In-One For Dummies
978-0-470-53943-9

Web Analytics For Dummies
978-0-470-09824-0

Word 2010 For Dummies
978-0-470-48772-3

WordPress For Dummies, 4th Edition
978-1-118-07342-1

11-37870